Analysis & the Fullness of Reality

Other Books

by

Richard H. Jones

———————

Science and Mysticism

Mysticism Examined

Reductionism

Mysticism and Morality

Curing the Philosopher's Disease

Time Travel and Harry Potter

Piercing the Veil

Nagarjuna: Buddhism's Most Important Philosopher

*For The Glory of God: Christianity's Role
in the Rise and Development of Modern Science*

Indian Madhyamaka Buddhist Philosophy After Nagarjuna

One Nation Under God?

The Heart of Buddhist Wisdom

Analysis & the Fullness of Reality

An Introduction to
Reductionism & Emergence

Richard H. Jones

Jackson Square Books
2013

Dedicated to
The Memory of
Henry Cutler Torrey
(1911-1998)
for the talks on the boat

Printed and distributed by www.createspace.com

Printed in the United States of America

Library of Congress Cataloging-in-Publication Data:
    Jones, Richard H., 1951-
        Analysis & the Fullness of Reality: an introduction to reductionism & emergence
        / Richard H. Jones
        Includes bibliographical references and index.
        ISBN-13: 978-1481988988
        ISBN-10: 1481988980
        1. Reductionism. I. Title
        B 835.5 J67 2013

Contents

Preface

When I was a graduate student back in the 1970's at Columbia University, I once attended a lecture on astrophysics and afterwards attended the reception for the speaker. While helping myself to some of the refreshments, I overheard two older physicists arguing (in a friendly way) over whether they were "reductionists" or not. After listening to them for a little bit, it became clear that they were actually agreeing on all the material issues and were only disagreeing over the proper label. I politely intervened and pointed out that they really were not disagreeing over anything substantive but only over the use a word: they both thought everything in the universe was made out of only one type of stuff but had more layers of genuine causes than just submicrophysical ones and were merely disagreeing over whether the label "reductionist" applied. In the terminology of this book, they were both substance-reductionists and structure-antireductionists. (I forget the terminology I used at the time.) To my surprise, they actually seemed more annoyed with me butting in than grateful for the clarification. (Maybe they just enjoyed disagreeing.) In any case, I went back to the refreshment table.

That was my first attempt to bring some clarification to the dispute. My second was *Reductionism: Analysis and the Fullness of Reality* (2000), which grew out of my interest in science and religion. When I wrote that in the 1990's, philosophical discussions of reductionism were growing, perhaps prompted by the recovery of experience and consciousness as topics in the philosophy of mind, and the topic of emergence was also beginning to reappear. Since then, the discussions have dramatically increased in philosophy and science and even to some extent in theology. And the disputes have only intensified and positions hardened. To those of a reductionist bent, the whole idea of "emergence" is only a fad, with some philosophers and scientists jumping on the bandwagon without thinking it through or devising a coherent position; this fad, they are confident, will ultimately be replaced by the "real science" of causal reductive explanations (Kim 2006b: 190-91, 2010: 2-3, 8-9, 66-67). However, to emergentists we are seeing the dawn of a profound "paradigm change" in science (Murphy 2007: 1).

The philosopher Carl Gillett may be overstating the importance of the topic of "reductionism versus emergentism" when he says that emergence is "at the heart of perhaps the grandest intellectual battle of our times" (2006: 816), but there is no denying that since the 1950's reduction has been at the "forefront of discussion in philosophy of mind and philosophy of science" (Hohwy & Kallestrup 2008: 1). It is a central issue in philosophy of science and metaphysics touching on such basic "big questions" as what is real, what has causal power, the nature of science, free will, how the mind fits into a naturalistic worldview, and life after death.

One thing that is still needed today is a brief overview of the issues of reductionism and emergence in all its fields—philosophy, the natural sciences, philosophy of mind, society and culture, and religion—for the general reader who is not inclined to wade through the increasingly technical philosophical works or the scientific papers but is interested in the basic issues. (And it must be said that many philosophers write with an obscurity that would make Hegel proud.) This reworking and updating of *Reductionism: Analysis and the Fullness of Reality* attempts to fill that need. In addition, two substantive points need to be reiterated: the disputes can be greatly clarified with a refinement of the terminology, and mysteries about reality still remain whether one accepts reductionism or antireductionism. Even if all the issues concerning reductionism versus antireductionism cannot be resolved, some can and the underlying competing visions can also be made clearer.

This book has added much new material and also removed much more material from the earlier book. Only matters directly related to reductionism and emergence are covered in this shorten version. The general discussion has also been updated and revised, and so this book supercedes the first on all matters related directly to either reductionism or emergence.

Overview

Various distinctions, definitions, and issues are presented in Chapter 1. Chapter 2 gives a brief history of the ideas of reductionism and emergence. Next, the four areas in which reductionists and antideductionists do battle are covered: the natural sciences, the philosophy of mind, the social sciences, and religion. By looking at all of these topics collectively, the objective is to see the connections and differences between the strands of reductionism and antireductionism in various areas of philosophy. How the ideas of reduction and emergence impinge on so much that is basic in how we see the world becomes apparent. Chapter 3 examines the principal field of structure- and theory-reductionisms—the natural sciences. In the following chapter, the central field today for the dispute over substance-reductionism (as well as being important to issues of structure- and theory-reductionisms) is examined in more detail—the mind-body issue. That is followed by a discussion of individualism and holism, and structure- and theory-reductionism and antireductionism, in the social sciences. In Chapter 6, religion illustrates the question of the reduction of any cultural phenomena. It also highlights the ontological dispute between adherents of contemporary reductive philosophies (materialism and naturalism) and the various antireductive religious metaphysics concerning substance-reductionism. The general problem of the emergence or reduction of possible higher levels of organization is the subject of the final chapter.

1

The Age of Reductionism

The philosopher Robert Nozick labeled ours "the Age of Reductionism" (1981: 630), and most people in our scientifically-informed culture would agree. We want to understand the world, and under the influence of modern science we now want to know how things work in terms of material and efficient causes. Moreover, we are not fully satisfied with any suggested explanation of a phenomenon unless it is explained in terms of something we deem to be a basic reality. We search for the "true nature" of things—what is "really real." And this is where *reductionism* enters the picture: we want to get down to the reality that is the source or substance of a phenomenon. We take a phenomenon apart to see what makes it tick, or we retrace (Lat., *re-ducere*, "to lead back") the development of the phenomenon to its roots. A reduction thus proposes what in the final analysis is real in a phenomenon. We find that what was apparently real is ultimately "nothing but" its parts or something else more basic. Thereby, an apparent reality is "reduced" to something real, and our desire for understanding at least the reduced phenomenon is satisfied.

In science, a common example of a reduction is the explanation of heat. When we explain why one object is hot simply by pointing out that it is being heated by another hot object, we only explain why that one particular object is hot—we have not explained the phenomenon of *heat* itself. To explain heat itself, we have to refer to something that itself is *not hot*—i.e., something to which the concept of "heat" does not apply. For the heat of gas, scientists have advanced such an explanation in terms of the movement of molecules: the molecules themselves are athermal entities, but their movement generates heat. The temperature of a gas is reduced to the average kinetic energy of its molecules. Heat is not *caused* by molecular movement but simply *is* nothing but the movement of molecules. Thus, there is nothing left to explain about heat after this reduction.

Outside of science, the same type of explanation is also commonly proffered in different fields. It is not unusual to hear that all that is real is only the physical, the rational, the programmable, or whatever is given primacy. In general, wholes are commonly reduced to only the interaction of their parts. For example, a person is said to be nothing but a body—there are no souls, and our mind is really nothing but the activity of our brain. We are nothing but machines, robots controlled by mindless genes or inanimate molecules. Similarly, society is simply the interaction of individuals. In the area of religion, any transcendent reality (God, Brahman, or whatever) grounding a believer's way of life is explained away as an illusion—the only reality involved in religious experiences and ways of life is actually (depending on the theory) the individual, society, or something in nature.

These various reductions do not all proceed the same way, but what all reductions have in common is the replacement or explanation of one phenomenon by another reality of a different nature, one supposedly ontologically simpler or more fundamental. By this process, our picture of what is actually real in a phenomenon has to change: the "whole" and its structures are no more than its "parts" and their structures. Mental and biological phenomena, if real at all, are identical to matter, and only what physicists study is causally effective.[1]

What Is So Worrisome About Reductions?

It is important to note that reductionism is not merely a matter of the scientific *identification of the causes* at work in a whole. Rather, reductionists go further and claim that the parts and causes are all that is real in a whole—the reality of a whole is *nothing but that of those parts*. It is easy to see why many people are disturbed by such reductions: in moving from the more complex to the simpler in human beings, reductions deny what is distinctly human. More generally, reductionists "reduce the more valuable to the less valuable, the more meaningful to the less meaningful," and never the other way around (Nozick 1981: 628). If things are reducible to a reality below the surface, then much of human life loses its value. The effect on our lives is to undercut the reality of what is specific to being human—consciousness, free will, personhood, our cultural creations. What seemed special about human beings is dissolved into nothing but lifeless and soulless matter. Moreover, if a human being is only a complex amalgam of physical objects, we are deluded on what we think drives us. Reduction thus is dehumanizing—our autonomy, dignity, and worth are undercut in a leveling physicalism. Reductionism leads quickly to a nihilism in which all values are utterly groundless (see Frankl 1969). Even if this is an overreaction, reductions nevertheless do, as Robert Nozick said, "seem to explain away our valuable traits" (1981: 633-34).

Scientific reductions might seem more limited in scope and so less monumental in their consequences. But these reductions are still disquieting. Consider macroscopic objects. The astrophysicist Sir Arthur Eddington (1958: xi-xii) presented the paradox that he was actually writing on two tables at once: the *"everyday" table* that we experience (bulky, substantial, colored, comparatively permanent) and the *"scientific" table* (mostly emptiness with numerous electrical charges rushing about at great speed). The problem is how to reconcile these two very different realities. Is the table really solid and rigid, or is it mostly empty space? Reductionists have a very simple solution: only the "scientific" table is real—a swarm of quarks or whatever is all that is really there, and solidity only results from interaction of those parts. Thus, what we actually experience is not the reality. The color and other features of the experienced table do not really exist in the world independently of us at all: they result merely from the interaction of our sensory apparatus with some physical reality existing apart from us. Only the sensory apparatus and the physical reality are real, not anything "subjective." In the most important sense, colors, sounds, and so forth are not real features of the objective world but are only our own creations that disappear when we are gone.

If our sensory apparatus is responsible for all sensory reality, what is the world independent of us but a colorless and soundless void? And this leads directly back to the distressing question: if reduction does this to our sense-experience, what about the rest of our lives? If everything human is reduced to the merely material, how could the world be anything but indifferent to us and ultimately meaningless? Our actions all become meaningless. Any value, meaning, or purpose to reality is only something *we* fabricate, not anything in any way grounded in the universe independently of us. Reality is purposeless, void of value and meaning, consisting of the aimless and amoral interplay of natural processes dictated solely by physical laws (Vitzthum 1995: 231). As Alfred North Whitehead said in characterizing this issue, nature becomes "a dull affair, soundless, senseless, colourless; merely the hurrying of material, endlessly, meaninglessly" (1967: 54). Thus, more is at stake in "reductionism versus emergence" than simply a question of metaphysics.

Emergentism

Probably most scientists and philosophers today are reductionists of one stripe or another. But opposing them is a growing group of "antireductionists" or "emergentists" who believe that more is ultimately real than what reductionists accept. ("Emergence" and "antireductionism" will be used interchangeably here for both ontic and epistemic situations, although many antireductionists dislike the label "emergentists."[2]) Something is "irreducibly real" in the persistent patterns of higher levels of phenomena that cannot be accounted for solely by, or predicted from, its lower level components. In an ill-defined image, higher levels have "information" that the lower levels do not have and cannot produce that structures the higher levels without violating lower level laws. To some emergentists, emergence is very rare, limited only to life and consciousness or even to only the latter. To others, it is a common event even on the physical level: the wetness of water manifests a property through chemical bonding that the properties of the hydrogen and oxygen molecules do not. The biologist Harold Morowitz differentiates *twenty-eight* levels of emergence (2002: 25-38).[3] Emergence may not occur in the same way in each case, but there is a common pattern of complexity leading to new levels.[4]

Higher level structures "emerge" or become manifest in the universe over time. Emerging properties are *dependent* for their appearance on base-conditions—hence the idea of *emerging* (Lat., *e-mergere*, "to arise out of")—but the lower level properties do not completely *determine* the higher levels. In short, some genuinely new properties exist at each higher level. This combines dependency and autonomy, and continuity and discontinuity. That is, given the way a lower level is constructed, the next higher level did not *have to be the way it is*. The physical level of organization is *necessary*: the way our universe is set up, both matter and the physical level of organization must be present for the higher levels to appear, but the biological and mental levels do not "emerge" out of the physical level in the sense of being their products. Thus, if the reductionists' catchphrase is "nothing but," then the antireductionists' is "yes, but." More structures of reality are at work in the higher level phenomena than in their bases. Thus, a complete understanding of the lower level—the components and their interactions—will not explain the emergence of stable properties and processes on the higher level.

Emergentism today is solely a matter of structures and natural entities, not substances. Only thinkers with a prior religious commitment to a soul think of a new *substance* emerging (e.g., Hasker 1999). How new levels emerge is a problem for antireductionists. (Reductionists think it can be ignored since only lower level factors are involved in higher levels.) To them, the base-conditions are necessary but not sufficient—more is needed for the higher levels to appear. Antireductionists are not necessarily committed to special "emergent forces" that produce an upward thrust giving rise to more and more levels of organization, although some sort of configurational Aristotelean "formal causes" seem to be at work. Instead antireductionists can affirm merely that new forces (e.g., "biotic principles") become operational only as the universe becomes sufficiently complex, just as the physical strong and weak forces operating in atoms were not manifested before atoms appeared. That is, all the forces may have been present at the beginning of the Big Bang, but they only kick in when the right base-conditions are in place (see Shoemaker 2002). As reality ratchets up new levels of organization with new properties as it grows more complex, each new level must obey all the laws of the lower levels, but previously-latent principles now also come in play.

Reality's Two Components: Substance and Structure

We may think that being "stuff" is the only criterion for what is real, but it is important to note that the universe has two separate and equally real components: substance and something structuring it—i.e., both "matter/energy" and "information." Thus, the world is both one (in substance) and many (in structure). Defining either component is difficult. Substance is what gives being to entities or other realities. Physicists do not define "matter" or "energy" or explain it but simply presuppose it—science is about understanding *structures*, not the *substance* they are embodied in (see Jones 2009a: 87-90). Even if substance is inherently endowed with, say, electromagnetic properties, there is still the distinction between the substance and its properties. Things are not simply "matter in motion" but "matter being structured." "Structure" may not be the best word here, but it is meant to denote whatever in reality is responsible for the stable invariances (properties, causes, relations, order, or other patterns) among changing phenomena.[5] Whether structures are inherent properties of things, as "essentialists" argue, or are imposed on inert, "passive" matter and act as an external constraint need not be discussed here. That structure is different from matter is what is important.

Such structuring of matter cannot be denied by reductionists. For example, a working radio and a bag of the raw materials that could be shaped into the radio's parts may be materially identical, but we can consider them to constitute the same thing only if we can completely ignore structuring. In nature, putting carbon atoms together one way creates a diamond, but put the same atoms together another way and we get coal. Consider an analogy to language: a word is not just a collection of letters: "car," "cra," and "arc" all have the same letters (the substance) but the order (the structure) produces different words or non-words. Moreover, no amount of study of one or all of the letters alone will ever determine if a word is created or not: the structure constitutes another order of reality and must be studied separately. Words "emerge" from its constituent parts, depending on the proper structuring. There are also different levels of order in language (words and grammar). The distinction between the paper and ink of this book and the meaning of the words is also apt: no amount of scientific knowledge of the "matter" will aid in understanding the linguistic "information" (Polanyi 1968). We do not need to know anything about the chemistry of the ink and paper to understand the meaning of the text; nor can the latter be derived from the former in any way. In sum, language cannot be reduced merely to its "physical" parts (the letters) or whatever physical medium it is embodied in. And, antireductionists argue, the same is true in living and conscious beings. Persons cannot be made by assembling a pile of the appropriate chemicals and stirring it up. Even on the strictly material level, the various sublevels of structure cannot be ignored. For example, how much is the human body worth? As a simple pile of chemicals, it is not worth much, but at the level of organs, it is much more valuable—indeed, some useable tissues and organs are very valuable.

Almost all philosophers today agree that there is only one substance to the universe—"matter," i.e., the "stuff" that embodies structures. However, how many types of structuring there are is a major point of dispute between reductionists and antireductionists. To the former, there is only one type—the physical. But according to the latter there are multiple types of structuring, each irreducible. The failure to differentiate these two components obscures this issue. Unfortunately, the label "physicalist" as currently used covers *both* physical substance (matter) and physical structure; thus, often people who are committed to matter implicitly assume that by definition all phenomena (entities, states, properties, processes, causes, capacities) must also be completely fixed by physical structures alone—matter can have only physical structuring. Moreover, arguments for the reduction of substances are improperly taken to be arguments for the reduction of structures, with the need for further arguments for structure-reduction not even seen. However, accepting only one physical substance does not compel believing that there cannot be nonphysical (biological or mental) structures embodied in the substance. (To keep the issues clear, the term "physicalism" here will be restricted to only the idea of *substance*, with no inference about the nature of reality's *structures*.)

The Reductionist and Antireductionist Approaches

Both reductionists and antireductionists agree on one thing: to be *real* means to be a nonnegotiable feature of the universe—in a word, *irreducible*. But reductionists and antireductionists diverge dramatically over what substances and structures are ultimately real. The conflict comes down to a conflict of deep-seated intuitions: the primacy of the "objective" physical over the subjective in our sense of what is real and the success of physics in determining how things work lead us to think that only what physicists study is in the final analysis real and causally effective, while our everyday experiences tell us that we can consciously control our body and have free will and that what we directly experience is as real as the microphenomena physicists study. To reductionists, reductionism is implicit in the very nature of science. Resting content with emergence seems "contrary to the scientific impulse" or "scientific spirit" (Nagel 1998: 5, 7). But the antireductionists' counter-intuition also has two equally strong sources: our sense that such realities as self-consciousness are something more than merely physical, and our sense that the analysis of reality provided by physics does not exhaust its reality.

All reductionists share the conviction that there is a fundamental *simplicity* behind experience, both in substance and structure. They strive to explain the complexity we experience with the fewest number of fundamental types of realities and laws: the reducing theory always explains all that the reduced theory explained and more. Reductionists do not deny the reality of everyday phenomena—only "eliminationists" do. Instead, they claim that phenomena are merely the products of more basic realities or are in fact identical to them. Lower level factors do all the work. The drive behind reductionism is to achieve economy in different ways—in ontology (both in substances and structures), descriptions, and explanations. The reductionist attitude, coupled with Occam's razor, leads naturally in the contemporary West to the ontological simplicity of physicalism and to physics as the ultimately the only true study of structures. Antireductionists, under this view, simply fabricate realities where there are none by reifying our everyday concepts.

However, Occam's razor only requires reducing the number of independent types of entities and properties to *the minimum required to explain phenomena*—e.g., no chemist accepts "All is water" just because it is simple. And antireductionists insist that the microphysical level of organization alone is inadequate to explain all phenomena even in principle—more levels of organization (and for some antireductionists, more substances) make up our world. Thus, more categories of realities are in fact required in our final ontology of what types of structures are irreducibly real. That is, most antireductionists today agree that there is only one substance, but they insist that more levels of causes are at work in biological and mental phenomena than just lower level forces and that the latter do not determine the former. Thus, antireductionists too reduce the realities to a minimum number of types, but they believe the number required is higher than reductionists suppose.

Antireductionists emphasize the role of the structuring and organizing element of reality. Within science, antireductionists can also readily accept the primacy of physics (since all of nature has physical properties) while still insisting that other sciences are autonomous and hence not reducible. Few antireductionists today propose a holistic *reverse reduction*—i.e., that reality can only be completely understood at the highest level of complexity and any lower levels are reducible to effects of that level. But some wholes are not *aggregate sets of parts* but *integrated units manifesting new features*. For all their emphasis on integrated systems, no antireductionist in the modern West denies that *analysis* (dissection of wholes into their constitutive parts or identification of the physical "bases" of a higher level reality) also reveals important and irreducible aspects of reality. Their claim is simply that an "integrative" or "holistic approach" will always be needed in addition to analysis in order to understand reality as fully as we are able. In short, analysis can never lead to a *complete* explanation of any phenomenon.

Reductionists may view emergentists as fuzzy-minded dreamers who are still trying to give human beings a privileged position in the scheme of things and who cannot face the cold hard facts of reality. In their view, antireductionists rely on ill-defined metaphors of "levels of organization," "hierarchies," "emergence," "information," and "grounds." Antireductionists, for their part, criticize reductionists for losing sight of all of reality in their zeal for simplicity and explanation (or at least predictability). Higher level phenomena still exist and are fully real. Moreover, emergentists ask why the higher level phenomena exist at all and how their presence is to be explained. And, antireductionists would point out, the metaphors central to antireductionism are at least intuitively understandable, if not precisely definable.

Clarification of Terminology

The basic *terminology* in the debate over reductionism has long been established. However, there is no consensus on the *meaning* of the principal terms—indeed, the meaning of the terms seem to vary from one disputant to another. Sometimes the term "reductionism" is used simply as a term of derision for one's opponents or as a badge of honor for one's own position. Nevertheless, the term has very particular connotations related to the relation of phenomena on different levels of organization. (In science, the use is sometimes *inverted* from the philosophical sense—e.g., physicists say Einstein's theory *reduces* to Newton's theory under everyday physical conditions.) It does not mean merely any attempt at unifying, simplifying, or ordering confusing and complex phenomena, or reducing the number of explanatory posits. Indeed, many of the difficulties concerning reductionism versus emergence can be eased with some clarification of the basic terms.

Levels of Organization. The notion of the reduction of wholes to parts or of phenomena to their bases has a central metaphor: *"levels" of organization.* It is accepted by reductionists and antireductionists alike. To reductionists, higher level phenomena are *explained* by lower level mechanisms: they deny any higher level *structures*, but not necessarily the reality of the *phenomena*. By affirming levels of interactions, reductionists can escape the simplistic position that properties on all levels are merely the additive sum of the properties of the lowest level: each "level" has some properties that other levels do not share. Thus, "whole/part" reduction is a matter of *substances*, while reduction of levels is a matter of *structures*. The metaphor of "levels" is hierarchical in nature: each level "above" another "in" a "whole"—e.g., a chemical level "above" the quantum level. A less vertical image is of integrated, nested coherent "systems" or "webs" inextricably interconnected with each other. But precisely defining these ideas is indeed difficult. Specification is usually in terms of *properties*, but perhaps the most exact way of looking at "levels" or "systems" is in terms of *orders of causal interactions or mechanisms*.

Some argue that the entire idea of "levels" only reflects our needs and not any objective features in the external world: the concept is only a product of what questions we are asking, when in fact such complexity does not objectively exist. We erroneously reify the descriptions of reality that result from different points of view into a layered world of distinct levels (Ahl & Allen 1996). (Antireductionists should agree that we should not reify our concepts into a *disconnected* world of levels.) Under this view, the observable chair may seem complex for one set of our questions but seem to be a simple system for another, and nothing more needs to be said about the relation between levels. But if different levels of organization in reality have different *properties*, that is not so. Levels of organization are then a deep and nonarbitrary feature of the ontology of reality (e.g., Simon 1962; Wimsatt 1994). Issues of how these levels emerge and are related thus remain important.

Emergence. Emergence is not just any change of phenomena or the evolution occurring within the universe; it is the appearance of *higher levels of phenomena* emerging from "base-conditions" (i.e., the lower level conditions that must be present to allow a higher level phenomenon to appear) as a system evolves. Reductionists do concede higher levels of organization "emerge" in some sense from lower levels—after all, individual atoms do not digest food, and persons are not amorphous clumps of quarks. Heat supervenes on the motion of molecules, and consciousness supervenes on the activity of neurons. Reductionists contend, however, that no new levels of independent *causes* actually emerge: what "supervenes" *emerges* in one sense but is *completely caused* by its bases—all higher level properties are strictly determined by the lower levels, or are merely "resultant" properties (i.e., aggregates of the lower level properties), or are a mechanical assembly (e.g., radios) in which the higher level phenomena result solely from the structure of the lower level realities. (The term "*cause*" will be used here to denote the relation between levels, although some scholars prefer to restrict the idea of causation to a relation existing only among phenomena occurring on the same level, i.e., efficient causation [e.g., Morgan 1927: 28].) In this way, phenomena are entirely explainable by the lower level properties and hence are structurally reducible. Knowledge of the lower level phenomena is both necessary and sufficient for completely understanding the higher level phenomena at least retroactively. In short, there are no genuine "emergent realities" (entities, processes, properties, causes). Thus, if two worlds are physically identical, they necessarily cannot differ in their biological and psychological features (if such phenomena appear).

Emergentists dispute one or more of these last points: even if two worlds are physically identical, they may have different biological and mental properties. Often the idea of emergence or irreducibility is connected to *unpredictability*. That is, the higher level phenomena are considered irreducible because they could not be predicted even from exhaustive knowledge of the lower level phenomena. But prediction is an *epistemic* matter and need not entail *ontic* irreducibility. Reductionists can admit that in practice we may never know enough about the details of the phenomena on one level to predict higher level activity, but they still contend that the higher level is completely determined by the base. In addition, prediction is merely a matter of correlating phenomena, not explanation: just because we may someday have enough knowledge to *correlate* the higher and lower level phenomena does not mean that the lower level phenomena *caused* the higher or that realities other than those operating on the lower levels are not also at work. Indeed, mere correlation is not the explanation of anything. At most, ontic emergence is only indirectly connected to epistemic emergence since a genuinely emergent higher level reality cannot be *understood or explained* even *in principle* by a complete knowledge of the lower level phenomena and their relations.

Various concepts should be differentiated here, although again there is no agreed-upon distinctions and definitions. Different epistemic and ontic senses must be kept clear. "Weak epistemic emergence" refers only to limitations on our technologies and our ability to know all the details necessary to explain higher level phenomena reductively in terms of lower level structures. "Strong epistemic emergence" refers to a limitation on theories due to the structure of reality: higher level contain phenomena that from the point of view of the lower level have autonomous abilities. "Weak ontic emergent properties" are powerless epiphenomena of bases; aggregates may also be grouped here. But if these novel properties are not determined by the bases alone they cannot be structurally reduced. (Since bases allegedly *determine* what *supervenes*, "supervenience" will be treated here as solely a reductionist concept.) "Strong ontic emergence" relates to higher level properties having new causal power that the parts do not have and that cannot be explained in terms of the interaction of lower level properties.

Being causally potent is sufficient to be deemed real and emergent, but some emergentists argue further for something stronger: "top-down" or "whole/part" causation, i.e., that the new level of properties can affect their bases after they have arisen. (The idea that higher levels could affect their bases *simultaneously* with their initial realization is indeed problematic, but *later influence* is not; hence the distinction between "synchronic realization" and "diachronic influence.") Over time, such feedback can alter the base-conditions. Think of how the role of worker soldier ants in an ant colony affects the development of their jaws through evolution over time—the needs of the colony constrain the development of the jaw. To do so, downward causation need not violate or alter the laws of the base, although it would negate the causal closure or completeness of physical causes. To emergentists, downward causation is just another case of causation, even though it is interlevel (see Bickhard & Campbell 2000; Silberstein 2006). To reductionists, any interlevel causation is always only "bottom-up," and the very idea that higher levels could exercise any kind of control seems like magic (see Kim 2006)—at a minimum, it introduces a problem of overdetermination since physical forces are sufficient.

Three related concepts capture a progression of how real the higher levels are considered to be. The basic concept for all *"emergence"* is that some higher level properties are not completely determined by lower level realities and so are irreducible. Thus, some properties of the higher level are neither found among the lower levels nor caused by them but have emerged as the complexity of reality has evolved, and so knowledge of the parts and their relationships is necessary but not sufficient to understand the higher level as fully as possible. The higher level properties depend upon the lower, but not vice versa. *"Organicism"* goes further: the "parts" do not exhibit all their properties independently of the "whole," and so knowledge of the whole is necessary to understand the parts. *"Holism"* goes even further and reverses the reductive relationship: the basic unit is the whole. The whole exists independently of the parts and its architecture determines the nature and behavior of its interacting parts. The properties of the whole stand alone, and so the study of the architecture of the whole becomes primary. The parts are reduced to only patterns within the dynamic whole system. The quantum physical level is the commonly cited example. But *holism* is usually about *substance* and cannot be conflated with *structure-antireductionism*: one can affirm a holism for a level while still advocating a structure-reductionism between levels (see Hüttemann & Papineau 2005). Whether a whole can be explained by its parts still remains.

Analysis. It is important to remember that *reductionism* is not the same as the *scientific analysis* of a phenomenon (i.e., the identification of its component parts or its bases). Analysis is a reverse engineering of phenomena to see how they work and to identify all the different lower level causes and conditions at work. All too often people use the term "reductionism" when what they actually mean is only "analysis." Newton's prism may have destroyed the beauty and wonder of a rainbow for the poet John Keats, but it only revealed the spectrum of light involved—it did not *reduce* the rainbow to something less. Everyone agrees analysis is necessary for a complete understanding of a reality—it is the additional *metaphysical step of reducing the reality of higher-level phenomena to the lower* by identifying the whole with its parts or by claiming the higher level is merely a product of its bases that is problematic. We may analyze the components or bases of a reality or we may approach it mechanically without taking the further metaphysical step of claiming the lower level as revealed in those analyses is the only actual reality involved.

Reduction, reductionism, and antireductionism. Not every attempt to bring order or simplicity to a situation is a reduction: reduction involves *a relation between levels*. In a reduction of structures, phenomena on one level or sublevel are explained in terms of realities on what is deemed a more basic level or sublevel. (A "sublevel" will be defined as a division of organization within a broader group, e.g., the atomic sublevel as a subdivision of the broader physical level.) Without this *interlevel relationship*, there is no *reduction*. Changes of a theory on only one level do not constitute a reduction, although the prior theoretical posits may be deleted. Newton's laws of mechanics did not *reduce* Kepler's laws of motion—both involve the same sublevel of physical organization, and thus his modification and unification should be referred to as *replacing* the latter, even though this is sometimes called a "homogeneous" or "intralevel" reduction (Nagel 1961). Instead, reduction requires two different levels or sublevels. In a replacement, the theory and ontology of a domain are transformed but not transformed into those of a lower level. A replacement may be a matter of the "horizontal" expansion of a theory the same level (including into other subdomains), but reduction is a matter of "vertical" expansion of a theory into different levels (Dupré 1995). (Of course, to reductionists both are a matter of *replacement*.)

"Reductionism" is not merely a specific instance of a reduction. Rather, it entails a philosophical judgment of what is finally real. At any point, past alleged successes at reduction are the only empirical grounds for thinking that in the future a complete reduction will ever be accomplished, and that is no guarantee of the future development of science. But *analysis* alone is not reductionism: even a complete analysis of bases and their workings does not constitute a reduction. Rather, an extra metaphysical step is necessary: reductionism affirms that only what is revealed in an analysis is real. Analysis is also affirmed as ultimately the only legitimate approach for our understanding of the world and as the goal that all science should have. Thereby, it goes beyond successes (if any) in science to a more general view of the nature of reality and science.

"Antireductionism" contrasts with reductionism in being a more pluralistic program for research. Ontologically, antireductionists accept either more than one type of fundamental substance or more than one level of structuring or both. Epistemically, antireductionists deny that all cognitive approaches to reality will ultimately be reduced to physics. The essential role of physical analysis of component parts and structures is not denied, but other disciplines are accepted as autonomous. Antireductionists thus affirm a robust pluralism of approaches while reductionists affirm one approach will ultimately be exhaustive. Reductionists accept that a "integrative" or "holistic" approach may be heuristically useful and even necessary in our current state of research, but they claim analysis leading to final and complete reductions will eventually replace that approach entirely—in the end, science will have a string of reductions leading ultimately to final epistemic and ontic reductions. And that is precisely what antireductionists reject.

Reduced Phenomena. A "reduced phenomenon" is never deemed fully real, but it can be treated one of four ways: elimination, identity, production, or as an epiphenomenon. Under eliminationism, there is in fact no reality at all where we thought a reality appeared—the appearance of a reality is comparable to an optical illusion. Like a pencil appearing broken in a glass of water, the illusion still remains even after we know better, but the genuine reality behind the phenomenon has now been identified as something less than we thought. Strictly speaking, eliminationism is not a form of *reductionism* since the claim is there are no phenomena to reduce.

Reductionists eliminate structures, theories, and concepts—eliminationists eliminate *phenomena*. Eliminationism does seem counterintuitive—especially with regard to the mind—but this does not mean it is necessarily wrong. Philosophers of mind who eliminate the self, free will, or consciousness as mere mistakes and those in social theory who deny any social realities are the prime defenders of this approach. The second approach is probably the standard position today: an apparent phenomenon is really *identical* to another reality; two apparent substances are thereby reduced to one. For example, the heat of a gas is not eliminated, but it is actually only the motion of its molecules. Under the less severe third approach, a phenomenon is explained as the product of lower level factors—its reality is again affirmed, but it is the product of other realities. For instance, human beings are not just piles of quarks but are totally the product of subatomic forces alone. Under the fourth option, the reduced phenomena are still accepted, but they explained as mere *epiphenomena*—i.e., effects with no power of their own to produce other effects. The typical reductive account of sense-experience is an example of this type. Under the last three options, the higher levels have no independent causal power; and under the first option, there is not even any reality to talk about. In sum, under eliminationism, there is no *A* but only *B*; under identity, *A* is real but really *B*; under production, *A* is totally the product of *B* but has causes; under epiphenomenalism, *A* is determined by *B* and any apparent products of *B* are in fact products of *A*.

Thus, reductionists are not as austere as their opponents often portray them. Even reductionists, unlike eliminationists, affirm there is more to reality than what is identified in a scientific account: scientific accounts *explain* phenomena, not *explain them away*. It is not so much a matter of reducing *entities* as reducing the number of *structures* allegedly operating on different levels within one entity. For reductionists, sense-experiences, pains, and so forth are real—even identity-theorists must concede that there are two things to unite. The reduced phenomena simply are explained by factors in reality taken to be "*more real*" in the sense of having power to produce something else. Thus, "*reduction*" involves the *ontic identification* of two phenomena, and a "*reductive explanation*" involves explaining one phenomenon by means of other *structures*.

Under all three ways of reducing phenomena, higher level phenomena are accepted but can be *exhaustively explained* by lower level phenomena. Quarks and atoms obviously do not have thoughts or feel pain—only beings on a higher level of organization do. Few reductionists today claim that quantum level events directly cause life and consciousness—intervening levels of organization are involved. But reductive physicalists assert that the fundamental properties of the universe are physical and that the physical alone produces any higher level effects. The actions of any whole are produced by its parts' structures, and this explains the whole. Wholes cannot *do* anything the parts cannot. These parts in turn are explained by their parts' structures, and so on, until the physical bases are the only reality under study. Those who reduce structure may carry on the reductions ultimately down to the lowest physical sublevel of organization (if there is one). However, explaining macrophenomena ultimately in terms of microphenomena, even through a chain of levels, is not simple. And to defend epiphenomenalism reductionists have the formidable task of showing that, for example, consciousness is nothing but the product of physical forces and in fact has no causal power. Indeed, thoroughgoing reductionists have the even more daunting task of showing that something as simple as the mechanical interaction of two physical objects (e.g., a bat hitting a ball) does not involve real emergent properties of solidity but is in fact only the product of causal interactions on the molecular sublevel—i.e., showing that solidity is the product of molecular forces is only the first step toward showing that the interaction itself is an event that is reducible to molecular actions.

Types of Reductionism

In all its forms, the concept "reductionism" relies upon the same basic intuition that only what physicists study is "really real," but when it is used without further specification unnecessary ambiguity arises. Without specifying which types of the multifaceted term "reductionist" one is referring to, it can be confusing to call someone a "reductionist." For example, Arthur Caplan (1988) and Ernest Mayr (1988a, 1988b) hold essentially the same positions on the pertinent ontic and epistemic matters concerning biology, but the former adamantly claims to be a reductionist while the latter champions antireductionism. (In terminology set forth below, both are substance-reductionists and theory-antireductionists.)

To help remove this ambiguity, different strands of reductionism can be untangled from the cluster of related ideas. Today three strands of reductionism are regularly disentangled: ontic, epistemic, and methodological (see, e.g., Peacocke 1976; Ayala 1989).[6] The distinctions turn upon what is being claimed to be reducible—entities or other realities, concepts, theories, or methods. However, these three must also be subdivided: "ontic" covers the reduction of both *substances* and *properties*, and "epistemic" covers both *descriptions* and *explanations*. To that end, five types of reductionism should be distinguished: *substantive, property, descriptive, explanatory*, and *methodological*. To further complicate the situation, there are "weak" and "strong" varieties of several of these categories.

Substance-reductionism. How many types of substances exist in reality? Substance-reductionists are monists who hold that all of reality is composed of only one type of substance. The stuff may be divine (as in some religious ways of life), conscious (as in idealism), or material (as with physicalism).[7] For physicalists, whatever composes rocks is ultimately all there is to reality. Human beings are made of the same materials as the rest of the physical world: there is no additional soul, mind, life-force, or other reality in a human being or in anything else. Every entity is merely an arrangement of quarks or whatever is basic. But substance-reductionism is *not tied to atomism*: what is fundamental may be a field or nonparticulate. "Particles" or other "entities" may crystalize out of a field as level-effects: what is substantively real may not come in discrete chunks. But their position is that everything is composed of only the "stuff" that comprises microphenomena.

Structure-reductionism. The other ontic issue concerns what type of causal things—e.g., entities, fields, processes, properties—should be accepted as real, whether or not they are all composed of one or more substances. Substance-reductionists cannot deny matter is subject to a *structuring* that is also real. Matter has not just flown about haphazardly since the Big Bang. Instead, electromagnetism and other forces structure the actions of matter. Basic structure is as much a "brute fact" about reality (i.e., something impossible to explain further) as the stuff structured.[8] Some thinkers believe structure is *more* real than what is structured: mathematical structure, information, or whatever, is the generative principle of the universe and matter is just what happens to manifest it (see Ladyman & Ross 2007). In any case, the two fundamental ontic categories of the universe—substance and the structure organizing it—are both real and irreducible to each other.

Structure-reductionists assume that there must be one fundamental level of structure and that it is physical. They maintain that all the apparent structures of reality are reducible to physical structures and (for the more thoroughgoing reductionists) ultimately to the structuring at whatever is the most basic or fundamental physical level of matter.[9] There are no "genes" or even "electrons" —the only real entities or processes are on the lowest level of physical organization. Any apparent "levels" are at best complex sublevels of physical causes. It is only a matter of *scale* and not new realities. Everyday phenomena are merely extremely complex interactions of subatomic realities. All the properties of any complex whole are determined by its parts, and so any whole is explained exhaustively in a "mereological reduction" by the properties of its parts. Reductionists agree with emergentists that the features of reality must be understood in their *context*—they are only asserting that the features can be understood completely in terms of their parts in their total context and in terms of physical structuring alone. The difference between a working radio and a bag of its parts can be explained solely in terms of the arrangement of the properties of its parts. The working whole is "weakly emergent" at best. Thus, *configurations* are part of reductionism.

In short, all that exists is matter organized by physical structuring alone. Just as reality is composed of only one stuff, so too all of reality's structures are of one type. All properties at apparently higher levels of complexity result from the presumably simpler structures at a more basic level. The liquidity of water is a product of hydrogen and oxygen molecules' properties. Biological entities and processes are nothing more than the interaction of the molecules that bring them about, and so on down the line until we clearly reach a level of physical structuring. There is a *continuity* of levels of complexity—indeed, a *determinacy* relation—and no independent or autonomous higher level realities. For both eliminationists and reductionists, the only real causation takes place at the physical level. This variety of ontic reductionism can also be called "causal" or "organizational" reductionism. But the important point is that it is ontological in nature because it relates to what is real in how the stuff of reality is organized. (Unfortunately, it is sometimes considered *epistemic* since many physicalists can see *substance* as the only ontological issue.)

Structure-reductionists can be grouped into two types: those who affirm that all causes are chemical or physical, and those who reduce even those causes to only those of the lowest level of physical organization. The first group merely denies biological and mental structures—i.e., all causes are physical, and no further reduction of structures is necessary. Thus, life and consciousness are like machines: all we need to know are the parts and the rules for arranging them to understand them fully. Such a position is consistent and very popular. But for thoroughgoing structure-reductionists, only causes on the lowest quantum level are real. There are not even any higher level physical causes, i.e., physical causes unique to interactions on higher levels. Higher level physical interactions are all explainable by the lower level causes. Think of John Conway's computer game of Life: no new level of causes or laws are at work in the unexpected "emergence" of gliders and their actions, merely the simple rules governing each piece that produce them.

Substance-reductionism is probably subscribed to by virtually all scientists and philosophers who are not religious believers, but there is no unanimity among philosophers and scientists regarding structure-reductionism. Indeed, arguing over what is real in the structures of reality is the principal area of dispute in philosophical circles in the whole area of reductionism and emergence.

Concept-reductionism. When we turn from ontic to epistemic reductionism, the first thing to note is that reductionists often claim statements that are apparently about one reality are really about another. Since ontic and epistemic reductionisms involve a *reinterpretation* of phenomena, it may seem only natural that the terms of the reduced view have to be translatable into the vocabulary of the reducing view. Moreover, the common-sense distinction between describing and explaining a phenomenon also may not always be maintainable—i.e., how we *describe* something may be affected by what we take to be in fact real and thus affected by how we ultimately *explain* it. To description-reductionists, explanation dictates description. These interlevel redescriptions, in turn, would figure in a reduction of explanatory schemes into one unifying conceptual scheme.

But such a reduction of the meaning of terms (also called "predicate reduction") is not widely popular in philosophical circles today. Eliminationists and some reductionists may be "strong" concept-reductionists who advocate the total elimination of reduced terms by reductions: when the real factors involved in a phenomenon have been identified, the referents of the descriptive terms collapse into those of the reducing theory. That is, both the referent and content of statements on one level are really about something on a lower level. There is thus no need to retain the terms even for descriptions since only statements about the "scientific table" are actually needed. "Weak" concept-reductionists, however, are willing to retain the continued use of reduced terms as helpful conventions for the phenomena and regularities on each level of organization—talk of the "everyday table" is a convenient shorthand even if the causal reality is on another level.

Theory-reductionism. This reductionism is closely related to structure-reductionism since it also involves our attempt to identify the structures at work in reality.

But the emphasis here is on *explanations* rather than the relation of *realities*. In particular, how do theories from one field of science connect to theories from other fields? For example, how do theories devised for the biological level of organization connect to theories in chemistry? Overall, how should the results from the different branches of science be *organized*? (The relation of science to *other ways of knowing reality* also figures in here but will not be discussed.)

The answer theory-reductionists provide is that the theories and laws we develop in one field of science are no more than special cases of theories and laws in more fundamental fields—ultimately, elementary particle physics—and thus the theories developed to explain merely those higher level laws will eventually be no longer needed. Today some reductionists advocate bypassing the higher level theories entirely and going straight from the lower level mechanisms to explaining the higher level phenomena. A successful reduction will supplant all the explanations of the reduced theories without loss of the latter's explanatory power or range. Reductionists may accept that the concepts used to describe the data at each level will have to be retained, but the higher level theories, along with their posited explanatory structures, will be eliminated. Theories in the social sciences will be reduced without remainder to those in psychology which in turn will be reduced to theories in biology and then to those in chemistry and finally to those in particle physics. In the end, only particle physics theories will convey scientific knowledge. All other scientific theories will be eliminated, and in a "nomological reduction" their laws describing patterns of phenomena will be shown to be no more than limited cases of fundamental laws, derivable in some fashion from the physics devised for the most fundamental level of organization we can find.

Ultimately, there will be no hierarchy of theories in this vision of the unity of science. The conceptual side of science will be magnificently simplified. If, as in a saying that can be traced back to Plato, science is "carving nature at its joints," then for reductionists there is only one level of joints, and particle physicists are the carvers who will provide the explanations of the workings of reality that will be as final and complete as is humanly possible. Any failure of the theory-reductionists' program may be weak (simply because of limitations on our ability to predict) or strong (because reality in fact has multiple levels of autonomous properties).

Method-reductionism. The final category of reductionism relates to analysis as the method for studying a phenomenon, i.e., disassembling a complex whole into its simpler component pieces or identifying the lower level bases of a phenomenon and then studying the features and organization of the component parts or bases to see how it works. As noted earlier, *analysis* should not be taken as *reductionism*: we can analyze the parts and bases without a commitment to a substance-, structure- or theory-reductionism, and without claiming that such an approach is in the end the only legitimate approach. Method-reductionists make the controversial claim that the analytical method is ultimately the only legitimate method for studying reality, regardless of how it is composed. They make analysis a regulative ideal and the objective of all science. That is, regardless of what is real, analysis is the only strategy, procedure, rule or prescription for any study of nature. Weak method-antireductionists see any failure in practice as due only to our limitations.

Philosophy informs the practice of science here: when method-reductionism is combined with theory-reductionism, all that seems really needed to be studied are the lower level phenomena because only they are actually real. Thus, reducing all sciences to physics becomes the ultimate aim of all science and "disciplinary reduction" becomes a concrete research program. Reductionism then is a principle or prescription directing future research toward further analysis and identifying the results as what is real in a phenomenon, with the goal being a complete metaphysical and epistemic reduction, i.e., demonstrating that no more than the ultimate parts are causally real and needed for an explanation.

Types of Antireductionism

The antireductionists' responses to reductionism vary: emergence of novel properties, metaphysical dualisms (God and world, life-forces and matter, mind and body), epistemic holisms, and methodological pluralisms. Overall, these positions can be grouped to mirror the five strands in reductionism.

Substance-antireductionism. Antireductionists of this stripe reject some type of monism—supernatural, mental, or material. In short, there is more than one fundamental substance to reality. But today few people in philosophy or science (unless they are religious) reject the substance-reductionism that all that is real is ultimately composed of only one type of substance. For example, any form of vitalism in which a second substance—a "life-force"—is added to inanimate objects to create living beings has been rejected by biologists for generations.

Structure-antireductionism. In one way or another, all antireductionists reject the second category of ontic reductionism. Reality is not seen as having only a physical level of organization, let alone only one subatomic sublevel. Instead, reality is seen as a hierarchy of levels, each with structures that are *all equally real.* (Indeed, it is an interesting question whether in the quantum realm there might be no one base-level but levels "all the way down" [see Schaffer 2003].) Since each of the higher levels of organizations is as real as lower ones, their phenomena are not reducible to those of another stratum, either higher or lower. Higher level causes have a potency of their own: a higher level causal event does not provoke new causal events on a lower level but has a life of its own—the lower level components are simply carried along for the ride (Kim 2006: 561). Thus, even if there is only one ontic stuff involved in all realities, there still are various strata of complexity or nested systems, with each system being composed of other systems, from the lowest submicro-level to the macro-level of people, planets, and perhaps more. Thus, there are layers in our ontology of structure, not just one level.[10]

As the saying goes, "a whole is greater than the sum of its parts." In contemporary antireductionism, this means that each whole has some *properties* of its own that are more than the sum of the properties of its parts and that are not products of lower level causes. Of course, the weight of a pile of sand cannot be found in analyzing individual parts, but the property of any aggregate is simply the sum of the properties of the parts and is predictable in a simple manner from the parts' properties (see Wimsatt 1994). That is, in an aggregate no *new types of properties* appear in a whole. Similarly, relational properties of parts (such as whether a string is straight or knotted or the shape of a cascading pile of sand) obviously cannot be found in the parts themselves. However, in an *integrated system* the manifested higher level properties are not located in the parts, their sum, or their arrangement with each other. So too, a system is a whole with dynamically interrelating parts. Its parts are not interchangeable or readily replaceable, and so a system is structured in a way a structureless aggregate is not.

Indeed, even to speak of a "whole" and its "parts" is somewhat misleading since the parts do not collectively *create* the properties of the whole as with an aggregate: "parts" become "parts" only in the context of a functioning whole. The structure of the whole is not the product of the properties of the parts but is the result of other than the forces at work in the parts. This means the idea of a "whole" and its "parts" does not really capture the idea of *emerging* higher level phenomena. The mind is not a "whole" with "parts." A table's solidity is a feature of a physical system at a higher level of complexity than that of quarks. Parts at the lower level of complexity combine into new units with new and unpredicted higher level properties. But where reductionists see continuity and determinacy between levels, antireductionists see a discontinuity between levels that cannot be completely explained by lower level factors: higher level causes and properties are not determined by lower level phenomena and thus are "novel" (O'Connor 1994).[11] In addition, *how* the properties actually emerge is not explained by the lower levels. In other words, there are more levels of organization at work than just those producing subatomic properties: water is "nothing but" hydrogen and oxygen in the sense that no other substances are involved, but there are natural organizational forces involved that are not present on the level of atoms. The resulting higher level properties are nevertheless an irreducible feature of reality and hence as real as those on lower levels. The same holds for life and the mind.

The realities at each level are in this way independent of what lies below and above them. Of particular importance, *causes* do not operate merely at the lowest level of complexity. Higher level properties (e.g., the translucency of water) might be explained as the epiphenomena of lower level causes; but if causes operate on one level regardless of what is occurring below or above, they cannot be explained away so readily. Instead, they are as real as lower level causes. This moves from any "weak emergence" to "strong emergence" noted above. Higher level causes are an independent reality ingrained in the structure of reality and must be included in our inventory of what is irreducibly real. Wholes are not merely the product of the parts nor are they just different configurations of the parts and thus "less real," as reductionists hold. To reductionists, all higher level phenomena, including life and mind, are at best like machines emerging from the interrelation of their component parts or buildings emerging from bricks and wood—all the "supervening" properties of the phenomena are completely fixed by the properties of their parts. Structure-antireductionists too affirm the reality of the parts of a whole or the bases of phenomena, but they resist any reductive claim that these parts or bases *determine* the higher level phenomena.

In short, reductionists and antireductionists disagree over the number of fundamental structures to reality. Structure-reductionists contend there is only physical structuring to reality, but structure-antireductionists accept more types of realities in the form of properties or causes as real in the same sense that the lowest level of physical structures are real. Thus, for antireductionists each level contains "natural kinds" of realities that cannot be broken down into more basic elements on other levels and thus are fundamental, irreducible features of the universe.

Concept-antireductionism. This type of antireductionism is simply the claim that the phenomena and regularities on each level of organization require their own descriptive concepts. We cannot rewrite statements about heat in any expressions involving only quarks and leptons. Statements about phenomena on a particular level have a subject-matter and content unique to that level, even if the phenomena are constituted or completely explained by lower level phenomena. In other words, the issues of substance-, structure-, and theory-reductionisms are different from the issue of reducing the *description* of phenomena on any level to descriptive concepts appropriate to another level. The irreducibility of concepts is also needed if there are separate laws covering regularities in the phenomena.

It is obviously difficult to be an antireductionist of any stripe and reject descriptive antireductionism: if one attaches any reality to the phenomena of a particular level, then the concepts needed to refer to what is unique in that reality cannot be reduced without remainder to concepts designed for another level. Terms devised for describing the lowest level will not do even in principle for configurations of matter on all levels: each higher level of physical complexity produces its own genuine phenomena that require intractable, unique descriptive concepts and unique laws to describe the activity. A change in theory at most will require a redescription of the phenomena explained but not the elimination of the need for unique descriptive terms for each level. In addition, a further difficulty reductionists encounter is that terms from different levels are often *interdefined*; expunging one set would thus require reworking the other.

Theory-antireductionism. Theory-antireductionists reject the reduction of all scientific theories to those of physics, let alone of particle physics. Instead, they advocate a pluralism of scientific theories for the autonomous levels and sublevels of phenomena. This does not mean antireductionists must accept a *relativism* in which all conceptual schemes are equal and no standards exist to judge between competitors or a pluralism of theories for any one level of organization—antireductionists may readily agree that there is in fact only one correct theory for each level of organization. Their point is that each level presents a different and equally real aspect of reality. Scientists in each field of science must formulate different questions and explanations appropriate to the level of complexity under examination. In particular, we cannot exhaustively explain biological phenomena in physical terms.

A reductive explanation of x in terms of non-x is neither needed nor possible—each level requires an explanation in terms of causes operating on that level. Just as reductionists accept that the physical level of organization is a brute fact that cannot be explained further—since they see nothing more basic—so do antireductionists accept each level of organization as being equally fundamental. Each side reaches what they consider to be the irreducible realities and hence the basis for proper explanations.[12] Thus, they differ on what is an acceptable explanation.

Antireductionist explanations may include mechanics operating "upwardly" from below a given level, but they also include the causes operating independently on that level. Distinctive and independent concepts for each level remain entrenched, not merely as necessary for describing phenomena and their laws at different levels, but as integral components of the theories that remain independent of theories designed for levels above and below. As our sciences develop, some current theories may well be reducible to those of another level, but the cornerstone of theory-antireductionism is that some higher level theories will remain autonomous forever. The complete explanation of any phenomenon will require different accounts from all of its levels. This does not reflect the neatness and elegance of a reductive account, and many scholars consider any "multiple reasons" or "multiple causes" scenarios as a wimpy cop-out. But antireductionists maintain that only this approach can account fully for the way things really are.

The resulting "unity of science" is not the unification in physics, as reductionists hope, but is simply coherence of different theories. The causal activity on one level is irrelevant to theories on other levels (within the bounds of "upward" and "downward" causation, where phenomena on one level cause events on another), and so theories on different levels cannot in principle conflict. Biological phenomena must comply with the laws of physics, but their causal interactions are not reducible to laws of inanimate reality. Thus, these phenomena need their own level of theories since they cannot be explained by physical evidence, no matter how complete physics ever becomes. There is no neat hierarchy of deducible theories but a proliferation of autonomous levels of theory each operating in its own realm. Theories covering phenomena on levels above and below any given level of complexity will have at best a limited role to play in understanding the phenomena at that level. A "disunity of the sciences" becomes the working hypothesis for this vision of science (see Fodor 1974; Dupré 1993).

Method-antireductionism. With the possible exception of some holists, no one rejects analysis—i.e., isolating a phenomenon's component parts or identifying a phenomenon's physical or other bases—as one research strategy. Method-antireductionists readily concede that the heuristic dissection into component parts is necessary to advance insights and increases our understanding. Their concern is with treating such analyses as *exhaustive*, i.e., as revealing all there is to know about reality. Rather, they are method-pluralists who accept analytical and integrative approaches as *both necessary*. Strong method-antireductionists contend that reality is not so constructed as to make the reductionists' research program successful even in principle. Treating a living organism as if it were a machine may very well lead to a great amount of knowledge concerning how it works, but according to antireductionists that does not mean an organism *is* a machine. The same with the neural bases of the mind. The analytical and mechanical approaches simply do not provide a *complete* picture. Instead, such abstractions must be supplemented with more "integrative" approaches to generate as complete an account of reality as we are going to get. Ultimately, we can understand reality most fully only by accepting all of its complexity to be as real as any of its parts. Method-reductionists fail here by reducing this complexity to a series of lower components that they contend can be understood in isolation from the complexity itself.

As a corollary of this, antireductionists resist all attempts to reduce one science to another, either through concepts or theories and laws. Instead, each discipline is considered an equal. There is a division of labor between the different sciences: scientists in each discipline study a different but equally real aspect of reality and contribute something unique to the final picture. Method-antireductionists thus reject any attempted reduction of any science as the only way to true scientific understanding. Each level of complexity requires an autonomous discipline. Each level may also require its own techniques of study (e.g., biologists may need to use methods alien to physicists). But, even if not, the important point is that each level's theories have as their subject-matter a level of phenomena that is *irrelevant* to those of the theories covering the underlying levels, since the lower level events are neutral to the higher level events and since the higher level events involve factors having no effects among the lower level factors (although the problem of "upward" and "downward" causation remains). Each higher level is simply an accidental "boundary condition" from the point of view of scientists working in the sciences designed for the phenomena below.

Relationships Between Reductionisms and Antireductionisms

The relation between the types of reductionism is not always obvious. In particular, contrary to popular opinion, *theory-* and *structure-reductionisms* do not follow from *substance-reductionism*: one can accept that all living and conscious beings are composed of only matter and still deny that therefore physics can explain all aspects of them—all phenomena must obey physical laws, but there still may also be nonphysical structures operating in them. So too, one can be a substance-reductionist and yet reject concept- and method-reductionisms. Conversely, structure-reductive scientists may accept that there is more to reality than the type of substance open to scientific study—i.e., they may deny the substance-reductionism of naturalism. (According to polls, most scientists in America are either theists or deists.) So too, they may accept that only physicists study irreducible features of the natural order, or they may accept non-scientific ways of knowing.

If one denies structure-reductionism, one would have to deny theory-, concept-, and some forms of method-reductionisms. Theory-antireductionism fits naturally with structure-antireductionism, since any autonomous higher causes would then require their own level of theorizing and would not be exhaustively explainable by lower order structures alone. Conversely, how we could have a complete theory-reduction that does not also entail a structural reduction? The theoretical posits of the reduced theory would be supplanted. Theories give our explanatory accounts of phenomena, and thus they identify both the composition of things and what we take as really at work in reality. Thus, in any theory-reduction, higher level phenomena would remain, but higher level structures would be explained in terms of lower structures or would be eliminated as unnecessary. In short, structure-reductionism is where the ontic and epistemic issues most clearly converge.

As already noted, one can retain concepts as necessary for the *description* of particular phenomena while still maintaining any of the other types of reductionism toward those phenomena. We need not be committed to the irreducible reality of, for example, dreams simply because one makes statements about them—we can still argue that either the concept's real referent or its real content is about some other reality. Thus, there are no fundamental facts about the world that are entailed by our description of phenomena alone. Concept-antireductionism in this way is perfectly consistent with substance-, structure-, and theory-reductionisms.

Theory-reductionism and method-reductionism combine to raise the issue of whether there will ultimately be distinct sciences or only physics. The issue is whether phenomena can be completely understood by analysis into parts and bases and whether all theories will be reducible to those of physics. Will laws and theories in biology and the social sciences ultimately be nothing but special cases of theories in physics? This is the crux of the dispute for most disputants today.

The Impasse

Today what is obvious to many reductionists seems patently absurd to many antireductionists and vice versa. They state their positions with confidence and usually without advancing arguments for the basic positions of "reductionism" or "antireductionism." Nevertheless, the above discussion does show that reductionists and antireductionists materially disagree over how many ultimate substances and forces and brute facts there are. Analysis and integrative methods can well be accepted as complements, each supplying something the other omits. But again, analysis cannot be confused with the metaphysics of reductionism: *reductionism and antireductionism themselves cannot be complements* because of their different visions of what is real. Nor for this reason can any successes of analytical approach in science be taken as unqualified evidence for the *metaphysics of reductionism*.

Behind the various strands of the physicalists' reductionism is the intuition that there is only matter and that the physical forces are all that makes the world work. Their world is simpler than the antireductionists' in its components and mechanisms and more complicated in the interactions of these components. To use a metaphor philosophers never mean literally: when God created matter and however many fundamental physical forces there are at work in nature, he did not have to perform any other deed for all of reality to evolve into what it is today, even if some randomness is involved in the evolution of the cosmos. For example, after God created molecules in motion, he did not have to do anything else to create heat. And once God set up rules that enabled atoms to combine, he did not have to do anything else for everything to appear, including human beings. Knowing the parts in their construction and context is all we will ever need to know in order to understand any whole. If we knew all the details of all the phenomena of any two neighboring levels, we would be able to predict all the higher level phenomena and to deduce all the higher level laws. Once we know the details of the lower level of organization, the mystery of the existence of the more complex level goes away. In the end, an account of one level will be all that is needed.

Antireductionists of each type, however, think God would still have more work to do to create higher level phenomena such as life and consciousness. Their intuition is that since the physics operating in a stone and a plant are the same there must be more going on in the plant than just complex physical reactions. Other forces are at work in the world, and the structuring of reality above the physical sublevels of organization is as real and equally fundamental as the structuring of those sublevels. Higher level phenomena involve the emergence of genuinely novel features of reality that cannot be exhaustively explained from any amount of knowledge of the constituent parts and their interactions, even if they could somehow be predicted *post facto*, and so the higher level phenomena will always require their own irreducible laws and theories. Moreover, the process of the emergence of higher levels itself has not yet been explained—or, for that matter, how "supervening" properties are "realized" by their bases—and may well not be explainable by any known physical forces. In sum, if we focus only on the parts and their interactions, a central mystery about reality will always be missed.

With these distinctions, definitions, and issues as a framework, we can turn to how reductionists and antireductionists of the different varieties do battle in four areas: the natural sciences, philosophy of mind, the social sciences, and religion.

Notes

1.   A minority position today is that causation is not in fact a feature of reality. Bertrand Russell defended the position on the grounds that causation does not figure in fundamental physical equations (but see Cartwright 1979). Some philosophers today claim there is no causation on the quantum level or indeed in reality at all (see Field 2003). If causation is a level-effect, reductionists here must argue that there has one basic level.

2.   Many antireductionists today resist being called "emergentists" because of its association with the British school of emergentism from the early twentieth century (Crane 2001). However, at most there is only a difference in emphasis: antireductionists focus on the pluralism of real levels of organization, while emergentists focus on the process of the

continuing arising of new levels in the universe.

3.   An issue that is often missed is whether all emergence occurs in the same way or not—i.e., whether there is one common pattern of emergence (Johnson 2001) or whether different levels of organization emerge in different ways. So too, is evidence of emergence (or reduction) of one level *evidence for other alleged cases* of emergence (or reduction)? Don Howard (2007: 156-57) and Michael Esfeld (2001: 300-302) both caution against the extrapolation of "entanglement" in the quantum realm as a basis for emergence in other realms—as Howard says, patience, modesty, and humility are intellectual virtues as well as moral ones. Some emergentists may also agree that some higher level features are products of lower level forces or aggregate-features only, even if some features are not reducible.

4.   If nonphysical *structures* are responsible for producing higher levels, then higher level phenomena do not "*emerge*" out of the physical level of organization—the biological and the mental structures are simply other nonphysical structures organizing matter. Thus, the concept of "emergence" does not actually capture the idea of different *structures* well.

5.   Whether substance and structure have one common source is an issue. Stephen Hawking differentiates "matter" and "interactions" (e.g., gravity and electromagnetism) and advances a theory in which they represent different spins of particles (1980: 135, 144).

6.   It was thinkers with an interest in *science and religion* who first differentiated strands of reductionism (e.g., Peacocke 1976)—others had treated all strands as one.

7.   The term "materialism" has fallen out of favor since physicists have not found tiny discrete bits of *matter*. Reductionism may seem to be a vestige of the old metaphysical view of discrete particles to nature (Gk., *physis*), and antireductionism may seem easier to maintain with a "process" view of things, but "physicalists" still contend that what is ultimately real in the universe is only what physical structures are embedded in.

8.   Some consider such brute facts to be "contingent" or "accidental," or, for those with an existentialist bent, "absurd" or "irrational." But the point is simply that such facts have no further explanation and must be accepted as just the way things are.

9.   Ontologically, "basic" and "fundamental" mean "applying to the most phenomena" and hence to "the lowest," "most ubiquitous" or "most abstract." Epistemically, they mean "what cannot be explained in terms of other features of reality" or "primitive."

10.   How do antireductionists know that structures and causes above the lowest physical level are not all *physical*? But if some structures operate only in living entities or conscious entities, labeling them "biological" or "mental" is appropriate. How could the new properties be merely new *physical* ones? In combining a substance-monism with a structural-pluralism, antireductionists may also adopt a "neutral monism" (to use David Hume's idea) in which neither physical nor mental properties have ontological priority.

11.   Tying the notion of "novelty" to *prediction*—i.e., higher level properties not being predicted from our knowledge of lower level phenomena—is risky since we may be able to predict more someday if we have more knowledge. We cannot know today that something cannot "*in principle*" be unpredictable or that claims cannot be deduced from an ideal theory. That higher level properties remain in some sense *ontologically unique* compared to lower level properties is what remains important, not the *epistemic* claims about prediction.

12.   Theory-reductionists accuse theory-antireductionists of circularity in their explana-tions—i.e., using part of what has to be explained in the explanation itself. But there is circularity in the reductionists' explanations too: reductionists explain physical events—all there is to reality, according to them—in physical terms, just as antireductionists explain biological and mental events in their own terms. Either way, as with any fundamental metaphysics, at some point there is nothing more basic to use for an explanation.

2

The History of Reductionism and Emergence

The term "emergentism" was introduced only late in the nineteenth century and the term "reductionism" only in the middle of the twentieth century. But even if "reductionism versus antireductionism" has become a distinct dispute only relatively recently, the controversy has roots that can be traced to themes lying at the very beginning of Western philosophy.

The Roots of Reductionism

Reductionism has always been closely tied to the schools concentrating on analysis. The view that we should cut up reality to get to its "real" components has been a part of Western philosophy since its beginnings. But so has the competing more integrative approach of antireductionism (see Montalenti 1974). In Greece when the pre-Socratic philosopher Democritus claimed only eternal and unbreakable identical bits of matter (atoms) and the void they move in are real, he epitomized the substance-reductionist approach.[1] We normally take substance to be more ontically fundamental than structure, but Pythagoras took the other perspective when he declared "All is number." Today a structuralism has returned but one focusing on physical structures rather than Platonic mathematical ones. These structuralists give ontic priority to structure—especially in quantum physics—and downplay the "stuff" that the structures are instantiated in (e.g., Ainsworth 2010; see also Ladyman & Ross 2007).[2] They advance a realism based on the structures detected by scientists as fundamental, even to the point of denying the existence of any "entities"—all there is for scientists to find in nature are invariant relationships.[3]

But Aristotle took a teleological and holistic approach in biology and accepted a dualist cosmology of fundamentally different celestial and terrestrial realms. This reflects both substance- and theory-antireductionism. He also introduced the famous phrase "The whole is different from the sum of its parts." Substance-, structure-, theory-, and method-reductionisms all fit well with the atomic approach but are hard to reconcile with the Aristotelian approach. Indeed, structure- and theory-reductionisms are the natural enemies of teleology since the latter involves an independent directionality to events not explainable by lower level principles.

The Aristotelian holistic approach dominated over the atomistic approach through the Middle Ages in Western and Muslim natural philosophy. But by the dawn of modern science in sixteenth and seventeenth centuries, analytical and mechanistic approaches of breaking down continuities into manageable units and examining their interactions—in Francis Bacon's words, "dissecting and anatomizing the world"—gained dominance after René Descartes and became the sources of important discoveries in physics. Analysis led to a certainty and agreement in claims that people craved at this time of religious and political turmoil. Any Aristotelian purposefulness was rejected in physics and astronomy, and attention shifted to questions of Aristotelian "efficient" and "material" causes. (The teleological approach dominated the study of the "natural history" of the earth and life much longer, well into modern geology and biology.) Galileo increased the focus on structure in science when he stated that the "book of nature" was written in mathematics. By the eighteenth century, the idea that explanations in astronomy and physics must ultimately be in terms of the mechanical interaction of independently existing particles of lifeless and inert matter was well-established.

In the exemplar of the new approach—classical Newtonian physics—physical wholes are reduced simply to the sum of their parts, with the parts being isolated items that interact only mechanically on each other. No new higher level realities emerge; all things are only different physical aggregations of inert particles produced by forces governed by Newton's mechanical laws. This approach became more entrenched by the nineteenth century with the mathematization of nature through precise measurement and the application of Euclidean geometry. The shift was away from the question of what is the ultimate nature of things (the issue of *substance*-reductionism) to how things interact and what kind of parts they were composed of (the issue of *structure*-reductionism). With the shift in interest in the modern era toward more analysis of phenomena and more empirical approaches to theorizing, the focus in modern philosophical circles shifted to issues of structure-, theory-, and method-reductionisms. Thomas Hobbes aided the shift by arguing that all phenomena, including human beings, are only bodies in motion.

In this way, a conception of the universe and of our place in it evolved in the modern era that was conducive to the development of the general idea of reductionism. Reductionist tendencies became central to modern science and to the epistemologies and metaphysics that developed in light of reflections on the modern scientific search for simplicity and unity. But, contrary to many scholars' perspective, the Scientific Revolution and the Enlightenment were not the only sources of modern reductionist thinking. Another source can also be traced back to ancient thought: the quest for a viable monism.

Substance-Monisms

The simplicity expressed by monism—i.e, that is ultimately only one fundamental type of reality—is ontologically reductive. Today it is considered more attractive than ontological pluralisms of fundamentally irreducible types of substance (e.g.,

Leibniz's monads) or dualisms (e.g., Descartes' material and thinking substances). The monistic commitment that there is ultimately only one fundamental type of reality usually includes commitment to a plurality of actual entities of that type.

A metaphysical quest for simplicity and unity has pervaded philosophy since the Ionian philosopher Thales first advanced the claim that water is the origin (*arche*) or the one ultimate substance of all things. Usually Western monists claim matter is only one kind of reality, but physicalism has not been the only monism advanced in modern times. In addressing problems with physicalism, George Berkeley advanced an idealism (or "immaterialism," to use his term) in which all of reality is reduced to a collection of mental substances—all subjective and physical phenomena become merely perceptions in an individual's mind or in the mind of God. The world is thereby reduced to a collection of ideas. Baruch Spinoza's God/nature can also be interpreted as ultimately a strong monism of only one substance. David Hume in turn argued for a neutral monism in which the ultimate stuff of reality is neither mental nor physical. Bertrand Russell also advocated a neutral monism of events as basic. Contemporary physicalists and naturalists may not be interested in speculating on the ultimate nature of "matter," but they carry on this monistic tradition.

However, there is a stronger version of substance-monism: there is in fact only one reality, and the apparent multiplicity of objects we experience is actually only a manifestation of that one reality. Monists of this stronger variation include the early Greek Parmenides who reasoned that all reality is eternally one and all apparent change is ultimately illusory. Philosophical speculation is not the only source of monism. Another important impetus is religion: positing one transcendent reality in the place of the apparent multiplicity of the created world. Advaita Vedanta's nondualism is a nontheistic example.[4] Not all religions are ontologically reductive, but religion does show that physicalists are not the only reductionists. Nevertheless, the reductive approach that has most strongly manifested itself in this century in philosophical circles has not been religiously-based—it settles for an substance-reductionism of only matter. (Whether there was a religious motivation for the monistic tendencies of the scientists of the seventeenth century or whether more broadly reductionism in nonreligious circles has a deep root in the religious quest for an absolute and immutable reality will not be addressed here.)

British Emergentism

In England, the first explicitly antireductionist school arose in the debates over Darwin's evolutionary theory (Mill, 1872; Lewes 1875; Alexander 1920; Broad 1925; Morgan 1927; see McLaughlin 1992; on the Continent, Henri Bergson [1911] developed somewhat similar ideas on the emergence of genuine novelty). Emergentists attempted to provide a general philosophical understanding of the formation of phenomena such as life and consciousness. Their objective was to sail a middle course between mechanistic physicalism and the vitalism in the biology of the day. Physicalists appeared unable to explain life and consciousness, and vitalists were committed to a nonmaterial substance to explain life. In their place, emergentists proposed that everything is indeed made only of matter, but properties of wholes are "emergent"—a term introduced by George Henry Lewes (1875)—in that they are not in any way predictable from even complete knowledge of the properties and relations of the parts.[5] The behavior of the whole is understood and explained in terms of the structure of that complex system and not in terms of the particular components within that system. The properties of the whole thus are *genuinely emergent realities*—"novel properties" not reducible in any way to the properties of the parts but new and real features of realities Broad 1925: 23).[6]

Emergence is thus at least as much an ontic matter as an epistemic matter of what we can or cannot infer or predict from our knowledge of the properties of a whole's component parts. Emergent properties cannot exist without physical bases, but they emerge whenever certain conditions are present—the process of emergence simply occurs naturally and spontaneously. It is an unexplainable brute fact about reality that, in Samuel Alexander's colorful phrase, must be accepted with an attitude of "natural piety" (1920: 47). Such properties as the transparency of water or the rigidity of solids are irreducible, new features of reality. They are not merely unpredictable from our knowledge of the atomic and molecular levels but are unexplainable by those factors alone. Thus, irreducibility covers both the *unpredictability* and *unexplainability* of higher level phenomena.

To elaborate: As the universe has evolved, reality has become more and more complex—matter has not merely been clumped into larger and larger aggregates but has become integrated structurally to reveal genuinely novel properties. Thus, at certain points in this evolution, distinctively new classes of properties have burst forth. All British emergentists accepted at least these levels: the physical, the chemical, the biological, and the psychological.[7] In Alexander's more elaborate formulation, matter emerged out of space and time; life emerged out of complex configurations of matter; consciousness emerged out of biological processes; and deity emerged out of consciousness (1920).[8] There are properties specific to each level resulting from organizational relationships; their study and the formulation of laws governing their relationships require sciences other than physics.

More generally, the properties and behavior of any whole (including mechanical devices) cannot be deduced, *even in principle*, from even complete knowledge of the properties and behavior of its parts, taken separately or in combination or in their structural context (Broad 1925: 61, 77). The higher level properties are genuinely novel and can never be anything but novel. This is in contrast to unexpected events caused simply by aggregation. For example, if we keep adding sand to the top of a pile, we may or may not be able to determine when and in which direction an avalanche will occur. Nevertheless, an avalanche, even if unpredictable in its details, is the type of event we would *expect* to occur. It is at most a trivial instance of "emergence" since the whole manifests a property (the movement of the avalanche) that the parts do not, but it is one that reductionists can accept since no new forces are generated. Aggregation by gravity *produces* avalanches, but a similar aggregation of oxygen and hydrogen does not *produce* wetness, nor does an aggregation of neurons *produce* consciousness. We would never expect or even conceive in advance of actually seeing water's wetness that this would emerge from oxygen and hydrogen fusing together; nor would we expect simply from connecting more and more neurons together that the new level of consciousness would emerge.

Central to this view is that each level has *causal powers* that the lower levels do not. For these emergentists, *to be real is to have causal power* (Alexander 1920: 8). Merely being epiphenomena or a necessary part of an explanation was not enough. For example, biological organisms have powers (e.g., digestion and reproduction) that inanimate matter does not. Consequently, there are interactions on the biological level that are constituted exclusively by the interactions on the biological level and not on a subatomic level. In short, the biological interactions are not accomplished by the physical properties from which the biological phenomena emerge. But biological interactions, like all events in the universe, obey the laws of physics and thus remain subject to their restrictions.

Emergentism is consistent with the identification of the base-conditions on lower levels—or "correlates," as emergentists called them—out of which emergent properties arise. It is not consistent with a structure-reductionism that maintains that the base-conditions determine higher level properties. Nor is emergentism consistent with a theory-reductionism that would render unnecessary all theories from a higher science in favor of those of a lower science. C. D. Broad did go so far as to agree that, for example, the nature and configuration of chemical compounds *determine* the higher level phenomena of a living body, but he insisted the higher level properties were not *predictable* from any amount of knowledge of the base-conditions (1925: 67-68). For example, breathing is an activity that cannot be predicted by the laws governing the interaction of the parts of a breathing system (1925: 81). The laws governing phenomena on any level are in no way deducible from laws or theories of other levels. To Broad, the characteristic behavior of the whole could not, even in theory, be deduced from a complete knowledge of the behavior of its components, taken separately or in other combinations, or of their arrangements in a whole (1925: 59)—something about even the simplest whole is left unexplained by its parts.

Some reductionists argue that emergentism in at least some forms is in fact compatible with reductionism (e.g., Wimsatt 1976; Stöckler 1991). But their arguments rest on the idea that the higher level properties may be predictable. In the emergentists' view, however, the emergence of genuine novelty renders structure- and theory-reductionism impossible. It also renders predictability improbable, even in principle, although Broad still argued for the compatibility of predictability and genuine novelty (1925: 67). The higher level properties remain genuinely novel phenomena regardless of how they arose and as such are irreducible. Thus, a gap remains between the explanation of the higher level phenomena and their base-conditions. And, again, *how* higher levels emerge from base-conditions remains a mystery for emergentists. (Antireductionists today are more open to the possibility that scientists may be able to learn something of the "how" of emergence.)

Perhaps the emergentists' highlighting of a problem they could not resolve is why this school never became more popular. In any case, emergentism as a distinct school peaked in the 1920's and faded in the onslaught of the logical positivists' attack against all systems-building. Advances in our knowledge of chemical bonding, while logically irrelevant to the issue of emergence (Broad 1925: 62-63), also hurt its acceptability (see McLauglin 1992). It is important, however, to realize that such views have been defended in the history of philosophy. And, with the decline of positivism, certain of the emergentists' central doctrines have reappeared in the works of contemporary antireductionists in both biology and the mind-body area and of the general systems theorists.

The "Unity of Science" Program

Reductionism in all its forms in twentieth century Anglo-American philosophy is anchored squarely in logical positivism. This analytical school, a reaction to nineteenth century German romanticism and idealism (the world as will, value, or idea), attempted to find cognitive certainty and completeness in science. To accomplish this, positivists attempted to construe science as an epistemic matter only, unconnected to any metaphysical commitments. A major aspect of their quest resulted in their "Unity of Science" program. This program consisted of two parts. The first part aimed to establish a universal language for the sciences through a concept-reduction of all theoretical terms in the sciences (and the cognitive part of our everyday language) to observational terms. One such attempt was Rudolf Carnap's "reduction-statements." Both the meaning and reference of the theoretical terms were to be reduced by means of "correspondence rules" or "bridge principles" connecting these terms to observational terms. Thereby, the theoretical vocabulary would be defined in observational terms. In this concept-reduction, a homogeneous class of terms in a theory-free, physicalist "thing-language" would become the beginning point for all hypotheses and the testing point for all scientific claims. Every term, even if not strictly definable in thing-language terms, would be reducible to terms of the thing-language and ultimately to observable "thing-predicates"—all statements about theoretical entities would thus be reduced to statements about regularities in our experiences. (This led to "phenomenalism" in which statements about external entities were to be reduced to statements about actual or potential experience.) All scientific knowledge would then be secured on a foundation of observational terms. However, the founder of the positivist Unity of Science movement, Otto Neurath, opposed this reduction to observational terms and argued "thing-language" had to be retained for science. And the semantic reduction of theoretical terms to observational ones does not necessarily lead to theory-reduction or other reductions: Neurath, foresaw a *pluralism* of sciences (Creath 1996). For him, the "in principle" possibility of a microphysical description of phenomena held no importance for the rest of science. But many others since then have thought it should lead to such a reductionism. The project also included the social sciences: sociological terms would be reduced to psychological terms concerning the individual members of a society and their relationships to each other and their environment. The psychological terms would then be reduced by a physiological or behaviorist method to physical terms (Carnap 1949).

Positivists thought the language of observational terms already existed and anticipated no great difficulties in carrying out their program (Carnap 1949: 22). This also was relevant to the issue of whether a description and theory (and hence concept- and theory-reductionism) can be completely separated. However, the proposed reduction-sentences were found not to replace the reduced scientific terms without a loss of content—the reducing vocabulary never conveyed, without residue, all that the theoretical terms of science did. Indeed, in one of the first uses of the term "reductionism," Willard van Orman Quine refers to a type of concept-reductionism—that each meaningful statement is equivalent to some logical reconstruction in terms of immediate experience—as one of the two questionable dogmas of empiricism (1953: 37-41). Other attempts by later analytical philosophers to reduce our talk of physical objects or unobservable theoretical entities to talk of some immediate sense-experience have also been generally rejected. If nothing else, thing-statements specify the *conditions for the occurrence* of certain sense-experiences and therefore cannot be reduced to statements about the sense-experiences alone but involve reference to something outside them.

In the end, the part of the positivists' reductionist program related to the concept-reduction of scientific terms failed. But the idea of concept-reductionism played a prominent role in analytical philosophy of language—it was an important part of why it is called *analytical*—in the first half of this century.

Reductive Physicalism

Logical positivists believed that all issues of substance-monism, dualism, and pluralism were metaphysical questions on the order of whether what we call "physical" processes are, in the final analysis, actually spiritual or not, and that ultimately we will not be able to find any real content to such questions (Carnap 1949: 413). However, the commitment entailed by their beliefs is to a physicalism reflecting the dominant version of monism in secular circles in the contemporary West: whatever stuff physicists study is all there is.[9] All apparent biological and mental phenomena are aggregates of matter, regardless of the dispute over structuring. Abstract entities (such as numbers, universals, and facts) are nothing but mental states, which in turn are nothing but neurological events. All social and cultural phenomena (such as languages, religions, and ethics) are in some way substantively reducible to the physical or are totally subjective illusions. Progress in science is measured in terms of the expansion of reductive explanations to new domains.

Physicalism can be defined by what it denies: any mental, biological, or super-natural substances. That is, all realities are merely combinations of physical objects—they are exhaustively composed of only the most fundamental physical particles or whatever the ultimate nature of matter is. But how should we characterize "matter"? Democritus's idea of indivisible bits of matter in empty space floundered with discoveries in physics in the early twentieth century. Not only were atoms found to be divisible, but Einstein's famous equation "$E=mc^2$" showed that mass (the physicists' refined version of "matter") is convertible to energy and vice versa. It seems "substance" has no substance. Vibrating "strings," intangible "fields," and theories of matter as being only excited states of space-time, with particles popping in and out of existence, also present a problem for characterizing "matter." Other answers in terms of occupying four dimensional space-time or having weight have also been found wanting. Today the most popular conclusion by philosophers is that the physical is simply whatever physicists study. No further characterization is needed. Physicalists brush aside the issue that physicists' theories *change* and so future theories may involve different ideas of what is material. With such problems in actually defining "matter," one might wonder why physicalists are so insistent upon it, but their point is that all that is real is only inert matter—there are no *biological* or *mental* substances. Some physicalists think they must throw in at least a dash of mathematics to make physics, and hence physicalism, work. But any realist interpretation of mathematical entities creates a conflict between the physicalists' motto "all is physical" and the reality of abstract entities.

Even if some physicalists were to assert that the world is the creation from some ontologically deeper, transcendent reality—an idea not easily reconciled with the spirit of physicalism—such a deeper reality would nevertheless not be acceptable as an active force within the universe. In short, the universe is one all-embracing, closed system of exclusively material realities. But physicalists need not be determinists: they may accept that some events are in fact causeless and random. But even if there are random events, the universe is causally closed: it consists of causal chains and initial conditions for events that are totally physical. This includes any processes causing the emergence of various levels.

Physicalists do include *structure* in their ontology, not just what is structured. And here physicalists are not all of one mind, so to speak. There are two broad groupings: *reductionist* and *antireductionist*. For reductionists, only physical forces organize matter or space-time into everything from subatomic particles up to the realities we experience. There are only physical properties, and so all levels are structurally reducible to physical structures (or, to most physicalists, to only subatomic sublevels of organization). Nature does not make discontinuous leaps in structure: no nonphysical structures exist. There is only one level of structuring and the different higher level properties that we see result only from increasingly complex combinations fixed by physical forces. Thus, if we could duplicate the physical aspects of the universe, we would duplicate it all—if what is biological is accidental, it may not appear, but if it does, still only physical forces are at work. Reductionists thus need not claim that the higher levels are merely large *aggregates* of phenomena from the lowest sublevel of physical organization but only that the lower level realities somehow *determine* the higher level phenomena and that only physical structures are involved. The correlation of higher and lower level phenomena is sufficient in their eyes to establish that lower cause the higher, and once we understand the lower level phenomena in sufficient detail, no mysteries will remain—nothing else needs to be explained as to how or why the higher levels arise. There is a "completeness of physics." Why the universe generates any order at all or why so many levels of order arise is no concern of theirs, nor is how exactly matter gives rise to life and consciousness.

For this reason, reductive physicalists treat the problem of "emergence" as in fact something very trivial. New properties do arise when physical pieces are put together into complex wholes, but their existence is no more problematic than, to use J. J. C. Smart's example, the fact that when the pieces of a radio are connected properly they can receive a signal. The new phenomena are not evidence of any new level of natural forces, nor are there special forces causing emergence. Things just arise automatically out of lower levels of complexity in accordance with some laws of physics, and there is nothing else to explain about "emergence." Simply identifying correlations of higher and lower phenomena is all that is needed.

Thus, reductive physicalists may use the word "emerge," but they deny there are any truly emergent realities in the antireductionist sense. All that reductionists endorse is that more complex configurations of matter exhibit properties that their parts do not, not that higher levels have independent causal powers or that the higher level properties can never be understood at least in principle by complete knowledge of both the higher and lower level properties. There are no other structures at work but the structures and forces that operate on the lower level. Higher level properties may never even be predictable, but they are structurally reducible as being exclusively the product of physical structures. The solidity and rigidity of ice would not be found by examining hydrogen and oxygen atoms individually, but once we understand chemical bonding and freezing, we find that no forces are at work except those at the atomic level—the higher level properties *must* appear whenever these atoms are bonded to make a water molecule and the water is cooled enough. No "emergent" structures or realities are at work. Solid objects do interact, but their causal power is only a product of lower level forces. And the same applies to biological and mental phenomena. Thereby, all organization can be completely understood reductively. With only one level of causes, each event can have only one complete explanation. Thus, there could be no more than one theory for any event. Any alternative would lead to causal overdetermination.

This configurational approach precludes a naively atomistic conception of reduction in which the whole is just the additive sum of its parts: the properties of wholes emerge only with the parts in their proper context, but wholes are still no more than the sum of their parts on different scales. The properties of the wholes cannot be located in any part—indeed, these properties are distinct from any of the properties of the parts, individually or additively—but they are exhaustively *explainable* by the parts and physical structures alone.

Naturalism

In sum, reductive physicalism has three basic components: substance-, structure-, and theory-reductionism. But another contemporary school of philosophy is not so restrictive on these issues. "Philosophical naturalism" as developed in America is centered on the success of science. Naturalists are less concerned with ontological questions of the composition of things and instead in their metaphysics simply endorse as real whatever can be studied by any of the sciences (not just physics). All naturalists are committed to the substance-reductionism in which all of the universe is composed of one type of substance. Some naturalists are structure-reductionists, but many are structure-antireductionists, accepting that real nonphysical phenomena genuinely emerge out of physical bases. Some are also substance-antireductionists for whom reality is pluralistic in its fundamental make-up, with no one substance having a fundamental primacy; they also reject any physical determinism (Ryder 1994: 14-15). William James's radical pluralism exemplifies this (1977). For naturalists, realities do not have to be physical—consciousness and abstract mathematical entities may be real and yet not physical. But everything real, including human beings, is continuous with the rest of nature and is subject to scientific investigation. In this way, naturalists attempt to avoid the metaphysical difficulties of characterizing what exactly is "matter," although giving concreteness to what exactly is "natural" is itself difficult. Thus, there is only one dimension to reality: anything real is "natural" (naturalism's ontic component) and open to scientific study (its epistemic and method component).

Nature is taken to be a closed causal system with no possibility of influence from outside. Indeed, there is no "outside"—the realm of nature is all there is. No reality exists outside the domain studied by scientists. There is only the "natural order" and no underlying reality or source to the world unknowable by means of science. Naturalists deny the possibility of a supernatural divinity existing outside nature or of such entities as "souls" that are not open to scientific scrutiny.

Not all naturalists are as gung ho as reductive physicalists about the reduction of the social sciences to the natural sciences. Naturalists can readily accept that social scientists study phenomena resulting from structures that are not reducible to physical ones and that these sciences themselves may prove irreducible to physics. But again, naturalists rest with reducing reality to what is studiable by scientists. Thus, naturalists are more open to substance-, structure-, and theory-pluralisms.

By reducing reality to only what scientists can give an account of, naturalists can be accused of making human reason the standard for what is real. But the type of reduction most distinctive to naturalism is the reduction of all things human to natural properties. Naturalists do not eliminate such sociocultural realities as moral and religious values—they can even champion their importance. But the thrust of naturalism is that all such values have no grounding outside the realm studied in science. Naturalists need not claim nature is essentially impersonal or value-neutral, since human beings and our experiences, feelings, and actions are as much a part of nature as atoms. Human life—along with its purposes, goals, meaning, values, and ideals—is wholly natural (Ryder 1994: 21). In denying the supernatural, any ethical values or religious demands are reduced to natural properties. Any realism concerning the sacred or life after death is denied, and religion is reduced to ideals of human activity (Dewey 1934).

General Systems Theory

In the 1940's, a school of speculative thinkers—"general systems theorists"—arose that is antireductive in outlook but is more metaphysical than most contemporary antireductive physicalists (Bertalanffy 1968; Koestler 1969; Weiss 1969; Laszlo 1972; Zeleny 1981). These thinkers focus on systems-theorizing in the sciences —from physics to the social sciences to ecology to computer science to information theory—and are attempting to construct an integrated and comprehensive picture of reality with practical social applications. They look to construct an encompassing theory of systems in the various sciences, but they do not reduce all systems to one abstract master system for the entire world.

General systems theorists emphasize the structural organization of reality in an encompassing hierarchy of systems. Stable patterns and invariances of structure underlying transformations in states of affair, rather than the classical focus on entities and their causal interaction, are central. Each entity is a whole subject to the dynamics of a network rather than a bundle of linear chain reactions mechanically programmed at a subatomic level (Weiss 1969: 4). The focus is on synthesis rather than on analysis into isolated parts (although the value of the latter is not denied), on how sets of events are structured, and on how they function in relation to their environment (Laszlo 1972: 20). Since the Big Bang, reality has been evolving new coherent systems—both physical and nonphysical—with greater and greater complexity of properties that exist in states of equilibrium. The higher systems are composed of lower level systems; and each system, from the level of quarks up to the universe as a whole, is a whole having some properties that cannot be reduced to the properties of their parts added together. Each whole is "more than the sum of its parts," not in the sense of having some more *substance* than the parts collectively, but in having *properties* the parts can never have. Indeed, the properties of a whole are *other than* the properties of its parts or their sum. And this is what makes the whole irreducible: the "information" of the whole is a level of "information" that cannot be reduced to the sum of "information" about its parts (Weiss 1969). In sum, we live in a universe of constant emergent novelty in which the novelty of each new level is not reducible to any of the preceding stages.

What is central here is an emphasis on wholes and structures. These theorists substitute the complexity of *natural systems* for the "emergence" of the British emergentists. They see a hierarchy of nested levels of complexity, with higher levels of organization having properties that are not reducible to the properties of their lower level components. Open systems develop greater complexity if they are not in a state of equilibrium, and their properties are generated by the self-organizing interaction of the components. After attaining a certain degree of complexity, the systems come to possess a new level of physical or nonphysical properties. Beyond that, these theorists do not go into *how* the higher level properties arise. Nor is the issue of the nature of the stuff in which systems are realized—the nature of the ultimate stuff of the world—important to them, although they are monists in their denial of nonnatural forces at work in the universe. What impresses systems thinkers is the scientists' search for invariance in the organization of entities, processes, and events that supplies uniformity underlying the diverse transformations, regardless of the material constituting them. The shift in attention is away from entities in isolation or their individual interactions to the stable relationships recurring within working systems. Indeed, the classical distinction between "substance" and "attribute" is replaced with talk of "wholes," "parts," and "systems."

General systems thinkers attempt to give these terms specificity. A system is a *self-stabilizing, self-maintaining, ordered configuration* in which the regularities exhibited by its interdependent elements determine the behavior of the totality. A system's properties are dependent upon the structure organizing its parts. It is the whole that makes the parts "parts." This talk of structures and organization, however, should not be taken to mean that these theorists see reality as static: within each level there is virtually nothing but dynamic interactions. Each whole is open to influences and conditioning from its environment and in turn influences its environment. In this way, there is a mutual interaction between the whole and the rest of reality. To these theorists, structure-reductionists miss something vital by focusing on the parts: everything is part of a whole. It is the structured wholes and their interaction with their environment that is the central feature of reality.

Systems theorists contrast integrated systems (e.g., atoms, cells, persons, or nations) with aggregates (e.g., piles of sand) and artificial constructs (e.g., machines or houses). The properties of aggregates are simply the sum of the properties of the parts, and the properties of the constructs are determined by lower level properties. Natural systems are wholes with irreducible properties. Any replacement of parts in a system (e.g., the replacement of atoms in the human body) is subject to the structure of the whole. In this way, the wholes are other than the sum of their parts. Wholes differ from aggregates (where parts can be added or removed without affecting the integrity of the relationships) or constructs (where parts can be replaced) precisely in not being merely the sum of their parts; instead they have an invariance in their naturally-generated organizational structure that gives rise to genuinely novel properties. But parts themselves *do not generate* the wholes since the resultant properties are not created by the properties of the isolated parts. A whole is not *made up* of its parts but rather *is* a new "emergent" reality. For example, the interaction of chemicals can completely alter the atomic structure of the substances by the fusion of the electron shells: salt does not "consist" of sodium and chlorine atoms any more but has completely new emergent properties; the properties of the whole cannot be detected in the parts precisely because the whole has drastically transformed its components' atomic structure and thus something new has resulted. Wholes influence the character and behavior of parts and vice versa. The interdependence of parts generated in a system by its organizational structure define its nature, not the parts individually or in individual interrelations.

Thus, more is involved in general systems theory than simply a shift in emphasis from substances to structures. As antireductionists in general agree, genuinely new features of reality emerge in complex systems, features that are not reducible to subatomic structures or their products. Wholes are sometimes said to be "synergistic" to emphasize the integration of parts producing something more than a mere pile of the parts. Organisms, as impermanent and open centers of activity with unique properties and governed by irreducible systems laws, have been an influential model for systems theorists (Bertalanffy 1968). But this does not mean these theorists treat all systems literally as organisms. Atoms are not reducible to the sum of the properties of its parts, but they are not an "organism" in a biological sense. Nor is the earth or universe as a whole viewed as a giant organism (as with the early Gaia theorists). In short, growing organisms are prime exemplars of the "systems" idea but systems remains the more encompassing category.

The prospect here is of a *reverse* holistic structure-reduction in which the reality of parts is downgraded or even denied in favor of that of the whole. Systems theorists resist this by endorsing a hierarchy of equally real levels. In fact, they give more specificity to the key concept of "*levels of organization*" than do most other philosophers who address the issue of reductionism or emergence. They use such terms as "suborganic" or "organic" to mean levels or modes of organization rather than categories of distinct realities or substances (Laszlo 1972: 29). The nested levels are interdependent realities "within" an entity and can only be abstracted out for study. Our grammar may make us think of an entity as distinct from the molecules or processes going on "inside" it, but systems thinkers do not look at the situation that way. Such levels are organized hierarchically, with "higher" indicating greater organizational complexity and "lower" indicating the simpler and more "basic" in the sense that the higher level cannot exist without the lower. For instance, for Arthur Koestler, an organism is to be regarded as a "multi-leveled hierarchy of semi-autonomous sub-wholes," branching in turn into more sub-wholes of a lower order, and so on down to the lowest order. These organic "sub-wholes" are self-regulating open systems that display both the autonomous properties of wholes on one level of organization and the dependent properties of parts on another level (1969: 210-11). All of nature consists of subsystems that constitute the base-conditions for higher systems—each system is a whole and a component of a larger whole at the same time. A system may be "open" and even indeterminate within its own level, but it is "closed" with respect to what it provides as a base for the next higher level. And each whole is subject to forces of more encompassing physical realities. Each whole, including the entire universe, has structures, but these structures are not reducible to one master structure, i.e., the irreducible reality of the substructures is never denied.

Levels have evolved from the subatomic, where even quarks do not exist in isolation but in integrated relationships, to higher levels of physical and chemical organization to the biological to the personal to the social. There are also additional sublevels of organization within each broad level. The biological and higher levels do not introduce new substances but are only increasingly complex structurings of the same stuff as in inanimate structures. Each level is real and has equal status with all the others—no structuring is any more real than another. Entities and processes on each level may be discrete and causally interactive. What remains central in their theory is a hierarchy of levels within each whole above whatever is the most elementary level of physical structuring. The properties emerging at a particular level in the hierarchy of systems involve the irreducible invariances on that level. Because properties on different levels are independent, it also follows that the various natural sciences will remain autonomous as scientists continue to study and explain the invariances on each irreducible level. Analytical and mechanical approaches to reality may prove very fruitful, but they will always be artificial *abstractions* and *idealizations* of the fullness of reality. The realities of the systems will still need to be accounted for, and explanations exclusively in terms of the parts will never be sufficient. Thus, "holistic" or "synthetic" approaches will always be needed for the fullest understanding we can have.

Today general systems theory remains underdeveloped and is probably only about as widely accepted as its positivist counterpart. But it does show the vitality of one elaborate antireductive metaphysical scheme.

Antireductive Physicalists

Antireductionism in this country did not catch on in mainstream philosophy in the early part of the last century despite the efforts of Roy Wood Sellars. His idea of "nonreductive realism" was that life is not a nonnatural force coming from outside nature but is a new capacity that nature found itself having (1970; also see Pepper 1926; Lovejoy 1936). Antireductionism, however, has made a powerful return among physicalists today. But contemporary antireductive physicalists are not simply emergentists without the title. British emergentists and general system theorists are more speculative in outlook, while antireductive physicalists, like their reductive counterparts, are not particularly concerned with the actual mechanisms of how higher level phenomena arise. But these physicalists are convinced one particular problem rules out reductive physicalism: "multiple realization." The basic idea is that *widely divergent base-conditions* are capable of "realizing" *identical higher state phenomena*. This suggests that other structures are responsible for the stability and invariance of higher level phenomena. Structure-reductionists think that only more detailed studies of the bases are needed to dispel this notion. But antireductionists point to such obvious facts as that the functions of artifacts (e.g., a clock's time-keeping or a computer's information processing) can be realized in many different ways and with many different materials. Cultural realities in general are defined without regard to their physical or biological substratum (e.g., a dollar being realized in various metals or paper), and thus they can also be realized in many diverse ways.

This is not to deny that every higher level phenomena must be realized in some lower level base. But simply because a physical substance and certain physical structures must be present for biological and mental structures to become operative does not mean that the physical layer determines or otherwise causes these structures. Thus, structure-antireductionists claim that because something is *dependent* on lower level phenomena base-conditions in the sense that certain base-conditions must be present for the higher level phenomena to appear does not mean that those phenomena are *derivable* from the base-conditions or *caused* by them. For example, the physics of subatomic atoms cannot account for the structure of molecules—molecules with the same atoms may have different structures—and thus subatomic properties cannot account for chemical properties (Hendry 2010, forthcoming). Even something as basic as *rigidity* can be realized by lattice structures and amorphous structures (as in glass). For many phenomena, there appear to be too many bases for even a manageable disjunctive set of bases. Indeed, sets may be open-ended in many instances. In sum, reductions require "one-to-one" (or at least "one-to-very-few") relationships between higher and lower level phenomena, but reality exhibits "many-to-one" relationships here.[10] In sum, there are recurring and stable types (and perhaps laws) on higher levels that are not determined or fixed by changing physical facts. Any natural kinds denoting how reality is in fact cut up that may exist on one level do not map cleanly onto natural kinds on a lower level. As Jerry Fodor puts it, lots of different sorts of micro-interactions manage, somehow or other, to converge on much the same macro-stabilities (1997: 162).

Of particular importance is that any given *mental state* can be realized in a range of quite diverse physical structures. As discussed in Chapter 4, not even a finite set of alternative physical states can collectively "embody" a mental one. Any straight forward and simple reductive identification of a mental state with a physical state hence is impossible. (Neural plasticity also suggests downward causation by psychological causes on neural bases.) This means mental properties are not simply physical properties. But this has not impressed the reductively-minded: they merely shift their claim from advocating one broad reduction of a mental state to advocating many littler "local" reductions to various physical states (e.g., Kim 1992). For them, the lack of a "one-to-one" relationship does not preclude the reduction of mental phenomena any more than the fact that the same temperature of a gas can be multiply realized by different motions of the molecules precludes identifying temperature with the mean molecular kinetic energy in the gas. But to structure-antireductionists, this means only that higher level phenomena must be embodied in a physical stratum—it does not at all explain the existence of the higher level phenomena in the first place.

Contemporary antireductionists too negotiate a middle path between reductive physicalism and vitalism, but they are squarely centered in physicalism. They subscribe to the substance-reductionism that everything is made of matter, but they reject the property claim that only the physical level of structuring is real. Instead, at least all levels of organization recognized by natural scientists are accepted as equally real. Thus, when the reductionist physicist Steven Weinberg says "Of course, everything is ultimately quantum-mechanical" (1995: 41), he is, according to antireductionists, both right and wrong: everything is physical and has a quantum field level, but it is equally true that there is more than one level of organization to reality, and not all such levels are ultimately quantum-mechanical. No primacy is given to the subatomic realm as being in any sense "more real" than the biological—plants and animals are as real as whatever subatomic realities physicists finally settle upon. In the extreme, they contend that advances in our understanding of the microlevels of reality will not make any explanatory contributions to our understanding of the world of our experience (Mayr 1988b: 475). So too, each state of matter above the atomic level—gaseous, condensed matter, liquid, solid—is an emergent level. Mental phenomena too are merely physical phenomena, but they are not reducible to, or determined by, the activity of subatomic particles. Sound cannot be reduced to the properties of sound waves but have an extra, irreducible property—the property of sounding. Our feelings, sensations, and thoughts are not eliminated—indeed, they are not even "secondary," as with Galileo, but have an equal claim to reality. Some antireductionists extend their pluralism to include all cultural phenomena (e.g., moral and aesthetic properties) as properties of objects existing independently of our subjective experiences.

It may turn out that some properties on higher levels are indeed determined products of lower level phenomena and hence are reducible to those lower level phenomena, but the point of structure-antireductionism is that not all properties on higher levels are reducible. Any successful reductions provide reasons to look for more reductions, but the reduction, for example, of chemical properties to physical ones is not evidence for other reductions, such as the mental to the biological. Properties of matter organized at the atomic level cannot be used to understand and explain properties at the cellular level—the properties of an electron are the same in a rock, a flower, or a person.

Antireductive physicalists may reject the idea of higher levels "emerging" out of lower ones: all levels of organization depend on lower level bases but are autonomous and not the products of those lower levels, and thus they do not "emerge" out of them. But activity on higher levels is not derivable from the components constituting an entity's or process' lower levels and the laws governing their activity. Wholes have properties that are qualitatively different and independent of the properties of their parts. Understanding the role each part or level plays depends on understanding the whole and not merely the parts. In that sense, the whole is greater than the sum of its parts and different in its properties. The solidity of tables or the liquidity of water are not *parts* of the systems composed of molecules but are *features* of the whole physical systems at a level higher than that of molecules (Searle 1995: 217). The higher level forces at work in a phenomenon have existed as long, or as timelessly, as the first physical forces that manifested themselves—the proper conditions for them to be applicable simply did not appear until a later point in the history of the universe. Just as a magnetic field explains the "spontaneous" organization of a pile of iron filings, so do these structures explain events that physicists dismiss as random or contingent. Thus, higher level physical forces (such as electromagnetism) and the forces responsible for life and conscious-ness existed in nature prior to the appearance of those higher level physical phenomena. These forces permit the properties to arise necessarily and spontane-ously whenever the appropriate conditions are present.

Each level has a novel order of causal interactions. Subscribing to a determin-ism of a closed system of causal order and initial physical conditions in the universe is possible for a structural antireductionist, but the possibility of causes from different levels of organization intervening in lower levels (e.g., consciousness affecting events on the neural or chemical sublevels in the brain) would require a larger causal order to be considered. The physical is closed in a substantive sense, but more structures are at work than just physical ones. There is no "causal completeness" of *physical* causes—indeed, this is a central issue in the dispute between structure-reductionists and antireductionists. The closure of physical causes is a metaphysical principle since physics cannot imply its own completeness (Bishop 2006: 45). And antireductionists see no reason to reject a *discontinuity* of structures between levels, even if there is only one substance and lower levels must be present. There is discontinuity even if there is interactions between levels through "upward" causation (e.g., biological mutations caused by subatomic radiation) or "downward" causation.[11] Because of this gap, theories explaining the activity on each level cannot be reduced to theories devised for other levels.[12]

Antireductive physicalism is thus a monism of substance combined with a pluralism of equally real levels of properties and causes. Antireductive physicalists thus see more complexity to reality than do reductionists in the area of structuring. Most antireductive physicalists today do not speculate on the actual process of emergence or why there are real and irreducible higher levels. They may be willing to accept that something in nature other than the forces currently recognized in physics is responsible for the emergence—forces built into the structure of reality as firmly as the atomic and other physical forces that are at work in the arising and operation of higher level phenomena. But in any case, properties appearing at higher levels of phenomena are not explainable in terms of lower level properties.

Concept-antireductionism is the natural consequence of such a view. Physical and chemical terms do refer to the same phenomenon in one sense (e.g., water), but antireductionists insist these terms refer to different levels of organization within that phenomenon (i.e., the properties of atoms versus the properties of water molecules). That is, both sets of terms refer to the same bit of matter, but they refer to different types of structuring. Thus, the descriptive categories of the different sciences all designate genuine, irreducible aspects of reality. In sum, concepts and facts for one level of properties are not deducible from the facts of lower levels.

Method-antireductionism also follows from these views. Analysis of parts and lower levels is not enough to lead to a complete explanation of any phenomenon. Holistic approaches may even be needed on one level of organization. Equally important, there is no one way the world is that can only be described by physicists. There is no one way to unify phenomena, but many different "maps" of the same terrain, each compatible with the others. Different domains require autonomous sciences and perhaps different methodologies. Physicists' accounts will never exhaust our knowledge, even in principle, or express all that is true of reality. A "*disunity* of the sciences" becomes the working hypothesis for this vision (see Fodor 1974; Dupré 1993).

In sum, antireductionists advocate a minimal version of physicalism (substance-reductionism) that does not exclude emergent entities and properties. A liberal pluralism of theories and methods across levels of organization and causes is needed to account adequately for the diverse aspects of reality, since there is no interesting sense in which ontological priority must be accorded to the allegedly homogenous stuff out of which bigger and more complex things are made (Dupré 1993). The antireductive "emergent" component may seem mysterious, but it is certainly no worse in this regard than the reductive physicalists' total lack of explanations for the way reality is organized into levels or for supervenience.

The Classical Model of Theory-Reductionism

Philosophers reject the first part of the positivists' "Unity of Science" project, as discussed above—that of reducing the terms of science to terms in a unified "thing-language" and "thing-predicates." The second part of the project—the establishment of a unity of the *explanatory principles* in science—has been more influential. Physics is treated as the foundation of the hierarchy of disciplines, and the objective is to construct a set of physical premises from which all the various laws covering the regularities in nature could be derived (Carnap 1949; Feigl 1953). Some speak of a unitary science attainable through the cumulative reduction of wholes into parts: a mereological analysis of wholes to their parts will lead smoothly in a continuous line from the largest wholes to the smallest parts (Oppenheim & Putnam 1958). Others speak, not of theory-reduction, but of a reducing theory predicting the same observations as the reduced theory (Kemeny & Oppenheim 1956). All the terms and principles would thereby be reduced to those of physics.

Theory-reduction here is conceived as a purely formal deductive relation between systems of defined concepts and logically related sentences. The idea is that the laws from the higher sciences eventually will be *logically derivable* from the theories that are finally established as basic to physics. As elaborated by Ernest Nagel, the classical account of theory-reductionism concentrates on the logical structure of finished theories and treats theory-reduction as a matter of statements proceeding by a formal logical deduction between statements (1961). Nagel included under one account both theory-replacement (or reductions with "homoge-neous" vocabularies) and interlevel theory-reductions (or "heterogeneous" reductions where the reduced theory contained descriptive terms not contained in the reducing theory). To accomplish this reduction, two things are required: the connectability of all concepts in the two theories, and the derivability of one set of laws from the other. The first requirement is a semantic relation anchoring the reduced concepts in the set of reducing concepts, thereby keeping the second requirement from being only the specification of necessary or sufficient conditions for higher concepts. Thus, one theory reduces a second theory if and only if the first theory, along with a set of "correspondence rules" or "bridge laws" translating the concepts of the second theory and a description of upper level boundary conditions into terms of the reducing theory (since higher level theories do not contain the concepts of lower level theories and vice versa), logically entails the second theory.

The bridge laws are not necessary definitions but contingent and substantive empirical hypotheses about the necessary and sufficient conditions on a lower level for the instantiation of the higher level phenomena to be explained. As such, they are constructed independently of either of the theories they connect. In form, they are biconditionals: if conditions x obtain on one level, then phenomena y occurs on another and vice versa. The laws of the reduced theory are then deduced, as simple logical consequences, from the reducing theory and a description of the boundary conditions. Nagel saw this theory-reduction as purely formal and having no ontic consequences. The empirical phenomena and laws to be explained are not explained away—chemical properties are not any less real when chemical laws are reduced to physical laws. But the reduction does clean up the theoretical realm: the theories previously used to explain phenomena are now unnecessary and are superseded, and thus their ontic posits are eliminated. A simpler overall account of the explanatory (and hence ontic) structure of the world results and, more diverse phenomena are brought within the scope of fewer structures identified as actually at work in reality.

The bridge laws are not part of the reducing theory or the reduced theory. Indeed, bridge laws are not part of physics, and they themselves are in need of explanations. For example, a new physical hypothesis is needed to relate the thermodynamic sense of "temperature" and the statistical mechanical sense of "mean molecular kinetic energy" (Nagel 1979: 358-59). Philosophers cannot present them as new scientific findings but only as correlations of a philosophical nature postulated by reductionists. Moreover, bridge laws connecting phenomena are in themselves *irrelevant* to the issue of whether a phenomenon has emerged or is reductively produced. But to reductionists, they are not mere correlations: the correlations are weighted in favor of *reduction*. The direction of the relation rests on the prior commitment to reductionism—the entities and processes of the lower level have ontic priority, and the higher level accounts can be replaced. The real structures have been identified, and they are always on the lower level. And since the correlations themselves do not *explain* anything, they only represent the reductionists' metaphysical judgment concerning what are the real forces at work in reality. Advocates would also have to explain how this new *causation* works. Those who see the bridge laws as *identity statements* between two claims, as in the case of the reduction of thermodynamics to the laws of statistical mechanics, would disagree. These theorists think the bridge laws and other correlations are explained through ontic identity, but again this is a matter of their reductive metaphysics.

In addition, the work of Norwood Hanson, Thomas Kuhn, and Paul Feyerabend on the history of science revealed problems for both the connectability and derivability requirements: *the change of meaning of terms* when theories supersede other theories. The word "sun" does not mean the same thing to Ptolemy and Copernicus (it referred to one of earth's many satellites to Ptolemy, but referred to an unmoving orb of another nature at the center of the universe to Copernicus), and "mass" does not mean the same to Newton and Einstein (mass is invariant in the former's theory but is relative to a frame of reference in the latter's). The fact that Newton's classical physics is a good working approximation in everyday circumstances for relativity theory is irrelevant—the *fundamental understanding of the nature of the world* in the two theories diverges and hence so do the meaning of their terms. Thus, there is less continuity of meaning here than Nagel saw. Some of the key properties in each case are incompatible in the different theories, and this means one set of terms cannot be translated precisely into the other. (This is also a problem for any attempted concept-reduction.) This also means that bridge laws between theories will never connect concepts with the same meaning. This incommensurability renders the theories completely unconnectable except by very artificial maneuvers. Without a meaning-invariance of terms between succeeding theories, the succession of theories cannot be seen as the simple replacement or reduction of one theory into a more comprehensive successor. In short, the history of one science cannot be reconstructed as a logical relation between successive theories. The old meanings can never be the logical consequence of the new theory. Rather, there is a total ontological and conceptual replacement with each new theory and no way to deduce one theory from the other. Any bridge laws connecting them will not reflect reality but will only be our own artificial creations.

In sum, Nagel's account is wrong: there simply can be no logical deduction when the meanings change. The successor theories are right on the explanatory structures in a way their predecessors were wrong, and we cannot deduce *what is wrong* from what is right. In fact, the theories to be reduced at points *contradict* the reducing theory. Even Nagel's supporters admit that the reduced theories were "not quite logically compatible" with, or were only "strongly analogous" to, the reducing theories. Some have argued that the reduced theories had to be "modified," "corrected," or "revised" for the deductions to work (e.g., Schaffner 1984). The structure of theories has to be "relaxed" to permit a "reasonably close analogue" to Nagel's account to go through (Schaffner 1993: 480). Others have held that the deductions work only "more or less" or "roughly," or "approximately," and that they do not "exactly fit" his account (Nickles 1973). Or an "analog structure" of the actual reduced theory must be created for the reduction to proceed (Hooker 1981). Some defenders are forced to argue that Nagel's account is still useful even though not a single historical example perfectly exemplifies the pattern he describes (Nickles 1973: 189). As staunch an empiricist as Carl Hempel stated that Nagel's account was an "untenable simplification" and that in none of the cited examples of reduction in science did the supposedly reducing theory imply the principles of the supposedly reduced theory—on the contrary, it contradicted them and thus the notion of deductive reducibility of laws did not work (1969: 197, 190). Even Nagel, in response to criticism, admitted that a reduced theory is only "approximately derivable" from the reducing theory and that the deductions varied in their degree of "completeness," the conditions for the bridge laws must be "relaxed," and the meaning of the terms in the bridge laws must be "extended" (1979). However, these are not minor quibbles when one is trying to construct a *formal* system. (This project also assumes all the sciences can be formalized into axiomatized systems—a premise that is itself not unproblematic.[13]) These problems undercut the entire project: it is like advancing a rigorous mathematical proof and then saying "Well, the theorems more or less follow from the axioms if you aren't too picky."

The entire "reduction as logical deduction" account also misses something essential: any historical or philosophical explanation of a theory-reduction would have to explain both the successes of the reduced theory and its *failures*—how, for example, Galileo's or Kepler's laws were correct and how they were erroneous. Looked at in this light, any attempt to modify or correct the theory to be reduced so that it would fit a logical deduction is entirely misguided. The errors of that theory would then be included as special cases of the reducing theory. Correcting the theory in fact thus would hurt the reductionists' cause. Of course, too much correcting of the errors in a reduced theory or adding premises known to be false (e.g., that the speed of light is infinite, in order to deduce Newton's theory from relativity) simply in order to make the deductions fit the account would make the entire situation blatantly question-begging. In effect, reductionists would be reconstructing the history of science to force it to be philosophically correct.

The thrust of these objections is that reduction, if successful reductions do in fact occur in science, is not a matter of logical inclusion. The formal deductive account offered the simplest and strongest image of what a reduction must be. It makes the succession of theories look like an instance of theory-reduction only by employing a view of theory-change that is necessary for this metaphysical vision. Even for theory-replacements, the real relation of the predecessor and successor is more complicated and less rigorous, and the situation for interlevel reductions will be at least as complicated. Even Nagel's advocates now advances a looser, less "elegant" account for a derivation reduction (e.g., Schaffner 1993).

Post-Classical Theories of Theory-Reduction

Of course, the failure of Nagel's account does not mean rejecting theory-reductionism. Reductionists are still convinced some sort of theory-reductionism must hold. Most reductionists today now look for ways that a reducing theory can directly explain the data of a higher-level theory. Jaegwon Kim revived reductionism by focusing on "functional reductionism." Functionalism, as discussed in the next two chapters, is usually taken to be antireductive: it accepts higher level functions that can be realized through multiple lower level bases. But following the lead of David Lewis (1970), Kim argues that functionalism can get around the multiple realization problem and enable a structure-reductionism in both the sciences and philosophy of mind (1998: chap. 4; 2005: 164-65; also see Chalmers 1996: 42-51 and Wimsatt 1984). A higher level phenomenon is functionalized by defining it in terms of its lower level causes and finding the lower level mechanisms that perform the causal work. The higher level phenomenon is then seen as being caused by entities that are identical to configurations of lower level phenomena. For example, water is reduced by finding the realizers on the molecular level of its functions. Kim doubts this can lead to any realism about higher level functions (2010: 228-31). But he concedes that parts of *consciousness* cannot be functionalized and so that this approach cannot yet produce a theory-reductionism (2005: 174; 2011: 310). Nor does this approach avoid the problem of bridge laws since any functionalization of the higher level phenomena will be in different terms than the causes on the lower level.

More generally, the emphasis has shifted away from the linguistic construction of science as simply an ossified set of finalized theories. The actual on-going scientific activity in the dynamics of theory-change has become the focus, not after-the-fact reconstructions. In addition, such ontic matters as the posited entities or structures to be reduced and structural simplification between related domains of science have returned as a central concern. The focus in proposed reductions now is shifting to the general explanatory relation between a lower level theory or domain of realities and the higher level realities, not the relation between lower and higher level theories *per se*. Reductionists also now generally agree no single account of reduction can cover the relations of all theories in the sciences. And, more importantly, there may be instances where *no* reductions are possible at all (Sarkar 1992: 188). Some branches of science, such as evolutionary biology, have proven especially resistant to the reductive approach. Some phenomena may have no further explanation at a lower level, and for them there is no point in bringing up the issue of reduction at all (Wimsatt 1994). So too, theories on different levels evolve together, being revised in light of new findings and theories on both levels. As a result, scientists may have to modify their reducing theory to account for the new phenomena now within its scope. Indeed, the higher level work may greatly affect the development of the lower level science. In this way, there may be a *dialectical relationship* between the reducing and reduced theories (McMullin 1972: 96; Crick 1994: 8; Churchland & Churchland 1995: 76). Scientists working on the reducing theory may also gain completely unexpected insights concerning the lower level from working to reduce another theory.

One approach that also focuses on the causal conditions of the base is one that both reductionists and antireductionists are exploring. It bypasses the notion of theory-reduction altogether and instead concentrates on a type of structure-reductionism involving the "explanatory extension" of the range of lower level causes. But this approach emphasizes the *organization* on the lower level and tries to explain both the connections between levels and their limitations. No theories or fields of research are eliminated, but different fields become connected. Sometimes causes are characterized in interlevel or interfield terms as research hypotheses for extending the explanatory range of theories (Darden & Maull 1977; Maull 1977). Multilevel descriptions of causal mechanisms are needed because the levels of organization are not totally isolated from each other; different fields simply have different foci of attention.[14] Thereby, there is an interfield integration that shows how higher level causal properties are achieved by lower level mechanisms. (Sarkar 1998; Machamer, Darden & Craver 2000; Craver 2005; Wimsatt 2006). ("*Mechanisms*" here does not necessarily mean external, machine-like operations only but the *workings* on the lower level responsible for the higher level phenomena.)

This approach incorporates a structure-reductionism by completely skipping the formal relation of the postivists' notion of theory-reduction. Indeed, talk of "theory-reduction" misdirects attention from the actual practice of science. The former approach distorts the actual practice of science to make it fit the formal relation of a reducing and reduced theory. The newer approach concentrates on the explanatory relation between different sciences. Explanations are rooted in (sometimes messy) causal relationships. Higher level functions add constraints on the lower level mechanisms. This approach also highlights the actual dialectical interaction of scientists studying different levels to show how fields of study have been developing historically. But the distinctiveness and independence of levels of explanation and also of disciplines is accepted. The study of one level then illuminates the other, even if there are no strict reductions. The different fields of analysis and different theories retain their separate identity, but interfield theories coordinate new lines of research across the fields (Darden & Maull 1977: 60). This may lead to unifying science (Kitcher 1981, 1993; see Grantham 2004).[15] But interfield connections may be the only "unity" science is capable of (Maull 1977).[16]

Whether or not these attempts succeed, theory-antireductionists are satisfied that the relation between different levels of organization is much more complicated than reductionists suppose and thus that no "unity of science" even remotely like that advocated by positivists is possible. Science will forever necessarily remain pluralistic. But reductionists can concede many of the points antireductionists emphasize—e.g., that different sciences involve completely different questions and that we will never find answers to one level of questions in another level. And they can admit there are only rather messy multiple relations between different levels of analysis. Yet they still contend that reductions in some sense are occurring, even if they are not "true" reductions of one theory or science to another (Hardcastle 1996a: 96-101). But antireductionists do not accept that the lower level mechanisms are sufficient to explain the higher level phenomena (e.g., Gillett 2007: 207).

The key difficulty here for reductionism is multiple realization, as noted above. At levels of organization higher than those studied by physicists, there are states, processes, and properties that can be instantiated by an indefinite number of different lower level states (Fodor 1974; Kitcher 1984). The higher level activity in such biological processes as binocular vision has been realized in very different neural structures in different animals and in this way is completely independent of the activity occurring on lower physical levels. Laws one level cannot be identified with laws on a lower level. And even if there are no laws on the biological or mental levels, something more than the lower level features must be occurring in the higher level features. Thus, even if higher levels depend on one set of lower level conditions in every case, too many different sets of the latter are possible for a reduction to occur. In sum, what is to be explained in the higher sciences is in an important way wholly unconnected to what is explained in physics, and so no type of structure- or theory-reductionism is possible.

Multiple realization renders any reduction account based on bridge laws highly problematic—no bridge laws could connect descriptions of higher level properties with a vastly disjunctive set of descriptions of properties on another level. Under any model of theory-reduction, the laws on one level cannot be identified with laws on a lower level because of the diversity of lower level phenomena upon which the higher level depends. If reduction were merely a matter of prediction, reduction may be possible. The common example is that the same heat of a gas can be realized by multiple states of molecules in motion: since heat is nothing but the average kinetic energy of the molecules, the heat is not realizable by only one particular set of motions by the molecules. But even if there is no neat one-to-one relation, the same heat is produced by multiple different underlying states. Thus, to reductionists it is "intuitively correct" that the heat of a gas can be reduced "piece-meal" to molecular kinetic energy (Hardcastle 1996a: 89). That is, there is no factor other than some state of molecular motion involved in the generation of the heat.

Antireductionists, however, point out that no one denies higher level phenomena in some way *necessarily depend* on the presence of lower level structures—the question is whether new structures are operating in the higher level phenomena. How many different sets of necessary lower level base-conditions produce the same temperature is simply irrelevant to the issue of whether the latter is *reducible* to the former: there is still a higher level phenomenon (heat) that molecules do not possess and that must be explained, not merely correlated with states of molecules. Some reductionists—identity theorists—argue that heat is not *caused* by motion but simply *is* motion, thus denying there are really different phenomena here. But this bold move is not convincing: heat is still a different phenomenon than motion. The two phenomena cannot be equated simply because changes in each of them can be correlated very precisely. A true reduction requires more than *predictability* from correlations: it requires an *explanation or understanding* of how the higher level phenomena could arise at all and how they fit into our picture of reality.

Even if lower level causes somehow produce higher level phenomena, we can still argue that explanations at different levels nevertheless have independence. In Hilary Putnam's illustration, the everyday phenomenon of rigidity might be determined by microstructures, but *explanations* of interactions of *macro-phenomena* have to be in terms of macrolevel structures independent of what is occurring in the microstructures. The role of microstructures in causing rigidity is simply irrelevant to explaining the higher level interactions—e.g., why a square peg of a certain size will not fit in a round hole (1994: 428-29). Rigidity and solidity cannot be treated as epiphenomena if they play causal roles in events. In general, any laws of activity on the macrolevel will be independent of activity on lower levels events and hence irreducible. The same event will require more than one explanation to account for all the levels involved. For example, we can explain why a green plant turns its leaves toward the sun in terms of the survival value for the plant or of the biochemical mechanisms making the turning possible (Searle 1992: 88-89). These explanations do not conflict, but they also are not reducible to each other. Similarly, we can describe the events in a computer in two complementary and consistent ways—in terms of the events occurring in the hardware and in terms of the software—but no one would argue that a software program can be *derived* from the laws of electromagnetism. The "software laws" and the "hardware laws" are each fundamental in the sense that neither can be derived from the other (Davies 1987: 144-45). Thus, a multiplicity of physical, biological, and other explanations (and hence a plurality of sciences, each with different interests and questions) is needed to explain any phenomena completely. The theories will be compatible with theories of other levels, since the activity on one level is irrelevant to the causal order on another. And because of this irrelevancy, there can be no successful reduction of all theories to one type.

New Wave Reductionism and Neo-Emergentism

Reductionists have certainly not given up the cause today. In particular, in the philosophy of neuroscience, John Bickle advocates a "ruthless" or "merciless" mind-to-molecule reduction: molecular pathways and events within neurons directly explain behavior and cognition without any intermediate levels in between (2003, 2006). On the other hand, versions of antireductionism are thriving in the philosophy of mind. Outside of philosophy departments, a resurgence of interest in emergentism has occurred in the last fifteen years (e.g., Clayton & Davies 2006; Macdonald & Macdonald 2010). "Process thought" theorists have joined the discussion (see Deacon 2012: 179-80). Nevertheless, reductionists still feel structure- and theory-reductions will be forthcoming (see, e.g., Hohwy & Kallestrup 2008). And neo-emergentists in their enthusiasm miss the fact that vast majority of scientists in physics and neuroscience remain reductive in outlook. There may be a "waning of materialism" (Koons & Bealer 2010) in some circles, but in mainstream philosophy and science (including almost all neuroscience) substance-reductionism is virtually unquestioned and structure-reductionism is alive, even if eliminationism has seen better days.

So how overall do matters stand today on the issue of reductionism versus emergence? To begin with, it must be realized that, during an era that outside of philosophy is an Age of Reductionism, the majority of philosophers who have actually explored the issue have become antireductionists of one stripe or another. The 1960's was the high watermark of structure- and theory-reductionisms. Since then, structure-, concept-, theory-, and method-antireductionisms have been on the rise. (Substance-reductionism still dominates outside of religious circles.) Indeed, even reductionists concede that by the 1990's such reductionisms had sunk to new depths of unpopularity (Melnyk 1995: 320; Kim 1993: 265). But since then a more sophisticated reductionism has been accepted by many philosophers.

Differentiating substance-reductionism and structure-reductionism do enable philosophers to affirm physicalism with regard to substance while accepting multiple types of structures. Or physicalists may continue to see an identity of structures where antireductionists see diversity. But even if complete correlations of phenomena on different levels are ever established, reductionists must do more than dogmatically state the structural primacy of the physical over other apparently real and independent levels of organization. They must still defend giving an asymmetrical relation to such correlations weighted in favor of the lower levels over other levels that have also evolved just as naturally and must also explain why there is hierarchy of levels at all. Behind the physicalists' basic intuition is the fact that in the evolution of the universe the physical and chemical levels of organization occurred first and lasted billions of years before the biological and other levels developed. Needless to say, antireductionists do not deny this or the dependency of later levels on the presence of the earlier. But this historical fact about the universe alone does not establish physicalism or the structural primacy of the physical level of organization. Antireductionists will point out that arising later does not in itself undercut the reality of the later phenomena in any way: as with many physical properties, the proper conditions for the later phenomena to arise simply were not present earlier.

Is there any empirical way to determine if there is genuine novelty in nature or only reducible products of physical structures? As discussed in the next chapter, no possible scientific findings appear to be decisive. The metaphysical nature of both substance- and structure-reductionisms and antireductionisms will become more apparent in the next two chapters. And for the foreseeable future, both positions appear to be viable competing philosophical programs for providing part of our broadest accounts for the world and our place in it. Reductionists may have the harder task, with their methodical grinding down of apparently genuine realities, but this task may turn out not to be impossible. Structure-reductionists will also have to produce convincing arguments for the primacy of physical structures over others, and substance-reductionists will have to do the same for physicalism or at least naturalism. Antireductionists, however, do not have a simple task either: structure-antireductionism and the physicalist intuition do seem strange bedfellows. Something that in a vital sense is genuinely new pops out of structured matter whenever a new level of organization is present, but how this process occurs is not explained by antireductionists any more than reductionists can identify the mechanisms within the microphysical realm that cause higher levels or any organization at all.

Reductionism in all its forms is a last vestige of logical positivism in philosophy. The more pluralistic approach of antireductionism does fit better with today's antipositivistic climate. Most antireductionists do not advance grand unifying schemes but rest content with a permanent multiplicity of theories. Reductionism also fits better with the premodern and modern quest to secure unshakeable foundations for our knowledge and values, although some reductionists may try to temper this by claiming reductionism is no more certain than whatever certainty scientists can provide. But the excesses of some postmodern enthusiasts may cause the pendulum to swing the other way. What is at stake is our worldview in one important area: what fundamental types of substances and structures make up reality? No one wants to accept more in their ontology than there is in heaven and earth, but the position that one adopts on reducibility may depend in the end on one's broader metaphysical commitments alone, and, as discussed in Chapter 7, this may have practical implications on our view of what is important in our lives.

Notes

1.   The idea of physicalism was two hundred years older in India, but no historian contends that the Greeks got the idea from the Indians.

2.   What if there is no fundamental "base-level" of structures to reality? What if different levels of structuring occur "all the way down" even in the microphysical realm? What if reality does not get simpler as the scale gets smaller? Do, for example, the strings of string-theory have further layers of structure? Structure-reductionists assume only on *a prior* grounds that there must be a base-level of structures and that reality cannot be otherwise. But it is an empirical question. And if reality is in fact constructed without such a base-level, the structure-reductionist program has a major problem: there would be no set of structures to reduce other structures to, and no explanation for higher levels of phenomena could get started. For antireductionists, there would be no problem: no one base-level is needed for the other structures to become operative since there are separate structures built into reality from the very start. All that is needed for antireductionism is that on different levels there are qualitatively different properties. All such realities would then be ontically equal, including those of the macroworld. We would have "an equalitarian metaphysic which dignifies and empowers the whole of nature" (Schaffer 2003: 513).

3.   The physicist John Wheeler's idealist speculation that the universe somehow or other arose from "information"—"it" from "bit," as he put it—is also a type of reduction of the universe's substance to structure. And today there is a theory that the cosmos is only a three-dimensional hologram projected from two-dimensional information in the "real" world.

4.   An experiential basis to this is mystical experiences, which give a sense of unity. But, like any experiences, these experiences are open to interpretation and have been fitted in dualisms and naturalism (see Jones 2010: 30-36). And there does not appear to be any evidence that mysticism has influenced the reductionisms of the modern West.

5.   It should be noted that, although emergentists place much significance on the *unpredictability* of the emergence of higher level phenomena, it is questionable whether any changes of any kind are strictly and absolutely predictable. This was recognized well before contemporary chaos theory (see Pepper 1926: 243; Henle 1942: 489).

6.   British emergentists introduced the term "supervenience" to denote the *irreducible reality* of emerging higher level phenomena, but the term has evolved into a term with an implicit *reductive explanatory component.* It formally means only that there can be no

variation in higher level properties without an accompanying variation in the lower level base-conditions. But it has come to denote both dependence upon, and *determination by*, the lower level phenomena (e.g., Kim 2011: 12). However, something can depend on something without being determined by it: even if there can be no changes in higher level properties without changes in their base, other factors may still be involved in the arising of the higher level phenomena. For example, there may no change in temperature without a change in the physical states of particles, but this does not necessarily mean that the those states *cause* heat. Without the reductionist overlay, "supervenience" merely labels the mystery of the dependency or determination or emergence of higher level phenomena.

7.   Today neo-emergentists usually include these levels: the physiochemical, the biological, the psychological, and the social. They would also add that many sublevels, including many physical ones, are emergent realities.

8.   By "*deity*" Alexander did not mean the god of traditional theism: it is a further quality of existence beyond the mind but related to the mind as the mind is related to life and life to matter. The world is "tending" to deity and not dependent upon it.

9.   Defining "physicalism" is harder then it might appear. One problem is defining "matter" (see McMullin 2010). (And Richard Feynman reminds us that physicists have no idea what exactly "energy" *is*.) The philosopher Carl Hempel identified another problem (1969): if one takes current physics to define the "physical," then physicalism today is likely false (since theories in physics change and are likely to be replaced); but, on the other hand, if one uses an ideal or future physics to define "physicalism," then "physicalism" will be unacceptably vague or indeterminate (see Crook & Gillett. 2001).

10.   The opposite of multiple realization—a "one-to-many" relationship—will be discussed in Chapter 5 concerning sociocultural phenomena and physiological bases.

11.   One can be an emergentist without being committed to "downward causation": one must accept various levels of novel, real causes or explanations, but one need not accept that nonphysical levels of causes affect physical levels or that wholes affect their parts. Reductionists consider the very notion of "downward causation" to be ill-defined or trivial. For example, dropping a vase is an action that directs the course of the vase's atoms, but no one would speak of a substantive downward causation here (Kim 1999: 26). But a substantive notion of it can be defended (e.g., Hendry, forthcoming: chap. 10).

12.   Subatomic events may be indeterminate on their own level but still have determinate effects on higher levels when upward causation occurs (e.g., the random decay of a radioactive particle causing a Geiger counter to click). There also may well be more subatomic influence on the everyday world than is usually supposed (see Vedral 2010).

13.   Donald Davidson (1970) raises an additional problem for mental phenomena: the general absence of any *law-governed* psychological phenomena. This is one reason for the irreducibility of the mental level to any level governed by laws. This also may be true of the biological level. (Some reductionists argue that to be real is to be the variable of a law or a generalization; so if no generalization can be made about something it is not actually real.)

14.   Today there has been a proliferation of subdisciplines in the sciences, but recently "cross-disciplinary research" and "convergence" have come into vogue in universities.

15.   After World War II, a "unity of science" program also arose in America based more pragmatically on the developing interdisciplinary areas of science rather than the positivists' philosophical perspective.

16.   Robert Batterman (2002) argues that "asymptotic" reasoning in science concerning behavior when variables tend to extremes—the "no man's land" between theories—may better explain intertheoretic relations and the emergence of genuinely new causal properties.

3

The Natural Sciences

The question of reductionism is central to philosophy of science, impinging issues from the fundamental question of what science is to whether all sciences are ultimately only one to theory-acceptance to questions of scientific vocabularies. Classic examples cited as successful reductions include the reduction of chemistry to physics, the reduction of thermodynamics to the statistical laws of molecular motion, and the explanation of the laws of genetics by the structure of DNA molecules. In such cases, laws governing the activity of phenomena on one level are supposedly explained by theories advanced to explain phenomena on a lower level. But are any of the many alleged reductions in the natural sciences really successful? In fact, does science as actually practiced support reductionism or antireductionism?

Two points before proceeding. First, science is only one way of approaching reality—one selected point of view—and in itself it entails no implicit final metaphysical schemes. Reductionism and antireductionism, on the other hand, are *metaphysical* in nature: they go beyond empirical findings and provide views on the nature of scientific findings and suggest courses of research. This makes these positions more like physicalism and idealism than the practice of science itself. The final judgments as to whether science is reductive or antireductive in nature will be a matter of philosophical decisions; whatever facts about nature are entailed by the practice of science itself are at best only part of the considerations. We may decide to treat our sensations of colors and tastes as epiphenomena because scientists currently study only their physical correlates, but we are not forced to do so because "science says so." Reductionists may let physicists dictate to them the final answer as to what is real, but this is as much a philosophical judgment as those made by people who choose otherwise. Reductionists cannot describe themselves as simply being "objective" and "scientific" without revealing that they do not understand what they are doing—no such decision is required by the practice of science itself.

In fact, philosophy can inform science here: the metaphysics of method-reductionism makes a reductive explanation the goal of science.[1] Science progresses by unifying phenomena—e.g., Newton introduced "gravity" to explain the motion of falling apples, tides, and planets. To reductionists, reductions are simply part of the same quest of bringing more and more phenomena under fewer and fewer theoretical posits. Not only may a reductive strategy lead to powerful new scientific insights, to reductionists ultimately this is the only way to gain new scientific insights. However, nothing about the nature of science requires that it must be reductive in nature: what scientists analyze out of reality may be, but need not be, treated as the whole of the ultimately real. Scientists per se are not committed to the idea that only physical theoretical posits or the posits on the level of organization described by quantum physicists are ultimately needed. Nothing about the nature of the scientific enterprise necessitates that conclusion. Scientists may in fact end up accepting multiple layers of structure. Scientists may be committed to the fewest number of theoretical posits to explain the phenomena they are studying, but this does not mean they are forced to accept only physical ones—there is a different between simple and simplistic. To make reductive simplicity an absolute goal in advance of actual study is a Procrustean bed that is antithetical to the spirit of science. Scientists are no less scientific if they argue that the structures that biologists and other nonphysicists posit cannot be eliminated. It is equally difficult to argue that the *only* methodological approach must be analysis as long as testable claims through a holistic approach are forthcoming. In sum, we should not ask whether science itself is a form of reductionism but instead ask whether structure- and method-reductionists or antireductionists at present have a better program for the future course of science: is the better way to conduct scientific research for the foreseeable future to strive for structure-reductions or to understand phenomena in light of different levels of causes? The question then becomes an empirical one: which is more fruitful for practicing scientists today?

The second point is that reductionism involves a *realistic* interpretation of scientific theories. Under realism, scientists strive to find objective structures in nature (i.e., properties that exist independent of our ideas), not merely correlate data and ignore their causes. (But they may ignore metaphysical questions concerning "causation" and "causes.") If theories are accepted merely as pragmatic models of aspects of phenomena, there would be no impetus to reduce them all to one theory. Antirealism may be fashionable among philosophers and quantum physicists (although realism has resurged recently), but probably most working scientists are realists, believing that they are dealing with structures actually existing in the world and not just concepts generated by a scientific community. Unfortunately, it is often assumed that to be a *realist* is to be a *reductionist*: if there is in fact one real world, then there is only one level of causes and thus only one true, objective, and complete account of reality, and so the account must be reductive. But antireductionists can also argue for a realism having multiple levels of organization. Thus, the questions are: how many types of irreducible entities and processes have scientists found, and is there a drive in science to reduce these to only one type?

Reductionism and Scientific Explanations

Under the realist interpretation, scientists attempt to cut reality up into irreducible entities and processes, i.e., to identify the structures of reality.[2] Theories are the explanations that put the components back together again. They provide a conceptual framework, limited to events in the natural order, in which the phenomenon to be explained fits intelligibly alongside better known phenomena. "Explaining" involves making sense of the phenomena by showing how they fit into a larger picture of reality. The phenomena then appear "rational," "natural," or "to be expected." This usually involves connecting parts of the explanatory scheme to the familiar by means of analogies or worked-out metaphors (theoretical models). Predictability of a phenomenon is always a good sign that it has been explained, but whether prediction is necessary to explanation is a debated issue. For realists, predictions may be part of a complete understanding, but understanding requires more—accurately predicting tides is something different from understanding why tides occur. The generally accepted type of explanation in science involves identifying the *cause* of a phenomenon, i.e., conditions that are necessary and sufficient (and non-coincidental) for the phenomenon to arise. However, historical disciplines, such as evolutionary biology and parts of cosmology, have also proven hard to fit under this model of explanation because of the role of contingent events.

Is a structure-reduction a form of explanation? The first reaction is to answer, "Yes." Most causal explanations identify causes within the same level of organization, but reductions involve a different type of "cause" since they require more than one level. Indeed, some object to referring to this interlevel relationship as *causal* at all. Nevertheless, an interlevel determinism is involved. A reduction of *x* to nothing but *y* "explains" the appearance of *x* and so should constitute an explanation. But the final answer to this question will turn on what we accept as a complete explanation. Even if a reduction is intended to dismiss a phenomenon as a total illusion, still a complete theory would have to explain why there is even the appearance of the phenomenon. How is there a new level of phenomena and interlocking organization at all, even if they are the result of lower level causes? Theories in science do not yet address this: causal explanations of the conditions for predicting the appearance of higher level phenomena may make the *prediction* of the appearance possible, but they do not *explain* the mechanism for the emergence. Factors, as yet undetected and perhaps undetectable, causing the emergence and the correlation of phenomena on different levels may be active. Reductionists tend to accept a complete explanation of emergence as merely *prediction*—which in the context of reduction involves the *correlation* of phenomena from different levels —while antireductionists expect a scientific explanation identify the *structures at work in reality*, even if scientists have not yet identified the mechanisms for the arising of higher levels of organizations. (Those reductionists who deny any arising of higher levels of organization but claim all of reality is simply aggregates of matter structured by the lowest sublevel of physical structure must deny there are any *correlations* but only *identities*. All "higher level phenomena" are at best only more and more complex interactions of phenomena on one level of reality.)

Structure-reductionists may claim that interactions are so complex that as a practical matter the precise predictions necessary to demonstrate an explanation or a reduction may forever be foreclosed to us. But reductionists contend that the reductions can still be established "in principle": the higher level phenomena are *determined* by lower level conditions and causes operating upon matter, and we would be able to see this if we had complete knowledge of the lower level phenomena. After all, the movements of even only three bodies in each other's gravity field is hard to predict even with a computer. Thus, antireductionists cannot cite such unpredictability as evidence of a genuine emergence of irreducible phenomena.

A cliché among people outside of philosophy of science is that "all theories are reductions." This, however, badly misconstrues the nature of scientific theories. All theories involve a particular point of view and are selective in abstracting out certain structures as central in that theory's account of reality. All analysis must do that. But such selection is not a reduction of any kind. A theory becomes substantively and structurally reductive only if it denies the *reality* of features (e.g., causes), and simply focusing on particular phenomena for study or selecting certain features as central in explaining particular phenomena does not by itself deny the reality of anything—substances, properties, or causes. The theories and laws of quantum physics are neutral on the issue of whether biological structures occurring in the same entity are real, just as biological accounts of photosynthesis need not deny quantum level events are also occurring. Reductions enter the picture only when theorists take their theories to be not merely insightful accounts of certain features of reality but to be *exhaustive and complete accounts* of all that is substantively or structurally real in a phenomenon and hence the only ones needed.

Downward Causation

The idea of "downward causation" of a whole on the properties of its parts or of higher level causes on lower level properties is also a point of contention (see Andersen et al. 2000; McLaughlin 1992: 75-89). Structure-reductionists, of course, deny the very possibility: lower level structures determine all higher level properties, and the higher have no power to affect the lower. For example, they see a conflict between downward causation and developmental biology (Rosenberg 1997). Lower level mechanisms suffice (Craver & Bechtel 2007). But antireductionists disagree: each level operates with its own independent causes, and the higher level phenomena can exert a causal influence on the stable processes occurring in their component parts. This does not mean that a higher level bootstraps its own existence by causing the lower level base-conditions out of which it itself arises: downward action can only occur after the higher level phenomena have arisen. Nor need downward action interfere with the *laws* of the lower level. But the higher level realities can exert types of control on their bases, just as the higher level computer program constrains the activity of the lower level hardware without interfering with the laws of mechanics and electricity (Davies 1987: 149-50). Karl Popper also argued that higher level phenomena can operate as causes upon their own substructure, including operating as a selection among randomly fluctuating elementary particles (1978: 348-49). But downward causation would violate the causal completeness of the subatomic realm, and if biological or mental causes affect the physical, the causal completeness of the physical level. Whether any such emergence affects the law of the conservation of energy is also an issue.

The psychologist Donald Campbell applied the idea of downward causation to biological phenomena (Bickhard & Campbell 2000). Biological processes produce part of the distribution of lower level events and entities. All processes at the lower level of a hierarchy are constrained by, and act in conformity with, the laws of the higher level (and vice versa). In short, the whole organizes the parts and can affect aspects of the parts at lower levels. For example, the structure of the jaw of some soldier ants is so specialized for piercing their enemies that they cannot feed themselves. This requires a "downward" explanation in terms of the ant's role in its society; it cannot be simply explained "upwardly" by means of its chemical make-up (Campbell 1974: 181-82). Evolution in general affects the chemical make-up of the world in that animals and plants affect the quantity and distribution of certain chemicals in the world (e.g., oxygen in the atmosphere), thereby affecting the future course of the development of life and the planet itself. In this way, the lower level chemical phenomena are subject to higher level actions.

To reductionists, this physical interaction is not as problematic as the prospect of the mental intervention in the physical order. (Roger Sperry's example of a wheel rolling down a hill affecting the wheel's molecules' path would be the same.) The different levels of the phenomenon remain distinct, and, according to reductionists, are determined by physical factors alone. Nor does the fact that we now may be able to direct our own genetic evolution through genetic engineering require any form of antireductionism. But in a stronger form of downward causation, a whole or a higher level reality interacts downwardly with, for example, its molecules' *inner workings*. That would require either an efficient causal interaction or some new type, perhaps like Aristotelean "formal causes" (see Deacon 2012: 161-62).

How Do Higher Levels Emerge?

Antireductionists seldom discuss how higher levels emerge or posit new kinds of causes to account for emergence. Reductionists see no more problems here than with gliders emerging in the computer game of Life: complex interactions are merely complications for analysis but are of no metaphysical consequence.[3] Complexity theorists focus on how complexity may arise from simple physical rules alone (e.g, Bak 1997).[4] Other scientists and philosophers today adopt an idea on how reality gets from one level to the next from general systems theorists: higher complexity emerges out of the "*self-organization*" of systems (Bertalanffy 1968). Both antireductionists and reductionists utilize this notion (e.g., Camazine et al. 2001; Ambjørn et al. 2008). They argue that when base-conditions are far from being in equilibrium, interactions according to a few simple rules cause things spontaneously to organize themselves into functioning wholes. These rules may not be physical. For example, in light of the great mathematical improbability of accidents being the cause of life and consciousness in a universe of a finite age, some new structures may be needed to change the odds. The structure-antireductionist physicist Paul Davies accounts for self-organization by means of yet-to-be-discovered "organizing principles," over and above the known laws of physics, that harness interparticle forces and alter their collective behavior in a holistic way (1987: 143) and cites Erwin Schrödinger on the possibility of a "new type of physical law" (1999: 258). He speculates that there may be complexity laws that generate information (1999: 259). Aspects of social behavior may emerge through the interaction with the environment, leading to new life-forms (Hemelrijk 2005). Gaia-theorists argue that the earth itself is self-organizing and self-regulating. The biologist Stuart Kauffman advances a reductionist theory of emergence: sufficiently complex mixes of chemicals can spontaneously crystallize into systems having the ability to catalyze the very network of chemical reactions by which the molecules themselves are formed; complex wholes (including living organisms) emerge, not through some molecular Rube Goldberg machine slapped together piece by piece, but is ordered spontaneously by self-organization; such order is "free," arising naturally from physical interactions; and this order, along with natural selection, accounts for the emergence of higher and higher complex wholes; no higher level processes are involved; the interaction of parts under conditions of high entropy accounts for all the properties of the systems (1995: 24-25). Other scientists also now speak of "order out of chaos" or that "increasing complexity" and "instability" produce the emergence of higher forms of stability (e.g. Simon 1962).

But current ideas of self-organization, self-production (autopoiesis), self-assembly, and emerging order for complex adaptive systems are still incomplete. Do molecules spontaneously just happen to form into all the necessary building blocks of a living organism? Or, how does reality get from one-cell organisms to more complex organisms that have hundreds of times as much "genetic informa-tion" in each cell? Why do amoebas bond when food is scarce? Where does this level of order come from? Do the structures of "self-organization" represent a higher level of organization since not all chemicals organize themselves into living entities? Does the order come from "above," i.e., from higher levels of organization, and not from a principle on the chemical level? How could biological "information" arise from the chemical level? How can this order just happen randomly, without a cause? Nature does indeed love to organize, but *why* and *how* do new levels of complexity arise at all? Why, for example, are atoms set up to organize themselves into molecules in the first place? Why is there structure set up to permit such an incredible number of different molecules to form? Why is nature virtually made to organize higher and higher levels of complexity? Even if complexities and instabilities are a necessary condition, how do the new levels of stability emerge from the chaos? If new levels of organization are nature's way of removing complexity and instability by creating new stabilities, we still must ask what is the *source of ordering*. Why does adding energy to unstable systems cause new types of order rather than just more chaos? Why does the universe not revert to complete physical equilibrium on a lower level or convert to total chaos?

Most importantly, order does not arise "spontaneously," "randomly," "by chance," or "by accident"—some *structure* is always at work. Iron filings do not literally "self-organize" into patterns: they do so only under the structuring force of magnetism. Calling order "self-organizing" does not *explain* anything. Neither antireductionists nor reductionists can rest content with claiming stabilities emerge whenever increases in complexities destabilize lower level stabilities. The structures in reality that accomplish this process must be specified. Unless those mechanisms are identified, this approach does not answer how emergence occurs or explain the relation between levels any more than saying the emergence "just happens." This is better than saying it happens "magically" but not much. It is merely another way of saying that no human or transcendent agent is involved in the appearance of life and consciousness in nature. Even reductionists do not mean that matter literally "spontaneously self-organizes." Reductionists employ the analogy of how a few simple computer rules can generate quite intricate growing and changing designs without any other input being necessary (e.g., fractals). But such programming algorithms constitute the *structure* organizing what is created in computers—the computers do not create any configurations themselves accidentally or randomly. And without some identification of the structures for the "self-organization of matter," no scientific explanation of this problem will be complete.

The Sciences

Since the heyday of positivism, empiricist philosophers and scientists have advocated one "unity of science" program or another—i.e., a vision of a unity of the phenomena studied, a unity of methods, and a unity of theories. But what strikes us at first glance about science today is the *diversity* of approaches in the different branches of the sciences and a growing number of subdisciplines, like biochemistry at the interface of chemistry and biology. Nancy Cartwright (1999) makes the case that modern science is a patchwork of laws, not a unified system. But we like to think reality is integrated into a unity, even if it has different orders of complexity, and the different natural sciences appear limited to different rungs of the hierarchy.

A useful way to characterize a "level" is in terms of the place an entity or process holds in the *causal order*, i.e., what sorts of entities an entity interacts with, what sorts of forces or mechanisms it is subject to, and what sorts of perturbations it can withstand (Burian & Trout 1995: 190). Dependency between levels and the possibility of "upward" and "downward" causation complicate this picture, but the structuring of reality does appear to create different stable levels of causal order. A molecule does not interact with a quark, and an atom does not digest food.[5] Reality consists of layers of these different orders of interactions. Levels involve different internally-organized structures that give phenomena on different levels different properties. Thus, if a "gene" or "atom" has *causal power as a unit* that its parts do not, then such units are structurally *real* even if it is not substantively distinct.

An additional consideration is that some structuring apparently is always present: matter may be inert, but it is always structured by at least physical structures. There does not appear to be bits of "pure" matter in the universe free of all organization, no matter how small the parts examined. Matter is just what is structured by natural forces and some such forces may always be present. Currently, the smallest identified bits of matter are quarks. But even if quarks have no parts—a question in debate today—they still do not exist except in relation to other quarks. Activity governed by structures is always present. Thus, even if matter is inert, reality is not. The fact that some structuring is always present suggests that *relationships* are as fundamental to reality as what is related. Indeed, science is better seen as the study of these relationships (the structures as identified in laws and theories) rather than the study of the stuff structured ("matter in itself," assuming it can exist free of all structure). Thinking in terms of "inanimate matter" and "biological entities" instead of levels of organization misconstrues the nature of reality. Physics is not about matter in itself and biology about life: physics is about the *physical structures* of reality, while biology is about the *biological structures* also organizing matter. The issue of structure-reductionism is about whether these structures are ultimately one, not about "matter" versus "life."

We give primacy to physics because physicists study the most universal levels of structures since all of reality, whether animate or inanimate, apparently has them. The most general structures are on the level of quarks or any smaller entities and of fields of forces. In the end, there may remain more than one theory covering different properties on this one level, or the various theories may end up unified in one quantum field theory. Consequently, the laws that physicists discern for this level are considered most fundamental because they will likewise apply to a level of all of reality. New properties appear with each higher level of organization. This includes not just chemical or biological properties but higher *physical* sublevels of organization, i.e., those physical properties not present in quarks. Quarks do not have, for instance, electrical charge or valence; and they have properties unique to their level of organization (such as "charm" and "strangeness"). Thus, some physical properties are level-specific. (Robert Laughlin suggests there may be some as-yet-undiscovered physical organizing principles for the mesoscopic scale of things [Laughlin et al. 2000].) But as complexity of organization increases, leading to different scientific disciplines, generality decreases.

Any neat picture is complicated by the fact that there are different physical sublevels. Different physical properties (e.g., wetness and solidity) are added at higher levels, and physicists of different subdivisions study different ones. Physicists also study physical properties and structures on the everyday scale —mechanics, electromagnetism, and thermodynamics being prime examples. The picture is further complicated by solid-state (condensed matter) and plasma physics that add other sublevels of properties like superconductivity and superfluidity. In addition, other scientists also study the physical level of the world: chemists study the levels of atoms, molecules, polymers, and crystals; biophysicists and biochemists study the levels of molecules and macromolecules; geologists study the changing earth and its parts on the everyday level; astronomers, astrophysicists, and cosmologists study planets, stars, galaxies, clusters, and any other larger scale physical level phenomena. It is useful to speak of the "chemical level" and so forth to indicate the properties studied, but all are subdivisions of the physical level and cannot be totally separated. In fact, scientists from one extreme (astrophysicists and cosmologists) may need to know the physics of the other extreme (particle physics).

The second basic class of levels is the biological. (Of course, to reductionists all levels are ultimately only in one group—our current classifications of sciences is temporary.) This contains a set of much more complex sublevels than does the physical set—molecules, macromolecules, cellular organelles, cells, tissues, organs, organisms, breeding populations, and species. Biophysicists and biochemists study phenomena on the level of molecules and macromolecules. Cell biologists and physiologists study phenomena on higher levels in the body from organelles up to organs. Botanists, zoologists, ethologists, and evolutionary biologists study organisms, either individually or in groups. Ecologists study the levels of environmental systems, up to that of our entire planet; thus they study the broadest scale on the biological level but must also study the chemistry and physics of the earth. Neuroscientists and cognitive scientists also fit within this group. Even mathematics can be fitted in under one (not particularly popular) interpretation: all of mathematics will be reduced to set theory, set theory in turn to logic, logic to "laws of thought," and these laws to neural activity studied by neuroscientists.

This inventory does not cover all the sciences, but it is enough to show that the situation is not as simple as speaking of "a hierarchy of levels" of study might suggest. The advocates of interfield disciplines and interlevel connections argue that scientists need to study aspects of other levels to understand their own, although reductionists contend that eventually scientists will need to study only the lower levels. Indeed, the overlapping between disciplines renders the concept "levels of disciplines" of limited use for the relation of the various sciences. Thus, any "unity of science" program is complicated, but this does not rule out the possibility of the eventual reduction of the sciences. However, scientists today are distinguishing more and more levels of complexity, not reducing their number. The languages of the different branches of the sciences are becoming increasingly technical and diverse—they are *diverging* rather than *converging*, and there is no reason to think convergence will ever occur (e.g., Suppes 1981: 5-6). More people use the image of the Tower of Babel to describe the relation among the sciences today—even among subdisciplines within one science—than speak of a trend toward the unification of different vocabularies or concept-reduction.[6]

Nevertheless, reality does appear to be arranged into multiple layers of natural levels, although the problem of "upward" (and perhaps "downward") causation complicates the picture. Each higher level of complexity adds new properties, both physical and nonphysical. In short, there may be a porous "hierarchy" of causal levels of reality, but not a neat hierarchy of scientific disciplines or theories mirroring it. Instead, intertwining sciences are the subject-matter for the issue of the reduction of ontologies, theories, and concepts in science.

Are the Sciences Being Reduced?

The different strands of reductionism and of antireductionism all come together around the issue of whether each science will inevitably be reduced or will remain autonomous. Under the reductionists' vision, commitment to the analytical approach in science slides easily into a philosophical commitment to all the types of reductionisms. And once a science's theory, posits, concepts, and methods are all reduced, there is nothing left to the science. Thus, in the end nothing remains of any scientific discipline except physics. Nor does structure-reductionism naturally stop merely with the reduction of disciplines to chemistry and physics in general: the logic of reductionism requires that any physical science also must be reducible until the chain of reductions ends with only elementary particle physics standing. That is, one can be a *physicalist* without accepting only quantum level causes, but it is hard to be a *reductionist* and accept *layers of even physical causes*. All higher level proximate explanations will give way to ultimate lower level explanations. Physics will advance up through the hierarchy of sciences, conquering all other domains as it goes. In short, reductionists are "imperialists in the service of particle physicists" (Brooks 1994: 803)—everything is physical and is determined by the lowest physical level and is explicable completely in its terms. Once we finish physics, we will know all there is to know about all "levels" of nature, and all laws will be shown to be "special cases" of physical laws caused by physical complexities alone.

Antireductionists reject all that. They see no compelling reason, let alone necessity, for the sciences to be reduced to one. Instead, they predict the continuing autonomy of the different sciences. Each science will remain fundamental and irreducible—the only "unity of science" comes from the fact that different levels of organization are not totally distinct, and so interfield studies may be needed. This is a straightforward consequence of their endorsement of the reality of different levels of causes. Any phenomenon is a complex of such causes, and scientists in each field of science account for different levels of causes at work in any event. The sciences outside of physics provide explanations that have no physical counterpart. And, as Robert Nozick says, it is certainly not obvious why the reductionists' perspective—"from the bottom up"—yields greater understanding than the antireductionists' (1981: 633). Physics is necessary for a complete understanding of biological phenomena, but it will never be sufficient: explaining the atomic interactions in an organism does not explain biological interactions or answer whether apparent biological-level causes are real. No one level is ultimately more fundamental than the others because reality is constituted by a variety of equally real levels of structures. Thus, there is an equitable division of labor among all scientists in the study of reality, and there is no drive to unify the different sciences and theories. Scientists studying one level of reality can ignore most of the theories covering others. Chemists and biologists can carry on their work without waiting for disputes about quarks, superstrings, or any other new theory in physics to be resolved: the phenomena they study remain distinct, and their explanations do not require theories from the lowest level of physical organization (although they need to study the physics affecting their own level). Physics as a whole retains primacy as covering the most general structures of all phenomena in nature, but what are somewhat condescendingly called the "special sciences" also produce irreducible theories about the diverse causal factors above those of the physical level. Particle physicists under this view are not predators but only one group of scientists among equals—they are as limited in scope (in terms of *levels*) as any "special science." In sum, any hierarchy of the sciences has no foundation but only equal strata.

Because of the complexity of causes in any phenomenon, to antireductionists no one account exhaustively depicts the way the world "really is." Thus, there is no one scientific picture of our one world. Each science provides a different picture in terms of different real causes. Each account, from the quantum field level to the biological to the cosmological, is complete in that it covers all of reality but is also limited in that it covers only selected aspects of reality (i.e., different levels of organization). No one science covers all structures and levels. The accounts do not conflict since they involve different questions asked of different levels of reality. In other words, they in no way involve competing answers to the same questions. But most importantly, the various accounts cannot be reduced to any one account. Instead, each account supplements the other pictures, and only collectively do the different accounts give a complete scientific account of reality by explaining all of its different levels. (Niels Bohr's notion of "complementarity" is sometimes invoked on this philosophical, rather than scientific, point [e.g., Primas 1983: 349-51].)

Is reductionism or antireductionism a more fruitful regulative ideal for scientific research today? Reductionism becomes a methodological "ism" when it commands that the downward approach is the only legitimate approach for science and that other approaches eventually must be superseded. Indeed, the reductionists' ideal is not based on the history of science but is a regulative program for the future development of science. It is this prescriptive nature of reductionism that makes it doctrinaire and absolute and thus in fact contrary to the spirit of science (Agazzi 1991). A more empirical answer to the question is simply to let the sciences take their course. At present, analysis and synthesis are both proving very significant, and subdisciplines in the sciences are proliferating rather than coalescing. The future may change this. Perhaps scientists will follow the reductionists' prescription.

The diversity among the sciences today may seem to favor antireductionism, but it is also compatible with reductionism, since even reductionists concede that a successful reduction of entire disciplines can only be a long-term goal. Unlike with Eddington's "two table" problem, the ontological issues surrounding the question of whether sciences are reducible or autonomous will turn in the end on scientific considerations concerning structures. That is, how many explanatory structures must scientists accept? In particular, will scientists always accept causes on different levels above the quantum field level as irreducible? (However, a philosophical residue will remain to the question, as discussed below.) To decide if reductionists or antireductionists have the stronger case for our allegiance today, we must now look more closely at the situation with the specific sciences today.

Physics and Reductionism

Today there are two competing philosophies of physics: a reductive one in which current theories are low-energy approximations of a more fundamental theory yet to be discovered, and an antireductive one having a hierarchy of quasi-autonomous domains, each with its own ontology and fundamental laws (see Castellani 2002). To reductionists, there are no new structures, physical or otherwise, at work on the higher levels. All the activity in the universe is governed only by electromagnetism and the other physical forces, and this includes "living" entities. All the true work of reality actually occurs on the physical level of structure or its lowest sublevel, and this will be disclosed once we find the universe's cosmic physical "DNA code."

Indeed, the reductionists' story of the history of the entire cosmos is remarkably simple, if incomplete in its details. In the Big Bang, the *ur*-stuff of reality somehow generated space-time, or the universe somehow originated as an instability in the quantum field and began to expand. After a period of cooling, some unpredictable fluctuations in space-time somehow caused bits of matter to condense out of space-time as matter and radiation decoupled. These tiny particles somehow began blindly to combine, i.e., to self-organize into more and more complex combinations. And, as the physical chemist Peter Atkins notes, the rest of the evolution of the universe is (scientifically) "unimportant" (1992: 3). Events involve accidental circumstances that result in random combinations of inorganic matter; from that, all higher levels of organization appeared (Vitzthum 1995: 230-31). There is nothing more to explain about life and consciousness: they are simply different products of the constant random shuffling of matter as structured by physical forces alone. We may think we are necessary, inevitable or preordained, but we are only the purely natural result of a great number of contingencies (see Monod 1971). The actual course of development of the universe may be very sensitive to the vagaries of these random events, but the only forces structuring this evolution are however many physical forces that physicists find. Nothing more is of scientific interest.

Once the basic forces and particles came into play, nothing more had to be added for the universe to evolve as it has. In sum, after molecules learned to compete and to create other molecules, a universe pretty much like ours inhabited with creatures much like us was "inevitable" (Atkins 1992: 5). The actual course leading up to animals like us may involve many accidental and hence unpredictable events. Chance events are not only incapable of explanation but are not in need of explanation—they are just the randomness constituting history. To understand it all, all we need to do is to identify the physical forces and particles at the beginning of this process. Thus, very little about our universe actually needs any explanation. Atkins speaks for all reductionists when he says "there is nothing that cannot be understood, . . . nothing that cannot be explained, and . . . everything is extraordinarily simple" (1992: 3). Everything is simply epiphenomena of quantum events.

Reductionists face certain major difficulties in achieving their vision. First, consider some problems in what reductionists take as the exemplar of a reductive discipline and the goal of all reductions—physics. Is it at least reasonable to assume that in principle physicists could discover a simple level of organization or a simple theory to explain all phenomena? Without at least the prospect of this occurring, reductionists cannot maintain they are justified today in adhering to their program. But "elementary particle" physics today does not look as promising as reductionists once thought it did. Indeed, it has even been argued that quantum physics provides the most conclusive evidence for the existence of *structure-emergence* (Silberstein & McGeever 1991: 187.) There appears to be organizational complexity in matter all the way down. Physicists may not have yet reached the laws of the basic physical level—so far every time something is advanced to unify and explain microlevel realities complications arise. At one point, physicists thought there were only three subatomic particles; now they talk of dozens and dozens. They have also introduced new sublevels. Scientific findings such as quarks not being able to exist in isolation or the Pauli exclusion principle controlling the behavior of electrons favor structure-antireductionism rather than reduction to isolated particles. Structured relationships become as fundamental as what is related (see Ladyman & Ross 2007). Even reductionists should concede that holism on the level of quarks, gluons, and leptons and on higher subatomic levels rules out any simplistic, mechanical reductionism.[7]

It may be naive to think of "fundamental" or "elementary" particles as distinct, permanent, identifiable entities interacting mechanically through fields of force—attaching a distinct identity to each particle has proven difficult. At best, even to speak of subatomic "particles" requires thinking of each particle as part of a group; none can be isolated from the rest nor understood in isolation. In quantum field theory, even the quantum "vacuum" of space-time is a seething sea of "virtual" particle/antiparticle pairs emerging briefly and being reabsorbed or becoming "real" when the requisite energy is supplied from the outside. Particles, including some apparently without mass, seem to be only temporary manifestations of shifting patterns of waves that combine at one point, dissolve, and recombine elsewhere. A "particle" begins to appear to be no more than a local outcropping of a continuous substratum of vibratory energy. The simplest atom exemplifies the general systems theorists' view perfectly: it is an organized whole that has no truly isolatable parts and that manifests new properties that were not foreshadowed by the parts alone. Similarly, the two electrons of a helium atom do not appear as two distinct electrons but simply as one "two-electron" pattern. In particle physics in general, the properties of larger objects on the subatomic level are not merely a simple linear sum of the properties of its parts and their relations; rather each larger object involves the "superimposition" of its parts upon each other, thereby requiring an entirely new calculation of the larger object's own properties. Thus, an integrative approach is needed for understanding even in a science as basic as particle physics. The same problem continues up the line: new properties appear on the molecular level. The properties of water are a distinct reality from the properties of hydrogen and oxygen atoms—the whole does not consist of its parts because it has transformed its components' atomic structure, and something new has emerged. The internal organization of H_2O molecules generated by the bonding of atoms creates a new level of unique properties (e.g., wetness, electrical polarity, and so forth).[8]

Of course, it does not follow from the fact that the most basic sublevels of physical organization are integrated that all levels above it must also be, any more than the fact that there may be indeterminacy on that one level means events on all other levels of organization are also indeterminant. But the process of evolving complexity on the physical level apparently continues above the elementary particle level into our everyday realm. As noted above, those who study "complexity theory" claim that nature has an innate tendency to "self-organize" and generate higher levels of complexity (Coveney & Highfield 1995; Kauffman 1995).[9] The history of the universe is one of unfolding complexity, leading to life and consciousness. Some argue that this complexity by itself will require the acceptance of the irreducibility of emergent levels of reality. Reductionists, however, argue that the intricacies of nature may only keep a detailed reduction forever beyond our technology. For them, it is an epistemic matter of our own inability to penetrate a physical process, not an ontic matter of irreducibility. After all, computers can generate extremely complicated patterns from a few simple rules, and nature may be the same way, even if we cannot discern those rules. But such practical problems do not mean the emergence of complexity is not in principle understandable. A reductionist such as Stephen Hawking can say we know the basic laws governing the behavior of matter under all but the most extreme conditions and all the laws underlying chemical and biological phenomena, but we still cannot predict events in general—even with a Grand Unified Theory unifying theoretical posits of all subatomic forces, we would not be able to do that because, in addition to the Heisenberg Uncertainty Principle, we cannot solve the equations of any such theory except in the very simplest situations (1988: 168). In this way, such problems are irrelevant to maintaining reductionism in principle.

To all of this must be added the fact that there is opposition even among physicists to the claim that elementary particle physics is in any sense more primary or fundamental than the other branches of physics or the natural sciences in general (see Weinberg 1992: 54-55). Two Nobel Laureates—Philip Anderson (1972) and Robert Laughlin (2005)—in particular disagree.[10] It is primarily the reductionist vision that makes particle physics seem more basic. Particle physicists study a layer of reality all phenomena share, but to go further and argue that therefore other layers are not equally fundamental or are less real is not a scientific conclusion but a philosophical one. Even condensed matter physicists such as Anderson have little need for quantum theory. Some prominent physicists believe that life must be considered an elementary fact that cannot be explained by physics (Bohr 1958) or that we should expect to find new laws of physics to be operating in biological phenomena (Schrödinger 1944: 73). Are processes on higher levels unreal because they are not as symmetrical as processes on lower levels? Consider time. Is it unreal or the irreversibility of time on the everyday level of complexity an illusion simply because some elementary particle equations do not have time as a variable? Or is time an emergent reality? Any answer leaves science and enters philosophy.

This leads to a related way in which physics may mistakenly be held to require reductionism. Physicists have been able to abstract out of what we experience some simplicity by framing theories so general as to apply apparently to everything everywhere at all times. In this way, physicists have found a degree of comprehensibility to the flux of events we experience. But this does not mean that the world is in fact *simple*, or that physics has shown it to be so—it only means physicists have been able to abstract a degree of order from what we experience. And to go from this abstraction to claiming the physical is "*the* world" or "the only thing real" or "the way things really are" is to go beyond physics. Physics does not necessitate this claim and cannot prove it. To *reduce* the world to only what physicists concentrate on is a philosophical step that accepting science does not force anyone to take.[11]

TOE's and TOO's

In any case, let us assume physicists will be able to come up with one theory unifying all the subatomic particles into one simple scheme in terms of particles, superstrings, structural organizing realities like fields, or something. Let us further assume this theory will be a "TOE," a Theory of Everything that unifies the four forces that physicists currently recognize (electromagnetism, gravitation, and two forces at work in the nuclei of atoms) into one theoretical framework. (Not that all physicists think such theories are feasible [see Laughlin & Pines 2000: 30; Hawking & Mlodinow 2010: 140-44].) All the physical sublevels will be covered. The physics governing the very large (general relativity) will be united with the physics governing the very small (quantum field theory) in one equation. A TOE, in short, will be one theory by which all the current laws of physics can be explained. The quest for unity begun in Presocratic times will be completed in modern terms. There will be a oneness of structure to mirror the oneness of substance. The ultimate causal structure of the universe will then be depicted by one physical theory. Thereby, a ground for the possibility of structure-reductionism would be established.

But antireductionists can point out two things. First, even if such a causal account is ever accomplished, all that would be established is a *correlation* of phenomena on different levels—it is reductive metaphysics that supply the reduction between levels. Thus, the question of the *ultimate status* of the actual phenomena on every level would remain. Should we treat macrophenomena as real or as nothing but the quantum events causing them? Are apparent causes on different levels successfully discredited? Are higher level phenomena determined by quantum events in such a way that we can reduce them to nothing but really complicated quantum events—the juxtaposition of a huge number of different wave functions, or whatever—or is there something more involved in the organization of levels that warrants granting these phenomena the status of being real? A TOE is silent on this issue. Any further verdict on whether quantum field level events alone are real is not a scientific but a philosophical conclusion.[12]

Second, there is nothing in sight like an actual physical explanation of biological and mental phenomena. As things now stand, there are phenomena that have no meaning in terms of lower levels of organization. Reductionists may dismiss all biological and mental phenomena as random events and so as neither capable of a quantum physical explanation nor in need of one since random events are of no scientific significance. That is, there may be some simple rules underlying all of reality, but these contingent events produce an unpredictability that may render any simple scientific account impossible. Because of randomness, there may be no inevitable course to the development of events in the universe. The history of life, our planet, and indeed our entire universe has no one necessary course dictated by particle physics. Each layer of development may contain a tremendous amount of such contingent events. All we can do is provide a history of what actually has occurred. Seen this way, particle physics leaves many questions of reality unanswered. But particle physics' explanatory power thus is quite limited. In the end, it does not explain all that much of the fullness of reality at all.

Moreover, reductionists still must explain how such phenomena as life and mind are *even possible*—otherwise not everything is explained in any sense. Antireductionists see higher levels as being structured by higher level factors rather than occurring randomly (although they too can accept that some random events also occur). To them, the emergence of life from inanimate matter without a role for biological "information" is simply amazing. This means not only explaining the evolution of life by physical factors alone but also explaining the origin of the initial biological material (DNA or RNA) that became the template for all subsequent development—that alone appears too complex to have developed by chance. To use a simile attributed to the astrophysicist Fred Hoyle: to believe the intricate first cell originated by chance is like believing a tornado ripping through a junkyard full of airplane parts could produce a Boeing 747. Indeed, the first cell would be *more* extraordinary since the objects in the junkyard are already *fashioned parts* of a larger, finished whole. Reductionists either have to show how electromagnetism and other physical forces enable the creation of higher levels of organization or they have to admit that nonphysical forces are also part of the structure of reality. (However, progress has been made on finding a chemical origin to life.)

We also need to know all the initial "boundary conditions" of the universe, the identity of all forces and particles, all constants in nature, and so forth. (We could also add that scientists may well discover new structures, e.g., some ordering large-scale astronomical phenomena. And, for all we know, more structures may emerge in the future.) But many cosmologists and physicists do not want to leave any laws or states of affairs as simply inexplicable brute facts. They want to know why all things are as they are—from why there are only a certain number of quarks on up. They want to answer Einstein's metaphorical question of whether God had any choice in creating the universe. They hope to show that no natural law or constant is arbitrary, merely the result of the random vicissitudes of cosmic history, but is in fact a matter of logical necessity. Ultimately, completing this quest would require accounting in natural terms for the emergence of space, time, and everything else from literally nothing or proving they are eternal. This means bringing the factual conditions of the origins of the universe within the scope of laws governing the evolution of the universe. But if the universe arose in a Big Bang, there would be a "singularity" we could not get beyond and so the completeness of any account would be impossible. On the other hand, if our universe had no beginning but is eternal, then space-time would have no initial random conditions. There would be no room for initial variability for any laws of nature but only one possible set of laws. Thereby, there would be no contingency of laws that could prevent the completeness of science. To speak metaphorically again, these scientists hope to show that God had no choice when he devised the laws by which our universe operates. With such an account, no law or constant in the history of the universe will appear accidental. Any randomness at the level of quantum field events or above may keep specific events from being predictable, but all scientific laws will be reduced to "special cases" of one fundamental law. Every scientific fact will then follow as exclusively a matter of logic and necessity. Once we know the code, life and consciousness may (or may not) appear as inevitable as a fully developed human is from his or her DNA code even if the specific details of the history of the development of nature may depend on random events. Thus, in an important way cosmology will have traveled full circle and returned to the methodology of ancient Greek philosophy: the laws of the eternal world would be deductions following from the (now empirically-founded) first principles.

Thus, do the assumptions behind a TOE justify a commitment to a structural brand of reductionism? No. When physicists speak of a "Theory of Everything," they do not literally mean *everything*—phenomena outside of the physical would still not be explained. Even as staunch a structure-reductionist as Steven Weinberg realizes a TOE in physics would not put an end to science—many wonderful phenomena would still need explaining. As he says, a final theory is final only in one sense: it would bring an end the ancient search for principles that cannot be explained in terms of deeper principles (1992: 18). A TOE cannot tell us all that is knowable about the universe and matter; other kinds of knowledge are needed as well (Gell-Mann 1994: 129). Even Weinberg concedes that a TOE may not explain consciousness but only its objective correlates (1992: 45). And, as the reductionist Stephen Hawking admits, there may be no unique TOE (Hawking & Mlodinow 2010: 118, 143-44). Indeed, no scientific theory can prove itself by bootstrapping its own finality or fundamentalness. In addition, no scientific theory can answer the metaphysical questions that any scientific theory presupposes—i.e., why anything exists at all or why there is lawful behavior in the universe in the first place.[13]

In short, a TOE in itself is not a *complete* explanation of anything. By itself, accounting for the particles and forces on the basic physical level will not account for *all* realities but only *one level* of all realities. But to be a theory of truly everything, a theory will have to explain *all* levels of *all* phenomena. In sum, a TOE will only be a "Theory of (One Level of) Everything." Moreover, a TOE must be combined with a reductive metaphysics of an interlevel determinism of all phenomena by the fundamental physical level of organization to produce the structure-reduction that reductionists desire. Only with such a determinism will the inevitably of every law be revealed by a TOE. (Any type of indeterminacy presents a problem here.) With the TOE alone, physicists will achieve in one conceptual scheme no more than the depiction of the laws of nature for the basic physical forces. It is only the reductive metaphysical overlay that makes a TOE seem to accomplish more than it does.

As things stand now, neither a TOE nor any other theory in physics as currently conceived would explain the dynamic and creative *emergence* of more and more levels of complexity. Scientists can explain what happens when atoms are organized into molecules and how it is possible, but they cannot explain *why* this occurs—i.e., why nature is set up to permit this to happen. No theories of organization in this sense have been advanced. All science is proving to be static in this respect: it deals with the final, developed levels of the universe and not with the process of the emergence of levels. Reductionists rely on the model of gliders in the computer game of Life to explain *how* any higher level of phenomena arises. For them, the current approach of physics will ultimately account for all of reality that needs accounting for: the relatively simple rules of physics virtually had to end up producing a complex reality (Simon 1962). Emergentists, on the other hand, should look for a scientific account of emergence—a "Theory of Organization," or "TOO," as Paul Davies calls it (1987: 138). Of course, it may be that such a theory is impossible—our minds perhaps have not evolved to understand such things. If so, then the process of emergence may not be open to scientific scrutiny. But if it is possible, then an approach not exhibited in current physics will be needed.

In sum, physics provides less support for reductionism then is commonly supposed. Classical Newtonian physics may have exemplified at least analysis as the ultimate method for science. But the limited scope and power of even the physicists' TOE makes theory-reductionism shaky. A different kind of theory is needed to embrace those aspects of reality related to the presence of levels (a TOO). Scientists may attempt a theory along such lines in the future, but at present such an approach is not on the horizon. However, any reductionists' denial of the need for a TOO results only from the metaphysical nature of reductionism. Reductionism is not the required result of accepting physics. Enthusiastic statements of structure- and theory-reductionism (e.g., Weinberg 1992; Hawking 1997) are simply unabashed statements of faith that everything must be that way rather than anything necessitated by the practice of physics.

Has Chemistry Been Reduced to Physics?

Chemistry is usually unchallenged as "reduced in principle" to physics through showing a direct relation between the valence of an element to the number of electrons in the outer orbit of an atom (e.g., Oppenheim & Putnam 1958: 35; Nagel 1961: 362). In fact, this is discussed surprisingly little. The closeness of chemistry and physics makes them the exemplar for reducing a science: in the reductionists' vision, there are no chemical level forces—all the apparent causal activity on the chemical level is the product of, or actually is, atomic level activity, and so all chemical properties can be explained in principle in terms of atomic level physics, even if the complexities of molecular interactions render precise calculations impossible even with the help of a computer. In short, chemistry is simply fancy physics—the physics of complex molecules hampered by computational problems.

However, eighty years after the completion of scientific accounts of the laws of quantum physics upon which chemistry is supposedly based, most chemical properties have not been explained by, or otherwise reduced to, quantum mechanics. Many question whether such a reduction can ever be achieved (Primas 1983, 2004; Scerri 1994; Hendry 2010, forthcoming: chaps. 8-10). Nancy Cartwright agrees that we notoriously have nothing like a real reduction of the relevant bits of physical chemistry to either classical or quantum physics: quantum mechanics are important for explaining aspects of chemical phenomena, but its concepts must always be used along side irreducible, sui generis concepts from other fields—physics does not explain chemical phenomena on their own (1997: 163). That chemicals may adapt or evolve (Lehn 2002) also presents a problem.

In particular, quantum mechanics is holistic, but the realities chemists deal with are considered discrete entities. The periodic table cannot be derived from quantum mechanics. Elements themselves have no chemical properties as components, and molecular structures cannot be derived from molecular Schrödinger equations (Hendry 2010: 206, 213). The heavier elements also have a history that depends on cosmological considerations—quantum physics is never the entire story, and thus chemical properties cannot be exhaustively reduced to physical ones (Popper 1979). Chemists study both the molecular level and the three states of the next higher level of organization (gaseous, liquid, and solid). The relation of those levels is not as simple as we might expect: at present there is no satisfactory, detailed picture even for understanding any state of water in terms of its molecules (Primas 1983: 317-18; Needham 2009: 111-13). Indeed, the very ideas of solidity and liquidity make no sense in terms of molecules alone. Such properties are not mere aggregates of lower level properties. Scientists may be able to explain how molecules sustain solidity or other higher level properties through bonding, but molecules alone will not explain why reality is set up for bonding to occur and higher levels to emerge. Thus, more than the molecular level is needed to explain even bonding.

Is Biology an Autonomous Science?

The main tension today between reductionists and antireductionists in science is over whether biology will remain an autonomous science. Reductionists advance their position as the only alternative to the substance-dualism of "vitalism." Vitalism can be traced to Aristotle, but in its modern forms, as advanced by Henri Bergson (1911) and Hans Driesch, it is the idea that a nonmaterial substance—called an "entelechy," "vital fluid," "life-force," or "*élan vital*"—is added to matter that is responsible for the property of being alive. This second substance is supposedly a "current of life" that infuses inert matter, thereby creating living organisms and guiding the entire course of the evolution of all organisms in all their diversity and novelty (Hull 1974: 127-29). This position, however, produced no testable hypotheses and thus proved to be a dead end as a guide to biological research. Today all biologists deny the need for such a second substance and claim life can be completely explained in terms of the organization of the matter within living beings. Organisms consist substantively of no more than the same atoms and molecules as inorganic entities, and "being alive" is only a complex combination of inanimate material functioning as unit.

Today structure-reductionists push further and claim that the only alternative to vitalism is to accept that the theories and laws of physics and chemistry are sufficient for understanding living organisms. "Identity theory" is expanded from mind/body to life/matter. All living phenomena are merely distinctive arrangements of inanimate material; the horizontal emergence of new species and greater complexity in the evolution of life needs no structures other than physical ones. As the physicist Richard Feynman put it, "everything that animals do, atoms do. In other words, there is nothing that living things do that cannot be understood from the point of view that they are made of atoms acting according to the laws of physics" (quoted in Pippard 1988: 393). Biology becomes nothing but the application of quantum physics to complicated configurations of electrons and nuclei.

Francis Crick of DNA's double helix fame succinctly states the structure- and theory-reductionists' credo: "the ultimate aim of the modern movement in biology is to explain all biology in terms of physics and chemistry" (1966:10). What Crick calls the "central dogma" of molecular biology is that DNA molecules determine the higher levels. Biophysicists and biochemists will identify the bases of biological phenomena, and once we have a complete description of all the molecular interactions occurring within a living cell, we will completely understood the cell and from there we will be able to reduce all biological phenomena to their components and then to reduce those to their chemical and physical bases. The origin of each living entity, its growth, and all its mature powers will need to be shown to be the result of molecules responding blindly to local physical forces alone and yet somehow cooperating and integrating their individual behavior into coherent, ordered wholes (Davies 1987: 100). Life will then be shown to be no more than the product of the physical and chemical levels of complexity. Thus, in the most fundamental sense, there is no such thing as *life* but only inanimate material at work. Many reductionists, such as Richard Dawkins, think evolution will be shown to be a matter only of forces acting on genes; ultimately, no biological function is involved. Eventually all of biology will be explained in terms of the level below it and so on right down to the atomic level (Crick 1966: 14). (And apparently biology students today are flocking to reductionist-oriented courses and ignoring evolution [Hull 2002: 164-65].) Ultimately biology will not be necessary. Thus, the science of biology, while clearly of heuristic value today, will be replaced entirely by chemistry and physics (Crick 1966: 98).

Reductionists expect to find nothing at work in a cell that cannot be explained by physical structures. For example, the development of an embryo will be shown to be determined by the laws of chemistry or be nothing but chemical properties. However, it is a crude caricature of reductionists to picture them as hacking up plants and animals into smaller and smaller pieces to see how the pieces work. Elephants cannot be studied simply through a microscope—the whole, including its interaction with its environment, must be studied first before the lower level explanation will be forthcoming. Reductionists realize that each level of structuring must initially be studied intact, not dissected into isolated parts. Even if proteins or human bodies were treated as physical machines, still the parts have to be studied in their total context. This means having to study parts of organism *in their biological context*. Reductive molecular biologists are as much "compositionists" as antireductionists (Crick 1966: 13; Ruse 1988: 86). Similarly, reductionists can be as sensitive as antireductionists to the boundary conditions of biological phenomena (even if they treat such conditions as arbitrary and random) and to the "open-endedness" of living processes. In short, for reductionists the biological level of complexity is to be reduced, not dismantled or denied.

In fact, physics may have to be revised to account for findings discovered in the analysis of biological phenomena. But physics would still remain only physics because it would contain only *physical* structures. Eventually all of evolution and any apparently teleological biological activities will be shown to be determined by inorganic, physical events occurring below the macromolecular level. All everyday level events will ultimately be shown to be simply the product of, or aggregate of, a series of microlevel events. For example, the self-reproduction of DNA molecules may be shown to be the same type of process as the reproduction of inorganic crystals by their seeding of other crystals. In the end, all biological phenomena will be shown to be more complex than other molecular phenomena only by degree.

The current focus for this reductionism is genetics and molecular biology (see Bechtel & Hamilton 2007: 416-19). Reductionists are not committed to a simplistic genetic reductionism of the human personality, e.g., that there is one gene for each human behavioral trait.[14] Rather, genes—the vehicles that let biological information be inherited—will be shown to be the building blocks of all biological phenomena, and classical Mendelian genetics (covering population-level phenomena) will be reduced to molecular genetics. All hereditary phenomena will be shown to be nothing but molecular structures and processes. Thereby, all DNA coding will be reduced to physical and chemical bases and initial physical conditions. Reductionists can point to tremendous advances in our knowledge of genetics. Gene therapy is a medical success story in the area of hereditary diseases. But it must be noted that this does not aid the reductionists' quest to reduce genetics. Such medical technology is irrelevant to the issue of whether biological phenomena can be reduced, since no one denies the importance of the genetic level to something inherited. Antireductionists can readily accept that adjusting the genetic level can affect the higher biological levels of organization—this only means that the genetic level is *necessary* to the higher levels, not that the latter are reducible to the former. Indeed, the quest for genetic reductions has not proven nearly as easy as enthusiasts in the 1960's believed it would be. (And it should be pointed out that biochemists as a rule are not as gung ho about physical explanations as reductionists are.)

Antireductionists hold no hope for this quest. Functional biological properties have no physical equivalent (Nagel 1998: 5). No one denies that analysis has been at the forefront of biological advances for the last century, but to antireductionists the complexity of biological phenomena constitutes a much greater problem for structure-reductionism than do the problems in physics: just as parts of a clock make no sense except in the context of a whole, parts of biological wholes each have functions that are useless apart from the functions of the whole's other parts, and thus each part can be explained only in terms of how it fits in with the other parts of a functioning whole. In that way, biological wholes are irreducibly complex.[15] There is no chemical explanation for an organism's survival, or how it can adapt an existing part for another use (exaptation), or how it can act with intentionality as an autonomous agent. Organisms are not simply physical clumps of molecules but are defined entirely by their organization and the mutual interaction of their biological parts. Conversely, no cell exists independently of an organism, nor does any organ or gene exist or make sense independent of its organism as a whole.

Thus, simply studying parts *in situ*, as reductionists do, is allegedly not enough. Antireductionists need not subscribe to an "organicism" in which the whole exercises a measure of downward control on its inorganic parts. But even if scientists devise a complete account of the physical or chemical level of a biological entity, such an account cannot explain the presence of the new level of complexity on the biological level. Upper levels of organization require higher level principles. A particle physics account of evolution explains nothing. Evolution occurs through "natural selection" (and perhaps more) regardless of lower level mechanisms and cannot be derived from chemical forces. Biological functions simply represent a new level of "information" that is carried by the lower levels but that is not reducible to physical and chemical information. Such biological "messages" will be missed if we study the molecular level alone.

Most antireductionists also reject likening an organism to a machine, since the parts of a machine are removable and replaceable and their interrelationships are strictly mechanical. But both organisms and machines operate by a structuring that is irrelevant to the underlying physics (Polanyi 1968). The design of a machine in no way conflicts with the laws of physics governing their parts—indeed, the form must utilize that physics. But machines *function* by their own level of design alone. The function of the parts can never be found by studying the parts' constitution; study of the design of the whole is needed. The forces that cause the rigidity of parts of a car engine are irrelevant to how it operates, and so the laws governing the parts in no way *determine* how a machine works. Moreover, machines cannot be designed on the basis of our knowledge of their parts alone and hence cannot be *explained* by the parts' physics alone. The parts in fact are *formed* in light of the structure of the whole—they are simply the material through which the machine fulfills its function. Everything material about a bird's wings may be explainable in terms of physics, but the functional properties still represent a level different from the mechanical events occurring during flight. Any attempt to explain anything biological in terms of the mechanisms of the parts alone miss that.

Biological processes such as vision or reproduction cannot operate on the level of a single molecule or below. To antireductionists, they operate by their own causes and cannot be predicted from any amount of knowledge of those physical and chemical processes also operating within a biological being. Thus, neurons occur only in the brain, not in other parts of the body, in inanimate objects, or independently in nature; this indicates that something is at work other than physical structures common to all matter in their creation. Even a simple cell has many properties that are absent on the molecular level. This new level has its own real causes, and therefore accounts of this irreducible level of organization require their own distinctive concepts to categorize different entities (e.g., "cell," "gene," and "organism") and processes operating on different biological sublevels (e.g., "digestion," "vision," and "adaptation"). Such concepts are simply meaningless when discussing molecules and atoms and thus have no place in chemistry and physics. In addition, explaining the whole will always require more than analysis of the interaction of the parts on their own level. The biological level contains vast amounts of factual conditions arising from the history of the universe. The chemical and physical levels remain constant in these conditions, and hence chemical and physical laws are neutral to biological history. In other words, the conditions are simply outside the laws of chemistry and physics—indeed, to reductionists, they will appear random and accidental and thus "unimportant" (Atkins 1992: 3) since the focus is only on the chemical and physical levels (Gell-Mann 1994: 115). But to antireductionists, life is unfolding according to nonphysical structures.

From structure-antireductionism, method- and theory-antireductionism follow: lower level disciplines will never capture the biological information or history of life, since these lie outside of the laws of chemistry and physics. A physical analysis of the body will only reveal chemicals, not the structure of organs or of the living whole. Such analysis of physical and chemical bases will inform biological research but never replace the study of biological organisms, breeding populations, and species as wholes, since this analysis does not aid in accounting for the uniquely biological level. An inventory of the molecules making up an organ and their chemical interactions will never explain the nature of that organ—the independent level of how an organ functions in the body is required to complete the explanation (Mayr 1988b: 475). Today biologists may be making great progress by focusing on parts (the genes), but antireductionists insist that focusing on living organisms as wholes is also necessary if we are to understand the biological realities completely.

Most importantly, for structure-antireductionists the new level of genuine causes operating in biological phenomena requires its own irreducible theories to explain those phenomena. Biological phenomena are constrained by the laws of physics and chemistry, but biological phenomena are wholes whose properties cannot be predicted, even in principle, from the most complete knowledge of their components taken separately or in combinations (Mayr 1988a). From the point of view of chemistry, nothing new happens with life—DNA is nothing but ordinary chemicals. But the arrangement of the chemical material in DNA (the sequence of DNA's nucleotide "letters") conveys "information" that comes from the biological structure. Chemistry does not determine this information—indeed, chemical structures are irrelevant to it. Biological structuring may exploit the chemical properties of the building blocks, but it is not determined by the lower level chemical properties. In that sense, biological entities operate independently of their physical and chemical bases. Their interactions occur on their own level. Biological properties are distinct from their bases, much like the arrangement of words on this page is extraneous to the chemistry of the page and ink (Polanyi 1968: 1311). Knowledge of the chemistry of this book's ink and paper is irrelevant to understanding the meaning of the text—another level of structure is at work. The rules of chess are consistent with the physics of the pieces' movements but cannot be derived from the laws of physics, and the same holds for biological information. Or to use another analogy: trying to figure out the nature and development of biological processes from knowledge of their physical and chemical levels of organization is like trying to figure out our transportation system from knowledge of the parts of a car's engine (Rose 1987: 14). In short, "no biology in, no biology out" (Cartwright 1997: 165). Distinct biological causes, concepts, and theories will have to be employed. And this means biology will always be needed as an autonomous science.

Antireductionists present two arguments. The first, as in other areas, is multiple realization. Multiple realization in biology is tied to functions (e.g., Rosenberg 1994: 27-33)—i.e., the same biological function (e.g., flight or vision) is achieved by different chemical and physical structures and has evolved more than once.[16] The biological functions can be achieved through an indefinite set of underlying molecular base-conditions, and thus those constituents cannot explain the higher level phenomena. Biological structures are needed to explain even how the base-conditions are working. Reductionists generally reject the very idea of functional explanations in favor of causal explanations in terms of physical structures and composition. But antireductionists argue that this misses the point: even if we reject the functional type of explanation, multiple realization still occurs in biological phenomena. For example, the same phenotypic traits characterized by a single Mendelian description can be realized by different types of molecular mechanisms, and, conversely, the same type of molecular mechanism can produce traits that must be characterized differently in Mendelian terms (Hull 1974: 39). That is, many different chemical processes may underlie one biological process or vice versa. Thus, the problem is more than the usual "one-to-many" problem of multiple realization—instead, it is a "many-to-many" mess. Some reductionists who favor functionalism respond in terms of functional sub-types (Esfeld & Sachse 2011). But some who favor reductionism in general accept this point and conclude that, because the relation of biological and chemical phenomena is not simple in the way reductionism requires, the reduction of the biology to the physics is impossible: evolutionary biology may be reducible to molecular biology (and the principle of natural selection may be a new fundamental physical law), but genetic development cannot be reduced further to chemical and physical forces (Rosenberg 2006).

The second general argument is the historical nature of biology. Any particular electron has no real history, but every cell represents a history of more than a billion years of evolution (Primas 1983: 311). Physics certainly deals with dynamic phenomena, but biological phenomena's origin, development, and overall history constitute a dimension that physics misses. Indeed, this problem can be expanded to include the history of the entire universe. For example, Karl Popper pointed out that heavier elements have a history depending on such cosmogonic and cosmological factors as the heat inside stars that cannot be found by analyzing hydrogen and physical forces (1974: 267-88). If those factors had been different, the subsequent phenomena would have been different, but there is nothing in the initial conditions that speaks to those factors. Hence, the historical dimension is irreducible.

To expand the text/page-and-ink analogy, the historical development of biological and phenomena can be likened to the narrative of a text: physicists identify the building blocks (the vocabulary and its building blocks, the letters) and the laws (the grammar), but they do not deal with the level of organization guiding the construction of the whole (the narrative of the text). The inflexible physical laws are the boundary that constrains the development of the universe—just as the rules of grammar do in any book—but they do not determine the outcome. Each account of a book in terms of its alphabet, punctuation marks, vocabulary, and grammar is complete in its own terms but not exhaustive of all aspects of the book. Most importantly, no one account of the book can be deduced from another, no matter how complete. In particular, the meaning cannot be deduced from the other accounts. Similarly, the origin and development of individual organisms and the evolution of life on earth are not deducible from other accounts; they are topics that physicists *qua* physicists simply miss. The causes and the explanations in these areas are of a different type than those currently in physics. They have to tell a story in a way particle physical theories do not (Rose 1985).

Evolutionary biologists need not reduce causation to only the genetic level. Instead, they too can accept a hierarchy of levels at work within evolution. In natural selection, causally active processes occur on two levels: selection operating on an organism on the phenotypic level for increasing "fitness" of the whole organism, and variation operating on the genotypic level creating inheritable differences among organisms. Indeed, some add a third level—the group or population level, or a species as a whole, distinct from the survival of the individual organism—and argue that quibbling about what is the one true unit of selection is a metaphysical muddle (Sterelny & Kitcher 1985). Thus, even if variations on the genetic level were reducible to the interaction of inorganic entities, the biological phenomenon of evolution would still not be reducible. In sum, there is a pluralistic causal situation in evolution that is incompatible with reductionism (Dupré 1994).

Reductionists counter that biology is not a true science and so has nothing to reduce. Biologists have advanced a large number of rough-and-ready generalities covering phenomena, but these all have numerous exceptions (Schaffner 1993:

490). Whether the concept of "law" even applies has been questioned. These generalities are thus not like the mathematical laws of physics. Moreover, there is a problem with the few theories there are in biology. For example, the few historical explanations advanced in evolutionary theory are considered to be quite weak (Schaffner 1993: 522). Few philosophers treat the theory of natural selection in the same way as they treat theories in physics (e.g., Rosenberg 1992: 104, 134-35). Antireductionists may argue that this situation merely reflects the current stage of development in biology, a stage still rather primitive compared to physics or that the complexities of biological structures renders impossible any laws comparable to those of the simpler physical level. The study of DNA may well end up making biology more like physics. But to reductionists this simply means that biologists are dealing with the contingent boundary conditions that real scientists can rightly ignore. The reductionist-minded Alexander Rosenberg argues that biology merely reflects our very subjective needs and interests and thus will never be reducible to "objective" physics (1994). Biology simply does not "carve nature at its joints" and so does not identify any structures or laws to reduce or produce concepts that will link up one-to-one with concepts from physics.

Even the most rigorous laws in biology—those in Mendelian genetics—present a problem. Philosophers David Hull (1974) and Philip Kitcher (1984) have advanced many problems with the notion that Mendelian genetics can in principle be reduced to molecular genetics. Mention of one hurdle will suffice: Mendelian genetics is about the transmission and distribution of genetic material in the form of phenotypes (consisting of proteins and other macromolecules), while molecular genetics covers the development of such material (consisting of nucleic acids) through evolution; the former are the observable characteristics of an organism, and the latter are the lower level base-conditions that, in conjunction with the organism's environment, give rise to the former. The population-level phenomena explained by "Mendelian genes" are not what is explained by "molecular genes." There is the multiple realization problem that the units of DNA do not correlate with particular phenotypes. Moreover, the mechanisms of molecular genetics are simply irrelevant to the transmission explained by Mendelian genetics (Hull 1984: 475). There is no genetic code operating on the chemical and physical levels of organization. The genetic "information" from one level is not reducible to the genetic "information" from the other, even if the higher level information is transmitted through the lower level mechanisms. That is, molecular genes are the carriers of the Mendelian information, but the levels of organization remain distinct.

Biochemical causes may explain genotypes, but another type of explanation in terms of higher level realities is needed to explain the observable characteristics resulting from the interaction of genes and their environment. There is no molecular biology of genes but only of genetic material. No amount of biochemical knowledge of the structure of the DNA molecule or of how those genes work will produce knowledge of the phenotypic level. Completing the Human Genome Project thus did not put an end to the science of human biology. Theories at different levels divide up the world differently, and the subject of a theory from one level simply does not map neatly onto the other, and thereby reduction is rendered impossible. Mendelian genetics cannot be derived from the molecular except by artificially "correcting" it for the sole purpose of satisfying a reductive scheme. Even some reductionists admit that the absence of a fully explicated biological theory at the molecular level entails that no theory-reduction is possible (Sarkar 1998). There simply is no molecular biology of genes but only of genetic material (Kitcher 1984).

Ardent reductionists assert that reduction is at least possible in principle and a non-Nagelian account will someday capture this relation (e.g., Sarkar 1998). Some reductionist-minded philosophers invoke the concept of supervenience to try to circumvent the apparent impossibility of manageable connections between the two sets of properties (Rosenberg 1992: 22-23). Two organisms with the same DNA would also have the same Mendelian genes, and thus Mendelian entities and properties supervene on molecular bases, with the DNA molecules doing the actual causal work of the factors that transmit phenotypic properties from generation to generation. Regardless, reductionists think it is "intuitively" clear that a reduction in genetics has taken place (Brooks 1994: 804). The philosopher of biology Michael Ruse rather unconvincingly argues that, even though the conditions for theory-reduction do not strictly hold, the situation in molecular biology is still one of reduction because there is "continuity" between Mendelian and molecular biology (1971). He has little more to back up this position than a staunch metaphysical belief that only reductionism fits with the way things are. Of course, antireductionists do not deny correlations, but they argue that the nature of what biologists study will always prohibit any "physics of life." Indeed, the trend toward generality exhibited in the last hundred years of biology has nothing to with reducing biological theories to those in chemistry and physics (Maull 1984: 512).

And even reductionists must be willing to admit that the quest for reductions is not driving scientific research in biology today. In 1972 David Hull could say that no biologists were attempting to correlate systematically the terms of Mendelian and molecular genetics—nor could he see why anyone, other than a philosopher trying to fulfill the requirements of a formal theory-reduction, would be interested in doing so (1972: 499). And the same is true today. It is not a primary goal, aim, or value of even *molecular biology*. Reduction is of no value methodologically or epistemically to scientists working in the field. The reductionists' rejoinder that reductions are "in principle" possible obviously has no consequences, either practical or theoretical, for biologists, although it might have some metaphysical consolation. But it is a matter only of philosophical interest. Indeed, trying to view reductionism as a scientific research project may well be distorting the way scientists actually work in this field (Hull 1974: 44; Wimsatt 1979; Maull 1984).

Of course, we do not know what the future may hold. Perhaps physicists will be able, for example, to encompass the historical dimension of biology, much like cosmologists want to encompass the boundary facts surrounding the Big Bang. Perhaps they will be able to create an expanded physics that replaces the need for biological posits to explain biological phenomena. Reductionists will argue that the design of a machine represents a higher level of organization than the mechanics operating among the machine's parts, but this does not mean the design is any less physical, and perhaps the same applies to biological phenomena. But the upshot of the present state of our sciences is that antireductionists currently have the upper hand on the relation of biology to physics. Indeed, there is nothing to suggest that any knowledge of the physical and chemical levels of organizations will ever achieve a complete explanation of the biological level. In fact, more and more biologists today are questioning the reductionist approach (see Williams 1997). Structure-antireductionism may in fact be the consensus wisdom in philosophy of biology today (Rosenberg 1997: 370). Over all, there appears little reason at present—except for a prior metaphysical commitment to reductionism—to believe that biology will not remain an autonomous and necessary science.

Have There Been Any Successful Reductions in Science?

The difficulties philosophers have encountered on the issue of reducing biological structures and theories also bear on the next topic: whether there are in fact any true instances of a "successful" or "complete" theory-reduction in science. Remember that the requirements are demanding: the reducing theory must do all the work of the reduced theory—the reducing theory must displace all the explanations and theoretical structures of the reduced theory, without loss of explanatory power.

Unfortunately for reductionists, *no* reduction has actually been demonstrated in detail. Rather, reductions have been dogmatically presented only in broad outline. Reductionists usually only identify a few crucial lower level mechanisms and make a lot of promises (Wimsatt 1976). Mendelian genetics is the only current possibility in the realm of biology, and, as just discussed, even after considerable tinkering, no one can claim classical genetics has been, or is being, reduced to molecular genetics. So too, the much touted reduction of thermodynamics to statistical mechanics, when actually examined, is found to fail (Bechtel & Hamilton 2007: 415-16). Heat is still a novel property that is distinct from motion, and the laws of thermodynamics make no sense when applied to molecules since they have no temperature (see Needham 2009: 94-98). Nor can thermodynamics be deduced from mechanics—incommensurable concepts are involved. For example, "entropy" and "equilibrium" are central to thermodynamics but have no correlates in statistical mechanics (Sklar 1993). The same event can be described in either set of terms, but neither set can replace the other. Even a reductionist-minded historian concedes that the typical textbook account of heat does not really involve statistical mechanics at all but rather only a crude kinetic theory of gases in which statistical considerations do not play any essential role (Brush 1977: 552-53). More generally, all the philosophical discussions of reduction involve idealized examples taken out of their historical contexts and do not reflect what scientists are actually doing (ibid.: 565).

Reductionists do admit that reductions have proven to be surprisingly complex and problematic. In fact, they concede this a little too readily—they predict rapid progress, and then the stubborn lack of progress just does not seem to bother them. Their primary explanation for the lack of any demonstrated reductions is to concede that reductions in the present state of science are futile—scientific knowledge is currently simply far too incomplete—but in the future research will rectify the situation (E. Nagel 1979: 115, 116). Currently, biologists in the area of genetics are too busy with substantive scientific research to bother with an issue that is admittedly only of philosophical interest—reductions involve details of no interest or value to the scientists (Ruse 1971: 29) But this explanation has the unintended consequence of admitting the scientific irrelevance of reductionism. As noted above, the reductionists' reconstructions distort actual scientific research, both current and past. Reductionism's ties to science are thereby weakened and its metaphysical nature becomes more apparent. This explanation also brings out the reductionists' act of faith: any empirical confirmation of reductionism is put off to the indefinite future, but reductionists are certain that confirmation will definitely be found someday. Still, the problem is that we are left with no nonmetaphysical grounds to commit to structure- and theory-reductionism today. In short, why be a reductionist *today* if it is scientifically useless and is not clearly superior philosophically?

Reductionists also have a second response: even if reductionism is technically impossible, still the drive for reductions is the way scientific research should be directed. The prescriptive nature of method-reductionism becomes prominent. This drive will result in valuable "partial reductions" of biology to physics and chemistry (Schaffner 1984: 428). If this means only that reductions will never fulfill all the philosophical requirements of a successful theory-reduction but are nevertheless true reductions, then this position collapses into the reductionists' response just discussed. The alternative is that this is an endorsement of method-reductionism while denying structure- and theory-reductionism, i.e., reductions should be pursed as a regulative ideal even if scientists never achieve a complete reduction. But the distinction between reductionism and analysis must be reiterated. Antireductionists agree that identifying the physical and chemical bases of biological phenomena is valuable, but analysis not a *reduction* of those phenomena to the underlying bases. Such *analysis* is not an "unsuccessful" or "partial" reduction at all, and thus it cannot provide any support for the philosophical position of reductionism.

If these two responses fail, reductionists still have a fall-back position: simply declare victory and move on to other issues. The editors of the prestigious journal *Nature* (in asking whether one of Rupert Sheldrake's books on "morphic fields" ought to be burned) noted that the shock troops of reductionists in biology—the molecular biologists—have not been able to calculate the phenotype of a single organism from a knowledge of its genotype. Their reaction is "But so what?" Molecular explanations of biological phenomena have been shown since the 1960's to be possible and powerful (Editorial 1981: 246), and apparently nothing more is needed. Reductions are "intuitively" clear (Brooks 1994: 804; Hardcastle 1996a: 89), even if reality is too complicated ever to expect a detailed reduction. Approximations of real reductions are all we can hope for. Reductions may have to remain only *ideals* forever. So what we have now is the most we can ever realistically hope for. But as long as reductions are logically possible, reductionists can ignore the difficulties of spelling out the details and can assert that they have achieved success. Reductions are *in principle* possible, and this is all that is needed. Thus, not actually being able to demonstrate them in practice is no big deal. Nevertheless, the idea of reductions being only "in principle" possible cannot provide reductionists with much comfort. It merely restates the reductionists' metaphysical faith in their own position rather than providing any argument for it.

Needless to say, any defense that is left with nothing but a bald statement of the position is not convincing, and that is precisely what happens when we are left with only "in principle" reductions. It is certainly difficult to see how the idea of "reducibility in principle" could have any direct methodological consequences for current scientific practice (Sober 1993: 25-26). And, far from being dictated by science, the reductionists' position is not even an attempt to conform to the history of science. Reductionists must also concede that their view does not reflect the current state of science—and they will never need to be disturbed by a lack of successful reductions in the future. Reductionists may hold on to their position indefinitely: unlike what Imre Lakatos called a "degenerating research program" in science that scientists should not pursue indefinitely in light of failed predictions, reductionism is a form of metaphysics and suffers no such fault. Indeed, since reductions are "in principle" already accomplished, reductionism cannot even be described as "degenerating." We are left only with a metaphysics that reductionists should frankly admit does not reflect the state of science. But, in such circumstances, why we should be reductionists today is not at all clear, especially if the success of science is supposed to be the reason for reductionism.

Antireductionists can readily concede that some apparently genuine emergent properties are in fact only products or aggregates of lower level properties and thus that merely lower level causes are at work in those properties—it is only the complete reduction of all higher level properties and theories today or in the future that they deny. Perhaps, for example, parts of genetics, enzymology, or physiology will be successfully reduced to chemistry or physics. Antireductionists only maintain that not *all* causes and theories from a given level are reducible to lower level causes and theories. Indeed, many who question reductionism go further. Hans Primas surveyed the usual examples of reductions proffered by reductionists and did not find a single instance in which the requirements for a reduction were in fact satisfied (1991; see also Horst 2007: 50-54). Even a former champion of reductionism, Kenneth Schaffner, can admit that reductions in science are "largely a myth," although he thinks the patchy and fragmentary reduction-like interfield mechanical explanations that do exist are still important (2006).

Another possibility about the future course of science must also be considered. Even if any successful reductions are ever achieved, there is still the possibility that these may be overturned in the future as science progresses. Further research may reveal irreducible properties or other complications on the higher level nullifying the previous reduction. Reductionists can rest confident only when theoretical science and scientific research have come to an end—otherwise, there is the possibility that the reduction will be overturned by a later scientific advancement. Of course, a complete explanation of all higher level structures and theories by quantum field physics may spell the end of theoretical science, if reductionists are right, and thus once that is achieved the threat of reversal would end.

The antireductionist Karl Popper was the most prominent counter to Ernest Nagel. His antireductionism is part of his view of the world that emphasizes creativity, unpredictability, and indeterminism (1979). While stressing the importance of "partial reductions" (i.e., analysis) for science, he argued that no major purported reduction in science and mathematics is in fact completely successful. The one possible exception is Maxwell's theory of electromagnetism unifying electricity and magnetism, which, he argued, might be better viewed not as a reduction but as a radically new theory which succeeded in unifying two physical forces on one level—i.e., a *replacement*—since no reduction to new levels is involved. In all other cases, there has always been some unresolved explanatory residue left by even the most successful attempts at reduction. The deductions involved in reductions are not strict but involve various approximations, simplifications, and idealizations. In his view, all of reductionism is based on a mistake: the wish to reduce everything to an ultimate explanation in terms of essences and substances that is not capable of, or in need of, any further explanation. In fact, science will always remain incomplete in that respect. The lack of any strict or formal reductions should therefore not be surprising (Popper 1974, 1982: 163-74).

Problems with reductionism are also present in mathematics. A major barrier to reducing any formal axiomatic system merely to premises and deduction, such as Alfred North Whitehead and Bertrand Russell proposed for mathematics, is Gödel's Theorem. This theorem states that in every formal theory powerful enough to articulate basic arithmetic, there are true propositions that can be stated but not proven even in principle within that theory. In the words of Freeman Dyson, "Gödel proved that in mathematics the whole is always greater than the sum of the parts." This has made formalization in mathematics difficult to maintain. Any axiomization of physics or another science would have the same problem. Furthermore, even if physicists could bring the initial conditions of the universe within a TOE, any TOE would still be limited in its comprehensiveness as discussed above. This problem also has ramifications for any proposed reductive relation between the empirical sciences: even if all the natural sciences could be transformed into formal systems—something positivists would like—still a reduction of one science to another would have to overcome the fundamental problem that both the reducing science and the science to be reduced are, as formal systems, more than the sum of their parts. There may be more laws within the scope of any one theory, let alone any one science, than can be proven by that theory. Each system is formally incomplete, thereby making their deductive relation between sciences in a reduction that much harder to accomplish successfully.

Reductionists, blissfully unaware of these problems or at least unconcerned by them, may continue to assert that theory-reduction is "a normal and fairly commonplace event in the history of science" (Churchland & Churchland 1995: 71). But reductionists have a major problem with science: in what should be the cornerstone of structure- and theory-reductionisms, there is a very real possibility that reductionists cannot point to *any* example that actually fulfills their goal. At a minimum, they must concede that reductions are much rarer and much looser in science than they usually contend. Nor can reductionists maintain that seeking reductive explanations is the driving force in science as practiced in the past and today. Nor is there any drive for a grand reduction of all science. Indeed, if anything, the opposite is currently true, since higher level causes are thoroughly embedded in science today.

Of course, pointing out possible empirical problems with purported reductions is not the same as producing a strong argument in favor of emergent realities. After all, antireductionism, like reductionism, also predicts the future course of scientific research. But at least antireductionists can point to the actual history of science and the current practice of scientists as evidence against endorsing reductionism today. That practicing scientists can basically ignore the entire metaphysical issue in itself favors the more open-ended approach of the antireductionists. Reductionists come across as making highly restrictive demands on the nature of science—demands that have no scientific justification. In short, one day reductionists may be vindicated, but the prospects for this cannot be called "bright" today.

The Limited Relevance of Empirical Evidence

Reductionists are fond of saying there is no evidence for the antireductionists' claim that each level of organization has a structural independence, but they are missing the point: the reductionists' metaphysical outlook does not *permit* any evidence to support the reality of nonphysical causes. The current need for "special" sciences is, in their view, only temporary and therefore does not support antireductionism. Similarly, for them the fact that physical posits have not yet replaced the need for biological posits to explain and predict biological phenomena only points to the poverty of our knowledge. In principle, nothing antireductionists could advance could count against the reductionists' commitment that a reduction of causes will occur eventually or will still be "in principle" possible forever. But reductionists cannot appeal to science to support their metaphysical faith if they are not willing to let anything in the practice and history of science count against it.

Scientists could achieve the most thorough analytical knowledge of nature imaginable and still not accept any structural reductions. What reductionists need is the elimination of causes from one level in favor of those on a lower level, not merely more empirical knowledge of a phenomenon's parts. Even if scientists could advance a complete set of base-conditions for the prediction of a higher level phenomenon, more is still needed—the creation of the higher level phenomenon would still have to be shown to involve no other causes. Correlation or prediction is not enough to answer the "how" question or effect a structure-reduction. Reductionists cannot point to any area of current empirical research or even any empirical prediction to investigate that would affect the issue of reductionism one way or the other when all scientists can do is *correlate* phenomena from different levels rather than explain how the emergence of the higher level phenomena occurred. In short, how do we *test* what causes are real?

Indeed, it is hard to see how there could be empirical evidence that only physical causes, let alone quantum field level ones, are at work in reality. Consider the origin of life. There is a real question whether further scientific research will be able to answer the fundamental reductionist question: if scientists someday do somehow create life (e.g., in stirring up a prebiological "primal soup" of chemicals), are they in fact creating life from chemicals, or are they merely duplicating the lower *base-conditions* necessary for the structures of the universe that generate life to become engaged? Is life just a property of matter organized by physical forces in a certain way, or are there structures unique to life (and hence are nonphysical) also at work? The physical conditions may be *necessary* for the appearance, but do they actually *create* the emergence? May we conclude life is no more than the evolution of self-replicating molecules, or have scientists merely set up the necessary circumstances permitting the biological structures already existing in reality to kick in? That is precisely the issue in dispute. If emergentists are correct, all biological structures are an inherent part of fundamental nature of reality; they would be built into reality the same way that any forces recognized by physicists are and thus are equally real. Biological and mental structures would be as "fundamental" or "ultimate" to the architecture of reality as physical ones—they simply are not active in inanimate realities. Phenomena arise naturally by reason of these structures when the appropriate lower level organizational conditions exist.

In short, how do reductionists know these conditions are all that is needed in creating life or that this is the only way to create life? The "building blocks" of life may simply be the chemical platform upon which the biological structuring makes actual life. Indeed, as the antireductionist Karl Popper said, even if we do reproduce life, this does not change the fact that life is still an utterly new reality in the universe (1978: 342). And, he added, we may artificially reproduce life without still *understanding* what is going on, while a theory-reduction requires such understanding (1979: 291). In sum, artificially generating life in a lab will not determine whether nonphysical structures are involved. There also remains the entire issue of how one level of organization arises out of a lower level—what is going on in *between levels*, as it were. This is the issue for a new scientific approach culminating in a Theory of Organization. Without a TOO, the need to explain why reality organizes itself at all and how higher levels emerge would remain. There is also the very real possibility that any experiments, if possible, on how reality gets from one level to the next could be as easily reconciled with one position as the other: reductionists can still claim that only physical structures are involved while antireductionists can claim that the natural mechanism for emergence, whatever it may be, does not undercut the irreducible reality of the higher levels.

Even if we could construct a brand new universe from scratch—one that is identical to ours in all its physical properties and that has as its ingredients only matter/energy and the same physical forces as our universe has and that we know is devoid of any biological or mental structures—the issue may still not be resolved. If no higher level properties were generated, any determination of them by lower level physical forces alone would be disproved, and antireductionists may seem vindicated in advocating independent structures. But reductionists could attribute any negative results to random events that would occur in any universe and thus still maintain they are correct. Only if biological and mental properties did arise and we knew no biological or mental structures were present could reductionists rightly cite the result as evidence of lower level determination. But nothing short of this occurring in a new universe could resolve the dispute—any empirical finding in our world would be open to reductionist and antireductionist interpretations.

Thus, the central issue of structure- and theory-reductionism—whether scientists can exhaustively explain higher level phenomena by means of lower level phenomena—seems hard to decide empirically. It is partially "empirical" in that it depends in part, on how scientists develop science as a whole in the future. But at present reductive guidance does not play the part in science that reductionists believe. And, as discussed below, if science is eventually conceptualized along these lines, problems still remain that keep reductionists from claiming victory too quickly. And if anything, contemporary science is pointing more and more to the importance of wholes and their properties. This means a "systems" approach or some other holistic approach is required. This emphasis on wholes includes physics. As discussed above, even on subatomic sublevels—the most fundamental physical sublevels—nature acts in terms of wholes. This suggests accepting an antireductionist approach more broadly. The structures studied by physicists will retain primacy as the most basic, in the sense of "broadest" or "most general," since all realities have a physical level. But why should we consider reality as ultimately having only a physical level of structuring? Nothing in the study of physics requires the reductionists' answer. The antireductionists' answer that all the levels of causes studied by natural scientists have an equal claim to reality certainly has more "scientific" justification today. And, once again unfortunately for the reductionists, nothing today is pointing to the demise of the "special" sciences. If anything, other sciences are proliferating. That the antireductionist pluralism also conforms more to common-sense does not hurt their case.

The Final Picture of the Sciences

In sum, to the extent reductionism is an empirical issue today, the facts favor the antireductionists. Still, the important empirical issue is how scientists will finally decide to conceptualize the sciences: will they retain multiple levels of real causes or not? Nothing in the above discussion of science can offer much comfort to reductionists. It raises the specter that the reductionists' program really has much more to do with metaphysics than with science. They believe all forms of reductionism are entailed by, or in fact is the same as, scientific practice. But this is clearly not true: scientists can carry on their work perfectly well without a commitment to structure-, theory-, concept-, or method-reductionism. And that is in fact what is occurring today. The faith of reductionists remains a philosophical position of little significance to working scientists today.

Needless to say, this has not deterred many scientists from participating in this philosophical debate in their spare time. Usually they end up taking a reductionist stance, since they wish to deny any form of ontological dualism, and they (quite understandably) confuse a commitment to substance-reductionism as a commitment to all forms of reductionism. That the pluralistic ontology of structures in structure- and theory-antireductionisms is also consistent with substance-reductionism requires more reflection than most working professionals want to spend on a philosophical issue. In addition, nonphilosophical reasons may also enter into a scientist's decision on this issue: money, power, prestige, and politics are involved in any social institution, including science. Practical, everyday concerns, such as competition for funding and jobs, may prevail over intellectual concerns of a philosophical nature and move a biologist to argue for the autonomy of biology or a particle physicist to argue for reductionism to assure the primacy of that science.

Note that structure- and theory-reductionists and antireductionists, along with those scientists who are neutral on the issue, agree on three things. First, all (except the religious) are substance-reductionists: there is only one substance to nature. Second, all agree that analysis is essential to science. No one, including antireductionists, doubts the importance of analysis for the practice of modern science. All agree on the importance of examining a phenomenon's parts and identifying its lower bases to gain knowledge of the whole phenomenon. Third, all agree that at present the "special" sciences are of great value. No one suggests all scientists should abandon their current research and turn their attention to quantum physics. All the sciences are needed to advance our current knowledge of reality. But beyond that, reductionists' and antireductionists' visions on the future course of science diverge dramatically. The former are betting that ultimately quantum field level causes will replace all other causes; the latter are betting they will not, and that therefore the "special" sciences will always be needed to account for some causes.

Three courses of events are possible. First, if science continues as it is today, antireductionism can never be confirmed, since we do not know whether in the future some final reduction might not be developed; and, for the same reason, reductionism can never be refuted. Second, if science were to end in much the same situation it is in today, then antireductionism would apparently be confirmed, although reductionists may still deny defeat and insist that reductionism is still "in principle" possible. Third, the course of science may change and antireductionism may be empirically refuted by a final structural reduction (as outlined below), and reductionism will be confirmed by the same. (We must also assume theoretical science will stop developing after that, so as to preclude the possibility that the reductive achievements will be uprooted by further antireductive developments.) Thus, there is some asymmetry in the situations: where one vision is confirmed, the other is refuted (if science comes to an end), except reductionists may never declare defeat. If anything, this means reductionism is more secure from empirical findings and therefore is more metaphysical than antireductionism.

Whether reductionism can be confirmed turns on what constitutes a complete and final reduction. Such a final reduction is the structure-reductionists' Theory of Organization—a "Cause-Unifying Theory," or "CUT." A CUT would be a theory that explains and predicts all phenomena (to the fullest extent we could expect of any scientific theory) and in which the only theoretical posits and causes are those of the lowest physical sublevel. Without such a TOO, all that will be established is a chain of correlated phenomena—the mechanisms at work in the arising of higher levels will still be missing. Any principles linking the correlates or explaining how the higher level correlate arose must be derivable from the CUT's principles. Structure-reductionists will need to show what quantum field level events cause reality to "self-organize" and give rise to higher levels of organization. Thus, a true CUT requires a TOE as well as a TOO. All phenomena would be fully explained by physical structures and hence no chemical, biological, or mental causes would be necessary. The higher levels of organization will be explained as products or aggregates of quantum field level causes, and all claims of independent levels of causes will be shown to be unwarranted. In sum, a CUT will be a single theory that achieves total the comprehensiveness of a TOE and a TOO. It will extend over all levels of phenomena, not merely over one level as with a TOE alone. This is obviously a daunting task. Something more than what physicists currently attempt to depict would be needed. Nevertheless, anything short of a CUT would not confirm reductionism or refute antireductionism.

If there are no testable predictions covering emergence, the development of a CUT would not be an empirical question. Rather, reductionism would be a matter of the *conceptual* side of science, having to do more with a new explanation than prediction. In short, a CUT would be a matter of *reconceptualizing* rather than new research. It may still be considered part of science, but it would not be something established by empirical research alone. Reductionists are betting that eventually scientists will be inclined to reconceptualize scientific findings along the lines of a CUT. Antireductionists see no reason to expect that. But only with an *empirically established* CUT could reductionists confidently affirm that all higher level phenomena are completely caused by lower level conditions and are not genuinely emergent causes and other realities arising from other factors having some independent reality. A handful of successful reductions of lesser scope will not suffice.

And even if a final CUT were accepted, one more issue remains: the metaphysical issue of whether higher level phenomena are real but merely *caused by* the quantum field level phenomena or are in fact *nothing but* those lower level phenomena. This is the crux of the eliminationists' interpretation of Eddington's "two table" problem. On this issue, no scientific evidence is possible. There is nothing to be settled by further research or reconceptualization, and no way to speak of *scientific* vindication of either position. The choice between the eliminative and noneliminative alternatives will remain a philosophical decision.

The Prospects for Reductionism

Structure-reductionists today present only metaphysical arguments while antireductionists present empirical evidence based on the actual practice of sciences. But the reductionists' vision retains a great appeal, despite the fact that the vision is entrenched in positivism. Nor can antireductionists claim that reductionists are uninformed about the current philosophical issues. It has a conceptual neatness—one science comprehending our one world—that antireductionism never will. Their vision proposes a smooth continuity of causation in all levels of organization that would remove all the explanatory gaps between the emerging levels that antireductionists must confront. But anything less than a complete CUT would leave the reductionists' account of the process of emerging levels as mysterious as the emergentists'. But this means reductionists cannot rest with any explanation other than the ability to predict the occurrence of higher level phenomena, since explaining this process of how quantum field level events cause organization requires more than correlating phenomena. Antireductionists are also saddled with the problem of specifying the "something more"—the factors not currently covered by physics—at work in reality in the emergence of higher levels of organization. Most antireductionists do not deal with this problem, but anyone attempting a complete account of the situation will eventually have to deal with it.

Nevertheless, one has to question the reductionists' basic intuition in light of the difficulties outlined above. The basic vision sounds plausible until reductionists try to get beyond broad ideas. When examined more closely, their vision comes across as less in touch with (or less concerned with) the actual practice of science, both past and present, than their rivals' and as a more restrictive vision of the future. Nor is their quest for reductions of current scientific interest—rather it is a scientifically barren procedure only of philosophical interest.[17] Indeed, far from supposedly capturing the scientific spirit, structure-reductionism seems *antiscientific* in its *a priori restrictions* on what scientists should be doing (Agazzi 1991). In effect, structure- and theory-reductionists are trying to "philosophize" science—forcing it to conform to an a priori metaphysical program—rather than letting philosophy follow from science as naturalists prescribe. This gives reductionism an oppressive feeling that antireductionism, although equally metaphysical, does not share.

Reductionists have yet another problem to contend with: the specter that the end of theoretical science is at hand. Pronouncements of the imminent demise of science have proven premature in the past, but many prominent scientists think the situation is different today. The analysis, for instance, of smaller and smaller particles presumably cannot go on infinitely—someday we will reach the limit. Perhaps that day is near. The minority who hold this view believe we are reaching that limit because the greatest scientific success—identification of the ultimate laws of nature—is now in sight (Hawking 1980; 1988: 156). That is, we are coming close to the true fundamental laws of the world. However, the majority view on the impending demise of theoretical science is that we may be hitting the limits of what is scientifically knowable by human beings, limits imposed upon us by our own physiology and technology. New particle accelerators can only go so fast and reveal so much. And why should we think that creatures with the limited abilities that we have acquired through our particular evolution should be able to understand *everything*? We may be nowhere near any of the truly fundamental laws of the world. The intriguing questions—unifying quantum physics and general relativity, a TOE, or the origin of life and consciousness—may lie forever beyond our abilities. Perhaps no more major revolutions in scientific conceptualization can be expected in physics, cosmology, or biology—we may be facing the end of the age of great scientific discoveries, and all that is left for scientists is research to fill in the details of current theories. Such a prospect may sadden antireductionists, but it is a real disaster for reductionists. If science does come to an end before a CUT is established, reductionists will be left with an uncompleted research program. The feasibility of reductionism is closely tied to establishing *predictions from the quantum level*. If we are left with higher level phenomena not being predictable, reductionists will have nothing but an "in principle" metaphysical scheme that does not reflect the state of science.

The upshot of all this is that it is arrogant and imperialistic for reductionists to feel they can claim analysis, physics, or all of science as their own. Reductionism is not only not required by science, reductionists cannot make as strong a case as antireductionists currently can. Scientists are not marching inexorably toward a CUT. Antireductionism is also a metaphysical interpretation of science and its future course. But antireductionists' predictions may prove false—their commitment involves risk, unlike the reductionists' with its "in principle" catch. Only the future course of science will determine these issues of autonomy and structures, and the empirical limitations even here were noted above. But antireductionists in this field have demonstrated that naturalists need not be reductionists of any type other than substantive. And at present, the antireductionists' position appears more secure and less doctrinaire than their rivals'. Of course, nothing can prohibit reductionists from adhering to their metaphysical commitment, and one day they may be vindicated. But, at a minimum, even reductionists must admit that it is much more difficult to commit to structure- and theory-reductionism today than it was in the 1950's.

Notes

1.   Reductionism in scientific methodology can mean one of two things: (1) the drive to explain of higher levels in terms of lower ones as the ultimate direction for all scientific research, or (2) reducing the methods in the different sciences to those of physics. A general role for experimentation, or at least some controlled predictions, may be a "method" common to all the natural sciences, but there may be no one set of techniques or procedures common to all the sciences, and so no one "method" in that sense. At the extreme, Paul Feyerabend, the self-proclaimed Dadaist of epistemology, denies there is one way or set of ways to study nature or either to devise or justify theories in science—whatever works is

valuable, and so "anything goes" in science.

2. Antireductionists can accept the division of a phenomenon into parts (entities and processes) for studying how it works—breaking down a whole into parts to see how it work does not necessitate *reducing* it to those parts. Antireductionists insist that it a distortion of reality when we identify the phenomenon totally with its parts or lower level bases. They accuse reductionists of making the simple but philosophically illegitimate move of going from a particularly insightful method to the ontological claim that only what the useful method discloses is all there is to reality. But method does not dictate ontology—we need not substitute what is revealed by a convenient and highly useful analysis for the total reality, any more than physicists *qua* physicists need to reduce reality to only what is disclosed by their study. Karl Popper takes the unusual position of being a theory-antireductionist who rejects method-antireductionism and stresses only analysis, although he despairs of any final analyses and hence the "completeness" of science in this regard (1974: 277).

3. Currently a key for the emergence of the "classical world" from the "quantum world" is "decoherence," i.e., the disappearance of quantum parts' interference with each other producing stable higher level phenomena. For example, classical space-time may have emerged out of quantum entanglements through decoherence (Vedral 2010). But this does not explain why or how the higher levels arose—decoherence only cancels indeterminism.

4. The application of *computers* to analyzing complexity should also be noted. Whether this bolsters the reductionists' case or is irrelevant is a matter of dispute.

5. Higher level causation is sometimes described as "nonlinear," i.e., its effects are not the (linear) sum of the effects of the base-level causes acting individually (Scott 1999, 2004). Nonlinearity can be interpreted either reductively or antireductively—i.e., as simply a matter of complicated interactions or as producing something genuinely emergent.

6. Reductionists can readily embrace *concept-antireductionism* in science. They can admit that the use of chemical or biological terms is often not merely a matter of convenience but of necessity to describe phenomena unique to that level and its laws (e.g., Schaffner 1993). For example, there will not be a quantum level description of biological functions such as digestion or adaptation: the biological concepts are simply meaningless in terms of the physics of the lower level of complexity. Concepts appropriate to one level may be completely inapplicable to phenomena on another level. The concept of "temperature" cannot be rewritten in some convoluted expression involving quarks. Similarly, higher level laws may have variables that lower level laws do not. The higher level distinctions simply cannot be drawn using the tools from the lower level—their ways of cutting up the world appear groundless from the perspective of lower level taxonomies. In sum, the ultimate vocabulary of science may not be physical terms alone. But the causal issue of *structure-reductionism* still remains separate from the conceptual-reduction issue.

7. At present, a major problem lies at the very core of any reduction involving *physics*: quantum-scale theories apparently requires indeterminism and absolute simultaneity, while general relativity rejects both. Any laws unifying relativity with quantum level events will require the modification of one or both theories as they stand today.

8. Some properties such as the wetness of water may be aggregate effects on the molecular level, since it is hard to say that one water molecule is wet. But the point is that such properties occur at the molecular level and not the atomic. In an important sense, water does not "consist" of *hydrogen* and *oxygen*: they lose their identity by the fusion of their electron shells when they combine to form H_2O, although they can still be separated through electrolysis. Water "consists" of these transformed elements. (See Humphreys 1997b.)

9.   Complexity theorists need not be emergentists: complexity is compatible with a determinism. Complexity is simply about the sensitivity of events to initial conditions. Similarly, "chaos" is misnamed: there may be unpredictable events, but this does not necessarily mean that they are uncaused or that a physical determinism does not hold.

10.   Whether condensed particle physics exemplifies antireductionism is a matter of dispute. See Howard 2001; also see Esfeld 2001 and Hüttermann 2005 on entanglement.

11.   Scientists occasionally make statements to the effect that scientists must continue to be reductionists even though reductionism is *impossible*. This may sound like the words of religious fanatics. However, it is based only on an unclarity of terminology. In terms of explanations, it may mean always to look to expand lower level theories to explain as much of higher level phenomena as possible, even though there may be limits: some features of the higher levels may need their own level of explanations. Antireductionists have no problem with that. In terms of methodology, this saying may mean either that scientists should analyze reality as fully as possible, since that continues to provide insights, even though this procedure cannot go on infinitely, or that reality cannot be reduced to only the parts analyzed out. The first option is neutral on the issue of reductionism, since antireductionists too accept this; and the second option is an explicit denial of structure-reductionism.

12.   Few philosophers of science or physicists defend eliminationism, unlike in philosophy of mind and neuroscience. For example, heat and everyday objects are usually deemed real in some sense. What is eliminated are theoretical posits, not phenomena, and so a scientists's ontological commitments (as dictated by theories) decrease.

13.   Hawking believes that science can prove why anything exists. He believes he has shown how the universe spontaneously arises out of nothing. But at most he has shown only that the universe cannot remain stable in an unmanifested state but must become manifest because of certain physical forces, not why there is something already there that could become the manifest universe rather than nothing. If the universe is the result of a quantum fluctuation bubble (Hawking & Mlodinow 2010: 136-37), this still does not explain the presence of the medium out of which the bubble appeared. That is, there may be a zero sum between the positive energy of matter and the negative energy of gravity (and so no energy is needed to create the universe), but where did that "stuff" come from? The ultimate cosmological question remains, even if he thinks that philosophy is dead (p. 5).

14.   Genes appear much less deterministic than they did fifty years ago. There may a gene for some traits (e.g., eye-color) but not for behavior (e.g., criminal conduct). That human beings share ninety some percent of our genes with other primates and have far fewer genes than once supposed—less than twice as many as a fruit fly—suggests that structuring is at work in the development of organisms, not just genetic material. Why else are we so similar to some primates on a cellular level and yet so different? Many argue that once we acquired language and could pass on information that genetic changes occurred.

15.   Claiming biological phenomena are "irreducibly complex" should not be taken as an endorsement of "intelligent design." Biologists have routinely been explaining in ordinary biological terms what ID advocates advance as evidence of a transcendent designer.

16.   Simon Conway Morris argues that "natural selection" is a search engine that tends to arrive repeatedly at similar solutions—thus, something like the rise of human beings is virtually inevitable—and that no other biotic principles are necessary (2003). If so, natural selection would qualify as a biological structure.

17. If science remains a "patchwork" of laws, as Nancy Cartwright (1999) alleges it is, then there would be no scientific grounds for reducing all causes to physical ones or all the sciences to physics. The issue would then remain strictly metaphysical.

4

The Mind

When we feel hungry, we normally get up and walk to the kitchen. But how exactly does this happen? In particular, how does it *begin*? What is the difference between thinking about getting up and actually initiating the process? How, that is, does the "mind" get the "body" to do something? Despite all the advances in neuroscience on identifying the correlates of consciousness, we know no more about this most fundamental aspect of the process than did the ancient Greeks. Do brain events cause mental events, or do mental events cause brain events? Or is there some other relationship? More generally, how do brain events become subjective experiences? Are our minds actually nothing but the brains? Are "consciousness" and "person-hood" irreducible features of reality, or are they total illusions? Are our bodies in fact all there really is to us? Are consciousness, perceptions, intentions, feelings, freedom of the will, and desires part of the irreducible causal make-up of reality? Or are they merely epiphenomena, or indeed entirely non-existent? Are we in the end nothing more than gene-making machines, or soulless piles of matter?

Today these are the most active questions in the "substance" branch of ontic reductionism in philosophy. The starting point of the discussion here will be two assumptions shared by both reductive and antireductive physicalists. First, the reality of a material body will not be questioned; the focus will only be on the question of the substance-reduction of a person or the mind to the body. Second, it will not be doubted that the physical can affect the mental—the effect we all have experienced of illness on our mental processes is evidence of that, as are experiments involving chemical and electrical stimulations of the brain. Damage to the brain or the experimental disconnection of parts of the brain can also cause some or all mental activity to cease. These two assumptions combine to support the claims of dependence in some sense of the mental on the physical and of at least "upward" interaction from the physical to the mental.

Dualism

Accepting a dualism is understandable since our inner life *feels* different than an inanimate external object. René Descartes framed the issues concerning persons and minds for the modern West when he asked in his *Meditations* "Who am I?" and concluded he was "a thing that thinks" (or better, "that is conscious"). Under his dualist view, the mind did not emerge out of matter and indeed does not depend in any way on the physical. Instead, the "thinking substance" can interact with matter and thus cause physical events. Most philosophers today unconditionally reject any dualism of irreducible ontic categories of matter and a disembodied mind, soul, spirit, or consciousness. A substance-reduction of the mental to the physical is advocated by both reductive and antireductive physicalists despite their dispute over how many *structures* are in play and by most naturalists because they see any such dualism as conflicting with a scientific view of reality. Intervention by an immaterial substance would violate the principle of the causal closure of the realm of nature and also the law of the conservation of energy if "mental energy" would somehow be injected into the natural order from "outside." Thus, from their point of view, the scientific picture of the world simply has no room for the mental. Reductive physicalists see dualism as a fundamentally antiscientific stance, and they take the admittedly dogmatic stance that dualism must be avoided at all costs (Dennett 1991: 37). To them, the only scientific approach is to assume that we are simply physiochemical machines and that the mind is only a physical object.

Not only does an immaterial substance appear to have no place in a scientific picture of reality, it is not clear how something immaterial could even *interact* with the material. How can a mental substance cause a physical event, when by definition it does not have any physical energy to bring about a change in the physical? Gottfried Leibniz tried to circumvent the entire problem by arguing for a "pre-established harmony" between the mind and body; but even this approach must account for the "resonance" between the two. Descartes himself placed the interaction in the pineal gland. Today some physicists and others place it on the quantum level of brain-events, with the mind collapsing wave-functions to release neurotransmitters (e.g., Penrose 1989; see Stapp 2007). But even if there is a locus of interaction, merely identifying it obviously does not answer the fundamental question of how an interaction is *possible*. If mind is neither a material nor energy in space and time, how can it affect matter or vice versa? But since we know from experience that changes in the body can affect the mind, most philosophers conclude something must be fundamentally wrong with the entire dualistic picture.

Not everyone, however, has adopted substance-reduction. Some following Leibniz's lead, defend a parallelism between mental and physical activity, with determinism preserved in each realm (Mackay 1980). Others are idealists who take the physical world to be wholly constituted by the regularities in our sense-experience (Foster 1982). Other remain unabashed substance-dualists. For them, the brain automatically conducts awareness whenever its base-conditions are assembled properly, but it does not create it. Some thinkers still advocate a mental substance (e.g., Foster 1991). The neurophysiologist Wilder Penfield pointed out that electrical stimulation of the brain never actually *activates* the mind. Conscious patients whose brains are electrically stimulated to cause their arms to rise feel that they themselves are not raising their arm but that something is being done to them—i.e., something different is happening then when the mind is at work. He favored the view that persons consist of two semi-independent elements—the mind and the brain—each with its own form of energy. The mind acts as both a switchboard operator and the switchboard: it is switched on by the brain but then takes charge when we are awake and is switched off by the brain when we go to sleep (1975: 82).

The neurobiologist John Eccles and the philosopher Karl Popper boldly stated their position in the title of their book: *The Self and its Brain: An Argument for Interaction* (1965). They held that the mind and body are distinct entities that somehow interact. The self-conscious mind is independent of the brain. It works by searching through brain modules and selecting some; next it integrates them and modifies them to initiate bodily actions. The mind, that is, decides which neurons will fire and which will not. In this sense, the self plays on the brain, like a pianist plays on a piano. Only if both the body and consciousness have been causally effective could mental states and consciousness have evolved as parts of our natural environment—as Popper noted, from a Darwinian point of view, it is hard to see how an utterly useless consciousness should have appeared at all (Popper 1978: 350-54). And only such a dualism prevents us from being compelled to accept a physical determinism that reduces our cognitive activity to pure self-delusion. They thus concluded brain activity cannot be completely accounted for without including consciousness as an independent component (Eccles 1994). In fact, Eccles believed our experienced uniqueness can only be attributed to a self or soul of a supernatural and spiritual creation (Eccles 1989: 237). According to Eccles, the self is actually outside the evolutionary process, and so the evolution of the brain and the body cannot be fully explained by the natural evolutionary processes alone.[1]

Today William Hasker is one of the few dualists remaining in philosophy. He argues for an "emergent self": a fully real substantive soul emerging from a functioning brain (1999: 188-201). This is a theory of the emergence of a *substance* (a unified individual), not of a new structure (the mind) within a physicalist context. But few outside the religious who are committed to life after death adopt this view. What it is about the nature of mind and matter that permits such interaction and how this interaction occurs are still not explained by the new dualists. Nevertheless, the upshot is that dualism is not entirely dead, despite the reign of physicalism.

Are there any scientific grounds for deciding between reductive materialism, antireductive materialism, and dualism? Presumably Penfield and Eccles and their opponents are all aware of basically the same data. No data known to scientists rule out interactionist positions (MacKay 1978: 600). The differing conclusions may remain more a matter of metaphysical interpretations and alleged implications of the data than differences that could be settled by further research in new directions.

Reducing Persons and the "I"

Reducing the mind revolves around the larger issue of what constitutes being a *person*. In particular, there is a sense of personal identity during self-consciousness and a core of agency during actions that do not seem to be material. The sense of

"I" is experienced as different (if not distinct) from our body. This "I" cannot be localized anywhere within the brain, or indeed anywhere in space and time. Can this "I" be reduced merely to tissues? The traditional answer in many cultures is the dualist response that this "I" is a "soul," "self," or other substance that exists independently of the body and that firmly grounds personhood as an irreducible element of reality. One school of philosophy—personalism—in fact took the person as the primary ontological category: all reality is a society of persons, and personality is the fundamental explanatory principle. The more usual question, however, is simply whether personhood is one of several irreducible category of reality.

Reductive physicalists respond that it makes no sense to speak of a "self" independent of the body. For them, any talk of disembodied persons or impersonal realities without some physical vehicle for memories or continuity is simply absurd. A person is substantively only a physical body undergoing a causally-connected series of changes in physical states. Personhood simply "supervenes" on the continuity of mental and ultimately physical base-conditions. We are in fact, in the words of Francis Crick, "no more than a vast assembly of nerve cells and their associated molecules" (1994: 3). Some philosophers argue that the sense of a "self" is merely a creation of our language: because we have terms used for convenience—"I," "me," "mine"—we mistakenly believe some reality must correspond to them and so we posit an entity, the "self." But the "self" or "person" is no more real than such out-dated scientific concepts as phlogiston or the ether, and as we advance in our understanding we will see that. In short, "persons" become no more than mere fictions created only out of our way of talking. Daniel Dennett, following Marvin Minsky, argues that the brain generates "self-consciousness" and the illusory sense of "I," the unified center of mental activity, through a process of editing all the mental activity going on in the brain (1991). This posited source of the narrations occurring in the mind is an entirely fictional product of the brain and not a causal reality in any sense. Other philosophers try a middle course in which the self is still treated as a fiction but yet has some kind of causal power (Flanagan 1992). But, in the end, all that remains for reductive physicalists is the body.

Eliminationism is also popular among physicalists today. Derek Parfit's updated Humean "bundle of connected perceptions" theory is a prime instance: all the experiences of a "person"—memories, sense-experiences, a sense of identity—can be described without an actual person or self existing. That is, we can give a complete description of reality without invoking the category of "persons" (1984: 212). Parfit may not consider this "eliminationism" since he still refers to a person's existence (consisting of a brain, body, and series of interrelated physical and mental events), but his ultimate ontology contains no such category. Most substance-reductionists in this field are also concept-reductionists: all talk of persons can be reduced without loss of content to talk of physical states or processes. Thereby, the category of "person" can be eliminated from our inventory of reality. So too, ultimately the terms for a "person" or "self" can be eliminated from our vocabulary.

Structure-antireductive physicalists, however, do not agree. Even though they do not embrace any dualism of substances, they believe the concept of "person" is incoherent if we subscribe to the reductive physicalists' program—persons are a complex of physical and psychological components, no class of which can be reduced to the other. A person is thus a unique category of reality that cannot be eliminated ontologically or conceptually. Contemporary antireductionists, being physicalists, claim the physical is a necessary part of what it is to be a person but is not all of it. There is an irreducibly psychological character to persons that the reductionists' vision simply omits. A person is not a distinct, immaterial entity but is not identical to a body either. Persons cannot be reduced to parts of themselves, and hence persons are irreducible realities—the whole must be included in our inventory of what is real. Any concept-reduction of terms referring to persons is similarly rejected. "Personhood" remains a fundamental category of reality, advancing a level of organization to matter that is not captured by a reductive physicalist ontology.

Persons, Minds, and Indian Mystical Thought

Perhaps the most illuminating way to transition from "persons" to the mind/body problem is to note that not all cultures are interested in it. For example, classical followers of the Indian traditions do not dichotomize "mind" and "body" as we do and hence are not interested in the issue of their relation or interaction. Consider three mystical traditions that divide reality up along the lines that end up quite different than we do in what they consider *mental*.

For Advaita Vedantins, our everyday notion of a "person" has no reality: all that is real is one pure consciousness (*brahman/atman*) constituting all phenomena that we classify as "subjective" or "objective." This one fundamental reality is sometimes called the "self," but it is not an individual, "phenomenal" person (*jiva*). Thus, translating "*atman*" as "self" is misleading: there are no connotations of a personal "selfhood." Instead, the fundamental reality is an impersonal consciousness with no real object of consciousness, either external or internal. This is not, however, an idealistic reduction of all reality to "mind" in the modern Western sense: all individuality and what we consider "mental" are as unreal as what we consider "objective, physical" entities. All that is real is an impersonal, undifferentiated consciousness, unlike the contents of our unenlightened "individual" mind. Belief in an individual self is a delusion—indeed, it is the central delusion of the false world of plurality (*maya*) we create out of what is in fact real. This consciousness is not based in matter—nor is matter *emergent*—and there is no pluralism of individual consciousnesses: there is only the one permanent, unchanging consciousness constituting all of reality. There is no matter to interact with. Descartes took the one unchallengeable reality to be the individual consciousness experienced in self-consciousness, but Advaitins take the same experience of self-consciousness to be of the one fundamental reality constituting ourselves and all of what we take to be objective realities—no individual "self-consciousness" is involved at all.

Samkhyas present a classic dualism of consciousness and matter, yet they see things differently than in the West: they separate an inactive, pure consciousness from all physical elements, including perceptions and the other mental activities we take as making up the "mind." They identify pure consciousness as our true self (*purusha*) and distinguish it completely from the equally real physical aspects of the world (*prakriti*). The universe contains a multiplicity of such real selves; thus, unlike for Advaitins, there is no one reality. Each individual self is a separate permanent conscious unit that "illuminates" or "witnesses" thoughts and the other content of the mind but that exists independently of such content and continues to be aware even in the absence of any content. Thus, each self is free of all content and intentionality. The consciousness is unmoving and yet affects matter, like a magnet controlling iron filings. Most of what we classify as *mental* (e.g., thoughts and a sense of "I") are in fact *material*—the self only illuminates these material phenomena and makes them conscious.[2] In the words of the Upanishads, the self is "the understander of understanding and the seer of seeing."

Buddhists also do not treat "the mind" as a special category nor do most schools treat consciousness as fundamental. Instead, they reduce "persons" to an aggregate of impersonal realities. In this pluralistic ontology, "persons" (*pudgalas*) consist of five components, one physical and four that we would classify as mental: sensation, conceptualization, dispositions, and perception (*vijnana*).[3] The whole is not ultimately real or a unity but impermanent—there is no unchanging consciousness or physical base to consciousness.[4] Thus, Buddhists replace the mind/body dichotomy with a larger plurality of impermanent parts. Each "person" is a temporary aggregate of parts, like (to use their simile) a chariot having its parts replaced. Each component of a "person," like all components of reality, is impermanent—i.e, without an unchanging "self" (*anatman*)—and conditioned by other components. There are no underlying, permanent entities but only streams of impermanent mental and physical components that we label "persons." Thereby, we end up with "selfless persons" (Duerlinger 1993; Siderits 1997). The way Buddhists see the person—indeed, all of the experienced world—converges with how David Hume saw the mind: there is only a bundle of components succeeding each other in a continual flux. Our causal question of how the components of reality interact with each other has never been a significant issue for Buddhists, let alone "mind" versus "body." (However, this metaphysics encountered the problem of accounting for the sense of identity over time and the sensed simplicity of personhood.)

Reductive Physicalism

In contrast to these Indian traditions, the core belief of reductive physicalists is that everything ultimately is only matter and physical processes. All events involve only aggregates of matter ordered by physical structures alone. What we think is psychological is not mental at all but inanimate physical events. Sensing is just a physical event involving sense organs, and thinking is just a physical event involving the brain, even though it may *feel* different than an object. There are no psychological diseases but only brain defects and chemical imbalances. Thus, consciousness and all other mental states, properties, and events can be reduced without remainder to a state, property, or process of the brain. For any human action, there is a deterministic chain of physical events from a neural event to the action and nothing more. Thus, how can beliefs and desires start neurons firing unless they too are just physical processes in the brain? All mental activity is strictly the product of physical forces and thus reducible to the behavior of the brain—it is at best merely a by-product of neural activity, with no causal power of its own. In sum, the idea that there is something outside of the physical is, in the words of philosopher J. J. C. Smart, "frankly unbelievable"—"I just can't believe it."[5] Each thought will ultimately be found to be the product of things that cannot themselves think. All mental activity is simply a naturally-evolved product of matter and physical processes alone, with the development of our brains being continuous with those of animals. Consciousness, like any mental activity, has no causal power in the physical realm, either because it does not really exist at all or because it is merely an epiphenomenal product of brain activity without any causal power of its own.

The first option is again eliminationism: all apparent mental activity (beliefs and reasons, desires, intentions) is in fact unreal—there is no mind. The appearance of consciousness and its content is explained away as being no more than an illusion (Dennett 1991). Eliminationists thus go through the same thought-processes as anyone else, but they know consciousness is actually only a persistent illusion, just as we know the earth is turning even though it still looks as if the earth is standing still and the sun is moving across the sky—the *appearance* of mental activity will remain, even though electrical impulses in neural networks are all that is really working. In effect, we are robots programmed not to realize that we are robots. The belief that the mind is real is only part of a "folk psychology" (i.e., our uneducated common-sense) that will eventually be replaced by science (see Stich 1983).

The most famous eliminationists are behaviorists. They propose reducing the subject-matter of psychology to stimulus inputs and behavioral outputs. Any mental activity that may or may not be going on in between these observable events would not enter the picture—the point is that any purported mental reality is not in fact causally active in our actions. Some philosophers also believed that, at least for explanations of behavior, statements about the mind could be translated without loss into statements about behavior and dispositions to behave (Ryle 1949). Feeling pain is only a bodily condition and a disposition to behave in a certain way—this disposition is no more "mental" than is the disposition of glass to shatter under certain physical conditions. All mental terms can be translated into the language of stimuli and responses. Nothing real corresponds to psychological terms, and so this vocabulary should be replaced with that of physiology and ultimately physics.

Functionalists also view mental properties without any need for consciousness. In an analog to the "mechanisms" approach in philosophy of science, mental properties are defined by the function they perform (i.e., their causal role in physical events) and are directly identified with lower level properties realizing that function. Thus, in perception we respond to sensory input by producing some specific behavioral output, and no subjective "visual consciousness" enters the picture—only the observable physical causes and effects exist. Mental activity need not be limited to life-forms: any object (e.g., a computer), regardless of its physical composition or internal structure, that responds to stimuli by producing the same response we do "*thinks*" and "*feels*" as we do. This type of reduction is very popular in philosophical circles, and it is the backbone of most research in cognitive science today.

Behaviorism and functionalism may account for much of mental activity (e.g., cognition or perception), but they have proven unsatisfactory to most philosophers precisely because our internal *subjectivity* of, for instance, feeling pain or sensing colors does not seem to fit with a scheme limited to physical input and output. Nor do they explain how the brain gives rise to the appearance of consciousness (Block 1980). That is, entities with the appropriate physical input and output setup might have very different internal experiences or none at all. Felt experiences and self-consciousness simply do not seem to be merely the activity of physical objects in the brain—there is *something more* to these mental states than physical states and behavior that is missed by this reduction. Pain is more than the stimulation of C-fibers. (That some wounded soldiers in combat are sometimes to busy to feel the pain until later indicates as much.) Still, most philosophers still embrace functionalism because they see no alternative if they are to accept a physicalism.

Eliminationists are also still active (e.g., Churchland & Churchland 1995). But this school is generally out of favor because of the common-sense objection that it is, well, frankly absurd. To eliminate a "self" as a separate entity may not be absurd, but to omit all our *inner experiences* from any account of our behavior produces too truncated a picture to be plausible. It is just plain obvious that having a headache or a visual experience involves something "inner" that is genuine in additional to any physical factors—in no sense are they *illusory*. Eliminationists cannot differentiate human beings, who have consciousness, from zombies, who have no conscious experience but whose actions are exactly like ours, not because zombies think and feel but because they think *we are zombies*. Being counter-intuitive is not fatal to a philosophical position, but eliminationism conflicts too baldly with our ordinary experiences of sensing, thinking, and so forth, to be an acceptable account of what it is to be a human. Its defense rests on the purely doctrinaire claim that mental phenomena must not be real because they are not the sort of things that physicists or biologists must recognize as scientists and therefore such phenomena would conflict with science. Thus, when it comes down to denying the obvious or accepting the irreducibility of the mental, eliminationists deny the obvious.

In any case, most reductionists conclude that mental states are *real*, even if they play no explanatory role in behavior. The principal form of reductive physicalism is a bold and straightforward mind/brain identity theory: each mental state is real but is *identical to* a brain state. Identity theory thus is both a substance-reduction, and a functional type of structure-reduction. There are no connections or gaps to explain. Pain is both a physical state and a mental property (a quale), but states are identical in the same way that the solidity of ice is identical to activity of subatomic activity within its molecules. The mental equated with the physical: our mental ontology is *nothing but* a physical one. The mental is not eliminated, but there is no separate mental substance or structure. Thereby, mental realities are not given equal status but are reduced to physical ones. Attempts to defend this position, however, as a matter of definition or logical synonymy, as positivists tried, have been found wanting since most philosophers now agree that we can imagine mental states without any corresponding bodily ones. Experiential and mental terms simply do not *mean* the same thing as physical ones, and so no concept-reduction is possible. In short, "mind" and "brain" are not interchangeable terms. Physicalists next argued that on empirical grounds that the identity theory still holds (Place 1956; Feigl 1958; Smart 1959). Either each particular mental event (e.g., each belief or perception) is identical to a particular physical event, or at least each type of mental activity (e.g., dreaming or sensing) is identical to a particular physical activity. Statements about mental and physical phenomena do not mean the same thing, but they are rendered true or false by the same neurophysical phenomena.

Identity theorists need not claim that a blind scientist who knows all there is to know about the neurophysiology of perception has the same knowledge as a sighted person. Sighted persons do have a set of experiences that the blind do not have. They know something of reality the blind do not—the "felt experience" of sense-experience. But the sighted have this added knowledge only because they have a different set of receptive nerve cells. The physicalists' point is that perception is still simply a physical event involving the irritation of these cells by light-waves and sight is identical to that event. In sum, the blind may not know all there is to know of reality but only because others have more receptive capacities; nothing nonphysical is involved in the sighted's greater knowledge.

Most reductive physicalists today are nonidentity theorists who grudgingly give mental states some minimal nonphysical existence, but they conclude mental events have no causal power in the physical realm, i.e., that they are no more than epiphenomena floating over the brain. Thought, as Thomas Huxley put it, is no more than the whistle of a steam engine—it makes a lot of noise and may appear to start the train, but the real cause of the motion lies in the boiler. Mental activity is a state or product of the brain, but it does not affect it any more than the music produced on a violin affects the violin. The music is a distinct phenomenon from the strings and wood, but the instrument totally determines it. Similarly, thought is totally produced by neural firings or other brain activity. The brain, and hence the mind, has evolved as the result of our survival needs, but the mind remains merely an epiphenomenal product accompanying that process. So too, the illusory sense of "self" may come from the brain interacting with natural and social environments as we evolved. In short, thinking is simply what the brain does.

The chief problem for both identity theorists and epiphenomenalists is to explain why there are mental states correlated with physical ones at all. This gives mental phenomena enough of a reality independent of neurophysical states and processes to trouble physicalists. In addition, how are mental states "instantiated" or "realized" by some physical state? In itself a one-to-one correlation between mental and brain events gives us no reason to claim that the mind is dependent on the brain. Antireductionists who affirm the causal reality of the mind can readily agree that introducing chemicals and electrical stimulation into the brain can alter mental states, since this cannot rule out that the mind could also be a cause—e.g., whether emotions can alter brain-conditions remains unresolved by the manipulation of the lower level. Thus, reduction cannot rest merely on the correlation of states. Instead, reductionists give ontological and causal weight to the physical, much like we say that the height of the flagpole causes and explains the length of its shadow and not vice versa. Reduction, in short, rests on the metaphysical claim that the physical bases are both necessary and sufficient for the appearance of the mental and thus explain them.

All identity and correlation theories run up against the "multiple realization" problem: the same mental states can be realized by means of completely different physical bases (perhaps including bases in other species and also in nonbiological entities). Even an indefinite set of disjunctive physical conditions cannot be correlated with one mental state. And even with a disjunctive set, we would still have to ask why such conditions give rise to a higher level phenomenon at all. Moreover, we would still not have a rule for distinguishing what is a base-condition from what is not—why, that is, does this set constitute the bases for mental phenomena and not some other conditions? Thus, even if a disjunctive set could be found, one would still wonder what is left of reductionism, since the lower level building materials would still appear irrelevant to higher level functioning, and this would raise the question of whether the lower level is in fact the only cause involved. Functionalists do not feel the multiple realization problem as acutely as identity theorists and epiphenomenalists. But even if they could circumvent it, any attempt at a reductionism based on mental functions collides with the problems functionalists encounter with the felt aspects of experiences and consciousness discussed below. These combined problems have caused most physicalists today to become structure-antireductionists. Indeed, many who endorse reductionism in the area of natural science nevertheless reject it when it comes to mental phenomena.

Mind/Body Antireductionism

Antireductive physicalists see the mental as grounded in the physical: there is no independent mental substance and no mind apart from matter. The mind also depends on the physical and biological levels of organization: these are the bases that must be present for mental phenomena to appear. Still, the mind is simply another level structuring matter. It does not "emerge" out of the physical or another level of organization—mental structures themselves exist timelessly, like the physical ones. Thus, the mind is another level of organization on a par with the physical, chemical, and biological levels. Once the mind arises, it operates on its own level in effecting our beliefs, emotions, intentions, and so forth. But the mental level is needed to understand the lower levels: we cannot truly understand the brain without comprehending the role of mind, any more than we can understand computer hardware while ignoring the role of software. The mind also operates downwardly in guiding events in the brain (and perhaps even rewiring of our brain through habits) as a causal factor in bodily actions. This interlevel action is simply another case of interlevel causation and is no more problematic than upward causation.

In sum, according to structure-antireductionists, the mind and its phenomena are genuine features of reality and must be included as equals in any catalog of what is real. Mental levels of organization are given an equal standing with physical ones, even if the former are dependent for their appearance on the latter. Most importantly, mental states have *causal power* within the mental and physical realms. With the mind, nature has produced a level of organization to matter that can causally enter into events on the same and lower levels of organization—the mental level is another natural level of causation on par with the physical. Because of these causal consequences, mental phenomena are as real and as autonomous as their physical and biological bases and hence irreducible to the physical level of organization. Thus, it is not the creativity of the physical level of organization that generates mental realities but the creativity of other aspects of the universe: matter is not somehow organized through physical structures, without more, into systems that think and feel—other equally real structures in the universe are also at work.

Antireductionists tend to ignore the question of whether there are forces giving rise to mental realities other than those examined in physics. Emergentists, of course, have no problem with such a commitment. Antireductive naturalists such as Daniel Chalmers also can accept consciousness as a fundamental force at work in nature: consciousness is comparable to irreducible physical properties, such as electrical charge (1996).[6] To explain the causal role of consciousness on the brain, one physiologist has proposed a "conscious mental field" (Libet 1996), a field that unlike a magnetic field can act upon its source (the brain). But we ask: how could we get from quarks to consciousness and feeling pain without some such nonphysical forces? More causes must be at work if the mind presents truly irreducible features of the world above the physical properties and is not just somehow an epiphenomenon of physical structures. Mental properties thus are natural properties of a physical being but not *physical or biological* properties (such as physiological ones), nor are they the *product* of physical properties or necessitated by them.

In this way, antireductive physicalists are sometimes called "attribute dualists" or "property dualists" since they endorse an irreducible dualism of mental and physical properties (or better, a pluralism including physical, chemical, biological properties). Unlike for substance-dualists, here there are no mental properties apart from matter, but some realities are capable of exhibiting qualities, properties, or relations that cannot in principle be characterized in purely physical terms. Someone's thought is not the same thing as neurons firing and an inventory of what is real must include both. Intentionality and other mental phenomena are constituents of the world as real as physical causes. Thus, the products of the mind, either general processes (such as seeing) or particular events (such as each individual thought), will never be accounted for solely by neuroscience, physiology, and biology, let alone by physics. Concept-antireductionism is also central to this property dualism: mental concepts and facts cannot be replaced by biological or physical ones without any loss of meaning. If we abandon the apparatus of a vocabulary to describe the mental *as mental*, our ontology will omit these real features of the world.

Even many antireductionists who endorse the reduction of various physical sublevels (e.g., the rigidity of a table as a necessary consequence of molecular activity) stress an unbridgeable gulf between the physical and the mental. Reality has made a "quantum leap" into another level of organization when consciousness arose. This difference leads to an explanatory antireductionism that denies that any one unified account of reality is possible. Consciousness is unlike anything else in the universe, and so no understanding based even on metaphors or analogies from other levels of organization is possible. In fact, the crucial difference between our mental and physical events—sense-experience, understanding, conceptualizing, and so forth, versus neural, chemical, or electrical events—can be stressed to the point of defending a dualism of immortal persons and impermanent bodies (Hasker 1999). But most antireductionists today are physicalists who do not subscribe to any substance-duality. Instead, they keep *both* physicalism and the mind by locating the differences in *levels of organization* structuring matter. The difference is no greater in type than the difference between atomic properties and biological properties.

Reductionists are not impressed with any current empirical problems within neuroscience in understanding any particular mental activity—the presence of any base-conditions is enough to support their metaphysics. Because of this attitude, antireductionists present more encompassing empirical problems with reductionism. The principal argument advanced by antireductive physicalists against reductionism has already been mentioned: multiple realization. There simply is no one-to-one or one-to-few relationship between mental and physical phenomena, as reductionists require. Every mental process may well have some set of neural correlates in every instance, but this is not enough to sustain structure-reductionism: reality apparently has an innate one-to-many structure with regard to the mental. There does not appear to be simply one human physiological state for each human mental state, and so something beyond the physical must be in play. Indeed, the same mental phenomena may well be realizable in physical systems other than those with human neurophysiology or perhaps even in systems with no biological level at all. The higher level events do not tell us anything about the underlying neural, chemical, or other mechanisms, and accounts of the latter in no way constrain accounts of the former. Moreover, such accounts cannot in any way explain why mental phenomena are multiply realizable in the first place.

The inverse of multiple realization may also be a problem. Not all perceptions can be correlated one-to-one with their physical stimuli, as Gestalt psychologists emphasize. The same physical apparatus and external stimulus could produce more than one actual perception, as in the different possible perceptions of Gestalt figures such as the Köhler duck-rabbit (and by extension all more typical perceptions) illustrate. This means the physical process of *sensation* is not the same as *perception*. Perception involves a level of structuring that the visual stimulation of the optic nerve by light-waves does not provide. Of course, a strictly physical explanation of the differences in structuring in different perceptions may someday be possible. But this problem does raise the possibility that the presence of a perception in our awareness is not the same as the neurochemical activity underlying it and instead involves another level of organization.

Subjectivity and Felt Experiences

The irreducible dichotomy of the physical and intentionality—the "meaning" content of our conscious states directing our actions—is central to various antireductionists' positions. Intentions are part of *subjectivity*, i.e., all our first-person experiences of thoughts, beliefs, sense-perception, pains, emotions, desires, and so forth. Subjectivity always has a private "inner" dimension that any corresponding physiological correlates cannot have. We simply cannot conceive of ourselves as merely a physical object. Our awareness of ourselves as subjects and agents is distinct from our awareness of ourselves as physical objects. Scientists may well be able to reduce some mental functions to the mechanical operation of physiological states, but this subjectivity cannot be reduced. Indeed, it cannot be studied at all by examining the electrochemical activity since science is limited to what can be produced for inspection by others. Thus, it cannot be studied by neuroscientists or anyone else—it is simply not an observable phenomenon. The "view from the inside" cannot be approached from the outside. We cannot reduce the first-person ontology to a third-person scientific one, as reductionists wish. In sum, first-person experiences are an irreducible field of reality all their own.

Thomas Nagel (1979) stresses part of this subjectivity: the irreducibility of our *perspectives* to any framework that admits only the physical. Intentionality and sensing manifest themselves only in subjective states but are no less real for doing so. A point of view or "something it is like to be" cannot be grasped by even an exhaustive physical analysis of the brain. It is something that we can imagine only from the inside. We can ask what it is like to be *a bat or a lion* because they presumably are conscious and thus have an "inner life," but it makes no sense to ask what it is like to be *a chair* since it has no inner life. This subjectivity is real and cannot be reduced to something else. There simply is no one dimension to the world, and the gap between the two is unbridgeable: God could not create conscious beings by piecing together a lot of particles having nothing but physical properties (1979: 189). Such a process would be logically, not merely empirically, impossible. A point of view cannot be constructed out of components that do not have a point of view (1979: 194). Subjective events have an "inside"—in terms of perspectivity, intentionality, and experientiality—that "objective" events do not and that simply cannot be grasped from the "outside." In John Searle's words, any attempt to reduce intentionality to something nonmental will always fail precisely because it leaves out intentionality (1992: 51). *Reasons* for our actions thus cannot be replaced with physiological *causes*—the ultimate explanation of our actions will always be in terms of reasons, even if there is a physiological basis to all our actions. Indeed, rationality itself—the capacity to recognize valid reasons and arguments—is not reducible to the biological (Nagel 1997: 137-40). The reasons for our actions may not always be well thought out and there may be motives we are not fully aware of, but the subjective "why" for our actions will always be part of the explanation, not simply mechanistic causes.

Also central to our mental life are the *felt aspects* of our "phenomenal experiences"—the greenness we sense when we look at grass, the hotness of touching a hot surface, and so forth. Philosophers call these phenomenal aspects (as opposed to objective aspects) of experiences "qualia." These are strictly subjective elements, as opposed to the physical input or resulting behavior. And whether they have any causal power is open to debate. They are in an entirely distinct category of reality from physical causes and results, and thus they are not reducible to them.[7] As Albert Einstein once said, science cannot explain the taste of soup. Even if we all experienced in the same way, qualia could not be reduced to the physical.

Reductionists realize they have a major difficulty with the presence of qualia in a physical world. There is no apparent reason why we have qualia—for all we know, other beings with exactly the same physiological apparatus may have radically different qualia or indeed no qualia at all. Even if qualia play no causal role in our actions, they are still there. And without a physiological explanation, their existence is incompatible with physicalism. Jaegwon Kim had to modify his position to "physicalism, or something near enough" (2005) because why qualia arise from neural substrates remains a mystery (2011: 310)—he simply can see no way to fit qualia into a reductive physicalist system. Some reductionists just awkwardly brush these phenomena aside and, in Francis Crick's words, "hope for the best" (1994: 256). Others blithely deny the obvious and simply eliminate them as completely unreal (e.g., Dennett 1991). Physicalists may redefine subjective terms in physical terms, e.g., "pain" as the physical damage or the resulting behavior (Hardcastle 1999), or sensing "color" as light-waves impinging the optic nerve. But this does not change the nature of experience—it is merely playing with the words and not making some new discovery about the world (Searle 1992: 118-24).

Antireductionists see all these ploys as a flat denial to face reality. Instead, they insist we should accept that there are in fact nonphysical features of reality—i.e., features that are not reducible *even in principle* to physical features. The sensation of color is as real and as much a part of the world as light-waves—it is just a feature that requires the mental level of organization to appear. It cannot be dismissed as "unreal," "illusory," or "reducible" just because it requires more than the physical level of organization. The sensation of color remains distinct from all the mechanisms enabling perceptions, and this appears to be an intractable problem for reductionists. We may be able to explain (i.e., structurally-reduce) memory, sensing, awareness, and learning physiologically, but not subjectivity and qualia.

Consciousness

For all physicalists, the "hard problem" in this field is how the physical workings of the brain produces any subjective experience at all—i.e., explaining the how and why of *consciousness itself*. (The "easy" problem is explaining such phenomena as memory, sensing, or learning that appear explainable in terms of brain mechanisms, although not that all such explanations have occurred yet.). Considering how familiar consciousness is, there is remarkably little consensus among experts over what exactly the term refers to, and this is part of the problem. Many mystics take consciousness to be a fundamental reality open to a direct experience of its "pure" state in the depth-mystical experience void of any sensory or intentional content, even if there is no observer distinct from what is observed. However, most philosophers writing on consciousness do no treat it as a reality independent of our mental activity but as simply the class of such activity (e.g., James 1977: 3-19). They reject any objectless or nonintentional consciousness existing independently of acts of consciousness. They may include all mental activity, including various states of awareness—the normal and such altered "states of consciousness" as dreaming, drug-induced states, and meditative states. But under the current view, consciousness is equivalent to being in any state of any type of wakefulness.

Some theorists in this field, however, do not treat consciousness as simply any mental activity occurring in some mental state but instead restrict the concept to what John Locke called an "internal sense" that focuses our attention on the *internal aspects* of a particular mental state. It is a subjective awareness of such mental states as perceiving, having a point of view, and even thinking (i.e., the awareness accompanying processing information). If awareness is focusing attention on something, then consciousness is *awareness of awareness*. In other words, it is a *second-order* awareness accompanying other mental activity. We can be aware of our own state of mind in a way that animals, which can perceive and perhaps form representations of their environment, may not. Thus, we are not always *conscious* when we are awake. This second-order mental activity is thereby central in a sense of personhood, a center of awareness (a self), and "self-consciousness" but is broader. (Eliminationists need not deny perceiving, feeling, or thinking or any other first-order awareness—they may only deny a mind or any second-order awareness accompanying those mental activities. If so, to them we are in the end no more conscious than a television set that is on.) We may assign a derivative status to appearances, but not to consciousness: it is not the *appearance* of some underlying reality but *is* the reality in question (Foster 1991: 155-56; Searle 1992: 121-22).

To see that consciousness in this latter sense is not equivalent to all of our mental life, consider this: this second-order awareness can be removed from all causal accounts of actions without loss. Indeed, not all purposeful activity requires consciousness, as the temperature-regulation by a thermostat shows. Or consider sleepwalking: sleepwalkers can play a musical instrument or even drive a car while asleep, totally unaware of what they are doing and surprised about where they are when they wake up. If we can do these things without second-order awareness, why did the capacity to experience what the brain is doing ever evolved, and why did evolution not weed out something we spend so much time and energy on? To reductionists, it has no purpose—if it had any power, it would only interfere with the real causality producing actions mechanically. Somehow nature evolved consciousness merely as an extraneous capacity. But why then would nature expend resources to produce and maintain it? (Dualists, of course, deny consciousness evolved from matter.) If reductionists are correct, consciousness as subjective experience is not part of the explanation of human behavior or of any causal account of the physical world and thus irrelevant to science. Nevertheless, even if much of our mental life is completely explainable in terms of the mechanics of the brain—e.g, sensation may be explainable in terms of sensory-stimulation and neural signals—why is there this accompanying awareness? We have as yet no idea how or why consciousness comes into being, although we are gaining understanding of the physical mechanisms accompanying it. As more and more neurons connect, the base for more and more types of mental activity increases, but how and why does consciousness appear? Even ignoring the issue of why aggregations of neurons form and grow, why should anything new emerge, let alone something so unexpected as consciousness? As David Chalmers puts the problem: how could something as immaterial as consciousness arise from something as unconscious as matter? Where does it come from? How do we get from, for instance, sensation to the inner picturing of alternative scenarios of external reality and the other second-order activity of consciousness? The mystery surrounding consciousness may remain until we gain a clear idea of how anything in the brain *could* cause conscious states (Searle 1997: 193). But it is not obvious how any increase in our understanding of the mechanisms at work in the brain or the function of other mental activity will shed light on the nature of this second-order consciousness accompanying the physical events being explained or how or why it has arisen.

Can Consciousness Be Explained?

With consciousness, physicalists realize they have a problem with something so foreign to the physical. Of course, eliminationists, while maintaining a straight face, simply deny there is any reality here at all—there is nothing to explain but only something to explain away. But for others, there is a reality here that cannot be dismissed so cavalierly. Structure-antireductionists accept consciousness as a fundamental, irreducible feature of the world, along side of physical realities such as space, time, mass, and electrical charge. That is, some positive fact about our world (the existence of consciousness) may not hold in a physically identical world. Consciousness may be tied to the brain somehow, but many argue that the natural sciences will never be able to tell us anything about its nature or how it is tied to the brain. Scientists may be able to find out what degree of neural complexity is needed for consciousness to appear, but many argue that *consciousness itself* will never be explainable in terms of physics or any third-person science, no matter how thorough our knowledge of the structural and dynamic properties of physical processes may become (e.g., Chalmers 1996). (Chalmers accepts that all of our mental life except consciousness is reducible.) The laws of physics cannot in principle encompass consciousness: it is impossible, even with unlimited computing power at their disposal, to deduce from the laws of physics that a certain complex structure is aware of its own existence (Pippard 1988: 395). Even to the reductionist Stephen Hawking, consciousness is not a quality that can be measured from the outside and thus is immune to scientific scrutiny (1997: 171).[8]

In sum, there is an *unbridgeable gap* between consciousness and the physiological mechanisms underlying it. Even if consciousness is strictly a physical event, we still lack an explanation for why the neural firings give rise to a *feeling* for the experiencer. An electrical discharge remains unconnectable to our subjective awareness. Even many who reject a gap between the properties of water and its molecules accept that something is left unexplained here—the character of the gap between levels seems different. If there should turn out to be laws of the mental realm, they would not be deducible in any way from physical ones but would be on par with physical laws as part of the basic furniture of the universe (Chalmers 1996: 213). Antireductive physicalists assert that we may never know why or exactly how consciousness has appeared. Indeed, we have no understanding of how consciousness *could* emerge from an aggregation of nonconscious elements, including computational devices (McGinn 1991: 214). (Of course, for reductionists who deny the existence of the mind or consciousness there is no "gap" or "hard problem"—all that needs explaining is the physiology.)

Thomas Nagel believes that reductive physicalism may still be correct but that attempts to develop a reductive theory of consciousness have failed for so long that it is time to look seriously at antireductive (but still physicalist) alternatives. Colin McGinn goes further and claims it is time to admit candidly that we shall never be able to resolve the mystery of how consciousness evolved (1991). He suggests that the way we are constructed cuts us off from ever knowing what it is in the brain that is responsible for consciousness. Our brain has evolved for everyday matters related to survival. We have evolved to look outward and not inward, and so we do not have an apparatus to observe a conscious state *qua* conscious state. Conscious states are simply not an observable property of the brain, and thus they will never be potential objects of our perception. The senses are geared to representing a spatial world, i.e., things in the world with spatially-defined properties. But it is precisely because consciousness lacks these spatial properties that we are incapable of resolving the mind/body problem: we cannot link the nonspatial consciousness to the spatial brain. It is not merely difficult to try to figure out how consciousness arose but impossible—we are not in a position even to figure out the right questions to ask. However, being a good naturalist, McGinn adds that this mystery lies entirely with us, not with nature. In short, the problem remains epistemic, not ontic. Consciousness is just a simple natural product, and there is nothing really magical about how the brain generates it—we will never be able to fathom the process, but it remains actually a rather simple natural fact and indeed its arising is not different from that of any other higher level natural phenomenon. In sum, our brains just do not reflect well on how they became the bases for consciousness, and there is nothing more to the problem. We create the dilemma by trying to make our brains do something that through evolution they were never intended to do.

Structure-reductionists could certainly agree with this last point. Julian Huxley could be speaking for more than just the reductionists when he said that how it is that anything so remarkable as a state of consciousness comes about as a result of initiating nerve tissue is just as unaccountable as the appearance of the Djin when Aladdin rubbed his lamp (quoted in McGinn 1991: 1). The reductionists' response is either to eliminate consciousness altogether as illusory or to admit that they do not have a clue as to how consciousness arises but still insist that it must be physical because physicalism is true. The blatant circularity of such a response is simply the result of an absolute commitment to their metaphysics. Even for noneliminative reductionists, the "why" of consciousness is a non-issue (Hardcastle 1996b: 13). Nothing needs to be explained because consciousness is perfectly natural: it simply supervenes on mental states, which in turn supervene on physical bases. Who cares why or even how it arises—all we need to do is to identify the physical or neurological correlates of the mental events. It may not be well understood yet, but that it arises is no more mysterious than the arising of solidity from quantum action.

Antireductionists, however, see a major mystery here in how—and especially *why*—our mental processing is accompanied by an experienced inner life. For them, this mystery cannot be brushed aside with a simple declaration that the mind must be a product of matter. Even if we knew every last physical detail about the universe, that information would not lead us to postulate the existence of conscious experience (Chalmers 1996: 101). And even if we ever establish correlations between neural processes and mental events, why consciousness should accompany the psychological properties or mental processing at all is left unanswered (1996: 115). The *why* and the *how* remain central mysteries surrounding a fundamental feature of reality. Certainly nothing is in fact explained merely by correlating consciousness with physical phenomena. Nor does the reductionists' claim that the mind is "realized" in the brain explain anything at all about how the mind arises. Nor does the fact that some mental may also be studiable objectively affect the fact that subjective experience is still different in type than the physical. Thus, to antireductionists, structure-reductionists have as much of a problem explaining the mind as dualists do and so reductionism should be rejected.

However, reductive physicalists are, needless to say, unswayed by the antire-ductionists' arguments. Jaegwon Kim argues that antireductive physicalism is in fact untenable because the mental properties can have no causal role in the physicalists' scheme of things (1993: 131-60). Reductionists are unwilling to admit conscious-ness as an irreducible feature of reality until antireductionists present evidence —other than subjective experience itself—of its independence from the physical. But what type of evidence could there be even in principle? As discussed above, scientific study of consciousness seems to be impossible. What more could there be than what is already occurring to us everyday?

The Mind as a System's Feature

John Searle presents a picture of the mind as simply a feature of a biological system. To him, the Cartesian assumptions behind the dichotomies of "monism" versus "dualism" and "mental" versus "material" are false, and the vocabulary used to express such dichotomies is obsolete (1992: 2, 25-26). The "mind/body" problem is insolvable and intractable if we persist in thinking in these dualistic terms. In fact, the solution to the mind problem is remarkably simple: mental phenomena are in fact *biological* ones caused by neurophysiological processes in the physical brain and are themselves features or properties of the brain (1992: 1). The brain causes such "mental" phenomena as consciousness, and these conscious states are no more than simply higher level features of the brain (1992: 14). That is all there is to it.

Consciousness is caused by the lower level elements and is simply a higher level feature of the entire neural system (1992: 167). (Searle, like most theorists in this field, does not address how or why the brain causes consciousness.) These systems have both intentional and nonintentional mental features. What we call a "mental" state is just an ordinary biological feature of the brain, and it plays a real causal role in our behavior (1992: 13). Consciousness is caused by neurobiological processes and is as much a part of the natural biological order as any other biological feature such as photosynthesis or digestion (1992: 90). In short, the "mental" is just another "physical" property. Mental phenomena are "emergent" properties only in the harmless sense that solidity is an emergent property of H_2O molecules when they are in a lattice structure as ice (1992: 14). Consciousness is a physical property of the brain in the same sense that liquidity is a property of systems of molecules (1992). It is caused by the behavior of neurons and so is substantively reducible as a product of brain processes (1992: 112, 116). But although consciousness is a biological process caused by lower level neural processes in the brain, it is still not structurally reducible to anything other than the mental (1992: xii, 116). It has a special feature not possessed by other natural phenomena—*subjectivity*. The ontology of the mental is essentially a first-person ontology in that every mental state has to be somebody's mental state (1992: 20). Behavior, causal relations, or anything else objective is irrelevant to the subjectivity of consciousness (1992: 69). The first-person features of subjectivity cannot be reduced without remainder to objective third-person patterns of neuron firings (1992: 117). And an explanation of intentional behavior in terms of third-person phenomena inverts the proper order of the explanation of human action (1992: 228).

Consciousness is crucial to explaining our behavior in the same way that other higher level features of physical systems (such as solidity) are necessary to explain those systems. Both consciousness and the solidity of the pistons in a car engine depend on lower level micro-elements, but both are still causally efficacious (1997:

50). Thereby, the higher level products play essential roles in any complete account of an event. Mental causation is not a problem since the mental is merely another physical feature of the brain. The subjectivity of consciousness is irrelevant to the mind's causal power. Reductive physicalists labor under a conception of reality that denies subjectivity as antiscientific. They cannot accept the reality of consciousness because of its subjective nature, but if they would accept it as just another physical property among others the mind/body problem would disappear (1992: 55). The causal role of the mind remains within the scope of science, although subjectivity remains outside the realm of objectivity studied by scientists. And since subjectivity is in fact just another natural product resulting from a natural system, antireductionists who accept subjectivity as irreducible are being no less scientific than reductive physicalists. Certainly, the structural irreducibility of consciousness in this scheme would not affect the scope and completeness of the realm of science.

For Searle, there is no distinct, nonphysical mental level of structuring that causally affects a separate physical organization or structures matter. Instead, all causal activity takes place on the physical level, with the "mind" being merely another physical feature of one order. There is no need to speak of "top-down" causation because the mental is merely another physical property. (Searle himself may not like being characterized as an "antireductionist" in any regard since he rejects such labels as "monist," "dualist," "property dualist," or "materialist" [1992: 15, 28].) To him, all the issues of "property dualism," "reductionism," "causal overdetermination," and so forth are merely symptoms resulting from the basic "dualistic" mistake in how we conceptualize the situation (1992: 220).

This excursion into Searle's ideas raises the question of whether the modern Western conceptualization of our situation itself creates its own problems. To him, the vocabulary of "mental," "physical," "dualism," and "materialism" generates philosophical problems that evaporate if we reconceptualize the mind, not as a distinct realm, but as just another natural biological feature of the body that does not need to be reduced to any other. With the mind, reality has generated another system that has causal powers continuous with the rest of nature. Consciousness is not separate from the body in any sense, and there is no "link" between consciousness and the brain (1992: 105). It is simply another systems-feature like liquidity or solidity. No "gaps" in the natural order are required for consciousness to work. Trying to conceptualize the situation in dualistic terms of "mind" and "matter" makes it impossible even to pose the questions appropriately (1992: 109). Reconciling reductionism and antireductionism here would be trivially easy if both sides would accept that the mind is a natural product of the brain (1992: 118-24). Mental phenomena would be accepted as just another product of nature as real as any other. But to reductionists, the subjective is simply too "unscientific." On the other hand, for most antireductionists, the mental is a different level entirely, thereby preserving the issue of the "interaction" of mind and body.

Contemporary Emergentism

Emergentists have no difficulty with endorsing the mind as a separate level of organization with full causal powers. For them, reality has produced in a person a new dynamic whole, i.e., a system with new irreducible structural properties. Some philosophers today accept the title "emergentist" for their position (e.g., Clayton 2004). But Roger Sperry, a Nobel-Prize-winning neurophysiologist famed for his split-brain experiments in the 1960's, came to embrace a fuller emergentism: consciousness is an emergent nonphysical property of the brain with causal potency that acts downwardly in regulating brain events (1985: 32, 92)—i.e., mental forces exert regulative control in brain physiology (1976: 165). Mental events are causes of neural events rather than epiphenomena of brain processes. They are real and causal as subjective qualities and are of a very different quality than the physical components from which they are built (1985: 100). Thus, they are not reducible to their physiochemical elements (1985: 79). Subjective mental phenomena are united with objective cerebral events within a single unified continuum in the brain (1976: 176). Only this position, unlike physicalism, dualism, or parallelism, gives a reason for our consciousness to have evolved at all (1976). Mental states are not observable or measurable at present, but they are still something accessible to eventual scientific description, at least in principle (1995: 23).

Sperry's view of mental activity is part of his grand holistic worldview. For Sperry, wholes and parts are both real. The properties of the parts are themselves in turn holistic properties of subsystems at a different level (1976: 167). The result is an array of hierarchically-interlocked forces, from the subatomic through the cellular, organic, cognitive, social, and even galactic levels, in a great pluralistic system of cosmic forces—a system in which the higher transcends the lower, and all are differentiated from, and united in, a common foundation (1985: 24). The hierarchy of increasingly complex natural systems exhibits diverse emergent properties at different levels that include the mental properties of the brain-mind system as part of one monistic natural order, although it is still useful to distinguish mind and matter (1995: 24-25). Any reduction of this hierarchy of levels that attempts to explain wholes solely in terms of their parts leads to an infinite downward regress in which everything is held eventually to be explainable in terms of what is essentially nothing, i.e., the emptiness constituting atoms (1976: 167). Instead, each level produces a new level of activity that cannot be reduced to its parts' properties.

Lower level laws cannot capture the higher level activity. In addition, higher levels can affect the lower: the activity within a brain cell is subject to higher level dynamics that determine the overall pattern of neuron-firings. The mind moves matter in the brain, just as an organism moves its organs or cells, or a molecule governs the course its own atoms travel (1985: 66). In exerting downward control, the higher level phenomena do not disrupt or intervene in the causal relations of the lower-level activity, but they "reconfigure" the course of events. For example, the motion of a drop of water in a whirlpool cannot be explained in terms of activity on the molecular level. (Note that this is not "downward causation" in the more extreme sense of affecting the course of events *within entities* on the lower level.) But there is a mutual interdependence between the parts and the wholes. In the case at hand, this means the brain physiology causes mental effects, and the mental phenomena in turn causally influence the physiology (1985: 59).

Thereby, we have the power to make genuine choices: our free will is affirmed as one element within a causal—indeed, deterministic—whole (1995: 28-29). This holism also brings human values within its scope: values of all kinds (e.g., ethical, aesthetic, or religious) are accepted as emergent mental phenomena and thus as positive causal factors in the sequence of brain events involved in human decision-making (1976: 175-76). Human values are not epiphenomena but noneliminatable causal factors (1995: 28). Indeed, values stand out as a universal determinant of all human action (1985: 10). Thereby, subjective values have objective consequences in the brain (1985: 60), and values must be part of the factors of reality accounted for in science. In short, subjective values and objective facts become part of the same discourse (1985: 68). This holism involves an "emergent evolution" that is not governed merely from below by chance gene mutations but is a gradual emergence of increased direction, purpose, and meaning among the forces that move and govern living things (1991: 248). Thus, Sperry sees his holism as restoring to human nature the personal dignity, freedom of choice, and inner creativity of which it had been deprived by behaviorism and other physicalist movements (1976: 176), all in a way that is consistent with science—indeed, the restored values actually become part of an expanded field open to scientific study.

Sperry admits the speculative character of his "emergent interactionism" (1985: 31). And how illuminating one finds his ideas will depend in part upon how strong one's commitment is to reductionism. Sperry goes beyond most antireductive physicalists in his metaphysical emphasis, but, as with Searle and antireductive physicalists, he is offering a way to view mental phenomena as purely part of the one natural causal order. Any dualism of mental and physical substances or any type of disembodied existence is rejected as clearly impossible. But when Searle and Sperry disclaim the label "materialist," they are really rejecting the label "reductive physicalist"—mental phenomena for them are "material," but they are not reducible to non-mental properties and are instead natural products of the same stuff that makes up all of the universe. Mental phenomena are no less real and no more problematic than the emergence of other phenomena.

Computers

One area often cited as a testing point for the legitimacy of substance-reductionism is the attempt to create artificial intelligence or artificial life. That is, assuming a computer will someday be built that completely duplicates all our thought and all other mental activity, then why should we believe our mind is anything but a by-product of physical processes? The brain becomes no more than a soggy computer producing the same ephemeral phenomena as computers made of metal and silicon chips. Similarly for artificial life: if we can create entities that self-replicate (or do whatever it is that constitutes "life"), is life nothing but just another mechanical process embodied in matter? Are we merely natural machines? In the end, are only matter and "lifeless" physical processes actually real? Would not success in this area finally settle the question of substance-reductionism versus antireductionism?

The issues can be seen by limiting them to one question: can computers think (see Block 1990)? Computabilists answer "Yes," or at least that someday computers will be able to think the way we do. Some try to win the argument simply by boldly declaring that the only real human qualities are whatever is programmable or able to be put in an algorithm (Drozdek 1990). In this computational theory of the mind, thought and all other mental activities are reduced to computations to make them encodable in computer programs. Many advance the software/hardware relation as an analogy for the mind/body relation—the mind is simply an information gathering and processing machine. However, enthusiasm for this image is waning, and reductive physicalists must concede that the parallel is not exact: the computer hardware does not produce or alter or affect its own programs in any way, and a person is still needed to design and initiate the programs. In sum, there are three realities here—the hardware, the program, and the programmer—while reductionists are committed to the view that the human "hardware" in fact programs itself. Any glitches in the software are not caused by the hardware of a particular machine and must be corrected on the level of software alone. Moreover, programs are not physical, even though they are "embodied" in some physical medium, but are a matter of manipulating signs (in binary computers, ultimately a matter of zeros and ones). Computing the value of pi remains distinct from any electronic property. In an instance of multiple realizability, the program constitutes a dimension of reality different from matter—it is "structure" and not the stuff structured—and hence is not reducible to matter, regardless of the material in which it is embodied (silicon, metal, vacuum tubes, wood, water). Thus, no physical description of the state of a computer's hardware will capture the program. All issues of the programs involve only problems of the relation of signs—something that is meaningless on the level of the hardware. But reductionists think any problems on the mental level are either caused by the physical alone or ultimately simply are physical problems. Thus, on the reductionists' own terms, the mind is not simply the brain's computer program.

In addition, most reductionists now agree that the classic "strong program" of Artificial Intelligence touted since the 1950's has failed to produce a true "thinking machine," duplicating our consciousness or our problem-solving ability. Classic AI projects involve sign-manipulation machines, and such an approach is unlikely to yield conscious machines. Even some ardent reductionists concede as much (Churchland & Churchland 1990). Such machines are not brain-like in structure, but their defenders argue that all that is needed is a duplication of *input/output functions*—identity of results, not identity of architecture, let alone of material, is all that matters. That is, sign-manipulation does not depend on the hardware's structure, and computational states are multiply realizable in different materials. Analog and digital computers may not "think" like us, but the results will show if they simulate the thinking brain in some way. If they do, some computational output could then be said to be the same in both the carbon-based and silicon-based systems. And, of course, any failure to accomplish this to date does not rule out the possibility that in the future other types of systems will be created that will in fact mimic the brain's parallel, collective, and simultaneous processing of signs.

Some philosophers, however, doubt the possibility that computers will ever be able to simulate all human thinking, let alone all of our mental activities. This is more than the basic claim that thought is one thing and electrical impulses in computer chips another. Rather, the arguments center around the notion that human thought is more than computation or sign-manipulation, and so the former will in principle always defy reduction to the latter. Hubert Dreyfus points out that the background knowledge that is always necessary to our thought cannot be fully articulated by any sign-manipulation (1992). Roger Penrose argues that there is a noncomputational element even in mathematics that current computers, operating solely with algorithms, cannot reach, and thus something in our consciousness transcends computation (1994). John Searle points out that understanding is not computational: computers' activity is a matter of sign-manipulation, and that never conveys understanding. Computation is defined syntactically in terms of sign-manipulation, and *syntax* (the rules for constructing sentences) will never generate *semantics* (properties of truth and reference—the "thought content" of understanding) (1984: 28-41, 1992: 197-226, 1997: 9-17). Thus, we too may calculate, but computers will never reproduce all of our thinking, even in principle. Searle also thinks that mental processes are *biological* processes that cannot be reduced to their functions. A computer may *simulate* part of our thinking, but we can simulate a tornado on a laptop without it being torn apart, and we can simulate thinking without concluding that the computer thinks. Equally important, simulating mental processes is simply irrelevant to explaining how it is produced in human beings.

Thus, we should not be misled by the technical term "information processing" into thinking computers actually think: there is no *information* in the ordinary sense of the term processed by computers but only meaningless signs. Computers are "sign-processors" and nothing more. This is not to deny that computers will achieve great feats of *computation,* defined as the performance of mathematically-describable operations. For instance, chess playing computers no doubt will soon routinely defeat the best human grand masters. But this will be by the staggering magnitude of calculations a computer can do in a split second. The finitude of each move and the limited number of options in each move makes chess perfect for computers. They will simply compute every possible future course of the game and choose the most likely winning scenario by some program initially supplied by human beings. Human chess players, on the other hand, arrive at their moves by means of experience and reasoning based on understanding rather than merely playing out every possible option in their head. In other words, humans are thinking and computers are merely calculating. Even computabilists must admit that at the very most computers here are simulating only part—perhaps only the simplest part—of human thought. But even if computing is part of what we do, this does not mean that the human mind can be reduced to a computer—the mind simply does too much more. By selecting only the aspects of the mind that resemble information processing, we are missing all other aspects, perhaps the most important ones.

At best, computers show that computation is multiply realizable, not that the mind is a computer. In fact, what computers do does not seem to be *thinking* at all. No one attributes awareness to mechanical adding machines when we use them to add numbers or thinks that we operate the same way, and computers no more think than do such machines. The operations we program into computers are simply more complex. Even if programs can learn from their own mistakes or otherwise teach themselves through feedback, it is only because of what we program in to begin with. Its "intelligence" tells us more about the intelligence of the programmers and designers than anything about the machine itself.

Of course, whether we want to call what computers are doing *"thinking"* is partially only a matter of definition. The real question here is this: would a complete duplication of every one of our mental functions present major problems for antireductionists? No. At most, we would duplicate the objective and observable results of our thinking. And even if we could duplicate these *results*, this does not mean we have created *consciousness or any other "inner" life*. Sign-processing simply does not require consciousness. The difference is also applies to first-order awareness—simulating all of our behavior and physical effects associated with, for instance, pain versus duplicating the inner dimension of feeling pain. Checking the "reasoning" of a computer can be done at least by checking the results, but how do we check to see if, for example, the computer is in pain? We may simulate behavior to satisfy perfectly the Turing "imitation of human behavior in a conversation" test for attributing intelligence to a computer but without there being any minds: regardless of the behavioral output, how would we know if any *consciousness* had been created? The reasons for rejecting functionalism mentioned above reappear here. Daniel Chalmers is willing to endorse even the strong AI program and still maintain the irreducibility of consciousness (1996). Even *dualists* could accept this: they would argue that all we have done is duplicated the base-conditions in another material for consciousness to be received. In sum, we may in fact one day duplicate actual consciousness, but its reality would still remain and the mystery of how consciousness arises in both natural and artificial bases would also remain—it would then simply now extend to something we manufactured. The questions of how consciousness arises and whether the structures responsible for consciousness are a nonphysical part of the fabric of the universe remain as unresolved as ever.

The conclusion must be that, based on computer technology, there is simply no reason to believe a reduction of the mind will ever occur. This may not deter enthusiastic reductionists in their faith that all mental phenomena are really only physical—after all, we do not know what may develop in the future. The ardent reductionists Paul and Patricia Churchland attach great significance to the claim that the brain is a kind of computer. But they concede that most of the properties of the brain and how the brain manages meaning remain to be discovered, and that in the end the brain is unlike any known computer. Still, they insist, the brain is a

computer nonetheless in a "radically different style" (1990: 37). In such circumstances, we might wonder why they still want to call the brain a "computer" at all.
Nevertheless, they cannot cite current computer technology for support in any way.
And reductive physicalists will never accept future failures to produce artificial
intelligence or life as counter-evidence to their fundamental metaphysical faith in
the reduction in principle of mind and life to the material.

Mental Causation

The differences between reductionists and antireductionists on structural issues
reach their highpoint on one topic: mental causation. For physicalists, whether
mental phenomena are real turns on whether they can make a difference on the
physical level or whether the physical bases in fact do all the work. (The issue of
mental causation is usually framed as if causation itself is unproblematic.) But if a
person has a physical component, most would agree that mental causation over the
material would be necessary if it is at all real. If the mind does not have such power,
it is difficult to see how a *person with free will* could be a reality—i.e., an agent
who has the *genuine power to choose how to act* and is not completely controlled
by material events in our brain or other parts of the body. The problem for dualists
and antireductive physicalists is to explain how distinct mental and physical
substances or levels of organization can interact with each other at all. And the
problem for reductionists is to explain away the appearance that our minds can
exercise some control over our bodies and that we are agent with causal power.
      Jaegwon Kim presents the reductive physicalists' case. The basic premise is
that the physical realm is causally-closed. Thus, if the mind is causally efficacious,
it must be reducible to physical properties and there is no causal problem (2005: 3).
To deny this would be to deny that in principle there could be a complete physical
description of physical events (1993: 209). Moreover, a sufficient physical cause
precludes the need for another (mental) cause. Thus, only the physical correlates or
bases upon which the mental phenomena supervene are in fact causally active—they
are the real causes at work when we mistakenly think the mind is affecting an event.
All the work still occurs only at the macrophysical level between physical realities.
Indeed, his argument against any robust mental causation can be extended to require
a thorough-going reductionism that accepts causation only on the lowest physical
sublevel. Kim has modified his views on reductionism (2005): the Nagelian model
of theory-reduction is out, and he concedes that physicalists have no explanation for
qualia. But his views on mental causation have not changed.
      Causation is thereby reduced to exclusively a physical phenomenon. To hold
otherwise, we either have to deny that physical causes account for all physical
effects or to accept mental causes as real but redundant (i.e., doing what physical
causes are already doing) and thus superfluous. According to reductionists, the first
option conflicts with science and so must be rejected. The second position is called
"overdetermination" (i.e., more than one sufficient cause), and under the rule of

Occam's razor it too must be rejected. Therefore, the only option left is to reject entirely the idea of mental causation, despite strong appearances to the contrary. Thus, mental phenomena are powerless epiphenomena. Kim realizes that this means evolution has produced a phenomenon with no power and no apparent reason for existing, but mental reality is a mystery of no concern to reductive physicalists.

Antireductionists uphold the first alternative that reductionists reject: non-physical causes are in fact among the conditions producing some mental and physical effects. There is some causal relation between the two substances of reality (for dualists) or levels of reality structuring matter (for emergentists and anti-reductive physicalists). It is hard to see our feeling pain as causing C-fibers to fire, but there is not reason to think that all mental properties must be like pain. For antireductionists, the problem of interaction between the mental and physical is nothing compared to the reductionists' problem of why there is even the appearance of consciousness. Affirming the obvious—that the mind has causal power—over eliminationism or epiphenomenalism is clearly the lesser of two evils despite its problems. The mental level is dependent on the physical (both matter and the physical level of organization) in that the latter must be present for the mental to appear, but it is equally real in its own right and exercises some causal power over matter. Our behavior results from intentionality and agency and thus these cannot be accounted for solely by the causal role played by physical forces. Conscious intentionality entered the picture once animate entities began to "self-organize." Agency too may be an emergent property (Kauffman 2008: 12).

Antireductionists have three options in defense of two-way interaction between the mental and physical. First, they can treat the mind as a separate level of organization, and the higher-order mental states as directly causing lower-order physiological events. (The idea of the "causal closure of the physical" confuses the situation since it does not distinguish *substance* from *structure*: to antireductive physicalists, the universe is physically closed substantively but not structurally.) Not all events have physical causes, and there is no deterministic chain of physical conditions in the universe. There is no overdetermination by mental causes: mental events are causes in the chain of causal antecedents not supplied by physical causes. Physicalists will object that this is unscientific: science requires the continuity that only a closed physical realm can provide. But if minds are a natural product of the universe, we should not construe science in a way that would exclude mental phenomena a priori (as discussed below). The subjective may never fall within the scope of science, but that does not mean it may not be real and have causal potency. The universe would then still be causally-closed, but the mind and the physical would both have roles to play, as Roger Sperry maintained. There would be no complete *physical* accounts of actions but nothing important would be lost.

The second option is to deny that any exchange of "*energy*" (as encompassed by the physical law of conservation of energy) occurs between the mental and physical realms or levels—only "*information*" is conveyed from the mental (MacKay 1978, 1980). This would mean that not all interactions involve an exchange of energy. The intentional properties of a physical system merely guide brain-events, in a way analogous to how computer programs guide the flow of physical events in the computer's hardware. In a computer, the flow of electrons in the integrated circuits is determined by the laws of physics, but the flow is also directed by the commands in the computer program as operated by a user.[9] Similarly here: the causal completeness of the physical is preserved—there are no "gaps" on the physical level in which the mind works—and there is no overdetermination of causes, because the mental does not interfere with brain mechanisms. Rather, the mental information guides the flow of energy. The physical account of events would thus be complete on its own level. But any account of only the energy in a brain or a computer will not be able to predict the course of events, and thus such an account will not be a complete account of the events. Nevertheless, advocates of this position still have to work out this notion of energy-free "information" and how the brain-dependent mind controls the brain.

The final option is to argue that the "mind" and the "physical" are illegitimate categories—in reality, the "mental" is another "physical" feature, and both are simply parts of one encompassing causal order. There are no separate "mental" causal level: there is only one natural causal order, and the mind is an integral part of it. The mind is just another systems-feature of physical systems. Consciousness is a level-effect of the brain that plays a real causal role in our behavior, as do the other features of our brain. This approach may also satisfy those antireductionists who believe biological and mental states are not *physical* states of our brain but are the products of other structures in reality that organize reality. The emergentists' idea of "downward causation" then is misguided since all systems are nested parts of one causal order.

For antireductive physicalists, mental causation thus is no more problematic than is any other level of causation—causation on a quantum or other physical level is not all there is. Events on the biological level (e.g., digestion) are not caused by quantum events and are thus not reducible to quantum events. The biological causes do not violate the causal laws of the physical level, but they must be taken into account in explaining any biological event. Mental causation is exactly the same: it is simply another level of natural structure, and thus of ordinary causation, that nature has produced. The mental is its own level on a par with other levels, even though it emerges only when the lower levels are properly assembled. The mind's causal power can enter into events in the same way as physical and biological powers. Thus, for a complete account of any event in which human agency is at work, the mental level must be included. The mysteries surrounding mental causation are merely a subset of the general mystery of how any level of organization emerges as an independent reality dependent upon lower levels of organization.

No causal overdetermination is involved here: the mind supplies causes the brain does not, and there is no duplication. To use Searle's example, when someone causes ice to melt by heating it, this event can be described as "The molecules were in a lattice but are now moving over each other in a random fashion," or as "I heated the ice." These are two different but consistent descriptions of the same events given at different levels (1995: 218-19). But each account reveals something different of reality—the equally real and distinct physical and mental elements at work in the event. A complete account of the physical level would not explain all aspects of what occurred. Each account tells us something real about the event that the other omits, and we need accounts of both the physical and mental levels to provide a complete account of the total event.

One consequence of the antireductionists' account is that it permits the possibility of genuine *free will*. Reductionists are committed to the denial of anything remotely like an agent's freedom of choice involving a mental event: we have no freedom of decision because all events are really physical, and all physical events are determined completely by previous and concurrent physical events (Crick 1994: 3). The antireductionists' approach allows a genuine role for human autonomy; or, to be more precise, it would require any determinism to embrace the mental as well as the physical realm (Sperry 1995: 28-29)—that the mental level is involved and is not determined by the physical level does not *guarantee* that there is free will. The brain affects the way we operate but does not explain all of how we think, desire, and decide—if free will exists, it is persons who are free, not brains. In sum, a complete account of even brain activity requires a role for beliefs and decisions, not just the physiological hardware.

None of these proposed solutions are entirely satisfactory. The reductionists' demand for evidence of the reality of emergent levels raises the question of what they would accept as evidence of a nonphysical reality—as far as they can see, all causation must be among physical objects. On the other hand, antireductionists do not present a complete picture either—they have the challenge of explaining *how* exactly the mind fits in with the physical realm. The emergentists and systems-theorists do make mental causation seem possible and even natural without dualism, but we are still left with the mysteries of emergence of higher level of organization and how the higher level can interact with the lower. Thus, we are left with the dilemmas connected to "interaction" or to the denial of the obvious.

The Strangeness of Reductionism

The bottom line is that both structure-reductionism and antireductionism (and even perhaps substance-antireductionism) are viable options today. However, antireductive physicalists present the stronger case today. Even if we assume dualism is not an option—and remember that there still are unrepentant dualists—the reductionists' arguments seem forced regarding structures. If you believe the Yankees are the best team in baseball or desire to do something about global warming, the belief and desire operate on a level that makes whatever is occurring on the physical level in the brain during these acts totally irrelevant—the belief and the desire are "realized" in the brain, but giving a chemical account, let alone a quantum level account, of the events would be unilluminating and pointless. The reductionists' accounts of the mind simply miss the central features of what is to be explained: *subjectivity* and *causal agency*. These features are so clearly part of our experience that it is hard to see why or how they would have evolved or survived in nature if they have no purpose or power. And reducing them to some objective feature of our world simply misses their very nature completely. Consciousness and other mental phenomena do not appear to be impotent appearances of some underlying physical reality but irreducible realities themselves. They may be open to explanation, but they cannot be explained away. In sum, we seem to be ontologically strongly emergent realities with causal powers.

If this is so, why are physicalists so reluctant to accept consciousness as real in the fullest sense of the term? And why is reductive physicalism considered so attractive? The basic intuition behind it is that the physical (both matter and the physical level of structure) existed for billions of years on earth before life and consciousness appeared and hence it must be more real in some sense. That intuition is then combined with the idea of ontological economy to produce both substantive and structural reductionism. Such economy is certainly a plus, but Occam's razor only requires that we not multiply realities *beyond necessity*. And if our experience requires a larger ontology than these physicalists are willing to supply, so much the worse for their doctrine (Wimsatt 1994: 208). Parsimony is useful if both sides share common ground and the dispute is over something else but not when the dispute is over precisely what is fundamentally and irreducibly real. In these circumstances, invoking Occam's razor can only be question-begging.

The reductive physicalists' second contention is that only their brand of physicalism conforms with science: only if we subscribe to a physicalist reduction of the mind can we arrive at a unified scientific theory of reality, since a scientific picture of reality has no place for such subjectivity as intentionality and qualia. But does science in fact require the denial of the mind as unreal in any sense? Reductionists require one particularly austere interpretation of what ontology we should accept. Unlike naturalists, who restrict our substantive ontic commitments to only what scientists must accept to practice science, reductionists go further and reduce the scientists' structural ontic commitments to only the physical level of organization.

However, there is a problem with this position. Just because scientists must approach all phenomena from the "outside," does that mean that no phenomena have an "inside"? Why does utilizing a third-person point of view require *denying* the first-person point of view? To practice science certainly does not require that. Scientists *qua* scientists need not deny there is more to reality than what they study. As noted in the last chapter, to practice science, scientists need not claim reality is reducible to only what they find. Certainly, just because the first-person phenomena cannot be studied by third-person scientific methods does not mean scientists have *proven them to be nonexistent*. If the private inner life were completely separate from the public objective realm studied in science, then obviously science has nothing to say on the subject—ipso facto, the mental realm would be beyond scientific affirmation or denial and would also be consistent with anything in the scientific realm. But mental causation would cross this gap, and so reductionists conclude that it is inconsistent with science. However, the idea of the mind and its powers as system-features of the human body shows that this alleged inconsistency only results from the reductionists' metaphysics: the completeness of *physical causes* is incompatible with any real mental causes, but the *causal closure of the natural realm* is not. The mind can in fact be simply one type of natural cause in one total natural causal order even if it is "subjective." Its action no more violates the causal closure of the natural realm or the law of the conservation of energy than does the action of stomach acid in digestion, even if how it works is not understood.

In sum, concluding that what does not fall within the scope of science is *unreal* is a philosophical judgment, not a scientific one. Actual science does not dictate any such judgment. And this leads to a second problem: the reductionists' metaphysics dictates what science must accept is real. But why should we accept the physicalists' reductive view of what structural commitments scientific practice entails? Letting reductive metaphysics dictate what scientists must accept to practice science is for naturalists putting the cart before the horse—it lets philosophy dictate the nature of science rather than follow it. Certainly, citing science as a reason for reductive physicalism in such circumstances would be clearly circular.

Here reductionists do appear to be blinded by their own metaphysical vision. They simply cannot take agency, qualia, or consciousness seriously. Their physicalist metaphysics requires summarily dismissing such phenomena as unreal since they do not fit in the reductionists' picture of reality as inert matter governed solely by the laws of physics. But today they cannot point to any detailed neurophysiological explanation of even the most elementary mental phenomenon—we do have correlations permitting predictions but not more. At best, reductionists only have a picture of what their metaphysics dictates must be the case. But why simply assume the mind must be only physical if we have no idea of how matter can generate the mental? Reductionists may argue that our neural systems are so complex that we cannot reasonably expect ever to accomplish a detailed, complete reductive explanation. This may be well be true, but how can that help their case? How can they argue from our ignorance that they must be right? They may instead argue that reductive explanations are forever beyond our grasp because of the complexity of the details are beyond our comprehension but that they are nevertheless always possible *in principle*. But how this differs from simply a dogmatic restatement of their metaphysics is not clear. Future failures at reductions would also not disturb them. Reductionism will remain a metaphysical program that will never have to be abandoned or even questioned by the lack of any empirical findings. Shielded from future failures, the reductionists' position remains impregnable but only in the way all speculative metaphysics is. With reductionism's metaphysical nature exposed, one wonders why one should be so committed to it when it flies in the face of our most entrenched experiences and science does not require it. Of course, reductionists can always fall back on an argument of last resort: we do not know what the future may hold—our current imagination cannot limit what might happen in future research. Needless to say, this is true—but that is no reason to subscribe to reductionism today. Such a ploy only reveals the faith involved in their particular philosophical commitment.

Antireductionists do have something on their side: the obvious. Our experience overwhelmingly indicates subjectivity and mental agency are real. Reductionists also have the basic problem that if one neuron is not conscious (let alone quarks), why should a network of millions of them, no matter how they are wired, give rise to subjective experience? And how? These concerns make a strong case for currently holding the belief that first-person experience is a fundamental category of reality. In short, it is more reasonable today to believe that consciousness is part of the blueprint of the universe. Antireductionists are split over the nature of the mental, but they all give mental phenomena some causal power in some way. However, they do encounter the mystery of how and why consciousness appears, how it is dependent upon nonconscious levels of organization of matter, how it arises, and how the levels can interact.

But the same basic mystery is also present for reductionists: how and why does the appearance of a reality arise when in fact consciousness and other mental phenomena are not real or have no power? Indeed, the mystery is in fact aggravated for reductionists: why is consciousness apparently there at all if it is "unreal" or impotent? Why should there be something like consciousness in a world that is ultimately nothing but bits of matter scattered over space-time regions (Kim 2005: 13)? Reductionists may settle for asserting that it is obviously a product of the physical or is something that they can assume someday will somehow be explained, but that does not mean that they now have any satisfactory explanation of it. It only means that they can ignore it because their metaphysics precludes it as a possibility. But in such circumstances, why should we subscribe to reductionism today? Why give one level of structure—the physical—causal priority when doing so provides us with no better understanding than giving more levels equal status? Why, especially when this metaphysics conflicts so drastically with our common experience?

Problems also arise when we look directly at the reductionists' metaphysical claim. How do reductionists know that matter and the physical level of organization is all that is involved in creating consciousness? How can they rule out that other factors may also be involved when they cannot specify how the mental emerges in physical terms? Even if antireductionists cannot specify the nonphysical factors or how exactly the dependence on the physical works, they are doing no worse than reductionists in specifying the mechanisms at work in the appearance of consciousness. Our experience only shows that the physical is a *necessary* condition for the appearance of mental phenomena in beings like us, not that it is both *necessary and sufficient* for causing it. That is, if we affect or remove the physical level upon which a mental property depends, then the mental also will be affected or terminated, but this cannot show that matter and physical causes are the only factors in the appearance of the mental.[10] But reductionists have trouble even considering the possibility of other factors since such factors would by definition be outside of physical structuring. Their metaphysical commitment forces them to conclude that the neural system is both necessary and sufficient for mental phenomena: the physical bases are not mere correlates of the mental but are all that is involved in its arising and the sum total of the causal power involved. Reductionists will also dismiss the dualists' contention that the physical base-conditions do not cause consciousness but only permit it to appear in physical beings or that the correlation of physical and mental phenomena is caused by a hidden cause.

The current neurophysiological approach will not be able to resolve this issue. All that neuroscientists are discovering are *correlations* of physical and mental states—they cannot prove the identity-theory or epiphenomenalism or establish causation. Questions such as whether the flow of adrenalin causes anger or vice versa or whether there is some other relation between them remain more metaphysical in nature. Even if we ever achieve a complete understanding of the brain's wiring, *how* experience arises from that wiring may yet remain a mystery. Moreover, no neurophysical theory may be able to explain *why* mental functions are accompanied by consciousness. In short, we would still need to know how and why the brain makes consciousness. In such circumstances, perhaps neuroscience should be conducted under a metaphysically neutral "correlations" approach rather than as part of a reductionist program.

If the possibility of a reduction "in principle" is the reductionists' fall-back position for when all else fails, then this untestability of subjectivity and the problem of "necessary" versus "necessary and sufficient" conditions become the antireductionists' counterpart. Which position we ultimately endorse will depend upon what types of factors we think are fundamentally real. We are left with a choice. And considering what is at stake in the way of the nature of a person and such phenomena as qualia and our possible freedom as agents, we should think hard before going with reductionism. The truncated view of a person that reductionists must endorse results from a doctrinaire metaphysics that is not required by science, let alone by our common experience. (And even reductionists must act *as if* they had free will. Indeed, it is hard to give up a sense of free will and simply let your body do whatever it was conditioned to date to do. To put the point ironically: we have little choice but to believe we have a choice. Reductionists only argue that ultimately this apparent choice is in fact an illusion and we are indeed only acting.)

But even though structure-antireductionism within the context of substance-reductionism should appear superior to naturalists than the commitment to the reduction of the mental level of organization to the physical, the mysteries of how consciousness arises and fits into the order of things still remain—antireductionists, no more than reductionists, have an explanation of how consciousness arises or why it exists. But these antireductive mysteries related to "interaction" are no greater than the reductive mysteries of how the physical gives rise to the mental level or why in fact the mental is present at all. Indeed, if reductionists were not obsessed with the simplicity of their metaphysics, they might see that the mysteries they must handle are greater—at least the antireductive mysteries are only a subset of the mystery of why any levels exist at all, a mystery reductionists too must face.

Perhaps these mysteries will always exist. After all, why should beings with our brains expect to be able to understand *everything*? Our descendants may develop an intelligence that makes ours look like an ant's, but the basic problem may well remain for any being with a brain evolved from our own or with a structure like ours. At most, all that philosophers can do in these circumstances is merely clarify the issues and identify problems—although, as John Searle has argued, philosophers since Descartes may in fact have done precisely the opposite.

Notes

1.   Popper was unconvinced by any form of ontic monism. Indeed, he despaired of any reductionism and argues instead for a pluralism of three realms: physical things, events, processes and forces; mental states; and products of human minds, especially works of art and scientific theories (including abstract entities such as numbers and classes) but also all social phenomena. The third realm is as objective as the other two—its elements exist independently of our minds. Thus, we invent numbers and equations but also discover objective features of reality about them. In his version of emergent evolution, the universe is highly creative, adding new realities with new irreducible properties and forces as it has evolved: first, the emergence of atomic nuclei and particles; next, life; then, consciousness; and finally, the products of the mind (1978). The physical realm has moved from being causally-closed to being open to the realm of mental states and events (1994). In sum, three different realms of reality have developed and interact with each other.

2.   See Puligandla 1991. In traditional Indian psychology, the thinking mind (*manas*) is merely a sixth sense, with the brain as its sense organ. Its activity is of the same nature as the activity of the other five sense organs and is not a separate entity such as the person (*purusha*) of Samkhya or a unified reality such as the *atman/brahman* of Advaita.

3.   To be more exact, Buddhist Abhidharmists delineate dozens of categories of reality, none reducible to the others and none (including consciousness) more fundamental.

4.   One Buddhist school, the Yogacara, dismisses all differentiation of independent objects in the external world as "mind only." This school also has a concept of a "storehouse-consciousness" (*alayavijnana*) underlying individual acts of consciousness.

5.   Such conviction usually appears in the context of religion. Thus, from astronomer Owen Gingerich, a Christian at Harvard: "Frankly, I am psychologically incapable of believing that the universe is meaningless."

6.   This leads Chalmers to suggest that perhaps *panpsychism* is true (1996: 293-99). That is, consciousness is embedded in every bit of matter like mass is, and when enough matter gets together with the proper structuring human consciousness arises. If panpsychism is true, physical particles have an innate *nonphysical* property.

7.   Many philosophers (e.g., Putnam 1999) deny the existence of qualia. But what they are questioning is whether phenomenal experiences can be reified into *distinct entities*, which then introduces the problem of the relation of these entities to the external world. But we can accept the reality of these experiences without that metaphysical move.

8.   Many theists today attach great significance to the failure to date of a naturalistic explanation of qualia and consciousness. In an argument for the existence of God going back to John Locke, they assert that consciousness could not evolve from matter and that nature could not produce such phenomena even in principle, and so a god must have created them.

9.   Actually a hierarchy of programs is required in a computer, each level of which is determined by algorithms applicable on that particular level but directed by a higher level program and ultimately by the data inputted.

10.   Reductive physicalists would also have to explain the placebo effect and why one's mental outlook can affect one's health in terms of beliefs being physical events.

5

Society and Culture

The conclusions of the last two chapters are that, while structure-reductionism is still vigorously defended, antireductionists currently have the upper hand. When attention shifts to the levels of organization above the psychological—the social and cultural—are there good reasons to assert the autonomy either of the levels of organization or of the disciplines studying them? Many philosophers and scientists, even among those who endorse the autonomy of the various natural sciences, think social and cultural phenomena are reducible without remainder to the actions and interactions of individuals. Social and cultural phenomena are merely our own subjective creations, and so are only psychological in nature. Thus, they are reducible to their neurobiological bases. And so the disciplines involved in studying these phenomena will eventually also be reduced to the natural sciences. On the other hand, many structure-antireductionists accept a realm of social and cultural sublevels as real, even if individuals are the agents for their appearance.

The sublevels of organization at issue—the social (any group-level phenomena) and the cultural (phenomena such as music, literature, architecture, technology, and philosophy representing our ideas, interests, and values)—will be called here collectively called the "sociocultural." And there should be no assumption that all of these levels are limited only to human beings. The issues surrounding these levels will be examined in two parts. First, is the sociocultural realm and the disciplines in the social sciences and humanities studying it reducible to the biological and physical levels and sciences? Second, if this realm is autonomous, must all sociocultural sublevels also be accepted as causally effective? To examine this second issue, the topic will be limited to one particular question: whether religious phenomena must be accepted as a causal part of the sociocultural realm. The first topic will be the subject of this chapter and the second the topic of the next.

Sociobiology

The first issue here is whether sociocultural phenomena can be reduced to biological phenomena.[1] An effective way to explore this issue is to look at one case: sociobiology. Sociobiology is the systematic study of the biological basis of sociocultural behavior in all organisms, including human beings (Wilson 1975: 4). Practitioners in the field (and in its offspring, evolutionary psychology) are routinely accused of advocating a form of biological reductionism commonly called biologism: people are no more than animals (the proverbial "naked ape"), and that all human social and cultural phenomena can be explained entirely in terms of biology.

Sociobiologists are concerned with finding a genetic foundation to all social behavior. Where sociobiologists differ from most scientists in genetics and evolutionary biology is in postulating the *gene* as the sole unit of selection in evolution, with no role for the whole (the *individual* or *group*). Evolution is seen in terms of the genes that are best able to replicate themselves in subsequent generations. Evolution as adaptive behavior for the propagation of genes by inheritance becomes the framework for explaining all human and animal sociocultural phenomena. All cultural creations and social activity—including any altruistic acts that apparently decrease the chance of one's own personal survival in favor of someone else's —must then be explained by how they contribute to the survival or disappearance of the genes of the individual engaged in that activity.

In short, all our activity centers on generating more of our own genes. At least some sociobiologists assert that forces apparently supplied by groups and individual members are causally irrelevant. For instance, Richard Dawkins claims "[w]e are survival machines—robot vehicles blindly programmed to preserve the selfish molecules known as genes" (1976: ix). We are "throwaway survival machines" created by selfish genes to propagate themselves. In short, genes are the only real forces. Organisms are nothing but DNA's way of making more DNA. There are no causal realities above the level of genes—no real societies, not even any ultimately real individuals, but only genes pulling the strings indirectly like a computer programmer (1976: 56). Indeed, even to speak of *individuals* is to use only the language of convenience; only the language of individual genes is literally true (1976: 71). Thus, the lumbering "survival machines" are structurally reduced.[2]

But the zoologist Edward Wilson, the founder of this discipline, has made it clear in responding to attacks on the issue of the role genes may play in explaining human social behavior that at least he is not a structure-reductionist. According to him, we do have a hard biological structure unaffectable by sociocultural factors, but once life reached the human level, genes gave away most of their sovereignty over behavior, although they still maintain a certain amount of influence in at least the behavioral qualities (1975: 550). Human cultures are created and shaped by biological processes while the biological processes, in a case of downward causation, are simultaneously altered in response to cultural changes—in short, culture can transform heredity (1978: 184-85). The genes do keep a leash on human behavior, but it is a long leash (1978: 175). In the dispute between those who think human social behavior is infinitely malleable (and hence subject to a complete determination by our social environment alone) and those who think it is completely fixed by genetics, he places himself closer to the environmentalist pole than the genetic. Indeed, in repudiating genetic determinism, he claims perhaps only 10% of human behavior is determined by genes (quoted in Wade 1976: 1151).

Wilson's opponents feel that sociobiology is simplistic and a vestige of nineteenth century materialism: there is no scientific evidence for *any* role of genes in directing human behavior (Caplan 1978: 259-64, 280-90; Harris 1979: 119-40). For them, behavior is a new level of reality, perhaps constrained by the lower levels but involving an entirely new set of irreducible causes. Thus, they deny any form of genetic determinism. For them, human behavior has to be explained almost exclusively in terms of sociocultural mechanisms: genes or other biological level phenomena have little or no significance on higher levels—it is the sociocultural forces that make us human. As with antireductionists in other fields, causes on one level are basically or totally independent of what goes on beneath that level, and it is the higher levels that are central to understanding the whole (here, human level phenomena). Nevertheless, the idea that one's genetic hardware influences, if not determines, some human action by establishing at least a *predisposition* to act a certain way is generally accepted today. And in denying this "upward" action and limiting the causation of human actions solely to the sociocultural level, antireductionists among social scientists are more extreme determinists than Wilson is. For the extremists, human phenomena are 100% plastic, determined not by genetics or any biological "human nature" but only by human social and cultural phenomena.

Moreover, Wilson and a colleague advance a theory of gene and culture coevolution (at least for human beings): culture is created and shaped by biological processes, while the biological processes are simultaneously altered in the response to cultural change (Lumsden & Wilson 1983: 118). In short, genes affect cultural evolution, and culture in a feedback effect affects genetic evolution. This involves a freedom of choice on the human level that genetic determination would not permit. It also involves the antireductionists' idea of downward causation from the cultural to the biological. Wilson and Lumsden speak of "culturgen" as the equivalent unit to the gene on the biological level (1983: 121). Dawkins also attaches at least some importance to cultural evolution for human beings and speaks of "memes" (1976: 206), although they are supposedly unconscious and "self-interested." Anthropologists have asked whether such individual, unconscious units of culture could be the objects driving evolution. In addition, cultural determinists reject the entire idea of coevolution with genes. But the important point to be noted here is simply that not all sociobiologists are committed to forms of genetic reductionism. Wilson sees culture as a new force in the evolution of life, with a capacity to transform heredity far greater than has been generally appreciated (Lumsden and Wilson 1983: 153). It becomes a matter not of whether genetic causation is all or nothing but of what is the appropriate less extreme percentages to attach to the genetic and to cultural components at work in a particular human phenomenon. He has also recently come to consider "group selection" over "individual selection."

Thus, Wilson is a structure-antireductionist. Even though he believes culture is ultimately a biological product and its evolution is channeled by rules that are genetically prescribed, any determination of our actions would not be limited to the biological level of organization. The sociocultural level receives prominence —indeed, it apparently dwarfs the former. Methodologically, Wilson accepts the need both for analysis of complex systems into manageable parts and for synthesis (the reassembling into whole systems) (Lumsden & Wilson 1983: 172). Wilson also concedes that the full array of the social life cannot be predicted from a knowledge of the genetic programs of the individuals alone. The phenomena of the sociocultural level must obey all the laws of the level of organization below it, but the upper levels of organization require a specific arrangement of the lower units, and this in turn generates richness and the basis of new and unexpected principles. Biology is the key to human nature, and social scientists cannot afford to ignore its developing principles, but the social sciences are potentially far richer in content; eventually they will absorb the relevant ideas of biology and go on to dwarf them by comparison (1978: 14).

However, Wilson also has made comments that social scientists find threatening: the social sciences and humanities are to be drawn into the modern synthesis of neo-Darwinian evolutionary theory by means of sociobiology (1975: 4, 547). The new neurobiology would cannibalize psychology and become the set of enduring first principles for sociology (1975: 575). This suggests that the social sciences and humanities are to be reduced to branches of biology and that sociobiology would play a major role in a "unity of science" program. But Wilson's remarks in *Consilience: The Unity of Knowledge* (1998) suggest that he does not envision a reduction of theories to physical theories or of the social sciences to physics. Instead, the various natural and social sciences together form a seamless whole, with chemistry being unified with physics, biology with chemistry, psychology with biology, and sociology with psychology. But in Wilson's view, there is not a chain of reductions; instead, the sciences remain intact. Biology stands as the "antidiscipline" of the social sciences, affecting their development but not replacing them (1978: 7-11; 1998). The social sciences are "biologized" only in the sense that social scientists must take account of the biological information shaping social behavior. Biology may revolutionize the social sciences, but it will not absorb these disciplines, any more than biology is to be absorbed (in Wilson's view) by chemistry and physics. All are needed, and none will be eliminated. In particular, sociology will be needed for studying the advanced literate societies that are most removed from the kinds of social systems in which the genetic basis of human social behavior originally evolved and thus in which the genes constrained actions more. Thus, advanced societies are most likely to display properties not predictable from a knowledge of individual psychology. Sociology is thus not reduced but aided by biology.

In short, Wilson rejects any attempt to explain social behavior on the human level exclusively in terms of genes. He is thus a theory-antireductionist with respect to both the social sciences and biology in addition to being a structure-antireductionist with respect to social phenomena. Dawkins is clearly a reductionist, but Wilson shows that sociobiologists can practice their profession without reducing human social behavior to genetic actions. This means more generally that not all scientists in the area of biology and genetics have to be structure- or theory-reductionists.

If sociobiologists—the scientists most often accused of being reductionists in this area—do not speak with one voice on these issues, then there probably are fewer reductionists in the area of human behavior than is usually thought. Indeed, there may well be more sociocultural determinists than biological reductionists working in the field of human behavior today. In any case, the upshot of this discussion is that natural scientists may study the genetic level of human actions without reducing all sociocultural phenomena to the biological or the social sciences to the natural sciences.

Sociocultural Causes

The variations in cultures revealed by cross-cultural studies naturally lead to the conclusion that all of human societies and cultural products appear to be entirely the product of our minds. For obvious reasons, very few social scientists subscribe to eliminationism. The phenomena of the entire sociocultural realm are rarely denied *in toto* or explained away as one grand illusion (although there are social eliminationists, as discussed below). Even social scientists who propose both applying natural scientific methods and a reductionist explanation of culture do not deny the existence of the sociocultural phenomena explained (e.g., Harris 1979). But some social scientists would reduce the *causes* that are apparently social in nature to psychological ones. In turn, many physicalists advocate the ultimate reduction of any apparently psychological causes to neurobiological ones. All intentionality or other subjectivity is eliminated in favor of neural firings. Thereby, the sociocultural realm will be connected to the natural sciences in a "unity of science" program. Any allegedly mental causes would be eliminated in favor of causes in physical systems. The closure of the chain of physical causes would remain intact.

However, structure-antireductionism concerning sociocultural causes is more popular in general among social scientists. Many social scientists may deny some apparent levels of causes in favor of lower ones (e.g., some apparently group-phenomena may be explained in terms of individual psychological causes) or some areas of sociocultural phenomena (e.g., religion) may be denied any causal potency. That is, a social scientist may claim to have identified the real sociocultural causes at work in a given phenomenon, thereby reducing or eliminating other causes within this level. But most social scientists today would stop the structure-reductions there and affirm that some causes on the sociocultural level are not reducible.

Antireductive social scientists endorse some form of *agency* involving a mental level of organization to explain most, if not all, human actions. The agency may be individual or collective, but the sociocultural antireductionists' theories entail a commitment to agency as a real cause. Social scientists all accept that human beings (and perhaps some animals) act at least sometimes to achieve goals. And they want to explain *why* we act as we do, not the physiological mechanics of *how*. They answer this "why" question in terms of our beliefs and desires. These beliefs or desires related to our goals may be our objectives, intentions, and motives for our actions, but they are also *causes* of the action as far as any potential explanation is concerned. To antireductionists in the philosophy of mind, not all causal explanations need to be in terms of impersonal, physical realities or events alone: explanations in terms of agency (i.e., with our intentional actions as causes) is a subgroup of causal explanations. Social scientists may discount the reasons we advance for our actions as mere rationalizations and purport to identify the real motivations. This may include causes other than rational thought—that has been an issue since Thomas Hobbes put forth the idea of the significance of the nonrational in human behavior. Our motives may be reduced to an unconscious level, but the unconscious even in Sigmund Freud's sense still involves a mental level above the strictly nonconscious physiological level. In sum, a role for the mental level as equally real and causal will always be included.

If the mental level of organization can be part of the causal chain of our actions, it is not a large leap for sociocultural antireductionists to include irreducible sociocultural causal factors in the explanations of sociocultural phenomena. And this means that, unlike in the natural sciences, explanations here will involve a level of organization involving the "purposeful" or "intentional" content of our minds—the reasons, beliefs, desires, or whatever else on the sociocultural level that propels human action. Thus, causal agency involves another layer of organization to reality in human actions that is missing in other natural events and that requires its own explanations. This means psychology, political science, economics, sociology, anthropology, and the other social sciences will differ from the natural sciences in necessarily utilizing irreducible causal intentionality.

Do Social Theorists Practice Science?

The irreducible sociocultural causes will always differ from causes in the natural sciences because of the role of human agency, but does this role for mental causation mean the "social sciences" can never really be *sciences* at all? Or do social theorists seek to accomplish something else? Dichotomies have developed from debates in the nineteenth century over whether the social sciences should be "humanistic" (*Geisteswissenschaften*) or "positivistic" (*Natureswissenschaften*): "understanding versus explaining," "interpreting versus explaining," "reasons versus causes," "subjective versus objective," "qualitative versus quantitative," "sympathetic versus detached," and "insider versus outsider accounts." The real scientists, many argue, seek the latter in each of these pairs, while social scientists seek only the former. The conclusion often reached is that the social "sciences" are thus not really sciences at all—there are no theories or disciplines to reduce because social theorists do not produce anything remotely related to real science.

The crucial requirement to be a "science" appears to be the search for *causal explanations* of phenomena. But some argue that merely including *intentional phenomena* as causes does not rule out the possibility of causal explanations, although it does expand the notion beyond the notion of "cause" in the natural sciences. But social theorists from John Stuart Mill and Auguste Comte to the founders of the social sciences to empiricists such as Carl Hempel have asserted that a search for causal explanations is needed for a science of human action. The basic requirement for such explanations is to identify constant relationships of "same cause, same effect" among various individual, social, or cultural phenomena. If established, such relationships would be enough for statements about human action to be laws permitting predictions, and these laws in turn could be explained in the framework of a theory. In short, there still could be causal explanations even though human agency is involved. For example, Freud believed our conscious and unconscious mind is subject to investigation in terms of lawful generalizations exactly as any nonhuman entity is; and his theoretical terms (e.g., "libido" and "repression") function like any other theoretical terms in a scientific theory.

But are there, as an empirical matter, such laws in the sociocultural realm? The complexity of human circumstances may make any causal relationships very hard, if not impossible, to discern in practice. At present, there may be handy generalizations about the sociocultural realm that help our understanding and that may loosely predict some general likelihood among future events. But finding a good example in the social sciences of an exceptionless causal law leading to exact predictions is even harder than in biology. Of course, many social theorists argue that these sciences are still in their early stages (even after a hundred years of work) and that in the future solid laws will be forthcoming. Others argue that even as "hard" a social science as microeconomics does not involve the study of real objects or features of the world—either it is a normative enterprise advocating a particular economic or political position (rather than being a descriptive/explanatory enterprise), or it deals only with the formal relations existing between ideal entities (e.g., an average consumer) unconnected to the real world (Rosenberg 1992; Ross 1995). In either case, it is not an empirical science involving natural laws. If so, there are no sociocultural causal laws, theories, or sciences to reduce at present.

But many social theorists argue today that the aim of their disciplines is not to produce causal explanations. Instead, the aim is to "interpret" or "make intelligible" the *meaning* of sociocultural phenomena in order to understand *why* the members of a group do what they do. Such meanings, unlike causes, do not exist in objects independently of the participants' intentions, and so the theorist's objective is to understand the participants' point of view. The role of intentionality and agency irreparably separates sociocultural phenomena from other natural phenomena and forces a different type of inquiry. It gives human events an "inside" that cannot be reached by an "outside" scientific point of view (T. Nagel 1979: 196-213). Rather than "explain" phenomena by identifying any alleged sociocultural or lower level causes accounting for a phenomenon, as in science, we are to "understand" the intentional elements on their own level. The same view has been raised for studying history: the historian is not a scientist but is concerned with understanding human actions (Collingwood 1946; Dray 1957).

The roots of this approach lie in the *Verstehen* methodology of the philosopher of history Wilhelm Dilthey. In contrast to the explanation that is possible for the lawful phenomena of nature, an intuitive understanding (*Verstehen*) involving a "total awareness of a mental state and its reconstruction based on empathy" is needed when we approach social and cultural life (1976: 181). We must enter into and "relive" the subjectivity of the people under study by reflecting on those experiences of our own that we think were analogous to the experiences of the people being observed. The sociologist Max Weber (1963) favored this approach: there is an "inner" meaning to human actions, not just outward behavior, and sociologists have to get at that meaning. The objective of sociology is to understand the uniqueness of each culture, not to attempt to discover universal laws to explain societies in general, although for him this understanding process was to lead to causal explanations. His paradigmatic types, such as "charismatic prophets," were not advanced to explain all phenomena cross-culturally but only to aid us in our understanding of specific cultures. This "understanding" approach is an attempt to see sociocultural phenomena from the participant's point of view, rather than to give an external explanation of the phenomena. But to many, the an "empathy" approach of trying to "relive" the experiences of others seemed to require some spooky intuitionism. It has now been rejected in favor of attaining the same goal of seeing the phenomena from a participant's point of view but through observational procedures relying more on empirical observation and testing than intuition.

The anthropologist Clifford Geertz is a leading exponent of the "interpretive" approach. For him, culture consists of "webs of significance" we ourselves spin, and the objective of the social scientist is not to search for causal laws explaining them but to interpret their expressions in a search for their meaning (1973: 5). All human action has a meaning, and this requires studying societies holistically to discern our intentions and not just in terms of "thin" descriptions of their mechanics. Such study is possible because there is nothing private about the meanings in a society. (Most philosophers agree that all sociocultural creations—including all of language—are public, not private, realities, and that meaning is fixed by the social world.[3]) Meanings can be deciphered by observing the actions in a culture. Others agree with him that the local specificity of human culture greatly limits any possible illumination that can be gleaned from theories claiming to apply across the entire range of human cultural diversity (e.g., Dupré 1995: 375).

Geertz wants to retain the label "science" for this enterprise—granted, it is not an "experimental" science, but it is an "interpretive" one (1973: 24, 5). But since interpretivists deny that there will be any predictive sociocultural laws or causal explanations or general theories as in natural science, whether the term "science" should be applied is debatable. Still overall this approach is strongly antireductive concerning structures and theory. Its practitioners treat the phenomena of the cultural realm as free of any general law-like activity that even in principle could be reduced to any level of causes below the "webs of significance" we have created. And the social "sciences" themselves would also be autonomous since social theorists are not doing anything even tangentially related to what the natural scientists are doing. Thus, the interpretive approach is incompatible with a structure-reductionism since its practitioners deny any causal explanations are possible for sociocultural phenomena. Advocates of this approach need not deny that there are biological constraints on our actions but only that these determine our actions. No "thin" description of our actions, no matter how complete on the physiological level, will ever be a complete account of our actions. We may still advance "thick" explanations of sociocultural phenomena of the understanding type answering *why* the participants are doing what they are doing. These interpretive explanations will account for the phenomena in terms of patterns of beliefs, goals, and so forth, placed within a wider sociocultural context that make the participants' action appear rational (Winch 1958; Nozick 1981: 638-42). Such explanations will be a matter of meaning, not physiology and physics. They will be in terms of what the participants say about their actions rather than what a sociocultural theorist thinks about the real sources of the actions. Whether theorists can offer any such explanations that are not open to the charge of being obscurantist, as interpretive accounts often are, is an issue. But such explanations would be antireductive and would never be continuous with the causal explanations of the natural sciences.

Where does this leave the issue of whether the sociocultural phenomena or disciplines are reducible? It seems too facile to say explanatory and interpretive approaches merely involve different questions—interpretive explanation remains *incompatible* with causal explanations, since its practitioners deny any universal social forces and thus that any laws governing human behavior are in fact possible. In other words, there is still a real conflict if the causal approach is indeed complete on the sociocultural level: there is no need for intentionality and agency as an explanation if sociocultural causes supply a complete explanation of sociocultural phenomena; conversely, if intentionity and agency provide a full explanation, then no complete causal accounts are possible. Until this issue is resolved, the issue of reductionism in these matters will also remain unresolved.

Structure- and Theory-Reductionism in the Social Sciences

The reductive physicalists' position here is obvious: any social phenomenon will be reducible to the behavior of individuals, and this in turn will be reducible to nonintentional actions of neurobiological causes. Reductionists point out that the only things we ever directly observe are the actions of individuals, not the actions or properties of some social whole. Cultural phenomena are not denied but are instead explained away: people and their ideas (e.g., ethics and laws) are already present when we are born and thus these ideas are imposed on us, but they are still simply people's own subjective creations—there is no other reality to study. Although some theorists are social level eliminationists, social phenomena are not usually denied—their causes are simply identified with individuals' actions and properties, and any social level forces that direct individuals' behavior are denied. A society's members are not the "neurons" from which a higher level social analog of consciousness emerges. Individuals are not merely base-conditions of higher realities—the lower level links through which social realities manifest themselves—but are the end of the line. The social level is merely an aggregate phenomenon, not a genuine emergent reality at all, and is explained away as such: all the properties of a society are simply the sum of its individuals' decisions and behavior, their interactions, and lower level biological and physical conditions.

Thus, any alleged social dynamics or feedback between individual actions and social forces is really only the interaction of individual causes. The antireductionist Émile Durkheim explained the higher suicide rate in Protestant countries than in Roman Catholic ones as due to the fact that the Protestant traditions give individuals more freedom of inquiry, and hence Protestants had the greater opportunity to doubt the meaningfulness of life (1951). But reductionists reply that this does not imply there is a social reality ("Protestant culture" versus "Catholic culture") that imposes itself on individuals—all that is involved is still only individuals making their own decisions in light of their beliefs. Similarly, a society is "capitalist" only because most of its individual members decide to act that way—there is no grand economic reality but only the aggregate of individuals' actions and attitudes. Any group-level laws in economics can be replaced, at least in principle, with laws about individuals' behavior and preferences in the market place. There are no real "market forces" operating independently of the individual members. Reductionists interpret Adam Smith's saying in *The Wealth of Nations* that the "invisible hand" of competition leads private selfishness unintentionally to a societal benefit as being about an economic institution (the capitalist system) that consists only of individuals' attitudes and interactions, not about an independent structure to reality—any observed regularities only result from everyone acting on the same beliefs. Social and political institutions can be treated as merely entities we reify from terms that do not correspond to anything in reality. For example, there is no "corporation" but only corporate material assets, employees, and so forth. Any apparent human agency of the individuals is reducible in turn by behaviorism or the identity theory to neurobiological or chemical causes. Structure- and theory-reductionists may also insist that we need to include causes from the natural environment to complete our explanation of sociocultural phenomena. But the point is simply this: all that is required to explain the phenomena are physical causes (matter and physical-level causes), and all social theories (if any) will eventually be reduced to those of the natural sciences. Sociocultural phenomena "supervene" on those base-conditions (e.g., "being the capital" would supervene on a physical city) but are determined by physical bases.[4] All causal power thus remains in the lower level conditions alone.

According to reductionists, trying to understand phenomena in the way interpretivists advocate would at best be a heuristic step leading to the causal explanations and laws that supersede any other type of explanation, and these explanations will always be in terms of lower level causes. Methodologically, the focus should be on analysis and the identification of underlying bases. Eventually, there will be no need for social sciences, as natural scientists complete their job by explaining all sociocultural phenomena. In sum, these sciences will be reduced in a "unity of science" type program: history, political science, economics, sociology, and any other social level science will be reduced to psychology, which in turn will be reduced to neurobiology and chemistry. Physics may not aid sociologists at present, but all sociocultural phenomena will eventually be shown to be the product of strictly physical factors, despite appearances to the contrary.

Sociocultural reductionists may also be concept-reductionists who advocate expunging all social terms from the scientific vocabulary or to treat terms such as "class" as no more than a convenient shorthand for the cumbersome correct descriptions in terms of individuals and their actions. Thus, to positivists, any investigation of a group can be described in terms of the members and their relations to each other and to their environment (Carnap 1949: 420). But sociocultural reductionists may agree that statements about social wholes do not *mean* the same thing as statements about their members. For such reasons, theory-reductionists here might be willing to subscribe to concept-antireductionism (see Nagel 1961: 537-40). That is, they may admit social concepts cannot be redefined without descriptive loss in terms of individuals, their interactions with others, and their material environment. They only assert that the actual *causes* at work are all below the level of sociocultural complexity, and so all *explanations* of these phenomena must be in terms of those causes. Thus, they can accept statements about group-level phenomena as referring to facts that cannot be stated without such concepts and need not treat them as merely elliptical statements about the actions and attitudes of individuals.

However, structure, theory, and concept varieties of reductionism do not represent the view of many working social scientists. Some social scientists may reduce aspects of the sociocultural realm—e.g., religion as a causal force—but few would reduce the entire sociocultural level. Some social scientists are physicalists who envision the ultimate demise of their own disciplines, but most who advocate this view are reductive philosophers with little interest in the social sciences. Indeed, under this view, a detailed analysis of social phenomena is not needed, since in the words of Rudolf Carnap it is "easy to see that every term of this field is reducible to terms of the other fields" (1949: 420). Most reductive physicalists are confident that a reduction is inevitable as the natural sciences progress. At worst, the complexity of the events on the sociocultural level may render a detailed account of the reduction impossible, not because other causes are at work but because such complexity renders sociocultural phenomena beyond our ability to analyze from a practical point of view. Still, reduction *in principle* is enough for reductionists.

Structure- and Theory-Antireductionism in the Social Sciences

Antireductionists in the social sciences see social facts as involving properties or features that cannot in principle be reduced to the mental and physical properties of individuals. Retelling, for example, the history of the Revolutionary War only in terms of individual soldiers and their interactions with each other would not only prove very difficult but would miss the causes of the events. Culture is a distinct level, like the program in a computer—it cannot work without specific hardware and the hardware constrains what it can do, but the program is still independent of it. Their main argument here is once again the "one-to-many" problem of multiple realization. The simplest to the most complex sociocultural phenomena can be realized in many different physical base-conditions. For example, being a piece of money is a social fact that can be realized in an indefinite number number of materials (paper, metal, wood, shells, and so forth) (Fodor 1974). Any material object attains value only because people decide it is valuable, and any material can be fashioned into a carrier of value. Thus, one cannot deal with economics in terms of the physical characteristics of the currency in a particular culture. Another level of organization is responsible for the ordering of the material bases. The same problem exists between social properties and properties of individual psychology. In addition, if there is the lack of any strictly causal laws among intentional phenomena, there are no laws to reduce even in principle to biological or physical laws or to be explained by physical theories.

Thus, to antireductionists, the sociocultural realm is autonomous: intentional phenomena are not reducible to neurological ones. People with the same genetic makeup have devised totally different social organizations. The role of human agency introduces a level of complexity that is simply not explainable from a knowledge of only the physical and biological conditions involved. In Hilary Putnam's view, we can deduce such physical macrophenomena as the rigidity of solids from knowledge of their microstructure, but we cannot deduce that, for example, capitalist production will exist from knowledge of the microstructure of the brain and nervous system: the same biological creatures exist in pre-capitalist and socialist societies. Thus, the laws of a capitalist society cannot be deduced from the laws of physics plus a description of the human brain—they depend on conditions that are accidental from the point of view of physics but essential to the description of a situation as "capitalist" (1994: 430). As discussed above, there is a *meaning* to human actions that is not explainable in any terms other than sociocultural ones. A neurological explanation of signing a legal document is simply irrelevant to the possible significance of the physical action—what is being signed and whether it is being executed properly depend on social factors alone. The social framework explains the action; physiology, let alone physics, does not.[5]

For most antireductionists, there are two basic sublevels to the social realm: *individuals' actions and beliefs* and *social realities*. Some antireductionists have argued that the social sublevel is literally sui generis. Cultures operate on a different level from social realities with its own structures, just as the symbol-systems of computers are independent of the electrical signals they guide in the hardware. Societies become the primary realities with supra-individual forces (e.g., a national destiny) controlling the actions of their parts (the members making up the society at any given time). The social whole thus entirely explains the individual, not vice versa. Jean Jacques Rousseau advanced such a holism: a society's general will exists independently of the members of a society at a particular time. In fighting the biological reductionism of his day, Durkheim advanced a sort of social vitalism: there is a superorganic "collective consciousness" or "group mind" (*âme collective*) in addition to individuals in a society (1915). But this is a structural vitalism, not a substantive one: individuals are the sole substance of any social reality (1982: 251), with a level of organization above the individual. Societies constitute a nonphysical reality that has its own properties and that is at least as real as its members. He likens the relation between individuals and social properties to that in biology: a living cell contains nothing but molecules of matter, but biological properties do not reside in the inanimate parts (1982: 128-29). The social whole constitutes a reality completely distinct (in the sense of being both different and independent) from the individual parts that manifest that reality (1982: 54). But Durkheim clearly went beyond any standard antireductionism of today. He discounted psychological causes altogether: the *social forces* (economic, demographic, geographic) are the real causes, and the *psychological mechanisms* (individual intentions) of individual persons are at best the means by which the social forces realize their effects or are merely useless by-products. Thus, any explanation of a social phenomenon directly by a psychological phenomenon is, to him, obviously false: the social reality is distinct from the sum of its parts and their relations, and the explanations of the social facts lie exclusively in the social realm. Maintaining that the explanations must lie with the individuals who make up societies is no more reasonable than demanding the reductions continue down to the physiological (and then physical) components making up the individuals.

But for most antireductionists, the idea that the social whole is more than the sum of its parts means there are two types of facts—one social and one individual—each of which needs an explanation. Some sociocultural antireductionists try to explain both types of facts with only psychological mechanisms. However, other antireductionists have maintained that a psychological explanation of social phenomena is always inadequate without positing other realities. The British emergentists treated all intentional phenomena as a level of complexity emerging from the lower level systems. The more recent general systems theorists treat the properties of the group as irreducible to the properties of its individual members. However, for many of these theorists, these properties are not truly emergent because they are reducible to the properties of the group's individual members plus their relationships with each other. Society is not, on the one hand, merely a collection of independent individuals, nor, on the other, are there any social forces or realities existing totally independently of persons. The properties of the social systems are not properties of the *individuals* who constitute their parts but instead arise out of their *interactions*. (In terminology introduced below, they are "relationists.") This pushes general system theorists closer to reductionists here than elsewhere. But social properties still are an irreducible matter of the wholeness of the system. Even if the social organizational properties were reducible to the properties of individuals, they would still have to be dealt with as wholes because social relationships and interactions are hopelessly complex (Laszlo 1972: 29).

More generally, most antireductionists in this area today do not deny a physical base to the higher levels—virtually all who are substance-reductionists with regard to any purported social realities. Antireductionists argue that the sociocultural structures cannot be reduced to biological and physical structures and that it is the resulting phenomena that make us uniquely human. But they do not all agree on how many sociocultural sublevels there are. The principal issue is this: are social institutions also real causal forces? Those antireductionists who are committed to social realities may also disagree on how many types of social causes (political, economic, religious and so forth) operate in the sociocultural realm.

Most physicalists in the social sciences also accept *free human agency*. The only exceptions are the most austere physicalists, such as the Marxists. Karl Marx stressed that individuals act according to their material interests—such economic interests are the real causes at work in history—and that all forces at work in nature are material, including those on the social level. Much of culture is dismissed as epiphenomenal "superstructures." This can lead to a sociocultural determinism, but Marxists adamantly oppose any biological determinism of human actions.

In any case, for most antireductionists today the *social* sublevels involve irreducible causal forces: group-structures that underlie individual behavior. Some theorists treat them as cultural systems that we ourselves create; these systems then have the reality and objectivity to impose themselves on us (Geertz 1973). In sociology, the mainstream position is a mild form of social antireductionism. In the sociologist Peter Berger's words, "society is a dialectic phenomenon in that it is a human product, and nothing but a human product, that yet continuously acts back upon its producer" (1967: 3). Reductionists agree that society is nothing but a human product, but they do not agree that it is in any sense a sociocultural reality that can act causally downwardly; instead, for them, only individual decisions and actions are involved.

For moderate antireductionists, we create a reality by means of the symbols we devise that acts back upon us. We are a "symbolic species" that becomes entangled in the self-organizing, emergent semiotic webs we generate, producing a tremendous causal force (Deacon 1997). No one can escape from social infrastructures. Most importantly, no one can become *human* apart from this matrix other human beings have made. Thereby, much of our mental life may really be social: while our physical and mental levels exist prior to enculturation, it can still be argued that our "self" and many psychological states are *social* creations that develop only through interactions with others. Indeed, an argument can be made for placing the social level *before* consciousness and much of the rest of the mental level, since social behavior was well-entrenched in the animal realm (e.g., among insects) before the distinctly human mental realm arose.[6] So too, all of the categories encoded in any particular language, including the categories about our inner psychological states, have arisen and developed only in a public context. The categories and rules of language in turn influence, if not completely determine, our thinking; all human thought thus has a social source. Language and our brain may co-evolve. Moreover, all reasoning and standards of rationality have a social, not an individual, context. In sum, many properties that appear individualistic have an irreducibly social element because all are formed only in social contexts and are understandable only if we examine those contexts. Whether there are universal properties or all human properties are dependent on a particular culture is not the issue here—the point is that social realities are what make us human. In short, we are biological creatures, but we also are what we are as much because of societies. For all antireductionists, the social and psychological levels are both real, even if they are interconnected. However, for reductionists and moderate antireductionists, there is no supra-individual social or cultural reality existing apart from human beings: the levels of organization to reality end with our own mental products. Stronger forms of emergentism include the social and cultural levels of organization as independent levels of reality that are as irreducible as the biological and mental levels are.

More extreme antireductionists, such as Rousseau and Durkheim, go further and see social forces as having a more independent reality and a primacy over the individual. A social holism controls the parts. Social entities are not simply our projections but have the same reality as physical and biological realities. In short, a new level of organization to reality emerged. Most social theorists agree social realities (e.g., countries) are not identical to any collective set of individual entities existing at any one time and thus must be included in our ontology. Social facts are neither nonexistent nor epiphenomena of psychological realities. But under more extreme views, a structure is involved in the whole that is not generated by the parts but that controls the parts. Society becomes seen as a type of organism. But even under less extreme antireductive views, a social structural reality exists that must be described and explained in concepts designed for its own level.

Thus, for these more holistic theorists, any social institution has properties that are independent of the sum of the properties of the particular persons (including their intentional properties such as beliefs) who constitute the parts of that structure at any given time. For instance, "market forces" exist in reality that operate on individuals working in an economy like any other natural force; they are not merely the sum of the decisions of individuals. In short, people are only "social animals" but parts of social entities. Social forces causally act downwardly on the individuals in ways that are not reducible to the individual interactions of the "parts" but that represent another level of organization to reality. Some theorists extend this idea to *animals* that exhibit the social level even without any conscious intentionality; it is possible to treat, for example, an ant colony as the primary entity, with the individual ants being the atoms from which it is made.

In sum, for both the more holistic and the less holistic social level antireductionists, there are higher level causes and not just individual actions, and these will require their own level of theory. Theorists will need to account for at least human social action on its own level in terms of desires and agency. Sociocultural theorizing will never be the case of explaining x in terms of non-x, as is the case with reductive explanations of sociocultural phenomena. Physical and biological causes play roles in human behavior and thus the study of them may be necessary to complete our understanding of various cultural and social phenomena. And indeed some sociocultural causes may in fact be reducible aggregates or products of lower level causes. But according to antireductionists not all higher level causes will be reducible and lower level causes will never provide a complete account. The interpretivists' claim concerning the impossibility of a causal science of the socio-cultural realm should be also noted again. The bottom line for both types of antireductionists becomes: if a causal explanation is possible, that explanation cannot be reduced to lower level explanations; if it is impossible, the autonomy of the sociocultural realm is assured, and thus theory-reductionism is impossible.

Methodologically, social level antireductionists argue that the study of individuals even in context is never sufficient for reaching a full explanation. Autonomous higher level sciences will always be required, to the extent that such sciences are possible, to make these phenomena intelligible. No unification of the sciences by means of the reduction of causes or theories is feasible. The natural sciences may contain complete accounts of certain levels of organization operating within, and constraining, sociocultural phenomena, but reality involves more levels to explain. Which sociocultural sciences are needed is a matter of dispute among antireductionists, with the usual disagreement being between the need for more than psychology or not. Mario Bunge advances the unusual position of endorsing, in effect, both the irreducibility of the mental realm and the eventual replacement of psychology as an independent discipline by an expanded neurobiology and sociology (1990). Most sociocultural antireductionists, however, give psychology an irreducible place among the sciences.

But the global scope of each science presents a complication: the potential for *conflict* between disciplines. If each social science explains *all* sociocultural phenomena, the different social sciences compete in a way the natural sciences do not: they attempt to provide complete accounts of the *same level of organization*. Everyone agrees that the natural sciences at present concern different levels or sublevels. Natural scientific laws on any level will be *compatible* with laws on other levels since they involve different phenomena, and the theories explaining them are at least for the present supplementing each other. Even under the reductionist interpretation, we still must wait for physicists to complete their hegemony over the other sciences and bring the levels now studied by others within their scope. The situation among the social sciences, however, is different: the disputants cannot even agree there are different sublevels of organization. In particular, there is the dispute over whether social levels exist or only the level of individuals does, and whether psychological mechanisms can explain social facts.

Thus, theorists may use their own explanations to explain the same phenomena as theorists from other disciplines. For example, reductive psychologists typically advance their theories of religion as not just explanations of the psychological aspects or sublevel of all religious phenomena but as a complete account of all the real factors at work in all religious phenomena. Reductive sociologists usually do not claim to explain only some phenomena or some aspects of phenomena but to give the only explanation needed of the sociocultural phenomena being studied. Typically each account is meant to be the most comprehensive, accurate, or complete one available for the phenomena under study. This holds whether social scientists are providing causal accounts or "understanding" accounts. So too, the conflict is not merely between reductionism and antireductionism but also among all antireductive approaches. Each account is presented as comprehending the same phenomena as the various social level accounts, and the proponents of each account implicitly or explicitly claim no other account is needed to complete our understanding. But this means that all accounts cannot be equally accurate or useful: some must be wrong in a way one is not. Only if sociocultural theories, however, can be understood as limited in scope to different sublevels—in particular, between individual and social—can they be understood as compatible (as discussed in the next chapter).

Individualism and Holism

Structure- and theory-antireductionists in this area are divided into two groups, usually termed "methodological individualists" and "methodological holists" or "collectivists" (see Winch 1958; O'Neill 1973; Sober 1984; James 1984; Bunge 1996: 253-61; Kincaid 1997).[7] But although the groups are described as "methodological," the discussions cover both *how to study* sociocultural phenomena (should social scientists study, for example, armies or only individual soldiers?) and *how to explain* sociocultural phenomena (should all explanations ultimately be in terms of individuals or social wholes?). The groups thus could be just as well be labeled "explanatory" or "theory" individualists and holists. One's stance also determines what data to ignore and the nature of what theories are acceptable. Also, note that here "holism" means *any type of social substance-antireductionism*, not merely the more extreme forms of it like Rousseau's or Durkheim's. The debate has died down, with a consensus emerging that we must explain social phenomena by studying individuals in context and that social structures and constraints are products of human agency (Bhargava 1992). But this has not resolved the basic dispute over the nature of a human being: are we individualist or social in nature?

The underlying dichotomy is between individual persons and their beliefs (and perhaps people's interactions) and social institutions. The dispute is over the ontological status of the social sublevel: are the social institutions real mechanisms that constrain the actions of individuals? Is a nation a construct or an emergent system? Holists here advocate the reality of social phenomena and also the need for social level explanations. The individualists' contrary position can be traced back to such social thinkers as Wilhelm Dilthey, John Stuart Mill, Jeremy Bentham, John Locke, Thomas Hobbes, and much earlier to the Sophists. (Locke attempted to formulate individualist laws for social institutions to mirror Newton's laws.) Karl Popper was a prominent advocate. John Rawls's theory of justice is also individualistic. So too is Edward Wilson's sociobiology: culture is determined by the mental development of individuals, and there are no sociocultural natural kinds to reality (1996: 110, 112). Even some general system theorists can be construed as individualists.

Under individualism, human beings are the only causes in history, and no explanation of a social phenomenon is complete until we have arrived at an account of it in terms of the dispositions, beliefs, actions, resources, and interactions of individuals and their physical environment. In short, we hold our destiny in our own hands and are not being pushed about by supra-individual forces. Individualists may be extreme "atomists" who claim only individuals existing completely independently of each other are needed to explain social phenomena, or they may be "relationists" who affirm that relations between individuals are also real and needed for explanations. Although atomism apparently underlies rational choice theory, few other social individualists are atomists since most theorists agree that interactions constitute an irreducible part of being a person. In short, contextual understanding is vital (Bhargava 1992). The issue is how *to explain* our nature and actions, and individualists see no reason to invoke any social level realities. A "society" has obviously preceded us and shaped our character from the day we are born, but this only means that we learn from other individuals, not that there is some independently-existing, supra-individual reality affecting us. Institutions (e.g., laws) simply reflect our agreement to act certain ways backed by sanctions in the form of the potential actions by others. All social roles are simply a matter of individuals' beliefs and actions toward others. Being a bank clerk or a king is purely a matter of an individual's psychological state and how other individuals react. We learn our social roles, and we may unconsciously reify our learned concepts and attribute such properties to alleged social and cultural realities, but in fact no other realities than individuals and their mental states are involved. When we change our mind, social institutions collapse (as with communism in 1989).

Thus, no social level reality withstands an individualist interpretation. In the end, there is no genuinely emergent higher level social realities but only the aggregate of individuals' interactions, however complex those interactions may be. But for relationists, the character of the whole is fixed by the properties and relations of its parts. Any social whole is thus nothing beyond those interactions of individuals with each other and their physical environment—it is no more than the sum of its interacting parts, and hence it can be successfully reduced to the properties and relations of the individuals involved. Eventually no social level sciences will be needed. Macroeconomics involves only aggregates of individuals' actions, not any social level realities, and so can be translated into individualistic terms. All economics will ultimately be microeconomics in the extreme—the interactions of individuals alone. Indeed, all social sciences should also be reducible to psychology, with the natural sciences completing the explanations.

In sum, the central tenet of individualism is that we have to explain social facts individualistically. To be thorough, individualists must also explain all the symbol-systems of a culture (including language) in terms of individuals deciding to think and act a particular way. Only then can individualists assert that there are no social level causes and no social realities for individuals to interact with. Most individualists may concede the irreducibility of social facts and social concepts (e.g., Flew 1995: 64), but both atomists and relationists are also *eliminationists* with regard to all apparent social realities. There is no social whole that is affected by the actions of its parts—there are only the parts. There are in reality no social institutions or other phenomena, and thus nothing to reduce. In the words of former British prime minister Margaret Thatcher, "I don't believe in Society. There is no such thing, only individual people, and there are families" (quoted in Flew1995: 61). "Society" is merely the label we give to the aggregate of individuals and not a reality in itself at all. Being a citizen of a country merely describes the dispositions, beliefs, and actions of individuals—there are no entities in reality called "countries" (or, for that matter, "families") beyond our own imagination. In short, our social creations are not natural kinds making up reality and cannot constitute part of any ultimate explanation. They are no more than mental fabrications that individuals create to focus their attention. Concept-reductionism follows naturally from eliminationism: all concepts referring to social wholes are no more than terms of convenience that must ultimately be eliminated, not just from explanations of sociocultural phenomena but from the description of them (since there are no such realities), even if the new descriptions are rather messy (see Gellner 1973: 248-49).

For all individualists, the fundamental elements for sociocultural theories are only individuals. There are no social level theories because only lower level realities at work. Even if there are social facts, still the only causal mechanisms at work are in individuals or their relationships. Social entities are at best only aggregates or epiphenomena with no causal power. To Karl Popper, they at best have only a "derivative" ontological status: that we are "biologically social animals" does not imply that social entities have a more fundamental, or even independent, status than individuals (1974: 222). Theorists who advocate individualism (e.g., Nozick 1974) do not reduce the forces at work beyond the psychological level. But to individualists, holists are no more than social vitalists. Moreover, relationists can also accept the importance of the *interactions* among individuals (e.g., the agreements to divide labor) while still denying that any social regularities compromise the integrity of individuals' intentionality (Pettit 1993).

Relationists are also methodological holists: we need to study individuals *in their social context* to understand them fully, since their social roles are learned and acted out. Social roles are an essential part of what we are, and so studying individuals atomistically (i.e., each individually without regard to their social environment) will not reveal the mental states behind their behavior. Interactions and social context are necessary parts of the explanations. This leads some holists to wonder why individualists are so insistent on being labeled "individualists" (e.g., Lukes 1970). Indeed, most holists today are "structure-holists" but not "substance-holists": they accept individuals as the only substance of the social wholes but affirm social level causes. The individualists' burden then is to try to explain all social phenomena strictly in terms of individuals as the only causal realities. The fact that individualists have to use a phenomenon—language—that is thoroughly *social* in nature to accomplish this is, to say the least, ironic.

But to individualists, their position is obvious and beyond dispute (Flew 1995: 62). On the other hand, social antireductionists insist that group-level structures are always needed to complete any explanation. To Auguste Comte, a society is no more decomposable into individuals than a geometric surface is decomposable into lines or lines into points (Lukes 1970: 76). Even if we could manage to *describe* a triangle in very complicated terms of the location of each particular point to each other, nevertheless other structures (lines) still are the realities creating the triangle, and thus we would have to invoke those structures to *explain* it.[8] And social antireductionists claim the same is true of social wholes: more levels of organization are at work in structuring social wholes than just those of their members.

More extreme holists see social realities as existing independently of their individual members. Social institutions are independently existing wholes that exert pressure on individuals, thereby revealing that they have powers not possessed by individuals. Individuals do not so much *create* the social wholes as *participate* in the realities that shape them and determine their role in the social wholes. Sociology has its own distinct subject-matter—an order of facts that other sciences do not study—and the data that sociological theories explain must be limited to social facts. There thus is a break in continuity between sociology and psychology, as there is between biology and the physical sciences (Durkheim 1982: 129). Friedrich Engels and the later Karl Marx also saw the need to explain history independently of the actions of individuals: history in the final analysis is not made by innumerable individuals interacting—the real driving forces at work are the nonconscious, social "classes." Individuals are directed and controlled by the nonconscious intentions of these realities that they themselves cannot control.

However, most social antireductionists are not so extreme. Moderate holists see social wholes as the creation of individuals that have the power to act back upon individuals; individuals thereby interact not only with each other but with another level of organization. Our biological commonality limits the differences in communities, but human society has distinctive underlying structures—even animals may have a "collective intentionality" (Searle 2010). All sociocultural creations are like language: we create it, but then it takes on an existence of its own that acts back on us constraining our thought. Its existence cannot be explained or even understood in individualist terms. Similarly, all social institutions and cultural symbol-systems have a causal reality of their own that acts upon our actions—their power is not simply the sum of the causal power of the individual people involved. Individuals and social wholes are *both* causally active and interact with each other. Some social level realities may only be aggregates of individuals' actions, but some are causal realities that somehow constrain individuals' actions.

Thus, social facts require social causes to explain them: actions of individuals must be explained at least in part by social wholes. So too, both "upward" and "downward" causation between levels is involved here. Under this view, we cannot understand the actions of individuals unless we assume societal facts and laws are as ultimate as psychological ones (Mandelbaum 1973a, 1973b). There are wholes that cannot be explained by their parts alone; they comprise a causal factor that cannot be reduced, and thus they are real. Such wholes are structurally irreducible, even if individuals constitute their entire substance and the wholes cannot act except through individuals. For example, explanations in economics of a market exclusively in terms of the sum of individuals' choices will never suffice. (Nor would most antireductionists reduce persons to only producers and consumers of material goods.) For all antireductionists, we can replace all the members of an institution and the institution will retain its character, not because of continuity of the beliefs of the individuals in the overlapping change of "parts," but because the institution itself is also a reality. Institutions do change, but their evolution is not the result of individual level factors alone but also social level causes.

Social antireductionists go beyond saying that the basic nature of a human being is social—something relationists can admit and think they can explain—and claim instead that social structures are at least as fundamental as individual ones. Few social antireductionists today, however, advocate the reverse reduction and contend that a social explanation is all that is needed and that individuals' decisions play no part in the complete explanation of a social phenomenon. But for radical holists, all mental development actually occurs only on the social level, and so only a social level explanation is needed; mental factors are no more explanatory here than are the biological and physical. In a reverse reduction, social wholes are the sole causes, and psychological factors of individuals and their relations are reduced to epiphenomena of the social wholes. Individuals are reduced to the functions they serve; they are empty nulls shaped entirely by the social forces present in their context. Individuals cannot alter the flow of history because social level forces are in fact determining the course of events. Individuals become merely the vehicle by which the whole acts. Radical holists would claim Julius Caesar was totally a product of the late Roman Republic—if this particular general had not taken over (and become "Caesar"), the social conditions would have created another one.

But again, most social theorists are less extreme and reject such "sociologism."[9] Instead, they see individual persons' actions at work in any social phenomenon in addition to social forces (as well as physical and biological factors). Accounts of all the levels of organization involved must be included in any complete explanation of a social phenomenon. To individualists, an explanation would be simply the sum of the explanations of each person's action; there are no other "social conditions." But moderate holists see both upward and downward causation between levels. Each factor is an independent cause, and integrating the two types of causation into one overall account having reference to both levels may prove difficult. But social facts are never reducible to psychological ones for any social antireductionist.

Antireductive Explanations

From the above, it is clear that individualists and holists differ in what they take as explanations of sociocultural phenomena. But they can agree that at least two types of explanations of such phenomena are possible for those who do not reduce the sociocultural realm to the biological or physical. First are historical narratives of the origin and development of a phenomenon. Human agency and intentionality can be fully acknowledged in such an explanation. Second, some relationists and holists advance functionalist explanations. These explanations start with the premise that everything must fulfill some beneficial service for a social whole within which it exists or there would be no reason for its continuing existence. Functionalists explain a phenomenon by the role it plays in a larger phenomenon. For example, in biology the heart is explained by the role it plays in maintaining the body, or in sociology the actions of a king are explained by his function in a given society. Functionalists need not reduce the explained phenomenon to no more than the function it fulfills—they need not deny that there is more reality to it than its role. But once we have explained what function is performed and how it is performed, functionalists are satisfied that we understand why the phenomenon exists and thus that we have explained that phenomenon as fully as necessary.

Certain problems are often pointed out concerning functionalist explanations. For example, if multiple realization is correct, then there may be more than one way, or indeed an indefinite number of ways, a particular function may be satisfied. More than one base-phenomenon may "explain" the same benefit, and functionalists thus will not be able to establish that a particular phenomenon is necessary and sufficient for a particular function. Similarly, a sociocultural reality may satisfy more than one function in a society. Most importantly for the issues at hand, functionalism will never account for the sociocultural realm *as a whole*. Functionalists only purport to satisfy our need to make sense of individual elements within a given level and not to explain where the level came from in the first place. Such an approach presupposes the irreducibility of the whole system within which the part functions—the part cannot explain why the whole exists any more than the heart can explain why the body exists. Reducing the part to the role it plays within the whole—e.g., reducing all of religion to the functions it fulfills for an individual or a society—does not explain the existence of the whole. Thus, functionalists may be reductionists with regard to some particular elements within that level, but they may be antireductionists with regard to the sociocultural level as a whole.

Nor will functionalism account for the *origin* or *changes* of sociocultural elements but only the *persistence* of those elements, including seemingly arbitrary and bizarre elements. The functions do not *cause* the phenomenon to come into existence in the first place, and this is what is behind the objections of empiricist philosophers of science to the idea of a functional "explanation" (e.g., Hempel 1965: 297-330). In their view, an explanation of what causes the original existence of the phenomenon is what is needed. For such theorists, parts create wholes, not vice versa, and the explanation must start and end with the parts. Identifying the role of the heart plays in a body does not explain the heart at all and only partially explains the body. The heart is a cause within the whole that can explain its effects, but it itself is a part whose existence needs a causal explanation, and its function does not provide that. In short, causes explain consequences, not vice versa. To reductionists and antireductionist causal theorists, the functional approach may be a useful heuristic device, but, like the "interpretive" approach discussed above, they doubt that it ultimately satisfies our need for making sense of things.

Social level holists add a third type of explanations: social level structures.

Adding an independent level of structure to reality above the mental is what separates holists from relationists. Such structures operate through "downward" causation to constrain the actions of the parts. They are responsible for ordering the "parts" into functioning wholes and explain why social realities can be multiply realized in different material bases. Rupert Sheldrake's social "morphic fields" that shape individuals' behavior is an example. Extreme holists have no problem with these types of structures, and whether even moderate holists can avoid utilizing some type of social level structures as part of their explanations is debatable. But a problem for holists is identifying any *mechanism* by which nonconscious, supra-individual social forces impinge upon and constrain the mental level in individuals to complete the causal chains producing individuals' actions.

Are the Social Sciences Autonomous?

Do the differences between reductionists and antireductionists concerning the sociocultural realm aid in any way to resolve their fundamental disagreement in all areas? Not really. The social sciences are too theory-heavy with the competing metaphysical visions to provide independent aid in resolving the issues. Both sides can easily fit any data from the sociocultural realm within their differing philosophical points of view. (The general problem of finding any empirical grounds to decide between reductionist and antireductionist theories will be discussed in the next chapter.) Indeed, the theories in this area have more of an a priori air than do those in the natural sciences. These accounts do, however, bring out more clearly the philosophical nature of the dispute. Reductionists see no reason to change their position that ultimately the sciences of the sociocultural realm (if there are any) will be absorbed into biology. They are little concerned with the relative lack of theoretical progress in the social sciences—all sociocultural phenomena will be explained in terms of lower level causes any way, and so no sociocultural theories are necessary to begin with. Just as biology advanced with the study of DNA, so too sociocultural phenomena will be better understood when natural scientists finally advance their disciplines enough to explain this realm.

On the other hand, social antireductionists are just as certain that sociocultural phenomena are unexplainable by physical and biological phenomena. They see no reason to embrace reductionism when human nature seems radically unfixed on a sociocultural level, even if it is a natural kind on the biological level (Putnam 1994: 439). In their view, biology is necessary for a total explanation of a phenomenon, but it is completely unable to specify the cultural properties of human behavior or their variations from one culture to the next. The "social sciences" may not be "sciences" in the natural science sense of the term—either because there are no causal regularities among social phenomena, or, if such regularities do exist, they are too complex for us to comprehend, or because the intentional phenomena of the sociocultural level of organization require their own unique approach. But some autonomous disciplines will always be needed for the various sociocultural sublevels, whether explanations prove ultimately to be causal or interpretive.

Both sides face problems. Both reductionists and sociocultural individualists have to contend with the fact that many social phenomena seem impossible to describe and explain in terms of individuals. Concept-reductionism is especially difficult to maintain: attempts to define social terms in terms of individuals' collective actions and dispositions are not likely to be successful. If social facts are indeed as primary as psychological facts, then concepts used to refer to the social facts cannot be reduced without remainder to terms referring only to the actions and beliefs of individuals (Mandelbaum 1973a). Social statements are not merely elliptical statements about individuals that could in principle be stated fully. Many terms referring to individuals as members of society only gain their meaning from social terms and so would have to be redefined completely if the social terms were all deleted. Of course, this does not foreclose structure- and theory-reductionism, but it does present reductionists with the difficult situation of making plausible any attempts to reduce social facts to individual facts and to deduce any sociocultural laws from biological laws (or any social laws from individualist laws).

On the other hand, social antireductionists—both moderate and extreme—have a major problem of making plausible the entire notion of causal realities on the social level, i.e., social wholes not structurally reducible to the reality of interacting individuals and their properties. They are forced to approach these alleged realities through the actions of individuals. Antireductionists need to make intelligible both the attribution of some kind of intent or causal power to a supra-individual reality and how it interacts with individuals. Presenting such an account of social level structures appears especially important since affirming the causal reality of social wholes does not carry the same degree of intuitive plausibility antireductionism has for most people regarding the biological and mental levels—i.e., we cannot *see* social realities the way in which we can see such other alleged emergent properties as the wetness of water or the purposeful actions of living beings. In biology, it may appear plausible that forces operating on individuals may explain through downward causation some changes in our genetic make-up, but we cannot see such an operation of economic forces or social classes in the social realm. Social antireductionists, however, reply that we can see many social phenomena (e.g., the procedure of a court) while many features of individuals are not observable (e.g., intentions) (Lukes 1970: 80). It is only the reductionists' perspective that prevents them from seeing the forest for the trees. Many philosophers argue for a realist interpretation of mathematical entities and equations, i.e., that they are not our mental creations but have a reality independent of us equal to that of physical objects and that we merely come across them (e.g., Popper 1979). Perhaps a comparable argument can be made for social and cultural creations. But currently most substance-reductionists probably think of the social level and all cultural phenomena as purely human creations in no way reflecting any causal realities existing in any sense independently of us.

Reductionists accuse antireductionists here of having nothing but an obscure vision to back up their position. Antireductionists see reductionists also as having nothing but a metaphysical intuition of what the nature of all realities must be—one unsupported by any actual detailed reductions in any field. Relationist individualists accept a middle ground, accepting genuine mental activity (intentional acts) while denying both the causal reality of supra-individual wholes and atomist individualism. Individualism may be more intuitively plausible to many Americans: if social realities are composed of individuals, then all explanations must be in terms of individuals. (Indeed, individualism is arguably a root-cause for the drive for reductions in general.) Or, people may not give the social sciences much thought and conclude that because the natural sciences according to the reductionists' view proceed by reduction to parts, so must the social sciences.[10]

But even if individualism has more intuitive plausibility, social holists can still ask whether there really are any good reasons why explanations should have to conform to this intuition—perhaps progress in explaining here, as in other sciences, can be made by abandoning widely-held intuitions (James 1984: 75). Like any deeply entrenched view, individualism is inclined to be self-sustaining (James 1984: 8), but this is no reason to continue to maintain it. Even if individualism is more intuitively plausible, it still has to be worked out in detail; and when we look at attempts to work out the position, it loses its initial advantage. In sum, just because societies are composed of individuals does not mean other factors may not be at work on them—the explanatory issues cannot be conflated with that ontological issue (Kincaid 1997: 10-11). Of course, antireductionists still have the problems of making the social level realities seem plausible at all and of identifying how these realities can act upon individuals.

In the end, we are left with the same basic philosophical divergence as with the natural sciences and the mind: reductionists have not yet presented any account of reduction in detail, and antireductionists appear to rest with the argument that the arising of the sociocultural level is merely another instance of the emergence in general of irreducible higher levels of organization. Reductionists are not worried about the future, since the reductions are always "in principle" possible, and antireductionists are not discouraged by their more complicated ontology. Reductionists like to think of themselves as being more empirical in these matters (since they do not posit any mental or supra-individualist realities), but the conflict is more over competing metaphysical directions of explaining and theorizing.

As discussed in Chapter 3, even in the physical sciences, reductionism is not simply an empirical issue. Deciding such issues as whether history is driven by individuals or by some overarching, impersonal social powers or by both turns more clearly on our general metaphysical outlook. The disputants cannot now point to empirical evidence for their positions and may never be able to. Needless to say, the arguments articulating the competing metaphysical intuitions have not been too convincing to those who do not share that underlying intuition to begin with. The situation is more open by degree than in the cases of the last chapters where antireductionists appear to have the edge. For the present, we are left with having to treat sociocultural phenomena as at least temporarily irreducible and the disciplines that study them as therefore autonomous, whether or not they are "sciences" in the sense natural sciences are.

Notes

1.   Reducing human behavior to cell biology or DNA has led to eugenic programs and is greatly affecting social policy in the United States today (Nelkin 2002).

2.   Critics ask how can a single gene be isolated from others as an individual unit of inheritance. They also point out that Dawkins is loose with his anthropomorphic use of language—in particular, how can an inanimate molecule be "selfish" or "purposeful"?

3.   Relationists in sociocultural studies also stress that meanings have a social dimension and that intentions are not merely conscious states of individuals. Rather, the intentional content of beliefs and actions is irreducibly social and can be realized both in individual minds and actions as well as directly in collective actions (Bhargava 1992).

4.   Antireductionists may also refer to sociocultural facts as "supervening" on lower level facts (e.g., Kincaid 1987), but they do not deny the irreducibility of higher level causes.

5.   The problem of attempting to reduce social phenomena below the biological is nicely illustrated by considering a simple social factual claim: "George was allowed home from prison at last on Sunday." How can the language of physics convey the meaning of "Sunday," "home," "allowed," "prison," "at last," or "George" (Midgley 2003: 35)? Any talk of quantum events or other physical properties involved in the event is simply irrelevant to understanding it. How then could physics explain any social aspect of the event?

6.   Many also argue that our brain evolved through our interaction with our environment, both social and natural. This would be an instance of downward causation.

7.   Social scientists also speak of "micro" versus "macro" in this regard. This may sound more scientific, but there is no consensus on the meaning of these terms.

8.   Consider the analogy further. There is a paradox at the center of geometry: points have no dimensions, and yet we can string them together and a one-dimensional line emerges. (So too with lines to two-dimensional planes and planes to three-dimensional spaces.) Is the line a separate reality? Is it the primary reality, with points being only abstractions? In any case, the reductionists' focus on points along does not explain the line.

9.   Sociologism should not be confused with the "historicism" popular in postmodern circles (i.e., that one's historical and cultural milieu completely shapes one's thinking). Under individualism, each culture at any particular time is totally unique, being completely shaped only by the thoughts and actions of the individuals present at that time. Such a total denial of history, cross-cultural universals, or social forces is disquieting to many theorists.

10.   Of course, antireductionists disagree on the nature of the natural sciences. And for them, the failure of reductionism anywhere makes the point of methodological individualism obscure (Dupré 1994: 184). Considerations of political philosophy may also enter the picture: those who espouse conservative views gravitate toward individualism, with its entailed beliefs in individual control and responsibility, and away from holistic points of view that envision using laws and other group-level restraints as means of social change.

6

Religion

Religion is a useful subject for understanding how theorists deal with apparent causes in the sociocultural realm because of the range of its treatment among sociocultural antireductionists.[1] (Theorists who would reduce the entire sociocultural realm will not be dealt with here.) On one extreme are those religious believers who think a sacred level of reality is causally active in all events of the natural order of the world—in fact, medieval "occasionalists" in Christianity and Islam thought God was the *only* real cause at work in the world. On the other extreme are those who think that all religious activity is a powerless epiphenomenon of other sociocultural causes. For them, religion is explained away by identifying the real causes that are actually at work in religious activity. In the middle are those who believe that the fact that believers engage in religious ways of life is by itself enough to make their beliefs, intentions, motives, and so forth into causal forces in the social realm—whether they are true or false, such beliefs are on par with other sociocultural causes. Theorists who believe sociocultural phenomena should only be "interpreted" or "understood" rather than causally explained may treat religion the same as any other sociocultural phenomenon, but beliefs about whether religion is merely an epiphenomenon or not may also very well enter into that approach.

All theorists here treat religion as a natural phenomenon. No reductionist denies the obvious—that religious phenomena exist and apparently motivate believers' behavior. Instead, religion is to be explained as any other part of the sociocultural realm is. And for antireductive theorists, religion is not in a privileged category separate from other sociocultural phenomena. The question is: is religion a unique causal factor among other causal factors in the sociocultural realm whose power cannot be reduced to other sociocultural phenomena, or should it be explained away as no more than a cultural epiphenomenon of social or psychological structures? Is religion always a dependent variable, or is it an independent variable helping to shape personality and to create, reinforce, or challenge forms of social organization (Glock & Hammond 1973: xiii)? Thus, the issue is the structure-reduction of religion: do we need to be structure-reductionists (and hence theory-reductionists) with regard to religion?

A related issue concerns what are the basic units of sociocultural reality. Should a theorist provide a comprehensive theory of religion in the abstract or only deal with some much more specific phenomenon of a religious tradition? The founders of the various social sciences and religious studies dealt with religion comprehensively, i.e., they provided explanations of the origin and nature of religion in general. More recent historians of religions and at least anthropologists tend to focus more on the phenomena from various religious traditions and less on grand theories of religion in general as an abstract entity, thus treating only the various concrete religious phenomena as causes or epiphenomena.

Religious Studies

But first a note on a relatively new player in the field: the academic study of religion as a sociocultural phenomenon—"religious studies." This differs from theology in that the objective is not to expound and defend a particular religious point of view but to understand religious different traditions's practices and beliefs from point of view of their participants and to explain them.[2] The first two parts of this discipline focus directly on empirical research. First is the "history of religions": describing religious phenomena in terms acceptable to the religious practitioners themselves and constructing scholarly histories of the world's religious traditions. In the words of Huston Smith, the objective is to convey the meaning religions carry for the lives of their adherents, i.e., to get into the heart of living faiths to see and even to feel how and why they guide and motivate the lives of those who live them (1965: ix). The second part is the comparative study of religious phenomena, such as the "phenomenology of religion": the comparison of religious phenomena from around the world and the attempt to construct a systematic typology of religious phenomena. The ultimate aim of these two enterprises is to understand, and to make intelligible to others, the behavior and mental universe of the religious (Eliade 1959: 162). The third part of this field involves explaining the religious phenomena and theorizing about the nature of religion. Theorists do not believe that this explanatory part must be in terms acceptable to the religious participants themselves.

The dispute over structure-reductionism is over the role of realities transcending the natural order in the explanations of sociocultural phenomena. To religious studies reductionists, even if a transcendent reality exists, religion is still not a causal force among sociocultural phenomena. Thus, they reject any religious explanations in terms of transcendent entities in favor of the social scientists' natural explanations. Antireductionists believe religious purposes, intentions, and reasons retain a distinct sublevel of sociocultural structuring and so require their own explanation and must play a role in the complete explanation of such phenomena even when they are treated as simply human phenomena—the theorists themselves may reject the existence of any transcendent realities, but the fact that the religious participants do suffices for making religiosity a sociocultural causal structure.

The roots of religious studies can be traced to David Hume's *The Natural History of Religion* written in 1757. The founding of religious studies as a distinct discipline is credited to Max Müller and his idea of a "science of religion" (*Religionswissenschaft*). Although devoutly Christian himself, Müller was nevertheless a reductionist concerning earlier forms of religion. In his search for the origin of religions, he rejected all appeals to a divine source. Instead, for Müller, myths resulted from a "disease of language": in ancient languages, natural phenomena could only be depicted anthropomorphically; archaic people thereby came to think in terms of actors animating the natural phenomena depicted; thus, the language was mistakenly taken as referring to distinct entities (the gods and other supernatural entities) behind events (1882).

Contemporary advocates of reductionism in religious studies are very unclear on what they mean by "reductionism." Even the most adamant advocate, Robert Segal, never explains exactly what he means by "reductionism" (1989, 1992, 1994; Ryba 1994: 15). Antireductionists in religious studies are no better. Apparently each scholar assumes the term has an unambiguous meaning, but different scholars in the field, reductionists and antireductionists alike, use the term "reductionism" differently. Some have very idiosyncratic uses. Others use the term simply to denote analysis or social science as opposed to an approach favored by historians of religions. But, as should be clear by now, analysis or identification of any sociocultural aspects of religious phenomena is not a substantive or any other type of reduction. This lack of clarity leads scholars to speak paradoxically of a need for both reductive and antireductive approaches when they actually mean only that social scientific and "history of religion" approaches to religion are both needed for the most complete explanation of religious phenomena. Other scholars speak of all theories being reductive because any theory selects only some factors for ordering and explaining phenomena. But simply because a theorist must select a point of view, which of necessity must be limited, does not make a theory *reductive*—just having a perspective does not mean one must *reduce reality* to only what is revealed by that perspective. Thus, if one advances a sociological theory and says that a psychological theory is still needed for a more complete comprehension of the phenomenon in question, one is not being a reductionist.

Many reductionists in religious studies think their opponents equate "reductionism" with the *elimination of the phenomena* under study. But apart from individualists in the social sciences (who claim there are no social realities), there are few eliminationists in the sociocultural field.[3] Contrary to what some reductionists in religious studies think, reductionists in the natural sciences who deny biological structures do not deny that *biological phenomena are biological.* Biological functions are still accepted. Rather, reductionists in the natural sciences believe chemical theory *explains* biological phenomena. The phenomena themselves are never questioned. In Ernest Nagel's example, a headache is still a headache even if the detailed physical, chemical, and physiological conditions for its occurrence are ascertained (1961: 364-66). All that is eliminated are the posited explanatory *structures* of the superseded theories. And in the sociocultural field, no one (including Durkheim, Marx, and Freud) argues that religious phenomena are really nonreligious in nature or that there are no religious facts. Rather, sociocultural structure-reductionists are *epiphenomenalists* who claim that the religious level is determined by other real factors and has no causal efficacy of its own—religious phenomena remain religious even though the actual underlying mechanisms causing the appearances have been identified and the phenomena are structurally reducible to other sociocultural factors.

Some reductionists in religious studies do see the difference between eliminationism and reductionism but surprisingly conclude that antireductionists should not be concerned about the latter since the phenomena are saved—all that reductions involve is a relation between theories (e.g., Penner 1989).[4] These reductionists stress that they do not attempt to reduce religion but only to reduce the *explanation* of it (Spiro 1966). But if reductive theories are accepted, religious phenomena remain but are powerless *epiphenomena*. Indeed, the phenomena are now shown to be *delusions*: the real factors producing the phenomena are shown not to be what the religious practitioners thought they were. In short, reductionists here do not bracket the question of the truth of religious ontic belief-claims but answer it negatively. Thus, reductionists in religious studies adopt both naturalism (thus accepting natural explanations as complete accounts of religious phenomena) and a structure- and theory-reductionism of religion as a human phenomenon. Life is not threatened if biological phenomena are ever shown to be the product of quantum level events, but religion is radically discredited by a naturalistic reduction—any transcendent realities are not explained but replaced by natural phenomena.

A related issue involves concept-reductionism. Many reductionists in religious studies think that antireductionists should be concerned only with religious phenomena being described and understood in religious terms and not with structure- and theory-antireductionism. Thus, when antireductionists such as Mircea Eliade (1959) denounce reductionism, all they are really concerned about is *saving the phenomena* and not about how the phenomena should be *explained*. Thus, antireductionists should be satisfied if scholars do not try to reduce the *descriptions* of the religious phenomena themselves (e.g., Proudfoot 1985: 190-216). This once again misses a crucial issue: no one disputes the need to use the participant's religious terminology to *describe* religious phenomena. Everyone studying religion today agrees that concept-antireductionism is needed to discern the *intentionality* of the religious. This also holds for social scientists, regardless of their position on the forms of reductionism: they all accept the need to have references to transcendent realities in the description and initial understanding of any religious phenomena to be explained. Reductionists in religious studies likewise should accept concept-antireductionism for the description and understanding of religious phenomena prior to their explanation. The difference between reductionists and antireductionists here is over whether references to transcendent realities are needed in the *explanation* of religious phenomena. To talk of the "true meaning of religion" (Segal 1989: 9-11) without distinguishing those two contexts only introduces confusion into the matter of reductionism. (Is the *true* meaning the participants' or the theorist's? Does it involve the intentional object or the theoretical explanation?) Thus, antireductionists are also mistaken in thinking that reductionists must deny the participants' religiousness when it comes to explaining the religious phenomena.

Cultural symbol-systems in general may be independent of psychological and social structures, like computer program being independent of the hardware. But antireductionists here insist that religious symbol-systems are independent of other sociocultural systems and that religion must be treated as one causal factor among the set of sociocultural factors in order to understand both religion and the sociocultural realm completely. Religion may be the controlling cause in some cultural phenomena (especially in archaic cultures) and more marginalized in others (especially today in the West). That a reductive or antireductive point of view may control how all the factors are weighted will not be discussed here. Antireductionists insist, however, that religion is not always an epiphenomenon but is also a cause (whether constructive or destructive) in at least some human phenomena.

To reductionists, antireductionists in the history of religions in accepting the religious explanations of religious participants and in accepting religion as a causal sociocultural structure are themselves committed to the reality of transcendent realities. Like scientists under the realist interpretation of theories, they are committed to the reality of the explanatory entities they posit in their theory explaining the phenomena under study. If this is so, religious studies would be like theology. "God" under theistic approaches becomes a causal explanatory posit of a transcendent kind for a religious theory of natural and sociocultural phenomena and of the final meaning of reality. Mircea Eliade is one historian of religion often accused of being a crypto-theologian. The claim is that he did not merely concede that religious believers embrace the reality of the sacred, but that he actually endorsed its reality by explaining religious phenomena in terms of the sacred or the real (e.g., Segal 1989). He, however, claimed he was not engaging in philosophical speculation about whether the sacred is real but was merely dealing with the sacred as an element in "the structure of human consciousness" (Eliade 1978: xiii). For him, human beings are essentially religious—we are *homo religiosus*—but not necessarily as the result of encounters with transcendent realities. There is a universal and irreducible human striving for the sacred, and the sacred is the intentional object of religious experiences. However, Eliade was trying to be neutral on whether the sacred exists independently of human consciousness. In other words, he was advancing an explanation of religious phenomena as the products of some innate structures in human beings that make us all specifically adapted to have experiences we label "religious" while remaining neutral on whether there is a transcendent source of these structures or a reality experienced. What this means is only that historians of religions can in principle advance explanations that are structurally antireductive without a commitment to the substance-antireductionism of denying naturalism. They need not *endorse* transcendent realities, as theologians do. Even if religious experiences involve transcendent realities, religion scholars can treat religious phenomena as human phenomena: the "worldly" elements can be studied by neuroscientists and social scientists—antireductionists simple deny that religious phenomena can be *reduced* to those worldly elements alone.

A related confusion concerns whether religious phenomena are "sui generis." On the level of description, this phrase means only that a religious phenomenon, while certainly human, must be grasped as religious and not merely in terms of physiology or any nonreligious sociocultural category. Antireductive historians of religion stress that a dimension to such phenomena is missed by any nonreligious analysis (e.g., Eliade 1958: xiii). For Rudolph Otto, the nonrational sense of the "numinous" (i.e., the sacred) is a sui generis mental state of a mysterious, awesome, and terrifying wholly other power and thus is an irreducible, primary category undefinable in terms of other categories (1958: 7). On the explanatory level, "sui generis" can have two more meanings. Religious phenomena may be considered sui generis in the sense that they are sociocultural phenomena that need their own unique level of explanation—i.e., they are strictly human phenomena but are causes themselves and thus not structurally reducible to other sociocultural factors. Or religious phenomena may be considered sui generis in that they are human phenomena but reference to transcendent realities is necessary to understand and to explain them fully because the participants utilize the idea of transcendent realities.

But some scholars believe antireductionists in religious studies are committed to a more extreme sense of "sui generis": that religious phenomena are *exclusively* a response to transcendent realities and have no dimensions except the religious (e.g., Segal 1989). Religious phenomena become literally self-generated: they are caused by transcendent realities and thus are unlike any other human phenomena in any way, and thus they are totally impregnable to nonreligious analyses. But no historian of religion denies that there are more dimensions to any religious phenomenon. In Eliade's words, there is no "purely religious datum"—manifestations of the sacred can only be expressed and transmitted in a particular historical context and thus of necessity will always have more than just a religious dimension (1969b: 7-9, 19). The religious level may contribute its own unique causes, but every religious phenomenon has other dimensions. Every religious fact, being a human phenomenon, is never "pure" but is conditioned by everything from the experiencer's physiology to all of his or her sociocultural environment (1969a: 31-32). In short, religious phenomena are also physiological, psychological, and sociocultural phenomena. What structure-antireductionists in religious studies are saying is that in order to get as complete an understanding of religious phenomena as possible they must also be understood on the distinctly religious level and not only as other types of sociocultural phenomena, and when it comes to explaining religious phenomena this unique level of organization also must be included. Thus, religious phenomena must be understood and explained on their own level and cannot be reduced to their "chemical constituents" (contra Spiro 1966: 123).

Antireductionists accept that a religious experience may also be a psychological crisis or related to a social movement, but it is not structurally reducible to the latter—both religious and nonreligious factors are always involved. The multiple dimensions of any religious phenomenon must be studied from different points of view. To adopt an image John Dupré uses for complex phenomena studied in the sciences, religious phenomena are a "causal thicket" too complex for any one perspective to clarify (1994). To accomplish such a pluralistic vision, antireductionists cannot merely state that we should accept every available explanatory approach. Instead, they will need *to limit the scope* of each approach—i.e., each approach must be treated as identifying only *some* of the causes at work in a human phenomenon, not all of them. For example, the antireductive anthropologist Edward Evans-Pritchard saw social accounts as only explaining religion as a factor in our social life—they cannot completely explain all of religion (1965: 121). Through different perspectives, each approach reveals something the others miss, and none reveals the "essence" of a phenomenon. Thus, antireductionists reject any one grand all-encompassing sociocultural theory and want a pluralism of approaches, while reductionists, in denying religion a causal role, are more inclined to see religious studies fitted into a "unity of science" program through a structure-reduction. Under the reductionists' program, religious studies scholars would merely provide data for their social scientific colleagues to explain through reductive approaches. Reductive philosophers of religion would complete the program by showing how the notion of a transcendent reality is nonsense and by providing naturalistic interpretations of natural explanations of religious experiences.

This means that under the antireductionists' approach the relation between the history of religions and the social sciences is less problematic than reductionists in religious studies think. Indeed, everyone agrees that social scientists contribute a great deal to the understanding of religion. As discussed in the last chapter, the social sciences, like the natural sciences, are not per se reductive, nor do they deal with the issue of the truth of religious claims about transcendent realities (contra Segal 1994). To say that aspects of religious ways of life can be explained socially or psychologically does not alarm anyone, but to say religion is "reduced" or "partially reduced" or "explained reductively" is problematic. Still, for reduction-ists, the only alternatives in explaining religion are either a commitment to a specific religion or accepting some social scientific theory as its complete (and hence reductive) explanation (e.g., Segal 1989). However, that is wrong: there is no forced choice between either endorsing the reality of transcendent realities or accepting a naturalistic reduction. Instead, structure-antireductionists advance a third position: endorsing religion as a causal human phenomenon without accepting or rejecting substance-antireductionism. Historians of religion can forego all high-level theological and philosophical explanations and still practice their craft more closely tied to the descriptive level, advancing at most low-level antireductive theories (e.g., phenomenological typologies) that are neither theological nor reductive while remaining neutral on the metaphysical issue of substance-reductionism. In short, religious studies need not be a form of theology.

The need for to clarify the ideas surrounding "reductionism" is greater in this field than in any of the other areas covered in this book, since the disputants bandy the word about freely while spending little time on what the term means. Many of the discussions in this field would disappear if, for example, antireductionists could see that structure-reductionists need not deny the existence of religious phenomena. So too, many scholars still speak of "reducing religion" when they mean only that the reality of transcendent realities or the soul is denied (e.g., Segal 1989: 27), not religion as a unique aspect of culture. But structure-reductionism does not follow from substance-reductionism: structure-antireductionists can affirm the causal potency of religions in the sociocultural realm without endorsing the existence of any transcendent realities. In short, the choice is not either a theological affirmation of God or a purely secular substance- and structure-reductionism. However, the latter approach is gaining strength within religious studies, as exemplified by the new interdisciplinary "cognitive science of religion" in which theories of the naturalness of religion effectively remove the transcendent from religious studies altogether (Lawson & McCauley 1990; Guthrie 1993; Rue 2005; Singerland 2008).

Religion as Epiphenomenon

Structure- and theory-reductionists in the area of religion believe that the true basic units of sociocultural causation do not include religion. Their reaction to religion goes beyond merely the naturalistic denial of any intervening supernatural realities that would make religion a privileged category. What reductionists claim is that all of religion is a human phenomenon that is explainable in nonreligious sociocultural categories—not just the social or psychological "dimension," "component," or "expression" of religion but all of it, including the apparently universal human urge for religious meaning that be naturalistically explained. The physiological factors and the real cultural, social, and psychological factors operating in religious phenomena are identified and applied. The content of religious belief is irrelevant, and the fact of religious faith becomes a phenomenon to be explained from a third-person perspective. In sum, religion even as only a sociocultural phenomenon is not a causal factor in the sociocultural realm but a powerless epiphenomenon.

The consequences of this approach are that the claims that religious persons advance about the real source of their beliefs and practices are always mistaken and that it is the scholars' job to identify the actual sociocultural forces at work in all religious phenomena. Reductionists may accept that we have genuine social or psychological religious needs, but they contend that there is no transcendent religious reality to fulfill them. They may even maintain a positive attitude to the presence of religion—i.e., they may feel religion is a useful social or psychological fiction—but they assert that in a fundamental sense religious persons are deluded as to the real forces at work in reality. The surface features of religion are in fact moved by natural forces that the religious are missing. What ostensibly motivates the religious can be dismissed entirely in favor of the real physiological, economic, social, psychological, or other factors that are identified as the real forces driving their actions. In this way, reductionists dismiss the justifications that the religious proffer as ultimately *irrational* and their actions are explained away.[5]

The search for the real sociocultural causes has taken two paths. Earlier social scientists tried to discern these causes in the early history of religion. The origin of religion was revealed in its earliest forms, and revealing this origin in human culture, along with detailing religion's subsequent historical development, provided a complete nonreligious account of religion. More recent social scientists have looked for the cause of religion's presence in the needs that religious faith satisfies in persons and societies today and thus cause it to remain active. The historical origin is irrelevant—early forms of religion are the same as later forms from this point of view. Instead, the objective is to identify conditions today in persons and societies that trigger religious phenomena as effects. In the reductionists' view, religion is constructed exclusively out of those needs (i.e., functions) and material considerations, and so there is nothing else to explain about religion.

A common concept social scientists use for this is "*projection*." This concept, the roots of which can be traced to Ludwig Feuerbach (1957), is that an idea arises in our mind and is "projected" upon reality. This may be meant neutrally: what is projected may or may not actually exist independently of our projection—all that is being emphasized in calling such notions "projections" is simply that the notions *originate* with us and are not imposed on us by reality. Everything from mathematics to music are projections that may or may not tap into a structure of reality. In short, religious and other ideas about the nature of reality are human constructs in that they originate with us and are open to psychological or social explanations as such. Whether our constructs correspond to a reality or are useful is another issue.

To reductionists, religious ideas, unlike those of science, are explained away as *only* projections. Religious ideas of transcendence are projections of our psychological or social needs or attitudes and do not reflect any other reality. There is nothing else behind them but only the natural phenomena causing the process of projecting—there is no transcendent reality that they "hit," or, if there is such a reality, hitting it would be only a coincidence since we have no experiential grounds or other reason to believe our projections should bear any relation to that reality. The belief-content of religious ideas is irrelevant, since such ideas mask the real psychological or social causes behind religious phenomena. The reductionist Sigmund Freud distinguished the two senses of "projection" when discussing "illusions": both his own theories and religious ideas are "illusions" in the neutral sense that they originate with us; but his own theories, unlike religious ideas, are capable of correction and thus are not "delusions" (1964: 53). Freud also called a belief an "illusion" when wish-fulfillment is a prominent factor in its motivation; its relation to reality could then be ignored (1964: 31). Illusions are not necessarily false—they may in fact conform to reality—but they are based prominently on wish-fulfillment and so warrant caution (1964: 47-53). It is their psychological nature, not their epistemic status, that makes them "illusions."

The history of the reduction of religion begins with the founder of positivism, the philosopher Auguste Comte (1975). Advocacy of any religious transcendent reality was to be displaced completely by the naturalistic position of science. (Comte in this regard tried to develop a naturalistic religion of humanity.) Religion and all other human phenomena become the subject of scientific study in a new empirical science of society. His naturalistic thrust gave the social sciences their initial reductive animus against religious ontological claims. The founders of the various social sciences had a negative attitude toward religious transcendent claims, leading to reductive approaches, although Émile Durkheim and Carl Jung thought of religion as a positive force facilitating the true sociocultural reality behind religious phenomena for the benefit of society or the individual.

The earliest social science—anthropology—was founded by Edward Tylor. For Tylor, religion is superstition, and its explanation lies in its historical origins: once we identify religion's earliest form, we can see what is essential to all religion and can trace its stages of development as cultures evolve (1871). Tylor found religion's original form to be "animism," the attempt to explain natural phenomena in terms of animation by spirits and gods. More recently, the quest for the historical origins of religion and general theories of its nature based on the study of tribal cultures supposedly uncontaminated by the modern world have not been as popular among anthropologists, having been replaced instead by concerns for the current sociocultural religious phenomena and detailed studies of the specifics of particular cultures. But natural explanations of religion are still the standard. Many anthropologists do not explicitly question the reality of the sacred. But, for example, Bronislaw Malinowski's theories about how social forces shape and are shaped by religion are scarcely consistent with a view of divinity as entering into and exercising control over human events (Glock & Hammond 1973: xiv-xv). Today physicalists' anthropological "cognitive science" denies the reality of any transcendent realities and explains religion away by structurally reducing it to the causal infrastructures of culture or to an epiphenomenal evolutionary byproduct (Boyer 2001; Atran 2002; but see Wilson 2002 on religion as an adaptive cause, such as shared religious beliefs and rituals promoting group identity).

Sociologists after Comte continued on the reductive path. For Émile Durkheim, religion is essentially social (1915: 423)—in fact, the only reality behind religious representations is society. The power of society and our dependence on it are projected onto reality as superhuman beings (the gods). The group, not the individual, is central, and the function of religion is to reinforce social solidarity. In this way, religion is essential to society, and in some form it will always be with us. As a social scientist, Durkheim was not concerned with speculation about the earliest forms of religion but only with what could be observed in his day. He concluded that totemism, the most "elementary" form of religion he knew, created both religion and a sense of society. Through a totem, the group represented itself by means of a projected symbol. That is, the god of the clan is nothing but the clan itself, personified and represented under the visible form of an animal or vegetable that serves as the clan's totem (1964: 206). Thus, the real power behind religious symbols is only *society*. In this way, religion is not denied—indeed, Durkheim valued it—but its power is explained completely in terms of society. Society is "the soul of religion," and religion is "the image of society" (1964: 419, 421).

Durkheim is not saying that by worshiping a totem, a group is knowingly worshiping itself, but he is claiming to have identified the only reality behind religious projections—the society itself—and is using that reality to explain the surface religious phenomena. Modern theists do not worship society, but the reality of God or any other form of the "sacred" (things set apart as superior, powerful, or forbidden) is reduced to only society. We must admit religion is religion, but we can explain away its power. Thus, no concept-reductionism is intended—the religious symbols still must be studied as intending religious realities. But there is a substance- and structure-reduction of the reality behind religious phenomena to sociocultural phenomena. There is nothing more to religion than its social fact. In his more philosophical musings, Durkheim does concede religious projections may reflect something more than society. Nothing, however, in the main body of his sociological work suggests that anything other than natural phenomena is involved in religion or that his explanation of religion is intended to be anything less than a complete reduction of all of religion to the social.[6] Many social scientists have followed Durkheim's views on religious projections. For example, the anthropologist Edmund Leach saw ritual action and belief as forms of symbolic statements about the ideal social order (1954: 14). The spirits of the Kachin of Burma are "in the last analysis nothing more than ways of describing the formal relationships that exist between real persons and real groups in ordinary Kachin society" (1954: 182). Similarly, many theorists see myths, which ostensibly are about the creation of the world or of particular natural or sociocultural phenomena or the interactions of gods and humans, as no more than symbolic narratives concerning whatever social, psychological, or physical phenomena are taken by the theorist to be fundamental.

The social reductive approach can also be seen in Marxist economic and political thought (McKown 1975). Karl Marx gave an explanation of religion in terms of economic and material needs. Our basic material needs (food, shelter, clothing, and so forth) are the base determining our actions; religious projections are merely part of the "superstructure" of beliefs determined by this base. To Marx, religion is a purely illusory ideology that legitimatizes the ruling classes' position of power and that has only negative effects on society. Its chief function is to keep the oppressed oppressed. Religion is simply the "sigh of the oppressed creature, the heart of a heartless world, as it is the spirit of spiritless conditions" (McKown 1975: 52). People have responded to their alienation by projecting an imaginary home for themselves in heaven where they will finally be happy. Religion is thus the "opium of the people," giving people some comfort while creating fantasies that keep them from rebelling against the true cause of our suffering. Thus, the abolition of religion as the illusory happiness of the people is required for our real happiness to emerge. Marx, unlike Durkheim, thought religion will eventually disappear from all societies. It will disappear when the economic conditions of society change: religion emerged out of our alienation from what we produce and from other people caused by capitalism and will wither away when this economic base ceases.

The reduction of religion in Marx's social and economic determinism is clear. All of religion is reduced to a mere passive effect of the material bases of societies with no substance of its own—a totally superficial epiphenomenon of no consequence. However, Marxists since the 1970's, following leads from as far back as Friedrich Engels, have been more willing to consider that religious systems are active, independent forces interacting with the material bases. Religion is no longer always treated as a subordinate element but often is considered an important part in the birth and consolidation of social structures (Maduro 1977). Nevertheless, in classical Marxist thought, religion is barely worth bothering with.

With Sigmund Freud, the reductionist approach switches to the possibility of reducing religion to something below the social level—the *individual*. Religion arises from biological and mental factors and serves the individual, not society. Freud saw his role as a scientist as simply to explain how this and other religious beliefs arose and why we still maintain them now that the truth of science has arrived. The answer he found lies in our *unconscious*: religion functions on the level of mind below the conscious, not on the rational level where its doctrines can be plainly seen to be simply absurd. Its power is solidified early in our childhood. In his rather fanciful attempts at the history of Judaism and religion in general, Freud traced the origin of religion to the origin of the incest taboo in the "primal horde" and the slaying of the "primal father" (1950, 1955). Religion arose to alleviate the guilt repressed in the unconscious surrounding that alleged historical event. The god of monotheism thus is nothing but an exalted father figure symbolically projected onto a purposeless and indifferent universe. This creation of a heavenly father is pure wish-fulfillment—the projection (in the pejorative sense) of a protective child-hood father. Religion is "the obsessional neurosis of humanity" (1964: 43). This makes religions "neurotic relics" to be outgrown now that science is here. But at present, religion remains the "universal neurosis of humanity." To him, religious persons do not know the real motives that impel them to their religious practices, but he had now identified the unconscious causes at work: religion is a coping mechanism in reaction to our insignificance and impotence in the harsh and hostile universe (1964: 32). In Peter Berger's words, for Freud, religion "is the childish fantasy that our parents run the universe for our benefit, a fantasy from which the mature individual must free himself in order to attain whatever measure of stoic resignation he is capable of" (1969: 56).

It is this wish-fulfilling quality that is central to Freud's treatment of religion. With religion, we have unknowing generated a picture of the world the way we would like it to be. All of religion is an illusion, not because it is necessarily an error, but because it is created only by our wishes (1964: 30-31). Religious beliefs are the "fulfillments of the oldest, strongest and most urgent wishes of mankind (1964: 30). Freud realized he could not judge its "reality value" because he dealt only with psychological causes and assessing truth-value does not lie within the scope of that inquiry (1964: 31, 33). He conceded that our wishes may in fact correspond to something real, but he believed such a belief would not be justified by anything we have experienced. His negative judgment toward religion extended passed religious ideas: religious experiences are, according to Freud, no more than purely subjective substitutes for sexual needs. The sense of any transcendent reality is dismissed as a self-delusion: the projection of the feeling of dependence upon one's father as an ideal. In sum, there is no more encompassing reality at work in religion than the mental and biological levels of the natural order (1964: 47-53).

Freud's former colleague and friend Carl Jung is usually considered to be anti-reductive toward religion, but the thrust of his thought is as reductive as Freud's. His attitude toward religion was certainly more positive than was Freud's—for him religion contributed to good mental health, while for Freud it was a neurosis—but in the end, the reality in religious phenomena was once again entirely reduced to biological and psychological forces. He saw psychotherapy as leading to the integration of the conscious and unconscious parts of the psyche (the "self"). This, Jung proposed, is also the real goal of religion. In particular, religious symbols mediate between the conscious and unconscious parts of the psyche (1938, 1964).

Jung shifted the locus of religion to the universal structures on the unconscious level of psychological forces. The level of the unconscious that we all share (the "collective unconscious") is populated with inherited structures or dispositions to symbolize in certain ways ("archetypes"). The particular content of the symbol becomes fixed only on the conscious level of the mind. But religious statements without exception have to do only with the reality of the psyche (1973: 102). All religious symbols have no objective referent other than the collective unconscious. Religious symbols are simply how the psyche symbolizes itself. Jung, like Freud (1964: 31, 33), claimed not to have been interested in the philosophical issue of whether God exists but only with psychological matters approached through science (1938: 2). He did not deny the possibility of such a reality, but he did deny the religious have any access to any reality beyond the collective unconscious. Instead, Jung reduced all religious realities to projections of the *collective unconscious*. God is reduced to a symbol of the integrated self. All religious experience is only the ego's experience of the content of the collective unconscious, and so all religious phenomena are aspects of that reality projected externally as if they were other than ourselves. The consequence of this "translating" all religious terminology into terms of his psychological theory is that the religious must be deemed to be mistaken about the true reality behind their claims and that this reality is in fact only natural (Jones 1993: 169-83). This is a reduction to different psychological and biological structures than was Freud's but no less thorough.

Today the most active issue in psychology of religion is whether religion offers anything unique to our psychological and social "well-being," and again the issue of whether religion is reducible figures centrally (Silberman 2005). Antireductionists argue for an interdisciplinary, multimethod research program in which religion is seen as a causal factor offering its own contribution (Pargament 2002). Reductionists may accept multiple methods too but not treat religion as a cause.

Functionalists are another group of social theorists who need to be mentioned. As noted in the last chapter, functionalists, rather than giving causal explanations, explain the persistence of a sociocultural phenomenon in terms of its useful effects or the needs it fulfills for a person or society as a whole. For example, for the sociobiologist Edward Wilson, religion serves a biological function: the successful forms of religion confer a biological advantage for the survival of the genes of its practitioners (1978: 182-86). The historical origins of religion and the culturally-relative beliefs and practices that practitioners use to justify or explain their actions are irrelevant. Any religious beliefs will do—the physical, psychological, or social functions beneath the surface of the phenomena are all that matter. Religion persists because of the various underlying needs it fulfills, and if those needs cannot be fulfilled in other ways—an issue functionalists do not usually address—then religion will remain with us forever, no matter how absurd the beliefs and practices appear to the scientifically-minded.

A functionalist approach need not be reductive—after all, each phenomenon in culture no doubt serves one or more functions in some sense, and its substance need not be undercut merely by identifying those functions. But in the case of religion, social theorists tend to equate its only reality with its function. That is, once we have identified the functions religion performs, there is nothing left to explain. Indeed, functionalists tend to *define* religion in terms of functions. Functionalists also are naturalists, and, as such, they deny any transcendent realities. Religion is thus substantively reduced to nothing more than its naturalistic functions. Other sociocultural phenomena are already exclusively natural, and so it is only religion that needs to be treated differently from how its practitioners treat it: its content is being summarily denied in a way that is not done for other activity. Thus, the effects of naturalistic metaphysics enter into the theory of these social theorists. However, functionalists are also usually structure-*antireductionists* since, in regarding religion as fulfilling a social or psychological function, they regard religion as an actual causal factor in the sociocultural realm. They could, however, be structure-reductionists if they argue that nonreligious social or psychological dimensions of religious phenomena are the only actual causal agents.[7]

Religion as a Sociocultural Cause

Structure-antireductionists' central tenet is that religious persons really do act for religious reasons—whether or not any transcendent realities exist—and not for unconscious social or other causes. Thus, religion is a real cause in human cultures on par with economics and the other sociocultural causes in shaping our beliefs and behavior. Max Weber was a champion of this approach: religion has been a factor in social change and economic development, and so no explanation of a social phenomenon is complete without the inclusion of religion as a causal factor (1963, 1984). The role of religion is complex: social, psychological, and cultural forces may shape religion, but religion in at least some instances can in turn shape those forces and so are not always merely epiphenomena. Nor can any sociocultural phenomena be reduced to exclusively a religious phenomenon. Economic, political, and other sociocultural factors may contribute to the explanation of the rise, persistence, spread, and fall of a particular religious tradition or any other religious phenomenon. But under the antireductive approach, there is more to religion than its social and psychological dimensions, and so it cannot be reduced to those factors but can enter into explanations as a causal factor of these sociocultural phenomena.

Theorists under this approach differ concerning religion's alleged cognitive content with regard to claims about transcendent realities. They may (1) endorse the cognitive content of one religious tradition or one more abstract philosophical interpretation of religion in general, (2) be neutral on the issue, or (3) be naturalistic substance-reductionists and deny the alleged cognitive content of beliefs entailed by all religious ways of life, or (4) simply ignore the issue. A theorist of the first type is committed to religious theories (either accepting some version of the participants' account or advancing one of his or her own) and so advance theological theories; one of the second type is not; and one of the third, implicitly or explicitly repudiates such theories. But all four types can treat religious beliefs, like all human beliefs, as projections in the neutral sense. The concern of theorists of the second type is that the *believers themselves* are motivated by their beliefs—i.e., that objects of faith exist at least subjectively for the believers is enough for religion to be a causal factor. Religious phenomena exist as social realities, and religious experiences occur, whether a transcendent reality exists or not. Similarly, theorists of the third type treat religious beliefs like any other motivating beliefs, even if the believers are considered to be drastically wrong about alleged religious realities. Thus, for the second, third and fourth types of theorists, the mere fact that religious believers are committed to a religious reality is sufficient to make religion a causal force in the sociocultural realm. In short, religion is structurally real in the sociocultural realm whether or not participants' intentional object (transcendent realities) really exist. We need not determine if the world is flat or not when the only question is whether a group acts on that belief. In this way, social scientists in accepting religion as a cause may remain neutral on whether transcendent realities exist. The only religious causal factor such theorists are committed to is simply religion as a sociocultural reality. (But by this reasoning, astrology and alchemy are *real sociocultural causes* as long as they have followers even though presumably they have no real structures in nature. So too, if religion eventually disappears through cultural evolution, it would lose any structural power in the sociocultural sphere.)

Thus, religion is not be reduced to social or psychological phenomena. Instead, a religious event is to be explained in part, for example, in terms of a historical narrative in which religious phenomena are treated as causes equally with other sociocultural phenomena. Antireductive explanations thereby treat religion as an element of a larger causal order of the entire sociocultural level, and antireductive interpretations of a sociocultural phenomenon's meaning include religion. Reductionists ignore the religious believers' explanation of their beliefs and practices since the religious do not really know what is going on—it is the theorist (each according to his or her theory) who knows why the believers are really doing what they do. Reductionists thus are not concerned with the content of religious beliefs. An account external to the believers is imposed. Antireductionists, on the other hand, must take the content of such beliefs seriously, not because they must accept the truth of such claims, but because the human phenomenon of religious intentionality itself figures as a cause among sociocultural causes. Antireductive theorists need to understand whatever significance or meaning the religious phenomena hold for the insiders to explain how they act. Moreover, they, unlike their reductionist colleagues, must be more interested in what makes religion a distinct sociocultural factor.

The sociologist Peter Berger is a prime example of a social theorist of the second type—i.e., when writing as a sociologist, he attempts to maintain a methodological neutrality on the issue of the alleged truth of religious claims concerning a transcendent reality. Under this approach, social theorists studying religion simply bracket the issue of the ultimate truth or falsity of claims regarding transcendent realities entailed by religious practices and deal only with what is empirically available, i.e., the complex of human experience and thought that purports to refer to the gods (1974: 125-26). In any empirical frame of reference, transcendence must appear as a projection (1969: 83). God is thus an objective factor in American culture because the concept motivates believers; whether there is a transcendent reality behind the concept is not an issue for social theorists. Treating religion as a projection does not distort the believer's perspective, since Berger requires, as a follower of Weber's "understanding" approach, that we see the phenomena "from within," i.e., view it in terms of the meanings intended by the believer (1974: 129). Thereby, the content of the believer's claims remains intact.

Within this framework, the religious projections can be dealt with as such—i.e., as products of human consciousness and activity—and the question of whether they may not also refer to something other than the human consciousness in which they originate is a philosophical issue that can be bracketed (Berger 1967: 100). Calling religion a "projection" in the neutral sense does not preclude the possibility that it may refer to something other than ourselves. As Berger notes, *mathematics* is also a projection of structures of human consciousness onto reality, but these structures have turned out to correspond to something independent of us (1967: 180-81; 1969: 45-47). Religious projections too may turn out also to be "signals of transcendence," but this is not a sociological issue (1969). Even religious believers who are committed to the reality of some transcendent realities can treat their ideas as projections for social scientific purposes and leave the philosophical issue of their possible truth or falsity for another day. This "methodological atheism" (1967: 100) is an instance of the "sociology of knowledge" approach in which what is accepted as knowledge by a group is examined as such, regardless of whether the alleged knowledge is correct or not. All beliefs are explained in terms of the supporting social *conditions*, and not by the *reasons* internal to science or religion supposedly determining the beliefs. Thus, social theorists can in principle bracket the issue of postulated religious realities and deal only with religious phenomena as real factors interlocking with economic, political, and other sociocultural factors.

Berger is much more positive than the reductionist social theorists discussed above: unlike Freud and Jung who advanced similar philosophical qualifications, Berger does not advance a reductive theory of religion but actually remains neutral. And, at those times when he does write as a religiously-committed believer using sociological data to infer the existence of God (1969, 1979), he realizes he "can claim no authority as a sociologist" for his position (1969: ix). He asserts that we need a substantive definition of "religion" in terms of the beliefs of religious persons, rather than merely a functional definition. Religion is not "flattened out" as a sociocultural phenomenon and treated like any other sociocultural phenomenon (1974: 128-29). There is also more to religion even when it is treated as a natural phenomenon than just the functions that religious beliefs and practices fulfill—the *content* of the beliefs and practices for the believers becomes part of what must be understood and utilized by social theorists. Human phenomena connected to belief in transcendent realities become part of the causal phenomena of religion. Thereby, referring to the sacred as something the religious believe in becomes a necessary part of social scientific causal explanations.

The third and fourth types of antireductive social theorist takes another tack on the philosophical issue, while attempting to maintain neutrality in the scientific study of religion. For these groups, the question of whether religious transcendent claims are true is answered negatively or simply ignored, although (unlike reductionists) they do accept religion as a sociocultural factor. Two students of the sociologist Talcott Parsons represent them. Parsons himself was antireductive regarding religion (he saw Christianity as an important and valuable social fact in Western cultures), neutral in his sociology on whether there is more to religion than just the sociocultural dimension, and very negative in his philosophical judgment on whether religious claims regarding transcendent realities are in fact true (1937).

The sociologist Robert Bellah follows Parsons on all three points. In granting religion an "autonomous sphere of existence" (1970b: 3), Bellah advocates a "symbolic realism" that denies any reduction of religion to the merely social or psychological or, indeed, to anything other than religion itself (1970a: 253). Under symbolic realism, religious phenomena have to be treated as religious. Only after the symbols have been explicated as religious is the critical issue of their social and psychological consequences to be addressed (1970c: 114). On the other hand, the reductive approach is, in effect, a theological judgment that science is superior to religion (1970c: 114). Instead, religion must be taken seriously as a "reality sui generis" (1970a: 253) and must be treated as a reality equal to the others studied in the social sciences. Only symbolic realism treats religious beliefs and practices as extremely important for both the maintenance and transformation of social and psychological structures (1970c: 114)—only this gives religion its due.

Bellah is thus a structure-antireductionist with regard to religion as a causal factor among sociocultural factors and a concept-antireductionist with regard to religious terminology. However, he is also a substance-reductionist concerning religious claims. In his particular naturalistic reduction, religious symbols are "nonobjective" and cannot be reduced to empirical propositions because they express another reality—"the feelings, values, and hopes of subjects," and other purely human phenomena (1970a: 253). They do not express any reality apart from human experience and certainly not a transcendent reality. Religious symbols have no "preterhuman" origins, nor do they tell us anything about the universe (1970a: 195, 1970c: 113). Religious claims are substantively reduced to something not intended by religious participants—religion becomes only a matter of feeling and subjectivity. Thus, when Bellah says "religion is true" (1970a: 253), we must realize this major limitation. Religion is not reduced to a social or psychological projection (1970c: 113), since it has its own independent significance; but this significance is still limited to the strictly human need for *meaning*. Only human phenomena, not any transcendent reality or dimension to reality, is involved.

Another of Parsons's students, the anthropologist Clifford Geertz, takes the fourth approach. His antireductive predecessors in his field include Edward Evans-Pritchard who attempted to get away from all-encompassing social explanations of religion and to look instead only at the "social refraction" of religion in particular African cultures. That is, social science only covers aspects of religion and is not a general explanation of all of it. For example, the spirits of the Nuer tribe "mirror" the social structure, but this merely shows us how the idea of spirit "takes various forms corresponding to departments of social life"—it does not enable us to understand the "intrinsic nature" of the religious idea itself. The sociological information does not help us to understand the specifically religious dimension any better (1956: 121, 320). For that, as well as its social refraction, we have to examine the Nuer's religion from the "inside," to see the Nuer way of life the way the Nuer do. For Geertz, culture arises naturalistically in the context of the social, psychological, and biological layers. But the "webs of significance" of culture are a layer distinct from the psychological and social bases and are not reducible to them. Culture constitutes a reality confronting and shaping us. It existed before each of us is born, and thus it creates us as much as we create it. Any explanation of religion that does not involve trying to grasp the system of meanings it conveys is like trying to explain a computer without mentioning a program or a book without reference to the meaning of the words (Pals 2006: 283).

But in his professional work Geertz shows no interest in the issue of the possible existence of a reality transcending the natural order. Such questions are for philosophers, not scientists. Still, his entire approach is completely naturalistic. He defines "religion" with no reference to a transcendent reality but only to a "general order of existence" (1966). This may or may not involve transcendent realities for the participant. Religion for him is simply a component of culture, albeit a central "cultural system" by which we try to make sense of our experiences. According to Geertz, this drive to make sense out of experience is as pressing as our biological needs. Thus, we cannot interpret religion in a reductionist fashion as nothing but a thinly disguised expression of something other than it seems to be—i.e., attempts to provide orientation for an organism that otherwise cannot live in a world it is unable to understand (1973: 140-41). In sum, any sacred transcendent reality is not necessary in his concept- and structure-antireductionism.

This discussion leads to one conclusion: social theorists can be structure-antireductionists concerning religious phenomena in the sociocultural realm while still agreeing or disagreeing with reductionists on the philosophical issue of substance-reductionism. The structure-reductionist issue is independent of the substance one, and only the former is relevant to the social sciences. Thus, contrary to a popular opinion, social theorists need not be structure-, theory-, or concept-reductionists toward religion to practice their trade. Antireductive theorists can be religious, neutral, or antireligious on the philosophical issue of the possible truth of religious ontological claims, or simply uninterested in the issue. No new emergent or underlying realities are accepted beyond the sociocultural realm, but religion can still be seen as an irreducible member of the set of sociocultural causes. Structure-reductionists usurp the role of philosophy when they assert that the substance-reduction of religion to merely what social scientists find is a *necessary consequence* of social science itself. Most often no philosophical argument is advanced for this maneuver; it is simply assumed that this must be the case. But the case of the antireductionist social theorists shows that one can practice a social science by sticking to the *structural* issue of the role of religion in the sociocultural realm without taking a position on *substance*-reductionism.

Metaphysics, Empirical Data, and the Social Sciences

Moreover, this means there is more to being a structure-reductionist concerning religion than merely having a negative judgment on the substantive ontological issue. One can be a naturalist and antireligious and still accept religious phenomena as causal sociocultural factors. Thus, explaining away religion does not turn on one's position on the cognitive content of religious claims concerning transcendent realities. It cannot be claimed that the rejection of religion as a causal factor in the sociocultural realm by such reductionists as Durkheim and Freud was a consequence of their belief that religious claims are false. The substantive and structural issues of reductionism cannot be related that simply. There must be more to why reductionists reject religion as a causal factor since antireductionists can agree with them on their philosophical judgment without following them in their reductive turn.

If structure-reductionism is defended only on philosophical grounds, it is as metaphysical as a position defended by religiously-committed believers on grounds related solely to their faith. Thus, for structure-reductionism to be a legitimate scientific option, advocates must defend it on social scientific grounds—i.e., by showing on social scientific grounds that religious phenomena should not be treated as causal realities. This requires showing that theories treating religion as an epiphenomenon are superior on empirical grounds to those that do not. Thus, structure-reductionists need to show that nonreligious social, psychological, or cultural forces actually determine both the impetus to be religious and the substance of all religious beliefs and practices. Only then would religion have been shown not to be a causal force and effectively explained away. Thereby, reductionists would have a theory by which religious behavior makes sense but is of no consequence.

However, if we accept an irreducible reality to the entire sociocultural realm, then antireductionists with regard to religion do have the *prima facie* easier and more credible case. Throughout history, religion appears to have been a force independent of its economic and other sociocultural bases. It has never been simply a private or trivial matter but has apparently been one cause in major economic and political changes throughout the world. Today religion still appears to be a causal force in the sociocultural realm in every corner of the world. Indeed, it often appears to be *the* cause of why the social world is as it is. So too, the rise of fervent fundamentalists in cultures around the world must be explained. That this is occurring in different religious traditions may indeed make it readily explainable by reductionists in terms of economics, social classes, or other social or psychological realities. But on the surface, the content of religious beliefs appears to be a motivating factor in the behavior of the religious, and explanations of them in other terms alone appears difficult. To refute the obvious, the initial burden must be on the reductionists.

In addition, another problem must be pointed out: the *metaphysical nature* of reductionism. The reductionists' metaphysics directs the course of their sociocultural theorizing and the interpretation of any data presented. The same does not apply to *antireductionists* since they can be neutral to a religion's metaphysical claims—again, one can be a substance-reductionist and still be a structure-antireductionist with regard to religion's role in the sociocultural realm. In addition, antireductionists have to study the content of religious beliefs and practices and their sociocultural context more closely to identify the various factors that they weigh against each other. Weber's detailed study of the rise of capitalism and Protestantism (1984), regardless of any problems his theory might have, is a good contrast to Marxist edicts on the subject. Because metaphysics is broader and deeper than any empirical findings, empirical studies cannot force a change in metaphysical commitment. Like anyone under the thrall of metaphysics, no empirical evidence could in principle refute reductionists' theories and reveal religion to be something other than an epiphenomenon. Their metaphysics dictates in advance that there is always a causal arrow from some other sociocultural factor or base to religion, and no social scientific study alone could possibly dissuade them from thinking religion is anything but a powerless epiphenomenon. Factors other than sociocultural data would have to make them change their minds.

The metaphysical nature of the reductionism presents a major problem for evaluating whether to accept or reject reductive sociocultural theories of religion. Reductionism is built into social scientific theories in the way speculative metaphysics is not built into natural scientific theories. As discussed in Chapter 3, scientists may be neutral on the issue of substance-reductionism. Moreover, the intricacies of any particular natural scientific theory are irrelevant to this issue and at best are of only limited significance to the issues of structure- and theory-reductionism. But in the social sciences, the metaphysics of substance-reductionism infuse theories of structural reductionists. In addition, there is no isolatable component of their global theories dealing with religion alone that can be evaluated independently of the other components. We have to evaluate, for example, Freud's theory as a whole to judge whether his reductive view of religions is credible. And it should also be remembered that Marxism, Freudianism, and Jungianism are not disinterested attempts at understanding and explanation but are attempts at practical systems for social or psychological change. Reductionism in Marxism and Freudianism has as one goal the complete elimination of religion. Trying to evaluate a metaphysical system is notoriously difficult, but trying to evaluate systems that can be likened to naturalized religions is even more difficult.

In particular, empirical findings end up being irrelevant to judging the competing reductive and antireductive claims. The problem, again, is that the metaphysical nature of the reductionist's commitment dictate how the theorists will interpret any data that might be found. For example, how could Marxists establish by an empirical test that the economic bases cause a change in religion rather than vice versa? Weber, for one, would reverse the causal arrow (1984). Antireductionists might seem to have the edge here, since they do more detailed studies and so they must know more about the phenomena under study; but reductionists think they have good reasons to ignore such content. A more general problem for any theory is how social scientists could prove by empirical data that in the complex circumstances of any given historical event the cause must in principle always be one factor or another and never religion. What type of data could be presented in principle that would be immune to obvious counter-interpretations by other social theorists and thus could be used to decide between the competing theories?

One basic problem here is that personal prejudice can shape one's metaphysical outlook more than any actual empirical results and that this determines one's sociocultural theory. The hostility and contempt Freud, the self-professed "godless Jew," felt toward religion as a sociocultural force preceded any research he did in medicine and psychoanalysis—indeed, it may have existed from his childhood—and thus his prejudice is not the product of research on religion but a prior cause of his reductive theory. Today, many academics suffer, in Thomas Nagel's phrase, from "fear of religion"—i.e., they *want* atheism to be true and are uneasy about the fact that some intelligent and well-informed people are religious (1997: 130). Wanting religion to go away may well affect how one approaches religion professionally. Indeed, many theorists in American political science largely ignore the role of religion in human affairs—despite its apparent importance in public affairs around the world—because certain social theories dominating political science circles predict the inevitable decline of religion; these theories dictate what political scientists consider important and what they consider irrelevant (Hertzke 1988). Indeed, even some sociologists accuse sociologists in general of frequently ignoring evidence; ideology, power, and network ties seem to determine what social scientists believe; and this has kept the social sciences from progressing (Cole 1996: 284-85). For example, to ignore the apparent religious motives in virtually every war around the world today seems incredible. The attacks of September 11th have not effected a dramatic change. We need not agree with George Bernard Shaw that religion is ultimately the only real force in the world to argue that religion must a factor in sociocultural phenomena. But for these theorists, religion is no more than a persisting folk custom with no causal force. In effect, because these theorists cannot personally take religion seriously, they cannot see how anyone could. Thereby, religion as a social force is filtered out of what reductive theorists consider causal factors in advance of any empirical research. In such circumstances, whatever they find would look to them to be a confirmation of their theory—but only because they have stacked the deck in advance against refutation. Their theories thus are not actually based upon data at all, and so it is hard to speak in any sense of *evidence* for their theories.

Because of their prior commitment to a metaphysical position, reductionists fall into the same position that the religious are routinely accused of: prejudice in conducting any psychological or social research on religion. Antireductionists remain more neutral since they can be favorable to religion as a sociocultural phenomenon without seeing this as a necessary commitment to the existence of any transcendent realities. One can be "religiously unmusical," as Max Weber claimed to be and still give religion a causal role in sociocultural phenomena. Nevertheless, the investigator's metaphysical commitments affect the questions asked, what is accepted as an answer, and what is advanced as an explanation. Similarly, any antireductionist's more detailed study can always be reinterpreted to show that the causal arrow runs from social-level bases to religious epiphenomena. And this has the result once again that it is very difficult to speak of any empirical evidence favoring one metaphysical position over the other.

Another difficulty reductionists encounter in making their position convincing is that the different competing and incompatible reductive social, economic, and psychological theories cannot be integrated into one comprehensive sociocultural theory. They are incompatible in that they all cannot be true at once (see Nozick 1981: 629-30). (Antireductive theorists, in giving religion causal force in addition to some other sociocultural factor, necessarily are more pluralistic and limit the scope of theories to different sublevels.) In short, if Freud is correct on what causes religious phenomena, Durkheim is wrong. As noted in the last chapter, these theories compete with each other in a way that natural sciences do not, since the different natural sciences account for different levels of causes in the world. Here the various reductive theories offer complete explanations of the entire sociocultural level. Each theory is exhaustive and at most only one can be right. That is, Freud did not offer an explanation of a psychological sublevel and Durkheim one of a social sublevel—each account presents a *complete* explanation of religion leaving no need, or even room, for the other theories. Each theory is only one-dimensional, but it covers the entire field. In Marx's theory, the psychological aspects of socio-cultural phenomena are explained by social and economic factors. Indeed, in reductive theories there is no distinction of scope into psychological versus social religious phenomena requiring different explanations. In sum, the various reductionist accounts compete with each other, not supplement each other. Nor can they be amalgamated into one theory by taking a little of each.

Marxism and Freudianism are rapidly losing general acceptance today, but their reductions of religion paradoxically are still popular. (Whether their reductions can be credible apart from their total theories is open to question.) Indeed, reductionism as an approach—in the abstract, unembedded in any actual theory—is still popular in academic circles, perhaps because of the general agreement that religion cannot be taken seriously, despite its apparent power today in societies around the world. It is easy for someone who has already dismissed religion to say, for example, "Religion just serves some psychological or social function and is nothing more," even if he or she cannot identify clearly what this function is or bother to investigate the issue. Reductionists cannot simply assert that one reductive theory *must* be right without advancing a specific theory—such a maneuver would again reveal the metaphysical nature of their enterprise. And antireductionists cannot be faulted for accepting the obvious—religion as a causal factor—as long as reductionists cannot present a detailed structure-reductive account that even convinces a majority of reductionists within a given discipline. In addition, the multiplicity of disciplines focusing on the sociocultural level also will remain firmly entrenched.

The central point here, however, is that there does not appear to be any empirical tests to favor structure-reductionism or antireductionism in general with regard to religion, let alone some specific theory. In such circumstances, it is apparent that whether a theorist adopts a positive or negative approach to religion must depend on factors other than considerations as a social theorist. In the end, whether a theorist accepts religion as a causal factor may not turn on philosophical (substantive) or social scientific (structural) considerations on the significance of religion at all but may be determined by other causes—including political, social, economic, psychological, and, according to antireductionists, religious ones.

The Transcendent, Reduction, and Emergence

The guiding topic so far for this chapter has been whether religion should be treated as a causal factor in the sociocultural realm. That is the issue of the structure-reduction of religious phenomena. The topic for the rest of this chapter is the metaphysical issue of the possible *substance-reduction* of alleged religious realities—a transcendent source of the world, spirits, the soul, and so forth. That is, can alleged transcendent realities be ontologically reduced to natural phenomena (i.e., phenomena that are parts of natural order open to scientific study)? Note that reductionists here reject the participants' own understanding of what they are doing. This means that, in the eyes of these social scientists, the religious participants, with their misguided commitments to the sacred, are fundamentally mistaken about the real factors at work in their faith, and thus their own self-understanding of the nature of their faith is irrelevant and can be ignored. But for structure-antireductive theorists, the participants' own meaning remains central but the explanation may be substantively reductive (e.g., Bellah 1970b, 1970c). For these social theorists, religious explanations of religious ways of life are no more than self-delusions based on projections that the religious create and that they mistakenly believe correspond to something existing outside of our own subjectivity.

As discussed in Chapter 2, physicalists and naturalists agree in their denial of any supernatural realities: all that is real is matter (physicalism) or the various realities constituting the spatio-temporal realm studied in natural science (naturalism). (For the rest of this chapter, physicalism and naturalism will be grouped together under the term "*naturalism.*") This position entails a commitment to the substance-reductionism that treats all of reality is reduced to what constitutes the natural universe. Such a metaphysical standpoint is inconsistent with the metaphysical commitments of all traditional religions. In the traditional understanding of all the major religions of the world, there is more than one ontological dimension to reality: there is the world we inhabit and also something more upon which this world depends that is not open to scientific study—God or a nontheistic counterpart in nontheistic traditions. That is, to the religious there is more to reality than the natural order of reality studied by scientists, and that other dimension is more fundamental. Naturalists explicitly reject any underlying or transcendent source not open to scientific study that would render the natural universe the creation, emanation, or appearance of another reality. Nor is the natural universe fulfilling some divine purpose or leading people to some fulfillment after death. In short, all of reality is leveled to the natural world. Similarly, any alleged entities such as angels or spirits that exist in realms or in ways not open to scientific scrutiny and that intervene in the natural order are also rejected. A "soul" or any other aspect of a person that could survive death also conflicts with naturalism for the same reason. As discussed below, alleged experiences of a transcendent source or a soul are all to be explained away by a natural explanation: such experiences do not have any transcendent reality among their causal roots but are nothing more than experiences produced by some natural phenomenon. All aspects of religion are to be reduced to natural phenomena and are as totally explainable as any other sociocultural phenomenon. Religious language can then either be eliminated outright or conceptually reduced to nonreligious language at least in principle.

Consider alleged transcendent sources to the world. For theists, God is a causal factor in the natural world and thus is a causal structure within the realm of natural world in addition to being a transcendent reality. Thus, the natural universe is not causally closed, and, in an *antinaturalism*, science no longer can give a complete account of all the causes at work in nature. Rather, God is also active in nature, either guiding events or as a cause in some events. Today the idea that God rather than nature is the ultimate source of "information" is getting attention (Ward 2010; Haught 2010). For example, the scientist/theologian Arthur Peacocke affirms the autonomy of the natural order but believes God is still acting immanently in the world: God is the underlying cause and sustainer of reality but is also active *guiding events* in the natural order through the input of "*information*" as a type of formal cause without the input of energy. God uses the materials of nature and acts within natural processes such as evolution to direct the emergence of new levels of organization (including life and consciousness). Scientists cannot find God, since God's activity is not part of the efficient causal chains in nature but occurs only on an underlying order guiding events (1986, 1993, 2010).[8]

Such a theistic approach gives all of nature a sacred aspect, but the problem is *how* the sacred could act through natural and human agents to accomplish a goal (Barbour 1990: 243-59). To explain this, some theologians employ downward causation. But the situation here would ontologically be actually the *opposite* of the mind/body and scientific situations since, if anything, the world arises out a transcendent ground of reality, not vice versa. That is, the transcendent does not *emerge* from lower base-conditions (as Samuel Alexander suggested) but is the source of everything else. Thus, God is not an emergent property or level of organization within the natural order but something else entirely. Nevertheless, God exercises a direct control on every level of organization, either without violating the closure of efficient causes in the natural order through an input of information or by becoming a factor in the natural efficient causal chains.

How such a reality can exercise control over the natural order is hard for theists to specify. Claiming that religious realities supervene on the physical in any way will not help since the religious realities would then depend on the physical as a prior base-condition. Using the analogies of the world as "God's body" or God as the "world soul" or the world as "a thought in the mind of God" may keep the closure of the natural level, but it leads to a pantheism or at least panentheism that disturbs many theists. It is also using one mystery—the mind/body problem—to try to explain another. Arguing that God guides the world like a computer programmer who alters the course of events within a computer's hardware would, like the mind/body analogy, explain how scientists could in principle give a complete account of the natural order (analogous to the electrical impulses in the hardware). But how God does this remains unspecified. And for many theists it suffers from the same problem as the mind/body analogy: it does not permit enough independence of either God or the world (Barbour 1990: 259). It leaves the world (including us) as too much of a puppet. Theists may try working out analogies from science (e.g., God as a kind of field) to get around this tension in the relation of the ground of reality to the natural order. But if no analogies from current science or nature succeed, leaving how God acts as simply a mystery, this renders this approach unsatisfying. The problem certainly hurts the credibility of theism in the eyes of the scientifically-minded. Theists nevertheless still have a fall-back position: the situation is unique and beyond our understanding, and so no analogies to any experiences from the natural world will work to explicate the situation for us.[9]

Reducing the Soul

The naturalists' opposition to supernatural entities extends to any idea of a "soul," "spiritual essence," "transcendent consciousness," or "immortal self" that could exist independently of our bodies or could continue after death. To naturalists, when we die, consciousness is simply no longer produced from its physical bases. Not all naturalists reduce consciousness the way reductive physicalists do (as discussed in Chapter 4), but consciousness is always treated strictly as a product of nature that cannot survive without a material base. Antireductive physicalists offer no more hope for life after death: consciousness and other mental functions arise from the material and cannot survive our death. Only William Hasker's idea of an emergent substance offers any hope of life after death (but only through a miraculous act of God) (1999: 232-35).[10] For naturalists, nothing arises through evolution or any form of emergence that could attain an existence independent of the physical. There is nothing in us that in fact could survive death. We are strictly a natural phenomenon that upon death decomposes totally into our physical components. Like any animal, we have evolved naturally here on earth, and there is nothing else to us. The only reasons naturalists see for accepting any idea even suggesting a dualism of mind and body are primitive religious beliefs in immortality that should have been rejected long ago on both philosophical and scientific grounds. All ideas that we are in any way a special creation or that we have a component that will survive our physical death are grounded merely in baseless hopes for immortality or for a paradise spun out of our own imagination to compensate for our suffering.

Some religious thinkers advance arguments outside of mainstream philosophical and scientific arguments in favor of the existence of some portion of the person existing independently of the body. The depth-mystical experience is quite naturally taken as revealing an eternal aspect of us that is in some sense identical with an eternal nonsubjective reality. Such paranormal experiences as out-of-body and near-death experiences are taken by many people as evidence of a separate soul (e.g., Geis 1995: 97-110). Of course, naturalists are not impressed—to the extent they take any notice of paranormal experiences at all, they dismiss them as illusory, explaining them away on physiological or psychological grounds. But even as convinced a positivist as Alfred Ayer had his "inflexible attitude" toward his belief in the lack of a life after death weakened when he himself underwent a near-death experience (1990: 198-208). Most scientists and philosophers do not take such experiences seriously enough to bother considering them when devising a theory of mind. When the field of experiences is limited to more conventional experiences, there few philosophers and scientists who advocate a dualism—Karl Popper and John Eccles being the most prominent examples. Only a very few argue for the need on scientific grounds to postulate a self (e.g., Tloczynski 1993). But this does show that dualism is not defended only by those with previous religious commitments. In the end, what one takes as the most plausible possibility here remains a philosophical decision that science cannot answer (Penfield 1975: 115).

Reducing Religious Experiences

The last point leads naturally to the next topic: what is most special experientially about religion—the religious experiences of transcendent realities that are the alleged epistemic ground of religious ways of life. However the class of "religious experiences" is delimited, naturalists will argue that the experiences can be exhaustively explained in terms of natural phenomena, and thus the religious are deluded as to the actual causes of their experiences.[11] The naturalists' view can be foreseen in the words of Voltaire: religious experiences are "supernatural visions permitted to him or her who is gifted by God with the special grace of possessing a cracked brain, a hysterical temperament, a disordered digestion, or, most of all, the art of lying with effrontery." No supernatural reality exists, and so in principle there is no such reality to be a causal factor in any of these experiences. Thus, religious experiences cannot include a supernatural cause in its chain to be completely explained. Instead, naturalists attempt to identify the set of necessary and sufficient natural processes at work in these experiences. Different types of religious experiences may require different explanations (i.e., different sets of physiological or sociocultural mechanisms), but only natural phenomena will be involved. If successful, naturalists would be able to duplicate a theist's experience of God without God actually being involved. A transcendent reality would thus not be a necessary cause of these experiences, and naturalists then argue that there are no grounds to believe that we have experiences of any transcendent realities.

Naturalists need not doubt the sincerity of the experiencers or deny people in fact have purported transcendent experiences—they simply argue that these experiences are always the product totally of natural causes and that the experi- encers are honestly mistaken about the real causes. Just as the experience of a rope as a snake is a genuine experience and can produce a real emotional kick that in turn produces real physiological effects even though there is no snake, so too the religious may have genuine experiences even though only natural phenomena are involved. All that naturalists contend is that they will be able to identify the specific natural factors that will explain how and why people seem to "experience God" even though no transcendent reality exists.

There are three types of reductive explanations: physiological, sociocultural, and philosophical. But the natural explanation of religious experiences is always substance-reductive: the only realities involved in the experiences are the experi- encer and elements of the natural world. Physiological reductionists attempt to find a set of biological or chemical conditions such that anyone under those conditions will have a particular type of religious experience. Recently there has been a surge of interest in the neurological study of spiritual experiences. The correlation of conscious states with the neurological or biochemical states of the brain or with physiological states of other parts of the body permits the stimulation of the same mechanisms at work in the religious experience. For a true correlation, there must be a one-to-one relation of changes in states of consciousness with changes in physiological states. All the phenomenological content of the experiences also must be reproduced. Naturalists argue that scientists can in fact duplicate every feature of various religious experiences and can also offer explanations for the strong emotional effects these experiences have on the experiencers. Thus, naturalists draw the conclusion that religious experience is nothing but brain activity.

Early in the last century, William James derided the "medical physicalism" that explains away Saint Paul's vision on the road to Damascus as a discharging lesion of the occipital cortex resulting from epilepsy, Saint Teresa of Avila as a hysteric, and Saint Francis of Assisi as a hereditary degenerate (1958: 29). More refined attempts to explain all the features of all religious and mystical experiences in terms of, for example, the stimulation of the temporal lobe structures of the brain are still popular (e.g., Newberg, d'Aquili, & Rause 2002; see Jones 2009b: 77-92). Whether chemical stimulation of the brain can trigger an experience phenomenologically identical to a mystical experience or only something similar to it also is open to debate (e.g., Beauregard & O'Leary 2007). Other physiological conditions are also used to explain visions. For example, the visions of light and deceased relatives in near-death experiences are explained away as merely wish-fulfilling hallucinations produced by a brain deprived of oxygen or as the brain's way of stopping the dying from struggling once there is apparently no longer any chance of survival. Near-death experiences still may well transform the life of experiencers who survive (and perhaps be the source of the ideas of heaven and life after death), but naturalists know the visions are only naturally generated when the brain is dying.

Other instances of the physiological type of naturalistic explanation are not based on experimentation or clinical observation but on more general scientific knowledge and naturalistic beliefs. One popular way to explain the sense of permanence and oneness in the depth-mystical experience is as merely a feedback effect: our brain has evolved to produce an intentional type of consciousness to deal with problems of survival; so when the mind is "on" but has no content with which to work, it malfunctions badly, producing the illusory sense of mystical oneness, timelessness, and so forth.[12] Others have attempted to explain all religious experiences in a very general way in terms of biological factors. Edward Wilson's sociobiological explanation of religion can also be placed in this category: religion, like all other human institutions, has evolved in directions that enhance the genetic advantage of its practitioners (1978: 182). Religion is seen as a positive force in our lives, but it is treated as totally a natural phenomenon; ultimately, the only purpose in religion is, as with all sociocultural phenomena, what it does for our genetic survival. The mental processes of religious belief represent predispositions programmed into the neural apparatus of our brain by thousands of generations of genetic evolution (1978: 214). (To fellow sociobiologist Richard Dawkins, religious ideas are merely a "virus meme" in the mind.) No transcendent realities are in any way involved in religion, only nature working itself out. Thus, religion as a product of an encounter with any transcendent reality is explained away.

Thus, physiological reductionists claim religious experiences are nothing but electrochemical activity in the brain or some other biological phenomenon. Sociocultural reductionists, however, find other mechanisms responsible for the same experiences. Psychological naturalists see, for example, belief in immortality as strictly wishful thinking in the face of the harshness of reality; ecstatic religious experiences are explained as, for example, surrogates for sex. Sociologists note that people with certain psychological dispositions are more inclined than most people to have religious experiences. Sociological and anthropological naturalists go beyond using social conditions to explain the inclination to have religious experiences—e.g., I. M. Lewis's theory that religious ecstasy is a means of access to political and social power for disenfranchised and marginalized groups (1989)—to the conclusion that social factors are the *only* forces at work in such experiences.

In the third category of natural explanations—philosophical reductions—the key idea here is that the alleged cognitive content of religious experiences is reducible to the experiencer's *prior religious beliefs*. The experience itself makes no cognitive contribution to the belief-framework. The basis of this reduction is the "constructivist" view widely held in philosophy today that all our experiences are conceptually structured. That is, the concepts we create become part of the filter by which the mind processes information. There is no "objective" experience in the sense that the world uniquely determines one experience free of any structuring input from a particular experiencer. *Moderate constructivists* still insist that the external world plays a role in constraining our creations—reality surprises us and resists our expectations, and thus theory-construction is not infinitely malleable. *Extreme constructivists*, however, attempt to assimilate knowledge totally to the nonexperiential and the social (Hesse 1988: 111-15). Scientific claims are accepted as "true," not because of any external reality but because of social considerations within the scientific community. The natural world has only a small or nonexistent role in the construction of scientific knowledge (see Cole 1996). Thus, moderates argue that reality and the structuring we supply are inextricably mixed in our experiences and our knowledge, but extremists conclude that concepts are simply our creations and have no connection to anything but other concepts. Extreme constructivists need not deny metaphysical realism (that some reality exists independently of the experiencer), but they contend that any configuration of concepts will do for coping with the world: we may need to adjust the parts of the conceptual system, but in the last analysis reality does not constrain our creation.

Constructivism does seem applicable to visions: experiencers do not sense a vague, amorphous presence but sense Jesus or some other figure from their own religious tradition shaped by their beliefs—Protestants never have visions of Mary and Muslims never see Krishna (although the Dalai Lama did have a vision of a smiling Mary at Fatima). Similarly, in the vast majority of cases, those who pray and hear a voice hear only confirmation of their prior religious and nonreligious beliefs. Whether constructivism can be extended to all types of *mystical experiences* is open to dispute (see Jones 2009b: 226-36). There is also empirical evidence against the constructivist interpretation of all mystical experiences (see Hood 1997: 227-28). Extreme constructivists reflect the tendency of philosophers to reduce religion to a matter exclusively of belief-claims and go beyond claiming belief is *one* component in religious experiences to claiming it is the *only* component (see Katz 1978, 1983). Even without that extreme, a mystic's conceptual framework is given all weight. Mystical experiences become "simply the psychosomatic enhancement of religious beliefs and values . . ." (Gimello 1983: 85). One postmodernist scholar questions whether memories of "mystical experiences" have any more transcendental "mystical content" than alien abductees' "memories" of their alleged abductions (Sharf 1998).

The cognitive substance of any religious experience for extreme constructivists is thereby reduced totally to the nonexperiential: the belief-framework brought to the experience constitutes the complete cognitive element of the experience. There is no possibility of an independent cognitive input from a transcendent source. Religious experiences thus cannot be sources of any potentially fresh cognitive input in anyone's system of belief. For the same reason, prior experiences cannot shape the conceptual framework one's brings to later religious experiences. In sum, alleged experiences of a transcendent reality cannot enter the cognitive picture at any point. Thus, under extreme constructivism, all religious experiences are no more cognitive than when Roman Catholics see the face of Mary in a rusted refrigerator on a back pouch. But extreme constructivism is popular in academia in the case of a religious experience. It neatly combines a popular philosophical position (constructivism) with two popular academic views on religion (naturalism and the reduction of religion to belief-claims).

Another variety of philosophical reductionism switches the emphasis to the *experiential component* but once again denies that it contributes anything cognitive to the total religious experience. John Bowker argued that LSD does not induce genuine experiences of a transcendent reality but only initiates a state of excitation that is labeled and interpreted from available cues as "religious" by some experiencers, due to the setting and the experiencers' background. The warrant for a particular label thus does not lie in the experience itself but in the conceptual background that created specific expectations and supplied the symbols to the structuring (1973: 144-57). Bowker presented this theory to discredit the notion that the idea of God originated in hallucinogenic drug experiences, but this idea can also be used to discredit the cognitivity of all religious experiences. Wayne Proudfoot offers this "cognitive labeling" approach to deny the possibility of any transcendent input in any religious experiences: experiencers unconsciously attribute religious significance to otherwise ordinary experiences. Religious experiences are simply general and diffuse patterns of agitation in states of our nervous system to which the religious give a label based on their prior religious beliefs in order to understand and explain the agitation (1985; but see Barnard 1992). Any extreme emotional state can be labeled "a religious experience" when experiencers believe the cause is a transcendent reality, but there are only cognitively empty feelings—bodily states agitated in ordinary, purely natural ways. A transcendent reality is not even indirectly involved as the source of the agitation. In sum, religious experiences are no more than cognitively empty feelings structured by prior religious beliefs.

Thus, philosophical reductionists go from the necessity of a conceptual element in most, but perhaps not all, religious experiences to concluding there is nothing more to them than natural factors. Overall, postmodernist reductionists in religious studies today downplay the significance of religious experience. They treat them as any other human experience, thereby ruling out the possibility that a transcendent reality may be involved. Instead religious experiences are strictly this-worldly experiences simply "deemed religious" (Taves 2009). That is, religious value or significance is given to unusual but otherwise ordinary experiences. "Religious experiences" are constituted solely by this-worldly elements and thus are exhausted explainable in the same manner as any other human experience. This approach allows postmodernists to focus exclusively on religious texts and discount any role for experience that may involve transcendent elements in the formation of religious doctrines and practices.

However, many philosophers find the total denial of any external input in all religious experiences as absurd as the denial of any external input in sense-experiences. These philosophers argue that religious experiences are potentially cognitive in nature and not simply intense internal states. In sum, one can be a moderate constructivist, such as John Hick, who argues that the mind contributes to every genuine religious experience but "the Real" does too (1989). Culture might explain why Christian visions are of Mary and not Krishna, but it does not explain all of the experience—in particular, why there is some "sense of presence" to experience in the visions in the first place (Bowker 1973: 42-43). Thereby, the cognitive content of religious experiences is not reduced to doctrine. For his part, Wayne Proudfoot explicitly denies religious experiences involve any transcendent reality (1985: 154); instead, all religious experiences are totally explained away in natural terms. In the end, whether one subscribes to any philosophical reduction appears to depend more upon whether one has a prior commitment to naturalism than anything inherent in the experiences themselves. This leads to the issue of the plausibility of proposed natural explanations.

Problems with Natural Explanations of Religious Experiences

If naturalists are correct, then even if transcendent realities indeed exist, religious experiences are still nothing but natural phenomena. Thereby, the alleged cognitive content of religious experiences and any beliefs based on them will be radically discredited. The religious are thereby left with no experiential evidence of transcendent realities. Religious faith and beliefs thus cannot be based in, or justified by, these experiences. And thus, even the minimal rationality of participants in a religious way of life is called into question. But before adopting this conclusion, problems with the naturalistic reductions of religious experience should be noted.

Only one such problem will be raised here: natural and religious explanations of religious experiences are in fact *compatible*.[13] Naturalists argue that if they can identify a set of necessary and sufficient conditions for a religious experience to arise, then the experience is totally natural and any transcendent reality cannot be a causal factor in the chain of events producing the experience. One strategy in response is simply to deny that any complete natural explanation is possible in practice—the complexity of any human phenomenon renders it impossible for scientists to be certain that they have identified all the conditions for an experience; certainly, no one to date has yet provided a good empirical reason to think that all religious experiences admit only a purely natural explanation. But let's assume that some complete and detailed natural explanation of religious experiences is possible at least in principle. It may be that different types of religious experiences have different natural mechanisms at work and so will require different explanations. But ultimately it is possible that each type of religious experience will have one natural explanation or another. We would then be left with a collection of explanations. But the issue still is: what do such explanations actually accomplish?

Consider physiological explanations. Naturalists claim that by demonstrating that all features of all religious experiences can be replicated by natural causes (drugs, electrical stimulation of the brain, or whatever, depending on the type of experience), theists cannot claim to have experienced God. But assuming every feature of every religious experience can be duplicated by some natural causes so that the natural experience is phenomenologically indistinguishable from the alleged religious experience, does the naturalistic conclusion follow? No. Theists can still respond that at best all naturalists have done is locate the *physiological bases* involved in the various types of religious experiences and stimulated them artificially. That is, if experiences of transcendent realities do occur, then obviously some mechanism in our bodies permits them to occur. All that the naturalists have done is to demonstrate how to stimulate the physiological mechanisms at work in those experiences by means other than the impingement of the transcendent. This cannot in itself rule out the possibility that other causes—transcendent ones—may also produce the same physiological effects.

Thus, if during some religious experience our brain produces a certain chemical, then scientists may well be able to identify this chemical and to manufacture a drug that will substitute for its natural production in the brain; this drug can then produce the same effects when it is artificially introduced into the brain. But scientists cannot conclude from that that during religious experiences occurring outside of the lab a transcendent reality cannot cause the brain to produce this chemical naturally—i.e., that God somehow uses the normal neurochemical channels of our physiology to produce the religious experience. If theists are correct, God may work behind the chain of natural causes in an undetectable way through the natural processes at work in our body, and all that the scientists will have done is located those parts of our physiological make-up. Such findings would only mean that some chemical conditions are necessary to set up the experience of the transcendent, not that nothing more is involved. Nor can naturalists conclude there must be no other ways to activate the same experience. Thus, naturalists cannot, without more, conclude from the fact that some chemical is involved that the resulting experience must be a purely natural phenomenon and no nonnatural factors are part of the set of causes. The drug (whether administered artificially or generated by the brain) may permit a genuine religious experience, or it may be a source of a delusion. The science itself will remain *neutral* on this issue of whether the experience involves contact with a transcendent reality or not. In sum, scientists may be able to demonstrate that a particular chemical is involved in the brain during a particular experience, but they cannot demonstrate that this is all there is to the experience: they can never demonstrate that they have eliminated transcendent realities as possible causes.

Thus, physiological demonstrations will at best only reveal a set of *sufficient* causes for the religious experience to occur—they cannot eliminate the possibility of *other sets of sufficient causes*. Scientists have located *necessary* causes, but it is simply the naturalists' assumption that scientists have also located the only possible sufficient causes. Theists argue that the experiences can also be produced by another sufficient cause, namely God. All scientists have demonstrated is at best something comparable to an electrical stimulation of the arm causing it to jerk: they have located the mechanisms at work in the event and stimulated them—they have not proven that no other source of the event is possible (here, the mind moving the arm). Scientists can push the button stimulating the arm movement all they want, but they cannot eliminate the possibility that there may be other ways nature causes that same movement. Similarly, no amount of artificial stimulation of religious experiences can prove that the experience cannot be caused by another means and thus is a purely natural phenomenon. In short, scientists simply cannot in principle demonstrate scientifically that they have eliminated transcendent realities as possible causes.

A related issue is the analog to the dispute between mind/body identity theorists and others over whether the electrical stimulation of the arm is the same experience as the mind moving it—the artificially stimulated movement does not *feel* the same to the experiencers as moving the arm themselves. That is, are the experiences stimulated electrically or chemically really the same as naturally occurring religious experiences, or are they in fact only part of the genuine experience the religious undergo? But more importantly, even if the natural causes exactly simulate every feature of a religious experience, the point remains that another cause cannot be ruled out. The naturalists' metaphysics require them to conclude that transcendent realities cannot be a cause, but nothing in the actual scientific demonstrations requires this philosophical judgment. In short, these natural explanations are *perfectly compatible* with religious explanations.

In sum, scientists will never do more than show that there are other ways of causing the same experience—if they are indeed the same—as those caused by transcendent sources. Thus, a physiological demonstration cannot invalidate the claim of a genuine insight into reality Thus, there is no forced *either/or choice* between physiological events and authentic encounters with such a reality: experiences can be both. This means that a complete physiological demonstration will not accomplish what naturalists think it does.

And the situation is somewhat worse for naturalists with sociocultural explanations. Sociocultural theorists can identify general correlations of sociocultural phenomena with religious experiences, but they have not been able to identify anything close to sufficient conditions for these experiences to occur. They are thus unable to predict which persons will or will not have those experiences or when they will occur. At best, their explanations will only be able to predict that certain persons or groups will have more of, or less of, a tendency to have those experiences than the population at large.

In one regard, social theorists are in the same boat with scientists experimenting on stimulating religious experiences with drugs. At most, ingesting the drugs set up the conditions enabling or permitting the experience to occur (by disrupting the grip that conceptual frames of reference normally have on the mind, or however the chemicals in the brain do what they do). The ingestion of a drug cannot guarantee a religious experience, even if administered in a conducive setting to a person with a religious background. Drugs never produce the experience on demand. Thus, the drug is not a *trigger* to such experiences. If it were, everyone or at least nearly everyone who is given a drug under specified conditions would have a religious experience. But the scientists' results are always that a much lower percentage of the subjects have any religious experience and that different kinds of experiences occur. And the situation is even looser in the social sciences.

Moreover, even if neuroscientists or social scientists do discover conditions that trigger a religious experience, the basic issue still remains: is the religious experience purely a natural phenomenon, or have the scientists merely identified the psychological and social conditions making a person receptive to the infusion of a transcendent reality? Perhaps mental stress or a severe psychological crisis is a way of breaking the hold our everyday life has on our mind, thereby setting up the physiological conditions necessary for a religious experience. Unusual psychological or social states may be sufficient to set up the base-conditions, but it does not follow that therefore the experiences are not insights (James 1958: 26). Or perhaps chemical imbalances or other abnormal physiological states brought on by drugs, breathing exercises or other meditative techniques, fasting or other ascetic practices, or whatever, are needed to permit certain religious states to occur. It is question-begging to assert without further argument that only experiences occurring in the states of consciousness that evolved to deal with survival give knowledge of reality. As William James noted, for all we know, a temperature of 103 or 104 degrees Fahrenheit might be much more favorable for truths to germinate and sprout in than our ordinary body temperature (1958: 30). Perhaps the mechanisms involved in schizophrenia are simply the malfunctioning of mechanisms designed for religious experiences. The important point here is that any physiological or social scientific finding in itself will be *neutral* on the question of whether the resulting experience has a transcendent reality as a cause or is in fact simply a delusion. Thus, the bottom line is that any forthcoming natural explanation and the theistic explanation will be *compatible*: for all we know, all that scientists have done is simply identified more of the conditions a transcendent reality uses to induce the experience. There is one qualification: if it turns out that only people with obviously *damaged brains* have religious experiences, then the presumption has to be that the experiences do not involve any insights into the nature of reality. Despite James's argument concerning fever, it would be hard to imagine a transcendent reality utilizing severely damaged brains as a vehicle for insights. But there is good evidence that religious experiences are widespread among normal persons (Hardy 1983).

From the above discussion it follows that the religious can provide an understanding of natural explanations consistent with their substance-antireductionism: as with any experience, there must be bases in physiological, psychological, and social phenomena for our capacity to have religious experiences, and scientists and social theorists may be able to identify those bases, but identifying those bases does not explain away religious experiences. Thus, the religious can endorse natural explanations as providing an understanding of the occurrence of the religious experiences but never as a *complete* explanation of them.[14] Physiological studies will identify the mechanisms active in these experiences and thus account for the body's reaction during these experiences. In this way, such studies explain part of the person having the experience but not all aspects of the experience itself. Socio-cultural explanations will identify such matters as the motivating forces for people to have the experience and the forms people use to structure the experience. But physiological or sociocultural explanations need not *deny* or *contradict* the religious claims: identifying that more is going on than the believers realize does not mean that the believers must be fundamentally wrong, but only that the phenomena involves more dimensions than simply the religious meaning (as noted above).

Natural Explanations and Naturalistic Reductions

One ambiguity that leads to problems here is that the phrase "naturalistic explana-tion" can have two meanings: the scientific account (a *"natural explanation"*) or one possible philosophical conclusion (a *"naturalistic reduction"*). It is only by confusing the two that anyone can conclude that the scientific accounts entail the philosophical conclusion. Physiological accounts of meditators may be complete in the way that a physiological account of seeing a tree may be complete, but they do not require the naturalists' conclusion that therefore only our own internal mech-anisms are at work in meditation any more than in vision. Drugs impair our ordinary cognitive and perceptual apparatus, but this does not rule out the possibility that they thereby may open up other levels of our consciousness. As just discussed, the science itself is neutral on all such issues and without more it does not justify the naturalists' philosophical conclusion that a naturalistic reduction is in order.

The consequence of this is that a scientific natural explanation cannot be used by itself as evidence against religion for a naturalistic reduction. The naturalists' conclusion that all these experiences are purely natural and thus that the transcen-dent, even if it existed, is not a cause in them follows only as a *philosophical* position and must be defended as such. The defense of the truth of their position will have to rest on considerations that are metaphysical in nature. In addition, the naturalists' commitment to science as the sole source of our knowledge of reality will itself also have to be justified on philosophical grounds.

In sum, the justification or rejection of the alleged insights connected to religious experiences will depend on grounds other than scientific accounts of them. Philosophers reject the "genetic fallacy" (that identifying the origin of a belief is reason to reject the belief itself), since true beliefs as well as false ones can have their origins in quite abnormal conditions and hence the origins are simply irrelevant to the issues of truth and justification. Some scientific ideas have arisen in strange ways (e.g., in dreams or during illnesses), but the truth or usefulness of the resulting scientific ideas is a separate issue from their historical, social, or psychological origin; it is an issue for empirical testing and other scientific concerns. So too, philosophers should they reject the broader "naturalist fallacy" (that a physiological or sociocultural account of a belief or experience is reason to reject the beliefs involved).[15] All beliefs, true and false, have sociocultural explanations. Social explanations of why someone is more likely than the population as a whole to have a mystical experience is no more relevant to the question of the truth of mystical claims than a social explanation of why scientists are likely to come from certain groups relevant is to scientific claims. Similarly, all experiences have physiological explanations, and no type of experience can be rejected as a possible vehicle of insights because of that. EEG examinations of scientists theorizing or identifying the neural correlates of a scientist making an observation are simply irrelevant to the truth or falsity of their alleged insights and theories, and the same holds for meditators. As William James said, "[s]cientific theories are organically conditioned just as much as religious emotions are" (1958: 29-30). The truth or falsity of a claim is simply independent of such accounts and turns on other considerations.[16] For example, if naturalists argue that scientific observations differ from religious experiences because scientific observations can be empirically checked, then, regardless of whether this is correct or not, at least they are conceding that factors other than physiology or naturalistic explanations matter.

It should be noted that it is not only naturalists who make this mistake. On the other side of the coin are those contemporary New Age enthusiasts conclude that scientists studying the physiology of meditators have *validated* age-old mystical claims. For example, the general shift of mental functioning in meditation from the left to the right brain-hemisphere (in right-handed males), a shift from the site of linguistic and analytic activity to that of nonverbal and synthetic activity, was popular back in the 1970's as establishing a physiological basis proving the truth of mystical claims. (Research now focuses on how the two halves work together.) But the grounds of this claim are as shaky as for the naturalists' claim: the science at best establishes the site of the neural activity accompanying the experience but is irrelevant to whether or not any claim is true. It does not establish that any insights into the nature of reality accompany the shift—the right hemisphere functioning without contact with the left may in fact be no more than a useless spinning of mental gears incapable of any true insight into the nature of reality.

Naturalists may concede may that a scientific account does not *refute* religious explanations, but they may contend that it still *lessens* the likelihood that such explanations are true. Religion scholar Robert Segal presents one such argument based on Freud's projection theory. Freud realized his theory of religious belief as a projection based in wishful thinking does not make these beliefs necessarily false (1964: 26-27)—an illusion after all is not necessarily an error (1964: 30-31) and a reality corresponding to our projection may in fact exist—but he argued that our projections are not grounds for believing they are veridical. Calling a belief an "illusion" relates only to its motivation and disregards its relation to reality (1964). Segal, however, insists that Freud is saying that it would be an *extraordinary coincidence* if a reality did match our projections since they are *primarily just* wishful thinking; thus, Freud's theory makes the existence of God *improbable* (1989: 80).

But Segal does concede that Freud believed religious claims to be delusions, not because of his own theory of projections, but on grounds of philosophy and natural science; his theory merely explained *why* humans succumb to the delusion (1989). Freud realized that what he said against the truth-value of religious claims had been said by others long before psychoanalysis came into existence (1964: 60). He did not believe his theory refuted religious claims but merely supplied an explanation for why believers believe what they do. He realized the "reality value" of religious doctrines could not be proved or refuted by his science (1964: 31).

Thus, for Freud, the issue of the truth or falsity of religious claims is a matter to be established on grounds other than the natural explanation itself. Freud's natural explanation itself does not make the belief-claims any less likely—even according to him, the psychological mechanism he identified is simply irrelevant to the possible truth or falsity of religious beliefs. Freud could not (and did not) argue that it is a coincidence or probable or improbable that a projection "hits" a transcendent reality and still maintain that he is writing as a scientist: issues of such probability do not turn on the psychological mechanism that Freud claimed is at work. Probability that religious claims are delusions turns on the philosophical and natural scientific grounds that Freud himself cited for accepting naturalism. Of course, as a naturalist, he no doubt believed it would be "very striking" and "remarkable" if human projections in this area proved in fact to hit something real; but the point is that he knew such an assessment of the truth-value of religious doctrines did not lie within the scope of his inquiry (1964: 33). Such a conclusion is a philosophical, not psychological, one. Freud's natural explanation only seems relevant to rendering religious beliefs less probable because it would supply a mechanism for why religious believers believe what they do, and this psychological "how" question is all that naturalists want to answer since they already accept that religious transcendent claims are false. Thus, Freud's mechanism indirectly seems to bolster a naturalistic conclusion that naturalists have already reached for other reasons. However, his theory renders religious explanations "less probable" only if we presuppose naturalistic metaphysics to begin with, and we are left to argue that point only on other grounds. Once again the issue is the basic philosophical one: naturalistic versus religious metaphysics. But Freud's actual position in the end only supports the contention that natural explanatory accounts in themselves are irrelevant to the philosophical issue.

However, even though a scientific demonstration does not *prove* some alleged religious experiences are not genuine, it does render religious explanations less probable in the sense that an *alternative explanation* is in principle available—i.e., the religious explanation is no longer the only candidate but now must contend with competitors. Of course, this in itself is not evidence against religious explanations of religious experiences. However, this does not mean that religious experiences do not count as uncontested evidence of contact with a transcendent reality. Some religious experiences may be veridical experiences of such a reality, but how can we know if scientists can duplicate all the features of the experience? That is, if religious experiences can occur whether or not God is present, then these experiences lose any epistemic presumption that they might have enjoyed in the absence of a natural explanation. We are left, not with proof that the religious explanations are wrong or proof that a reductive explanation is right, but in a more uncertain situation: these experiences may or may not be experiences of a transcendent reality but we can never be sure; hence, the experiences are not unambiguous evidence of a transcendent reality. Thus, the damage is not to the possibility of a genuine religious experience but to the experience's *philosophical value as evidence* in an argument in favor of transcendent realities.

Based on the science alone, religious projections are part of the sociocultural level of organization and may or may not be as successful in depicting something real as scientific ones. We are left with two alternative groups of metaphysical systems, neither of which is more compelling at present. Naturalists will then argue that natural explanations are at least as satisfactory as religious ones and cover the same ground, and so, under Occam's razor, they should prevail. But the religious counter that naturalists consider them satisfactory only because these explanations account for all the aspects naturalists think (on metaphysical grounds) are actually involved. In short, each argument will be construed within one's metaphysical position, and the issue of which position is correct will become one strictly of adjudicating between competing metaphysics. If reality is "religiously ambiguous," as John Hick argues (1989: 122-24), then this may remain our situation forever.

Thus, it appears that which alternative one chooses concerning what natural explanations actually accomplish will depend on one's prior commitment to naturalistic or religious metaphysics. Or one may try to remain open on the matter. It is a bald metaphysical dispute in the way that structure-reductionism in the social sciences is not. The religious are substance-antireductionists who think transcendent realities are somehow a causal factor and thus natural explanations will always be incomplete. Naturalists see some natural explanation in physiological, evolutionary, psychological, sociological, or philosophical terms as in principle fatal to religious transcendent belief-commitments. The extent to which the commitment to a metaphysics determines what is accepted as true or rational or even possible need not be entered into here. The point for the issue at hand is simply that our choice regarding what natural explanations can, at least in principle, actually accomplish will turn on metaphysical commitments—the scientific explanations themselves will not contribute to this choice.

Notes

1.   "Spirituality" is coming to replace "religion" in certain contexts. It refers to a personal quest for meaning whether one is affiliated with a religious institution or not.

2.   Theology will not be discussed here, but it should be noted that some Christian theologians and philosophers of religion have become enthusiastic supporters of *emergence* (see Clayton & Davies 2006; Murphy & Stoeger 2007; Davies & Gregersen 2010).

3.   Some thinkers such as Marx and Freud would like to eliminate religion as part of their naturalistic programs, but that is obviously a different point.

4.   Discussions of reductionism in religious studies end with Ernest Nagel's *The Structure of Science* in 1961. Reductionists speak of "positivism" and the "unity of science" program (e.g., Wiebe 1998). The scientist/theologian Arthur Peacocke made a major contribution to reductionism by differentiating different types of reductionism (1976, 1985), but religious studies scholars have not made any general contributions to the field.

5.   For most social theorists, there is an asymmetry of explanation: a *rational* action is its own explanation; only the *irrational* needs a further explanation (Hollis 1982: 75). If religious actions or beliefs were deemed "rational," the surface justifications provided by the religious would be included in explanations as sociocultural causes. That is, what a scholar deems rational will not be subject to a structure-reduction; only the irrational will. However, what is deemed "*rational*" will vary according to one's metaphysical commitments. So too, reductive sociologists of knowledge do not treat all symbol-systems equally as projections. They differentiate between the systems according to the alleged truth or rationality of their content and treat only those that to them are *false* or *irrational* as subject to their approach. As the anthropologist Edward Evans-Pritchard noted, if theorists accepted the reality of spiritual beings, they would not feel the need to advance sociological or other theories to explain away the behavior of the religious (1965: 121). In short, reductionists renounce impartiality and transform the "sociology of knowledge" into the "sociology of error" (Hamnett 1973). In the sociology of science, theorists adhere to a principle of "symmetry" between true and false or rational and irrational beliefs. All are equally open to "external" explanations in terms of political considerations or whatever—it is not that true or rational beliefs are open to "internal" explanations in terms of internal scientific considerations and false or irrational beliefs require only "external" explanations.

6.   There is a major difficulty for Durkheim's reductionism: how does society come to be mistakenly seen as a transcendently person or other reality by the religious? Why are people unaware of the true reality behind their symbols? All Durkheim said is that society, by its power over individuals, has all that is necessary to cause people to have the sense of the divine (1915: 207-41). But how is a social reality transformed or idealized into a religious symbol of the power behind all of reality? Even if social factors cause a sense of transcendence in the first place (and thus there is no independent religious sense), why do the practitioners not know the true reality behind their symbols? Durkheim needed to specify a mechanism or explanation for how the very process of projection occurs. Without that, his reductionism remains problematic.

7.   Functionalists have major difficulties here. First, social theorists disagree profoundly over what exactly are the needs that religion is supposed to fulfill. Obviously, psychological and social theorists will disagree in the manner to be expected over what our fundamental needs are. There is also the related problem of whether a search for the "meaning of existence" is a uniquely religious need or can be fulfilled by a nontranscendent realities. And if religion fulfills more than one function, then it can be argued that there is more substance to it than just any functions it fulfills. Second, functionalism with regard to religion shares the general problem with functionalism noted in the last chapter: in the eyes of causal theorists, we explain by means of causes, not effects; thus, if anything, we partially explain *society* by means of religion by identifying the functions religion fulfills, not explain *religion* at all (e.g., Spiro 1966). Its initial existence, not its persistence, is what needs explaining. Functionalism may be a good strategy for isolating salient causal relationships, but for causal theorists, such an approach will never suffice actually to explain religion.

8.   For theologians to speak of a "cosmic story" or "the story of the universe" implicitly gives the universe a purpose: it assumes there is a deep explanation—a narrative leading purposefully to a conclusion—and that there is a transcendental source telling the story. This begs the question against naturalist readings of the history of the universe.

9.   "Religious naturalism," which denies any transcendent realities and reduces religion to merely ethics, doctrines, or subjective experience, will not be discussed here. In effect, it simply gives naturalism a religious veneer and denies traditional religious ontological claims by "reinterpreting" them reductively in naturalistic terms.

10.   Hasker uses the analogy to magnetic fields for the emergence of a substantive self from the field of consciousness (1999: 232), but he realizes that the analogy breaks down since the magnetic field cannot exist independently of its source. All that Hasker can say is that perhaps God works a miracle in the emergence of an independent self (1999: 233).

11.   According to religious historians, pre-modern human beings *experienced* the world as sacred. That is, they experienced the world as having a transcendent dimension—they did not experience it as impersonal and unconscious and then offer explanations in terms of gods and spirits. Thus, all their experiences would be religious.

12.   It is possible to give a *positive* naturalistic reduction of mystical experiences—i.e., such experiences give an insight into the nature of our ordinary mind (e.g., perhaps revealing consciousness free of all objects) or into the natural order of reality but do not involve any "contact" with a transcendent reality. Under such an interpretation, such experiences cannot be explained away any more than any other natural cognitive event.

13.   For other problems, see Jones 2000: 279-88.

14.   Some religious believers may exempt their own religious experiences or beliefs from natural explanations while applying such explanations to all other forms of religion. If some particular religious explanation is better than other ones, then it is a matter of theology that will have to be shown on grounds other than natural explanations.

15.   This is different from the "naturalistic fallacy" in moral philosophy regarding whether normative statements ("ought") can be derived from factual statements ("is").

16.   It should also be noted that in the case of the Buddhists' "mindfulness" type of enlightenment the insight occurs outside of the "lucid trances" (*dhyanas*) related to concentrative meditation, although the mind is prepared by such concentrative exercises. Similarly, the enlightened state of the Advaita Vedantins is not a continuous depth-mystical experience but a state of consciousness that is outside of that experience and that results from that insight. The mystics' interest is in the *insight* into the nature of reality, not any unusual experiences, and whether these insights can be tied to specific states of mind or body is irrelevant to their religious ways of life and concerns. Failure to establish correlations of experiences and physiological states would be equally irrelevant. Studies of what to the religious are the physiological side-effects of the religious exercises are irrelevant to these claims of insight, however interesting they may be in understanding how the brain works.

7

The Mystery of Emergence

The conclusions reached above can be easily summarized: antireductionism in its various forms today appears more convincing in the areas of the natural sciences, the mental realm, the sociocultural realm, and in the role of religion, although the reality of a social or cultural level of organization is not as intuitively plausible as antireductive structures in other areas. Everything may have a physical component, but the simplistic reduction of all to the physical and physics must be rejected. Higher level concepts, causes, and explanations and holistic methodology all are thoroughly ingrained in the sciences today, and there is no reason to think the situation will change except for the reductionists' bald statement of their metaphysical prescription and claims of "in principle" reductions. Whether one rejects substance-reductionism or accepts transcendent realities turns more clearly on broad metaphysical considerations rather than issues related to reductionism alone. But reductionism in all areas still remains viable, with vocal advocates vigorously presenting their cases, especially in neuroscience and physics. In addition, there is not one undisputed case of strong emergence that antireductionists can point to. And, of course, we do not know how matters will develop in the future.

The Centrality of Emergence

One problem, however, concerning the plausibility of reductionism should be highlighted before closing: the prominence of emergence in the organization of things. Philosophers from William James (1977) to Henri Bergson (1911) to Karl Popper (1978) emphasize the active, creative nature of the universe. Novel realities appear that apparently are not reducible to what came before. Part of the universe's creativity is the unforeseeable *generation of new levels of organization as a regular feature of its development.* The only apparent overall plan of development to emergent realities is increasing complexity, accompanied by an unpredictability from what came before. From physical sublevels above the quantum field level to the chemical to the biological to the mental, this process of complexification, integration through "self-organization," and emergence of new realities has occurred constantly throughout the history of the universe. In fact, the universe seems to be a complexification machine, generating more and more complex but stable emergent realities—indeed, this seems to be one of the universe's basic features. Thus, a basic question that both reductionists and antireductionists must answer is why the universe has the habit of turning disorder into a new level of order.

Such emergence may end up being an intractable *mystery*—i.e., not just a manageable problem awaiting further scientific study but something forever beyond our abilities to know.[1] The emergence of higher levels of organization may be a basic, brute fact about reality that will remain impregnable to scientific analysis and explanation, as with why anything exists at all or why any order or lawful behavior exists in the universe.[2] Certainly neither reductionists nor antireductionists have an adequate explanation for this process at present. Antireductionists may accept the possibility that the process may be amenable to some type of scientific investigation (e.g., Davies 1987). Christian theologians and philosophers of religion have jumped at the opportunity provided by our ignorance to make God an underlying source of emergent creativity or "information" (see Clayton 2004; Clayton & Davies 2006; Murphy & Stoeger 2007; Davies & Gregersen 2010)—but finding a gap where theists can say "God did it" is not a scientific explanation. To date the best scientific attempts at an explanation are only to find a place for it within an overarching explanatory scheme of a metaphysical nature; this nevertheless does help to make some sense of it, even if it does not supply an empirical account.

Moreover, structure-antireductionists recognize this process as a *fundamental feature of reality*. Structure-reductionists, on the other hand, simply see no issue here. Their "less is more" approach does not *explain* emergence as a product of physical forces but *dismisses* it as something not needing any explanation because it obviously must be physical and is not needed for predictions. As long as scientists can correlate phenomena on different levels, they see nothing further of interest. The lower level conditions *determine* the higher, and so why there are correlatable phenomena is not seen as an issue. The "how" and "why" of emergence can simply be ignored. The physical level of organization (or the lowest physical sublevel) is the only brute structural reality—all explanations begin and end there. The emergence of higher and higher levels of stability to counter greater and greater complexity just occurs "spontaneously," "naturally," or "necessarily" as a result of the physical level of organization—there is nothing to explain or to be concerned about (e.g., Hardcastle 1996b). Just as a plant inevitably grows when given light and the appropriate nutrients, so too does the universe sprout levels of organization—all we need to know is the DNA code to explain the plant, and all we need to know to explain emergence is the cosmic code lying in the forces of physics. In sum, there simply is no mystery here. Only emergentists have a problem here: by believing there is more to reality, they create the need for explanations where none are in fact needed. The reductionists' attitude toward emergence is "It just happens. Just accept that it is all done by physics. If physicists can practice particle physics even though, in the words of Richard Feynman, 'no one understands why Nature behaves in this particular way,' so too can we move on to other questions."[3]

But such an attitude misses something fundamentally important. In their zeal to replace the complex with the simpler, reductionists are looking the *wrong way*. Reality has been getting more and more complex, but reductionists keep looking for the simpler and simpler as the only path to explanation. Complex levels are emerging, and reductionists are looking only for the lowest, most general levels. They are missing something vital that needs explaining. Reality is not a smooth, seamless whole but contains a series of "quantum jumps" in organization giving rise to apparently *genuine novelty*—i.e., given only the way a lower level is, the next higher level *does not have to be the way it is*. As Saul Kripke put this metaphorically, after God made firing C-fibers, he still had to perform another act of creation to make pain. The process of emergence is both extraordinary and yet recurring throughout the history of the universe. Reductionists have no reason to believe that another universe that is only physically identical to ours *must be* the same as ours, with some biological and mental phenomena accidentally or necessarily arising from the physical structures. At a minimum, reductionists need to be able to account for the very process of the emergence of more and more complex levels of organization in terms of only physical forces. Why is there a process of some realities "supervening" on others at all? Even if complexity can arise from fairly simple sets of rules as in the generation of "gliders" in the computer game of Life or of a full tree from the DNA in a seed, why is reality set up in the first place with rules that form more and more levels of interaction? Why did reality even get above the lowest level of organization? How did a pile of interacting inanimate material become alive (reproducing, self-maintaining, and doing whatever else constitutes "life")? Why is the universe set up for more and more complex forms of life? We can easily imagine a world where life is confined to single-cell organisms. Why did beings with specialized organs develop from cells with the same DNA? How does cooperation and integration fit into the process of evolution? Why do unrelated organisms arrive at very much the same biological solution (e.g., the wing)? Why did consciousness become attached to anything in the universe?

The emergence of *qualia and consciousness* is not merely left unexplained by structure-reductionists; it is not only an accident; it is downright *miraculous*. It is totally unexplainable within a reductionist's framework—all they have is a blunt declaration that it is not a problem and "hope for the best" (Crick 1994: 256). When Jaegwon Kim claims his position is "something near enough" to physicalism (2005), he is missing what a devastating blow these phenomena are to reductionism. Even if they were only epiphenomena, they still are there and do not fit at all. The anomaly of qualia does not only demarcate "the limits of physicalism" (Kim 2011: 333), it refutes the basis of reductive physicalism—such a view simply does not work as a metaphysics. Hand-waving does not make the problem go away.

So too, reductionists have no place in their scheme of things for any dynamic process of the evolving complexity of matter and the emergence of new levels of interactions—their vision screens out the issue entirely. Hence, its significance is missed and implicitly denied. But any scheme that has no place for something so obvious and fundamental to the universe is simply not plausible—it cannot be a serious contender for allegiance until reductionists can do more than say "Well, that's just the way things are—it must be something physical, even if we don't know why or the details of how it occurs." For antireductionists too, emergence may remain a mystery, but at least with their emphasis on a structural pluralism to reality, they recognize the process of emergence is occurring and realize its importance. Indeed, "emergentists" place emergence, although a mystery, centrally in their scheme of things. But merely by placing emergence within their outlook antireductionists win this important philosophical contest at present by default.

The explanatory skeleton scientists have abstracted is no substitute for the world in which we actually live and move. All we experience is *explained*, not eliminated, by scientists. It is the philosophers or scientists *qua* philosophers, not scientists *qua* scientists, who explain away apparent realities. It is the philosophers advocating substance-, structure-, or theory-reductionism who explain away the reality of a phenomenon by claiming it is "really only" or "merely" or "nothing but" something else. Only eliminationists actually deny the *existence* of some of what we experience. The thrust of the reductionists' drive, however, is to replace all of the scientific *structure* with that of the lowest level of physical organization. However, it is not obvious that the reductionists' perspective on reality—"from the bottom up"—yields greater understanding than other possible perspectives (Nozick 1981: 633), let alone that it is the only legitimate perspective. There is nothing in what we experience to suggest reality is put together this way. It is only an intellectual desire for a neat conceptual scheme that can motivate such a drive to explain everything in terms of the simplest and to ignore totally what is not amenable to such treatment. This approach misses the centrality of the process of emerging higher and higher levels of organization to all of reality. In short, reality is bursting forth with perhaps endless creativity, and reductionists are looking the other way.

Emergence and Levels of Organization

Structuring is obviously part of reality—the universe does not consist of quarks drifting about aimlessly. Instead, the universe is organized into levels of stable organization with dynamic interactions resulting in sets of different types of properties. Thus, structuring reveals something basic of reality. So an inventory of what is real must include both what is structured and some type of structure, each fundamentally real and equally primary—neither feature can be reduced to the other, even if the two features have some common source. While structure-reductionists stress the substance structured (and as physicalists, they accept matter as the only substance), structure-antireductionists stress the structuring, and those who are explicitly emergentists stress the repeating process of complexification and stable organization. Emergence is tied to the process of complexification: something real in nature other than matter is producing both the structuring and the upward development of higher levels of organization. For reductionists, only physical structures are real, but they offer no explanation of how these can produce the process of upward emergence. Subatomic particles have the ability to "self-organize," but why reality should be constructed to do this or why that process should lead to more and more levels of complex properties is irrelevant to the reductionists' scheme of correlations. Thus, as discussed, it is simply of no interest to reductionists and they have no explanation for it at all—they do not have even the promise of one. Nevertheless, emergence shows there are basic aspects to the nature of reality than fit in the reductionists' philosophy.

Integrated wholes (i.e., "systems") have phenomena that are irreducible in that they have properties that their components cannot manifest—or to put it differently, they *do* something their components cannot. They have a freedom and a causal power that obtains between events on their level regardless of the lower levels' activity. There may also be laws about activity on each level that are unique to that level. In short, there are facts about each level of reality that are independent of the facts about other levels. If nothing else, this means concept-reductionism must be rejected: there are levels of information that simply cannot be reduced. And when it comes to explanations, theory-antireductionists see all these levels of organization as equally real: processes and events on each level have their own causal powers and generate a complexity that becomes the base for another level; hence, none is ultimately more fundamental than another. Thus, phenomena resist explanations in lower level terms and instead require causal explanations unique to each level. And any explanation of how the process of emergence that produces new levels occurs would be as fundamental as explanations within levels.

But there is no scientific reason to believe that the four fundamental forces physicists concentrate upon (or however many they finally discover and settle upon) constitute the only structures at work in reality or are responsible for the process of emergence. Instead, accounts of various levels all at present reveal something of reality equal to that of particle physics. There is no sense in which subatomic particles can be treated as "more real" than, say, a bacterial cell or a human person, or (according to many antireductionists) a social reality (Peacocke 1986: 27-28). An account of a baseball play in terms of the quarks involved would not explain the action at all. Nor does the physics of quantum level particles help us understand chemical bonding, the periodic table, the appearance of life, mental properties, or human personal and social behavior in general. In short, the emergence of real novelty in the course of evolution should be regarded as fact (see Mayr 1988a). Indeed, for all we know more levels may emerge in the future—nature may not have fully unfolded yet. But the important point is that for antireductionists reality consists of multiple levels of properties, all *equally real* and hence not reducible to just the physical. To complete their argument, antireductionists must add that the reason the various levels of properties are irreducible is that there are independent, nonphysical levels of structures (forces, "principles") at work in reality.

This is where reductionists disagree. Reductionists must accept some structuring, but they insist that ultimately there is only one level of organization—the physical set of sublevels or perhaps only the lowest such sublevel—and that can explain all that there is to explain. (Again, structure- or theory-reductionists have not actually presented an account of the process of emergence in terms of physical forces—all they have produced is a metaphysical declaration of the way things must be.) That one level produces all higher levels of complexity. All ostensibly real higher structures are reducible to the physical. The higher level properties result simply from a very complex interplay of lower level forces.

Structure-reductionists and antireductionists, however, do not merely disagree over how many irreducible levels of organization constitute the scientific skeleton of reality. It is not simply a philosophical game about what are the fewest posits necessary. Indeed, naturalists should not be too concerned with that issue: accepting several levels of organization as unexplainable, brute facts is not that great a jump from accepting one—the basic mystery of why there are any such levels at all remains. And here the disputants face in opposite directions. Reductionists vote for simplicity and explanation as simply predictability, while antireductionists accept both complexity and perhaps our need to accept more mysteries as central to reality. Nothing in our experience or science suggests that only the physical level exists or is causally effective or that it causes the process of emergence—it is only the structure-reductionists' metaphysical vision that compels their conclusion.

This can be seen most clearly in considering human beings. For reductive physicalists, all that exists is matter in motion, with its activity controlled by the laws of physics—we are, in Francis Crick's words, "no more than the behavior of a vast assembly of nerve cells and their associated molecules" (1994: 3). When matter evolves into certain configurations, the basic physical forces, coupled with the pure randomness of events, cause life and mental faculties automatically to arise, and these higher level phenomena disappear when the configurations become disorganized. To structure-reductionists, the process that generated the highly complex brain as a base of consciousness is simply a fluke. All we are is only a physical activity of matter. We think more is involved only because our brain has evolved to look for agency and purpose. Substance-reductionists say this is not a bleak and dark picture at all—they feel at home in the universe, since everything is constructed the same way. The naturalist physicist Freeman Dyson, for one, says "I don't feel like a stranger in the universe." To them, it is the religious, with their dualism of soul and body or their separation as creatures from the creator, who should feel like strangers in a strange land, alienated from their true home.

But structure-antireductive naturalists offer another option: life and the mind are perfectly natural aspects of reality, reflecting real structures that are as natural and inherent in the fabric of reality as those that are physical. Reality is simply more complex than the reductionists want to believe. As Karl Popper put it, the world is far more interesting and exciting than is dreamt of in the reductionists' philosophy (1982: 163). The appearances of life and consciousness are not flukes or perplexing anomalies to be reduced but are regular emergent features that are as natural as the appearance of atoms and molecules. All our subjective, first-person experi-ence—everything from pains to sense-experiences to the creation of great scientific and artistic works—is as much a part of the fabric of reality as matter. Our experience of the Mona Lisa is no more "reducible" or "unreal" than the paint and wood—the appearance is as much a feature of reality as the physical constituents. Scientists can analyze energies, vibrations, and the neurophysiology of hearing, but it is absurd to say that this touches the impact of the reality of music on us. In the words of Erwin Shrödinger, "[s]cience cannot tell us a word about why music delights us, or why and how an old song can move us to tears." In short, experience is a level of reality that is no less real than the physical. Most importantly, consciousness and other mental phenomena do not occur randomly but result from innate structures ingrained as deeply into reality as those of physics. If so, consciousness is as fixed a part of the world as the atom or the brain. It may be a fundamental category, like space-time—i.e., something that cannot be derived from anything else—and the structural skeleton of reality cannot be described fully without including it. Thus, any ontology that eliminates consciousness or any other feature of a higher level of organization is simply missing something fundamentally real. In sum, under antireductive naturalism, we have the possibility of truly being at home in the universe—we are as normal and expected as anything else.

Theists may be able to adapt the idea that life and consciousness are built into the structure of reality and thus have a central role in the development of the universe to support the strong Anthropic Principle, i.e., that the laws and conditions of the universe must be such as to make the universe observable at some stage of its history. Or they may adopt some other form of teleological causation—in short, the universe is "designed" for self-organization and emergence. The religious may argue that the emergence of life and mind (or a place for souls) plays a central role in the very purpose of the universe. Indeed, a trend of increasing complexity may itself be evidence of some purpose (Davies 1999: 270). Most importantly for the issues at hand, emergence is central to the universe, and even if life and consciousness were the result of matter being structured by physical forces alone, reductionists still have no explanation of *how* this occurs, let alone *why*. Nothing in the reductionist vision accounts for an active process of emergence of higher and higher levels of interactions. Reductionists, in sum, have no reason whatsoever for why or how reality came to be organized the way it is—indeed, with their framework of what needs explaining, they cannot even in principle give a reason.

According to structure-antireductionists, "life," "mind," and "the physical" are equally fundamental categories of structural reality, none being reducible to another. Perhaps a better way to approach the situation is to see "matter" as simply how the "stuff" of the universe appears when only the physical level of organization is involved. We may well never know what this "stuff" is, but there is no reason to give primacy to its physical organization. Everything is *physical* in that every bit of the stuff constituting reality has a physical level of organization structuring it (if the physical level of organization is in fact present throughout the universe). But it is wrong to say "*everything is only physical,*" since some bits of the stuff of reality also have other levels of organization operating away in them. And there is no reason to believe these levels are the products of, or explainable by, only the physical level. Thus, the claim "*physics explains all of reality*" is true insofar as physicists explain one level of all of reality, but it is also false insofar as physicists explain only that one level of reality's structure, not other structures or emergence.

Conceptually separating *structure* from the *stuff structured* may lead physicalists to feel less compelled to reduce all levels of structure to the physical. For example, mental properties are physical in substance, but a nonphysical level of nature's structuring may still be at work. Looked at that way, there is no reason to think mental structures "come out" of the physical level of organization. Such structures may be totally distinct, although they depend on the presence of other levels developed to certain degrees of complexity to become operative in matter. More generally, it may be wrong to look at the entire issue in terms of the inter-action of fundamentally different levels of structure. Instead, we should start with the obvious: *the whole at work* in the immediate experience of awareness and human agency. Starting with the irreducibility of the human being—i.e., the primacy of the person and the lived body, according to William James and such philosophi-cal phenomenologists as Maurice Merleau-Ponty—may well tell us something more central about the nature of reality than trying to figure out which structures can or cannot be reduced, let alone focusing only on the lowest, more general levels of organization. The human brain is the most complex known bit of the universe, not by chance, but because the convergence of the different levels of structure are necessary for consciousness to appear. Human free will and downward causation appear more natural than claiming that only the lowest level of organization has causal power. To deny the reality of consciousness and these faculties or even to dismiss them as epiphenomena is difficult to maintain: why would they have evolved in nature or continue to exist in any way at all if they did not have real causal power in the world? If any emergence is genuine, then so are its products and their interactions. Such a view is more in keeping with the nature of a dynamic and growing reality than its denial. Once again, any scheme that looks only toward the simpler and has no place for emergence is unacceptable.

This point also has an impact upon Sir Arthur Eddington's "two tables" paradox (1958: xi-xiv). For reductionists, the everyday table we experience is, in the final analysis, only a convenient construct, something simpler than the literal truth that only subatomic activity is involved. To antireductionists, we are not forced to choose whether the table is "really" substantial or "really nothing but" insubstantial subatomic forces. The concept of emerging *levels of reality* allows us to avoid any paradox of a subatomic table versus an everyday table. The different descriptions of the same system are descriptions of different levels within the system and thus of different types of properties of the system. Both physical sublevels of reality are present in the one phenomenon. Even if the subatomic levels are one cause of the higher level property, nevertheless more of reality is involved in the higher properties. The higher levels have a reality too, a reality that is not described in particle physics. As the philosopher Gilbert Ryle noted, in a very real sense particle physicists do not describe tables and chairs at all—they are asking different questions about another level of reality (1954: 79). There are different but equally real levels of reality to all phenomena, and particle physicists simply do not deal with all of them. The higher levels are not unreal or an illusion or epiphenom-ena—anyone who has walked into a wall knows that solidity is not an illusion. Solidity and all the other higher level properties are still real factors in the world, even if they are factors that quarks and their interactions do not possess.

In short, there are features of reality that are not features of the subatomic particles. Tables are not just quarks, water is not just hydrogen and oxygen atoms, and people are not just DNA molecules. The higher level phenomena possess properties and causally interact with each other in ways that are not describable in terms of particle physics. Thus, there are real features of the world that are omitted from our accounts when the focus, as with reductionists, is on the lowest level alone. As the physicist Donald MacKay put it, the fallacy of reductionism—or, in his phrase, "nothing-but-ery"—is to suggest that once we have a complete description at one level, we have no need for descriptions at others (1982: 20). Reductionists may see particle physicists as having the magical key to the universe, but physicists need not see themselves this way (as noted in Chapter 3).[4] There is no one way the world is with regard to structures. Instead, the world exists in a different way at each level, and it "is" or "has" the properties revealed at each level.

What Needs Explaining

Structure-reductionists may respond that they do not deny the obvious—that solidity, life, and so on, exist—but argue only that the higher levels of organization and their properties are *completely caused by* lower level phenomena. They claim antireductionists are committed to nonexistent entities or forces. Indeed, reductionists see a robust antireductionism as the return of vitalism. Instead, quarks somehow combine and give rise to other subatomic entities that eventually give rise to atoms which in turn combine into molecules which in a lattice structure produce all of a table's everyday features (impenetrability and so on). Thus, even if quarks are not solid but only eddies in a sea of energy, their properties and interactions determine all higher level phenomena. And similar processes of bonding explain the wetness of water, the origin of life, and consciousness even if we do not know the details of these processes. Explaining the expansion of metal when heated does not require any new forces, and the same is true of all level effects. Higher level entities are simply configurations of lower level objects interacting in increasingly complex ways, and their features are simply features totally determined by the parts. Even the exemplars of emergence—qualia and consciousness—are only the straightforward products of matter and the physical level of organization. In the end there is nothing that cannot be explained, and everything (at least from a scientific point of view) is, as Peter Atkins says, "extraordinarily simple" (1992: 3). Once we finally understand all the levels thoroughly, we will see that higher levels of complexity are simply complex mixtures of lower level properties. Ultimately, if we had an account of only the one lowest level of organization in complete detail, we would be able to explain all the apparently "higher" level phenomena. All the complexities of the fullness of reality will then be explained by simple principles (if we can call quantum physics "simple"). Only the "how" of organization, not the "how" and "why" of emergence, matters. Antireductionists are missing the simplicity of it all.[5]

The reductive approach has the advantage of making it easier to construct one coherent picture of our one world, but this misses the problem with their approach. Even if scientists one day are able to explain (or at least predict) all higher level properties in terms of lower level properties—a big "*if*"—the problem would still remain why lower level entities combine at all to form higher level effects. Scientists may be able to discern the mechanics of how subatomic particles combine to form atoms, or how atoms combine to form molecules, or even how consciousness arises from brains, but why does this process exist in the first place? Is the universe structured to generate disequilibrium, and why is this complexity countered by higher and higher levels of organization rather than some stagnation or chaos on the lowest level of structuring? Why is it in the structure of an atom to combine and for complexity to lead to higher and higher levels of order? Scientists may be able to explain how life originates from its components, but that does not mean life can be reduced to those components (Popper 1974). Neurons combining do not form consciousness: they only form the base for it. Even the exemplar of a reductive explanation—explaining heat in terms of the motion of the molecules—still has the emergence of a novel property of the system (heat) that the parts do not have. Even if only the parts in context produce a higher level effect of the whole, why is reality set up to do this? Why do things in wholes behave differently than they do in isolation? Are some things set up to be parts? Is reality essentially relational? Explaining only the mechanics of "how" integration occurs does not touch the real problem that reductionists have from focusing only on the parts. In sum, if the world is set up reductively, the wonder of new levels only appears greater.

Antireductionists readily concede that the lower levels are a necessary part of the picture—the way reality is set up, the physical level of organization is always the first to appear, and without it no other levels will become active. But *dependency* on bases does not mean that the bases *cause or determine* the higher levels. So too, antireductionists can accept a chain of correlations of phenomena from different levels—correlations in themselves do not establish a reductive relationship or any explanation. But they ask why is there the very process of emergence of any higher level properties at all? Why, that is, does the interaction of parts lead "inevitably" or "naturally" to higher level properties? Even if scientists can explain the relations of "realizing" or "dependency," why are there levels for these relations to begin with? And why is there a hierarchy of levels? Indeed, why is the world organized into more than one level at all? Scientific correlations of phenomena are simply irrelevant to this issue. To ignore all that needs explaining is simply to ignore what does not fit the reductionists' Procrustean point of view. Even if after studying the complexity of mixtures of lower level factors under which conditions a higher level phenomenon appears, there still remains more to be explained—i.e., why the stable, coherent higher levels with their own properties emerge at all. Something more at work in reality must be explained in the emergence of higher level than can be imagined in the reductionists' vision.

The mechanisms that reductionists find important may not be the only ones at work in reality, or even the most important ones, since questions of the emergence of life and consciousness remain unaccounted for. To dismiss even solidity and wetness as only "level effects" of subatomic particles is to miss the emergence of new levels of organization completely. We have no reason today to think a few relatively simple rules are responsible for all the complexity of the fullness of reality. The world remains more complex and mysterious than reductionists like to think. Reductionists must dismiss altogether the idea that new causal units emerge because they have no possible explanations for how such wholes could form. But whether wholes are in fact more than aggregates or are merely parts in particular configurations, something real is omitted from the reductionists' vision.

Scientists routinely note that we actually know every little of reality. They abstract out those parts of reality that lend themselves to understanding under controlled conditions, but those parts are still only one aspect of a vastly more complex whole. As Bertrand Russell said: "Physics is mathematical not because we know so much about the physical world, but because we know so little; it is only its mathematical properties that we can discover." The abstractions are, to use a common analogy, small islands of intelligibility in an immense sea of unintelligibility. That physical laws are so abstract is hardly grounds for the causal "completeness of physics" (Cartwright 1999)—the argument is strictly metaphysical. In addition, that perhaps *95% of the universe* apparently consists of apparently unknowable "dark matter" and "dark energy" has only recently been discovered and should give reductionists pause: how much do we really know about reality, and what do we have to learn? And yet reductionists are supremely confident that they know the ultimate answer on the issue of reduction and emergence. The reductionists' simple metaphysics becomes a substitute for the true complexity of reality: with that as a screen, reductionists do not have to face (or perhaps cannot even see) the complexity and mystery engulfing the intelligible element. To many, it is arrogant to say we truly know anything of the fundamental nature of reality with confidence, let alone something not covered by science as currently practiced.

Antireductionists can be more open: any laws of higher level phenomena are not deducible from the laws of lower level phenomena because they depend, in addition to lower level conditions, upon conditions on their own level that are accidental from the point of view of all lower level disciplines (Putnam 1994: 431-32). Thus, we could never reconstruct the universe simply from a complete knowledge of the lowest level of organization (see Anderson 1972). There is no smooth continuity between levels but numerous ontic and explanatory gaps, and this feature makes any structure- or theory-reductions difficult even to conceive. If this means a form of "vitalism" for biology, then it would be in terms of vitalistic *structures* and would not share the problems of vitalistic *substances* (see Hull 1974: 128-29).

Can There Be a Science of Emergence?

The sciences as currently designed will always fail to explain one obvious feature of the fullness of reality: what makes the arising of layers of organization occur at all and perhaps be inevitable. It may well be only natural factors at work, but from the study of current science we would never be able to tell. Science as scientists have designed it to date simply cannot address the basic problem of emergence. Scientists produce particular abstractions of reality, but none of these abstractions are relevant to the issue of emergence. By looking at the world from different points of view, scientists have found different levels of organization to phenomena, and they have been able to correlate phenomena from different levels. As time goes on, they may be able to correlate more and more. But something is missed by merely correlating phenomena. Even the new sciences of complexity and "self-organization" do not help. What scientists need to answer is how the higher levels are an inevitable consequence of the lower—i.e., why and how there is an upward drive—and this issue is simply missed by the analytical nets scientists have been casting upon reality. Perhaps emergence occurs by chance. Perhaps systematic natural forces are at work. Perhaps something more is at work in reality than reductionists can accept. Perhaps not. In any case, scientists are not yet asking the relevant questions. What is needed is a theory of transition between levels. Can science build "staircases" between levels (Gell-Mann 1994: 112)?

Thus, what needs to be studied is how levels emerge, what goes in between levels to get from one level to the next, and the entire overarching upward drive of emergence. But even if scientists ever do establish a chain of correlations leading from the highest levels of organization to the lowest, they still would never be attacking the problem of *emergence* at all. Even if one glorious unifying theory is ever achieved, something very real and important about the universe will still be omitted from science if the existence of a process of emergence is not covered. As discussed in Chapter 3, a CUT without a TOO does not accomplish the reductionists' dream. A science based on establishing correlations demystifies part of reality, but it is simply not designed to deal with the dynamic dimension that the process of emergence adds, and so the mystery would remain.

Also nothing in the reductionists' vision of science could ever lead to evidence of emergence, let alone an explanation. Reductionists assert that, even if emergence is possible in principle, antireductionists have not presented "a scintilla of evidence" that there are genuine emergent forces in reality (McLauglin 1992: 90-91). What is needed is empirical evidence of a *mechanism* for emergence. Antireductionists at this time also do not have evidence of the mechanisms at work, but this does not rule out that there is the causal reality of the higher level phenomena. And what finding would reductionists accept even in principle as *evidence* of an irreducible, emergent reality? Reductionists rule out the obvious—e.g., the apparent causal reality of mental activity—as evidence of genuine emergence. Thus, they do not even get to the issue of a mechanism for such a reality. Doing no more than finding more and more correlations certainly is irrelevant to this problem. The problem is showing how the higher level phenomena and correlations arose in the first place. But again, the entire issue of such emergence is screened out by the reductionists' approach to research and theorizing. Reductionists would stop probing reality once the correlations are established. Thus, if there are emergent forces at work in reality, the reductionists' approach would simply not find them.

Certainly reductionists have not advanced any explanation of emergence solely in terms of physical forces. What they need is a new Charles Darwin who can explain emergence by means of the known physical forces, just as Darwin advanced a natural mechanism (natural selection) to explain evolution without invoking a preconceived plan. As things now stand, to use one example, gravity working alone only makes larger and larger clumps of matter—it does not integrate matter to form any level of organization, let alone make the process of emergence run. Thus, if gravity alone were at work, larger and perhaps more stable clumps of matter might develop, but no biological or mental level of organization at all would appear—in short, gravity cannot explain how nature integrates. The same is true for the other known physical forces, whatever their effect on particular physical sublevels. What in reality structures subatomic particles in such a way as to enable them to combine and for higher levels of combinations to arise needs to be identified. More generally, when instabilities arise, why do things form higher level order rather than simply coalesce into order of the same level or collapse into chaos? It is not clear how studying the known physical forces is much help in this regard.

Questions could also be asked concerning biological forces. While natural selection may account for complexity on one level, as it now stands it cannot account for how higher levels could emerge in the first place. For example, it may or may not account for why neurons arise or attain more complex configurations, but it does not account for how consciousness comes to be associated with them. More generally, natural selection does not explain why matter tends to organize in the first place or the direction of higher levels of complexity. Thus, it cannot deal with the issue of emergence. Indeed, one would not expect the forces producing lawful activity within any level to govern emergence—such forces would only organize the same activity over and over again within that level and would not lead to a higher level of organization. How, for example, could a chemical process give rise to a nonchemical property? (Of course, this is why reductive physicalists feel compelled to claim that consciousness and other apparently strongly emergent realities are only physical properties or must be in fact utterly unreal.)

Nevertheless, emergence may involve lawful structures that can be studied by science. If so, it will be studiable but only by a very different science with new approaches to research and new ways of looking at complexity in nature (see Davies 1987: 203). Analytical experiments may not be possible. Both reductionists and antireductionists agree that when things get too complex a new level of organization somehow emerges. For example, a complex physiochemical condition appears where proteins "spontaneously" arrange themselves into a reproducing organism. But as an explanation this sounds as convincing as the "spontaneous generation" of life sounded to biologists of an earlier time. Simply saying that a new structure "*spontaneously*" bubbles forth or that reality "*self-organizes*" does not explain anything at all—it identifies the issue but offers no reason for why it occurs. Things do not spontaneously fall into ordered states. Iron filings do not organize themselves—magnetism is at work. Ordering does not "just happen" or arise "for free" out of chaos—something in the structure of reality must make it happen.

In sum, we do get "something from nothing" or "more from less" or "a free lunch"—order only comes from ordering principles. Something structural has to be responsible for the process of emergence. Some factors organize phenomena on one level into base-conditions for the emergence of higher level phenomena. From a reductionist perspective, this may look like a very strong form of downward causation—e.g., a structure from the mental level causing neurons to develop and form the complex wholes necessary for consciousness to appear. But perhaps another type of force is involved. Perhaps the force responsible for emergence is a force comparable to the four forces physicists currently focus on and just as fundamental. Whether what is responsible for emergence is called "biological," "physical," or just "natural" is irrelevant. Indeed, a vocabulary for a science of emergence has not yet been developed. Since the factors responsible for emergence are different from an intralevel cause, even labeling them a "force" or a "structure" is problematic. Terms with a more epistemic than ontic flavor such as "code" and "information" have not yet proven very helpful. Perhaps it should be thought of in terms of a "field of force" not yet discovered or of organizing "principles" (Davies 1987; see Schrödinger 1944) that guide the course of development of the universe. Perhaps it is evidence of a design or purposeful blueprint to reality (Davies 1987: 203). Or, naturalists may argue that it removes the need for a creator god or designer. The principles would be like any other natural force and would remove emergence as a "gap" in the natural order to be filled by a transcendent agent. (Or more exactly, natural structures for emergence and irreducible biological and mental structures would be no more the result of intelligent design than physical structures like magnetism; whether all of reality's structures are designed by a transcendent reality would remain an open question.) All emergence would be built into nature from the universe's beginning—life and consciousness would come about as naturally as any other level of organization, even if they did not emerge until the later evolution of base-conditions permitted.

Perhaps no science will help us understand the reality behind emergence. Perhaps the process is like the problem of consciousness as conceived by the physicalist "mysterians" (McGinn 1991): a dimension of reality that is perfectly natural but that creatures with our type of cognitive apparatus are simply not equipped to study, and so we cannot expect to learn its cause. We are evolved to survive in this universe, not to know all there is to know about reality, and so some things may well remain forever beyond our understanding. If so, emergence will remain a mystery, impregnable to analysis and explanation. And ultimately, whether we attribute emergence to God, natural forces, or chance, we cannot explain why any of these sources should have the capacity to create new patterns of organization. But the reductionists' approach simply stops the discussion before it starts.

Whatever position is correct, the basic dispute between reductionists and anti-reductionists will not be settled by sciences based on only correlating phenomena from different levels. Scientists may decide to conceptualize their results along reductive lines, but they need not. As discussed in Chatper 3, without new empirical evidence, deciding to interpret scientific correlations reductively or antireductively would not be an empirical decision. Neither philosophical position is necessitated by either science or naturalism. Neither side can confer the imprimatur of science on their vision. This points once again to the *metaphysical* nature of the dispute. Reductionism seems more "scientific" only because reductionists ignore what is not explained in the current approach of science and are satisfied with correlations alone. As also noted in Chapter 3, reductionists need not fear their metaphysics will ever be disproved: they can maintain their position in light of any developments in science because it is always possible that future research will produce the details that reductionists need. But if science comes to an end pretty much as it is today, reductionists can argue as a last stand that the lack of establishing a physical engine for the process of emergence is only due to the fact that our technology cannot penetrate all the details of reality—"*in principle*" all is reducible and indeed already has been reduced through the establishment of correlations.

But again, the scientific correlation of higher and lower phenomena and predictions based on such correlating do not address the issue of emergence and hence are themselves neutral to the issue of reductionism. Antireductionists have no problem with the correlations themselves, no matter how detailed. They can accept correlations if they are established (since they too accept lower level bases to higher level phenomena), and they will not be disturbed if they are not established. But they ask how do these correlations, if they exist, *arise*? That must be explained by more than the correlations themselves. And the point here is that scientists do not address this issue today—indeed, even how to address it is far from clear at present.

Determining What Is Real and Its Implications

Reductionism is a central topic in considering *what we deem real in the world*. Both reductionists and antireductionists are going beyond science in their positions: what each side suggests is irreducible depends on their comprehensive view of what they consider real or fundamental. Such decisions on matters of ultimate ontology are logically prior to deciding what is reducible. If we see something as real, be it first-person experience or whatever, we are not going to explain it away by something apparently simpler but accept it as irreducible. And reductionists see much more of reality as reducible. But our best knowledge—the natural sciences—does not lead to the conclusion that only the physical level of organization is real or that the natural universe is the only reality—neither structure- nor substance-reductionism follows from any scientific finding. Science does not dictate what should be reduced, nor indeed do our experiences. Instead, we make a *judgment* of a philosophical nature concerning what is important. The philosopher Mary Midgley rightly argues that reductions are not value-free but are parts of a larger project for reshaping the whole intellectual landscape and often our general attitude toward life as well (1995: 133). Substance-, structure- and theory-reductionisms are meta-physically and epistemically ideological in that they encourage both a naturalistic metaphysics against a religious one and the view that the scientific abstractions of reality exhaust all possible empirical knowledge of reality.

The value-laden nature of substance- and structure-reductionisms, however, has practical implications going beyond a purely intellectual concern for understanding reality. The reductionists' downward focus and refusal to accept the full panorama of levels as equally real has a negative consequence: the more valuable is always claimed to be nothing but the less valuable—e.g., the performance of a violin sonata is "nothing but the scraping of horsehair on catgut" and "love is nothing but glandular secretion" (Nozick 1981: 627). More broadly, reductionism entails a view of what is real in the world and in human beings that has an impact on our values. Reductionists present a cold and bleak world devoid of purpose, meaning, feelings, and values—a nihilistic world in which people are a cosmic accident, randomly evolved into no more than survival machines for genes. Ultimately, we are nonentities, void of any significance. We are not beings with the capacity for free will; instead, there is only the behavior of a vast assembly of nerve cells (Crick 1994: 3). In the end, only lower levels of organization control actions. If we only had complete knowledge, we would know that causes from the lower physical sublevels of organization alone dictate all actions.[6] The reductionists' world has no place for value (Kauffman 2008: 11). The reductionist worldview is "chilling and impersonal," and according to reductionists it has to be accepted, not because reductionists like it, but because that is "the way the world works" (Weinberg 1992: 53). If the world-clock were twenty-hours long, *Homo sapiens* would have been around for less than a second—that in itself shows how insignificant we are in the scheme of things. Reductionists may be able to find some meaning to life in such a pointless world, but it would be totally subjective.

Antireductionists, even of the naturalist variety, see the world as a much more welcoming place. Reality is not essentially uncreative—a place in which events are random or controlled by physical forces alone. Instead, reality is intrinsically creative in that genuinely novel realities have emerged, not through chance, but because of the inherent nature of reality. Antireductionists see no reason why reductionists are so adamant that the physical level of organization is the only structuring force at work in reality, even leaving aside the issue of why emerging levels occur at all. In the words of the physicist Paul Davies, reductionists have an "extraordinary prejudice" in favor of the lowest physical level of organization, since there is no compelling reason why the fundamental laws of nature have to refer only to the level of fields and elementary particles (1987: 142).

To antireductionists, life and consciousness are as real as stones and quarks: they are as inevitable, given the right conditions, as any physical phenomena. Nor is it clear why the entire organization of reality should in any way be called simply "physical" since some structuring is present in animate realities and not in inanimate ones. Certainly just because the physical level of organization started structuring the stuff of reality before the biological and mental levels did does not mean the latter are the *product* of the former. The physical level of organization may have existed for billions of years before the proper physical conditions appeared for the other levels to kick in, but this does not mean that the latter structures are not independent or that they are any less *real and essential* to the overall scheme of things. It may mean only that the structures of consciousness require a physical base of a certain complexity to be present before they can begin to structure matter. Thus, life and consciousness "emerge" out of the physical level only in the sense that the physical level must be present first, not that the physical level causes them.[7]

The most direct and significant consequence of the antireductionist position is this: our mind is a causal reality, and thereby, the possibility of genuine free will and human responsibility is not revoked but is in fact routine features of reality.[8] Indeed, the devaluing of people, and of free will in particular, cause many antireductionists to speak of reductionism not only as a philosophical blunder but a *moral failing* (Nozick 1981: 631; see MacKay 1982; Midgley 1995)—if a rock or machine breaks or ceases to exist, there is no moral problem, but not so if a person or animal is a reality worthy of moral concern. Under the antireductive view, our humanness is not only real and not accidental but part of the fundamental blueprint of reality. (Theists would probably invoke a designer at this point.) To biologist Stuart Kauffman, this worldview beyond reductionism is one "in which we are members of a universe of ceaseless creativity in which life, agency, meaning, value, consciousness, and the full richness of human action have emerged" (2008: 2).

What we value too may also be part of the mental level inherent in reality (see Sperry 1985). Our social nature may also be central to the scheme of things; if so, social and cultural levels of organization could not be reduced to the activities of individuals who in turn could be reduced to the activity of physical particles. We may learn something about an equally fundamental aspect of reality by focusing on our mental activity and sociocultural creations as by studying quantum physics.

In sum, if antireductionists are correct, we are not an unexplained blip in a silent sea of energy and matter but are somehow programmed into the structure of the universe. We are connected to the rest of the universe in a meaningful way. We may be only tiny bits of matter from a supernova that exploded billions of years ago, but somehow we became animated and conscious. Exactly how and why this occurred may remain a mystery, but it is amazing enough for many naturalists to feel at home in the universe and to feel wonder at all that is. Whether antireductionists of the naturalistic variety can find this view of the universe "*meaningful*" when any transcendent source of meaning is denied is a point of debate between naturalists and the traditionally religious. The prospect of a transcendent meaning for the entire the cosmos would be gone, but the world or one's life may still have a meaning or a significance—indeed, the world may be suffused with value—that a reductionist perspective simply screens out.

To reductionists, antireductionists simply cannot face the world as it really is—the harsh reality that reductionists believe science compels us to accept. But to antireductionists, it is the reductionists who are being utterly unrealistic and cannot face the obvious: life and consciousness are as real as everything from quarks to large-scale physical phenomena. It is the reductionists who engage in a form of philosophical wishful thinking: they are presenting a warped perspective and are blaming it on science—as discussed, scientists need not reduce reality to the causal features they abstract from the study of nature. Human beings can be treated as physiochemical mechanisms to learn much about how we work. That is science. But it is quite another thing to claim that this abstraction is *all* a human being is. That is neither a scientific premise nor conclusion: we may be merely an evolved, complex form of animal life ceasing at death, or there may be more levels of reality at work in us, some of which survive death in some way—the scientific study of the body (the physical and biological levels) or the correlation of physical and mental states will never prove either possibility. It may show that the body is necessary to the appearance of the mind but nothing more. As the astronomer Sir James Jean said, we have no idea of the relation of life to the universe: life may be the final goal of the universe, an accidental and unimportant byproduct of natural processes, or a disease affecting matter in its old age. In short, "we are complex machines" is a claim within the realm of science, but "we are *only* complex machines" is a metaphysical claim. The reductionists' position is a *metaphysical* conclusion in no way entailed by the science itself.

It is the reductionists' qualifiers—"nothing but," "really only," "merely"—that turn straightforward scientific analyses of phenomena into metaphysical conclusions. It is the reductionists who make the philosophical move concerning the status of those abstractions as the final word on reality, not scientists *qua* scientists. The reductionists' move is an example of what Alfred North Whitehead called the fallacy of "misplaced concreteness," i.e., reducing reality to the abstractions of science (1967: 50-51). Scientific theories, like all thought, involve abstractions; they become distortions only when we remove them from their context of study and absolutize them into something more than they are. To antireductionists, it is a distortion of reality to claim that only those abstractions are real or that one abstraction (the lowest physical level) is either the substance of all reality or can ever explain all the features of reality. The ontological question of what is ultimately real must be kept distinct from the scientific questions concerning causes and must be defended on philosophical grounds—the reductionists' conclusion does not follow simply from the science. Indeed, if anything, reductionists are *antiscientific* in spirit since they are prescribing the course scientists should pursue rather than letting scientists decide the development of science unfettered (Agazzi 1991).

Thus, *science* does not compel either accepting the pointless world of reductionism or the richer and more optimistic world of antireductionism. Science does not say the universe is meaningless or that we have no free will. Reductionists do. Their stark picture of reality comes, not from science, but from their particular metaphysical interpretation of the significance of science. Reductionists believe, in the infamous words of Steven Weinberg, the "more the universe seems comprehensible, the more it also seems pointless" (1977: 119). But scientists *qua* scientists cannot find meaning to the universe, even in principle: the tool of science is not *designed* to find any meaning, purpose, or significance, or miraculous exceptions to laws. Any meaning to the universe would simply slip through the analytical nets scientists cast over the universe. To use an analogy used earlier, science is giving us more and more complete accounts of the "grammar" and "vocabulary" of the universe—but whether the "book" has *meaning* or is only a random set of grammatically correct gibberish will not be found in such an approach. The rules of grammar govern and constrain the construction of the book, but this does not mean all aspects of the book are reducible to grammar. Accounts of the book in terms of its alphabet, punctuation marks, vocabulary, grammar, or meaning-content can be complete in their own terms but are still not exhaustive of all aspects of the book—the question of the *meaning* of the book remains on a level that is not addressed by analyzes of its grammar. Similarly with science and reality: scientific accounts do not address the issue of the universe's possible meaning. To claim science has *disproved* any meaning to the universe in principle when scientists *qua* scientists could not find it in the first place is an egregious error. (But science may show that specific efforts at articulating a meaning cannot be correct, as with creationism.) Reductionists who think physics deal with meaning do not understand the difference between science and metaphysics (see MacKay 1982). Reductionism, like any metaphysics, may contain claims about the meaning or lack of it to reality, but such claims will have to be defended on philosophical grounds, as any meta-physics must. Science in itself no more "unweaves" the wonder of why reality is set up to reveal a rainbow by its analysis of how a rainbow works than it destroys the meaning of a book simply by analyzing the book's paper and ink.

The Choice

Ultimately, we are left with a choice between two alternatives on what forces run the universe, and, more importantly, on how we fit into the scheme of things. Under one, we are a fluke of no significance. We are the accidental realization of random physical events. The world is void of purpose and meaning (Vitzthum 1995: 230-32). All value—indeed, all first-person experiential elements—comes only from us and not from any reality independent of us. We would be, in Stephen Gould's phrase, a "glorious accident" but an accident all the same. Under the other alterna-tive, our first-person experiences are not illusions: our presence in the universe represents, not something incidental or fluky, but something fundamental about reality and also provides a deep and satisfying basis for human dignity (Davies 1987: 203). We are not rare and improbable but expected, and thus we are at home in the universe in a way that advocates of reductionism cannot imagine (Kauffman 1995: 25-26). We are very much at the center of the universe in a structural, if not geographical, sense in that all known structures meet in us.[9] We are an integral part of the overall scheme of things, imprinted in the very forces and laws of the universe. If the antireductionists' position is correct, intelligent beings are not accidents but are an expected and perhaps inevitable part of the cosmos.

Thus, antireductionists would predict that intelligent beings are likely quite common throughout the universe, not a rarity. Antireductionists can also make a second prediction: life elsewhere in the universe will have many similarities to life on earth, since life is structured by the same biological structures operating here on earth (assuming physical and biological structures are the same throughout the universe). That is, less variation would be expected than if only physical structures and a lot of randomness are involved in the appearance of life. There is also the possibility of life being realizable in other physical base-conditions since the physical conditions do not determine the biological properties. In this way, the search for life elsewhere in the universe becomes an empirical testing point between antireductionism and reductionism (see Davies 1999: 272-73).

Thus, we are left with a genuine *choice* (if we do in fact have free will). And what we choose directly affects what we think we are—what it is to be human—and how we view our lives and live accordingly. Those who choose to accept the obvious experiences of our lives as the starting point of what is fundamentally real and to reject structure-reductionism as implausible are not being "unscientific," "subjective," "fuzzy-minded," "obscurantists," "mystery-mongers," or any of the other rhetorical barbs that reductionists throw to try to win the argument. In fact, the two sides are presenting competing metaphysical manifestos of how we should look at things. The reductionists' vision is conceptually and metaphysically neater: it accepts only what can be explained by science and ignores the rest (here, any possible transcendent realities and the entire process of emergence). Antireductionists, on the other hand, emphasize the blossoming of reality and hence see more complexity and mystery within nature. The former approach leads to an austere ontology; the latter to a messy one. Other substance- and structure-reductionists may agree with the philosopher Willard van Orman Quine when he says he prefers the landscape of the desert to that of the jungle.[10] Those antireductionists who deny substance-reductionism may do so either for religious reasons or to create the elegance that a transcendent reality supposedly provides to a metaphysical scheme. (Whether this move in fact does supply final answers or only complicates the situation or is too speculative to be satisfying will not be discussed here.) But such a move, like that of reductionists', does attempt to provide an answer that removes a mystery. But naturalistic antireductionists should also be willing to live with the possibility of more unanswered questions.

The reductionists' confidence that they will inevitably prevail may one day be vindicated. But not knowing why or how levels form or why life and consciousness emerge is no reason to believe the lowest level of the physical order of organization is the only force at work in reality. However, psychological and social causes (if real) may be on the side of reductionists. More and more philosophers who actually study the issues may be adopting pluralistic structure-, theory-, and method-antireductionisms, but the corresponding forms of reductionism fit better with the physicalism prevalent among scientists and many academics. Moreover, physics quite properly retains central importance in the eyes of most people inside and outside of academia—but it is easy for many people to inflate its importance. Many of the scientists popular outside of academia also are substance-, structure-, and theory-reductionists when speaking *qua* philosophers (e.g., Stephen Hawking, Francis Crick, Richard Dawkins, and Carl Sagan.) The deepening trend in higher education toward fragmentation and specialization within disciplines and away from looking at the big picture or asking philosophical questions also favors gravitating to reductionism—i.e., if one has not examined the issues, one may well treat one's own research technique as exhausting what is "really real" about the phenomenon under study. Such extra-scientific and extra-philosophical considerations may well favor reductionists for the foreseeable future.

Still, in terms of more disinterested reasons, does reductionism or antireductionism offer a better account? The dispute may well remain philosophically unresolvable. In the mind/body area, what is discussed is so basic that opponents often cannot even take each other's ideas seriously enough to debate them. And the same may be true in the dispute between reductionists and emergentists—die-hards in each camp cannot believe their opponents could really believe anything so absurd. How compelling one finds either program will probably not turn on the reasons that proponents proffer. The issue will remain a metaphysical issue and not settled by science. In his notebook, the philosopher F. H. Bradley once characterized metaphysics as "the finding of bad reasons for what we believe upon instinct." Something like that could certainly apply here. The arguments each side advances on basic metaphysical disputes will never be remotely convincing to the other.[11] And we cannot realistically expect reasons alone to convert anyone here or on any issue directly involving any fundamental belief-commitments in how we look at the world. Our intuitions, our gut feelings, of what is important and ultimately real, rather than any reasoned analysis and arguments we might develop to justify these intuitions, will still determine which course we follow.[12] This may be best seen in the reductionists' and antireductionists' treatment of religious ontological claims, but it is just as true here concerning the issue of reductionism and emergence.

In the end, we may decide to ignore the obvious—the apparent genuine reality of the levels of organization emerging throughout the history of the universe—in favor of restricting our worldview to only what physics reveals. Or we may choose to be a little more modest about what we claim to know of the fundamental nature of reality and reject any grand, neat metaphysical systems in favor of approaching the world with more humility, impressed by the awe and wonder of it all. Indeed, from this point of view, only the reductionists' hubris exhibited by their claiming that reductions in fact have already been accomplished "in principle" permits them to believe beings such as ourselves can attain the sort of final answers reductionists espouse. Instead, we would have to live with more mystery in our intellectual life and accept more of the vibrant nature of reality as fundamental. All that philosophers can do when such a basic conflict of worldviews arises is to help refine the dispute by clarifying the concepts and issues and pointing out what the commitments entail and their price, raising questions, and presenting the difficulties with each position. The decision will still remain for each of us to make.

Notes

1. On the centrality of mystery in all that we take to be knowledge, see Jones 2009a.

2. Some theologians argue that the mere fact of *lawfulness* in the universe is evidence of God—without God, there would be chaos. But why would it be more natural that no structuring existed and everything was chaotic? It is no stranger that there exist *structures* that make the universe lawful than that there is *substance*. The existence of any state would be a mystery, and the absence of structures is not more "natural."

3. Actually, quantum physics cuts both ways: its supposed explanatory success is the basis for reductionism and the causal closure of physics, but if we do *not understand* it, it becomes a shaky basis for any metaphysics including reductionism.

4. Reductionism and naturalism should not be equated with *scientism*—i.e., the claim that science alone provides any genuine knowledge of reality and can answer all our personal and social problems, if there are answers. Neither reductionism nor naturalism entails this position about knowledge in general and values, but many reductionists do defend it (e.g., Rosenberg 2011).

5. Structure-reductionists reject a "biologism" or "psychologism" in which fully understanding how the brain works would explain "E=mc^2" and other subjects in physics. But they may well endorse a "physicsism" in which a TOE that finally unifies gravity with quantum physics and so forth will eventually lead to explaining how the brain works.

6. A strict determinism by lower level realities is a natural correlate of reductionism, since no other causes are possible; but reductionists can accept that some events in nature may have no causes at all but are purely random and purposeless.

7. Quine famously said "Nothing happens in this world, not a flutter of an eyelid, not the flicker of a thought, without some redistribution of microphysical states" (1981: 98). But even if so, it does not follow that the microphysical states *must have caused* these events.

8. A point that antireductionists often miss is that the existence of independent mental structures does not *guarantee* free will—there still may be a determinism on the mental level or in a person *in toto*. Whether there is genuine free will may be an empirical question that we cannot answer today or perhaps ever. Many events in the mind may be determined by the brain, but whether these merely present *options* for the mind to choose from is not clear.

9. Perhaps physics involves too great an abstraction from the fullness of reality, and instead biology should be the fundamental science for a more evolutionary scheme of cosmology. The biologist George Gaylord Simpson thought biology and psychology are more epistemically fundamental than physics.

10. Some reductionists dismiss the conflict between reductionism and antireductionism as unreal (e.g., Dennett 1995) or as only a matter of personal preference in ontology or of our attitude toward life and the world (e.g., Hardcastle 1996b: 10). Such an approach reflects the positivists' attack on all metaphysics as essentially meaningless. But considering the impact the diverging views have on our actions and values, it seems difficult to dismiss the problem as an unimportant matter of personal taste, even if we cannot resolve it.

11. In discussing consciousness, Valerie Hardcastle, a "convinced materialist," says she has "total and absolute faith that science as it construed today will someday explain [consciousness] as it has explained the other so-called mysteries of our age," and she realizes that she has "little convincing to say" to those opposed to her (1996b: 13).

12. On the importance of intuitions in philosophy (and the surprising lack of rigorous arguments even in contemporary philosophy), see Gutting 2009.

Glossary

Aggregates: wholes whose properties are simply the sum of the properties of their parts with no new types of properties appearing in the whole.

Analysis: scientific examination of the parts or processes within a whole that make the whole work. This differs from the substance-reduction of a whole to its parts.

Antireductionism: the general idea that higher level properties are not the products of lower level parts or processes or that wholes have properties that their parts do not produce.

Antireductive physicalism: the belief that the universe has only one substance (matter) but also layers of independent structures, not merely physical ones.

Bases: lower level conditions or processes necessary for higher level phenomena to appear. Both reductionists and antireductionists affirm such a need for such foundations.

Bridge laws and principles: postulated definitions connecting terms of a higher level theory or law to those of a lower level theory.

Causal completeness of physics: only physical causes operate in nature. Some structure-reductionists argue for the causal completeness of quantum physical causes.

Causal power: often taken as the key to the genuineness of emergence (Samuel Alexander's "dictum"). That is, if a higher level property has no causal power in addition to those of its lower level base components, then reductionists argue that the higher level is structurally reducible to the lower. Conversely, if the higher level as a causal power its bases do not, then it is a reality distinct from the bases.

Cause unifying theory (CUT): a theory combining a TOE in physics and all theories of other sciences with a reductive TOO—i.e, a theory that unifies all the theories in science and the metaphysics of reduction. Thereby, the lowest level causes in physics determine all phenomena.

Concept-antireductionism: the idea that terms describing phenomena on one level cannot be replaced by terms describing phenomena on a lower level. Each level of organization requires some unique descriptive terminology.

Concept-reductionism: the practice of reducing terms describing phenomena on one level to terms in a lower level theory. Part of either a semantic or an epistemic reductionism.

Correlation: finding regular connections between phenomena on two different levels of organization. Finding such correlations does not per se justify a reduction.

Dependence: lower level phenomena providing necessary conditions for the appearance of higher level phenomena. Not necessarily equivalent to lower level determination.

Determinism (reductive): the belief that lower level properties determine all higher level properties. No chance or another level of structures is involved in the appearance of higher properties or powers.

Downward causation: the process by which higher level structures alter the internal makeup of their base-conditions or otherwise affect interactions on lower levels. If this occurs, then the relation of base-conditions to higher level phenomena cannot be merely one of lower level determination. To reductionists, there is only "bottom-up" causation.

Dualism: the idea that there is are two or more substances (or structures) to nature or a person. Thus embraces a pluralism of substances or structures and rejects a monism.

Eliminationism: the metaphysical claim that an apparent reality is not in fact at all real but an illusion. Especially prominent in philosophy of mind. Distinct from any reductionism that affirms the reality of what is explained by a theory- or structure-reduction.

Emergence: the appearance of higher level phenomena from lower level bases, suggesting a discontinuity with the bases and an independence of structure. "Weak" (reducible) and "strong" (nonreducible) varieties concerning both theory and structure.

Emergentism: a school of thought emphasizing the emergence of levels of genuine causes and denying any structure-reductionism of only physical properties.

Epiphenomenalism: the metaphysical belief that, while a higher level phenomenon is not an illusion (as with eliminationism), it has no causal power—only the bases are causes.

Functionalism: the idea that properties are defined by the function they perform (e.g., their causal role) and thus are taken to be independent of the material in which they are embodied. Functionalization can be a based for a reduction or be antireductive.

Fusion: components losing their previous individual properties when combined into systems with higher level properties—e.g., atoms into molecules.

Hierarchy of sciences: the current pluralism of physics and "special sciences" studying different levels of organization. To reductionists, all will eventually be reduced to physics. To antireductionists, all sciences are equal and none are in a privileged epistemic position.

Holism: the belief that wholes are more than the sum of their parts. "Substance-holists" take this substantively, but moderate "structure-holists" hold that wholes are *substantively* constituted only by their parts but not *structurally*—i.e., wholes have levels of causes that their parts do not, and so the actions of a whole cannot be explained by the actions and properties of its part. This is not merely a matter of different levels of organization, but all of wholes in themselves being distinct causes. Nor must wholes have to be treated "organically" as living entities. To reductionists, there is no additional causal power to the whole but only the causal power of the parts, either individually or *in situ*.

Identity theory: two apparent realities are in fact identical (e.g., each mental state is identical to a state of the brain). Neither of the two realities is eliminated. This applies to substance-reductions and structure-reductions (e.g., heat is simply matter in motion).

Individualism: the denial that there are real social wholes. Everything social in nature is constituted by individuals, either as a collection of distinct individuals or in relations.

Levels of organization: qualitatively distinct spheres of stable properties and interactions. These can be seen as different levels of causal interaction.

Materialism: see Physicalism.

Matter: label for whatever is the substance of the objective natural universe, whether it is "substantive" or energy, or a field or discrete particles.

Mechanism: entities or processes organized to produce regular changes to a set of conditions.

Mereological reduction: the idea that the properties of the whole are determined by the properties of the parts. Thus, structurally, any whole consists only of it parts.

Metaphysics: theories of the general nature of reality. Such theories need not be a priori speculation but can express, for example, what is supposedly inferred by the nature of scientific research. But because it provides a general account of reality, it is largely impervious to new empirical data. The branch of "ontology" deals with what is real.

Method-antireductionism: analysis of wholes into their parts cannot exhaust our knowledge of how things works. We also need a holistic approach, perhaps even in a structure-reductionism. Its second component is that a pluralism of sciences will also always be needed to provide as complete a scientific picture as is possible of any phenomenon.

Method-reductionism: only analysis showing how the parts of wholes work is necessary to the final scientific picture. Any holistic approach is of temporary heuristic value at best. Eventually only the physics of the parts will remain.

Multiple realization: the antireductive claim that the same distinct higher level properties are realized by more than one combination of lower level properties. For example, the same type of psychological properties are realized within the same species by distinct neural properties. In short, there are different lower level means to the same higher level end. This suggests that the stable higher level phenomena are the product of higher level structures and not determined by lower level structures.

Naturalism: the metaphysical view that only what is in principle open to scientific study is real. Not materialism or physicalism, which is about the ontic nature of the "stuff" that constitutes the natural world.

Physicalism: the metaphysical belief that everything in the universe is made of the stuff studied by physicists. It is usually construed as having both a substantive and a structural component: there is only type of stuff and only the structures studied in physics (or, to microphysicalists, in quantum physics alone) are real; hence, the "completeness of physics."

Properties: any attribute or characteristic of anything standing by itself in contrast to events, states, and processes involving things.

Qualia: the subjective, sensed aspects of sense-experience, as distinct from the physiological conditions—e.g., the sense of pain or of the greenness of grass as opposed to physiological and other physical changes.

Realism: the metaphysical belief that entities or structures exist independent of our conceptualizations and beliefs. "Common-sense realism" is the belief that there is a world independent of our mind. Criteria for "what is real" are, however, unsettled.

Realization: vaguely defined as the role of base-conditions in the appearance of a higher level phenomenon. Reductionists consider the role of the base-conditions to be noncausal but still a determination of higher level phenomena. It precludes a structural identity of the base and the higher level phenomenon.

Reductionism: the general idea that some apparent reality is "nothing but" some other reality. It contrasts with eliminationism since the reality of what is produced by lower level causes is not usually denied, although the phenomena may be deemed epiphenomenal.

Reductive physicalism: not only is everything made of matter (substance-reductionism), but only physical structures are real (structure-reductionism).

Religious (transcendent) realities: realities that are, in whole or in part, not within the sphere of natural events and thus not open to scientific study.

Self-organization: the process by which entities "spontaneously" and "naturally" form functioning wholes by "self-assembling" components of their base-conditions. That is, only natural structures are at work in the process and no agent outside the whole is needed. But it is misleading to call this "autopoiesis" (literally, "to make itself") since causes and conditions are involved.

Structure: whatever in reality is responsible for the stable invariances—properties, causes, relations, order, or other patterns—among changing phenomena.

Structure-antireductionism: the metaphysical belief that there are causes operating in biological and perhaps mental and social realities that qualitatively different in kind from physical causes and thus are not reducible or explainable by physical causes alone.

Structure-reductionism: the metaphysical belief that all apparent causes or other realities are reducible to lower level ones and ultimately to physical ones (or to quantum level ones alone). Thus, structure-reductionists typically affirm the "completeness" of physical causes and deny any genuine emergence.

Substance: whatever it is in reality that structures are embodied in.

Substance-antireductionism: the metaphysical belief that there are two or more substances to reality (e.g., a physical body and an immaterial soul) and thus the denial of any substance-monism.

Substance-reductionism: the metaphysical belief that all phenomena within the universe are made of only one type of substance—i.e., the same "stuff" (however defined) makes up all that is real. Otherwise called "substance monism."

Supervenience: a term originally introduced to denote the *irreducible reality* of emerging higher level phenomena, but it has evolved to mean *determination by* lower level phenomena. It formally means only that there can be no variation in higher level properties without a variation in the lower level base-conditions—an idea neutral to reductionism and antireductionism.

Systems: the idea that wholes are integrated in such a way as to produce new properties and causal powers and to function as a unit. Thus, wholes cannot be reduced to atomistic parts.

Theory-antireductionism: the belief that at least some theories outside of physics have an equal epistemic status with those of physics. The result is that a pluralism of physical and other scientific theories is needed for our best scientific account of the natural world and will never be replaced solely by theories from physics. There may also be a "dialectical relation" or "co-evolution" of theories from different levels: theories on one level may place constraints on theories of other levels or otherwise cause theories of different levels to be revised.

Theory-reductionism: the belief that the theories of physics (or perhaps only of quantum physics or a TOE) will eventually give the complete theoretical understanding of the natural world, and all theories from other sciences will be superceded. Theories from the other sciences at best of only heuristic value today.

Theory of everything (TOE): a theory in physics that will unite all known physical forces. Such a theory will account for all of the physical level of organization.

Theory of organization (TOO): the structural analog to a TOE. It may be reductive or emergentist.

"Unity of science" programs: various attempts to connect the diverse scientific disciplines that exist today through common theories or causes or interdisciplinary approaches, or to reduce them to physics or to different applications of physical structures.

Upward causation: a cause from a lower level of organization effecting events on a higher level, e.g., radiation causing a Geiger counter to click or causing a mutation in a gene. This should not be confused with a *determination* of the higher level by lower level causes—it refer only to specific events within the higher level, not all of them.

References and Other Works

Agazzi, Evandro. 1991. "Reductionism as Negation of the Scientific Spirit." In Agazzi, ed., pp. 1-29.

___, ed. 1991. *The Problem of Reductionism in Science.* Boston: Kluwer Academic Publishers.

Ahl, Valarie and T. F. H. Allen. 1996. *Hierarchy Theory: A Vision, Vocabulary, and Epistemology.* New York: Columbia Univ. Press.

Ainsworth, Peter Mark. 2010. "What is Ontic Structural Realism?" *Studies in History and Philosophy of Science Part B: Studies in History and Philosophy of Modern Physics* 41 (January): 50-57.

Aizawa, Ken. 2009. "Neuroscience and Multiple Realization: A Reply to Bechtel and Mundale." *Synthese* 167: 493-510.

___ and Carl Gillett. 2009. "The (Multiple) Realization of Psychological and Other Properties in the Sciences." *Mind and Language* 24 (no. 2): 181-208.

Alexander, Samuel. 1920. *Space, Time, and Deity: The Gifford Lectures, 1916-1918*, Vol. 2. London: Macmillan.

Allen, Charlotte. 1996. "Is Nothing Sacred? Casting Out the Gods from Religious Studies." *Lingua Franca* 6 (November): 30-40.

Andersen, Peter Bøgh, et al., eds. 2000. *Downward Causation: Minds, Bodies and Matter.* Oxford: Aarhus Univ. Press.

Anderson, Philip W. 1972. "More is Different: Broken Symmetry and the Nature of the Hierarchical Structure of Science." *Science* 177 (August 4): 393-96.

Atkins, Peter W. 1992. *Creation Revisited.* San Francisco: W. H. Freeman.

Atran, Scott. 2002. *In Gods We Trust: The Evolutionary Landscape of Religion.* New York: Oxford Univ. Press.

Ayala, Francisco Jose. 1989. "Thermodynamics, Information, and Evolution: The Problem of Reductionism." *History and Philosophy of the Life Sciences* 11 (No. 2): 115-20.

___ and Theodosius Dobzhansky, eds. 1974. *Studies in the Philosophy of Biology: Reduction and Related Problems.* Berkeley/Los Angeles: Univ. of California Press.

Ayer, Alfred J. 1990. *The Meaning of Life.* New York: Charles Scribner's Sons.

Bak, Per. 1997. *How Nature Works: The Science of Self-Organized Criticality.* New York: Oxford Univ. Press.

Barbour, Ian. 1990. *Religion in an Age of Science: The Gifford Lectures 1989-1991.* New York: Harper & Row.

Barnard, G. William. 1992. "Explaining the Unexplainable: Wayne Proudfoot's *Religious Experience.*" *Journal of the American Academy of Religion* 60 (Summer): 231-57.

Batterman, Robert W. 2002. *The Devil is in the Details: Asymptotic Reasoning in Explanation, Reduction, and Emergence.* New York: Oxford Univ. Press.

Beauregard, Mario and Denyse O'Leary. 2007. *The Spiritual Brain: A Neuroscientist's Case for the Existence of the Soul.* New York: HarperOne.

Bechtel, William and Jennifer Mundale. 1999. "Multiple Realizability Revisited: Linking Cognitive and Neural States." *Philosophy of Science* 66 (no. 2): 175-207.

Bechtel, William and Andrew Hamilton. 2007. "Reduction, Integration, and the Unity of Science: Natural, Behavioral, and Social Sciences and Humanities." In Theo A. F. Kuipers, ed., *General Philosophy of Science: Focal Issues*, pp. 377-430. New York: Elsevier.

Beckermann, Ansgar, Hans Flohr, and Jaegwon Kim, eds. 1992. *Emergence or Reduction? Essays on the Prospects of Nonreductive Physicalism*. New York: Walter de Gruyter.

Bellah, Robert N. 1970a. *Beyond Belief: Essays on Religion in a Post-Traditional World*. New York: Harper & Row.

___. 1970b. "Confessions of a Former Establishment Fundamentalist." *Council on the Study of Religion Bulletin* 1 (December): 3-6.

___. 1970c. "Christianity and Symbolic Realism" and "Response to Comments on 'Christianity and Symbolic Realism.'" *Journal for the Scientific Study of Religion* 9 (Summer): 89-96, 112-15.

Berger, Peter L. 1967. *The Sacred Canopy: Elements of a Sociological Theory of Religion*. Garden City: Doubleday/Anchor Books.

___. 1969. *A Rumor of Angels: Modern Society and the Rediscovery of the Sacred*. Garden City: Doubleday/Anchor Books.

___. 1974. "Some Second Thoughts on Substantive Versus Functional Definitions of Religion." *Journal for the Scientific Study of Religion* 13 (June): 125-33.

___. 1979. *The Heretical Imperative*. Garden City: Doubleday/Anchor Books.

Bergmann, Gustav. 1944. "Holism, Historicism, and Emergence." *Philosophy of Science* 11 (July): 209-221.

Bergson, Henri. 1911. *Creative Evolution*. Trans. by Arthur Mitchell. New York: Modern Library.

Bertalanffy, Ludwig von. 1968. *General Systems Theory: Essays on its Foundation and Development*. New York: George Braziller.

Bhargava, Rejeev. 1992. *Individualism in Social Science: Forms and Limits of a Methodology*. Oxford: Clarendon Press.

Bickhard, Mark H. and Donald T. Campbell. 2000. "Emergence." In Andersen 2000, pp. 322-48.

Bickle, John. 2003. *Philosophy and Neuroscience: A Ruthlessly Reductive Account*. Dordrecht: Kluwer.

___. 2006. "Reducing Mind to Molecular Pathways: Explicating the Reductionism Implicit in Current Cellular and Molecular Neuroscience." *Synthese* 151: 411-34.

Bishop, Robert C. 2006. "The Hidden Premiss in the Causal Argument for Physicalism." *Analysis* 66 (January): 44-52.

___ and Harald Atmanspacher. 2006. "Contextual Emergence in the Description of Properties." *Foundations of Physics* 36 (December): 1753-77.

Blitz, David. 1992. *Emergent Evolution: Qualitative Novelty and the Levels of Reality*. Boston: Kluwer Academic Publishers.

Block, Ned. 1980. "Troubles With Functionalism." In Ned Block, ed., *Readings in Philosophy of Psychology*, Vol. 1, pp. 268-305. Cambridge: Harvard Univ. Press.

___. 1990. "The Computer Model of Mind." In Daniel N. Osherson and Edward E. Smith, eds., *Thinking: An Invitation to Cognitive Sciences*. Cambridge: MIT Press.

___. 1997. "Anti-Reductionism Slaps Back." *Philosophical Perspectives* 11: 107-32.

Bohr, Niels. 1958. "Light and Life." Reprinted in his *Atomic Physics and Human Knowledge*, pp. 3-12. New York: John Wiley.

Bowker, John. 1973. *The Sense of God: Sociological, Anthropological and Psychological Approaches to the Origin of the Sense of God*. Oxford: Oxford Univ. Press.

Boyer, Pascal. 2001. *Religion Explained: The Human Instincts that Fashion God, Spirits and Ancestors*. London: William Heinnemann.

Broad, Charles D. 1925. *The Mind and Its Place in Nature*. London: Routledge and Kegan Paul.

Brooks, D. H. M. 1994. "How to Perform a Reduction." *Philosophy and Phenomenological Research* 54 (December): 803-14.

Brush, Stephen G. 1977. "Statistical Mechanics and the Philosophy of Science: Some Historical Notes." In Frederick Suppe and Peter D. Asquith, eds., *PSA 1976*, Vol. 2, pp. 551-84. East Lansing: Philosophy of Science Association.

Bunge, Mario. 1990. "What Kind of Discipline is Psychology? Autonomous or Dependent, Humanistic or Scientific, Biological or Sociological?" *New Ideas in Psychology* 8 (No. 2): 121-37.

___. 2003. *Emergence and Convergence: Qualitative Novelty and the Unity of Knowledge*. Toronto: Univ. of Toronto Press.

Burian, Richard M. and J. D. Trout. 1995. "Ontological Progress in Science." *Canadian Journal of Philosophy* 25 (June): 177-202.

Camazine, Scott, et al. 2001. *Self-Organization in Biological Systems*. Princeton: Princeton Univ. Press.

Campbell, Donald T. 1974. "'Downward Causation' in Hierarchially Organised Biological Systems." In Ayala and Dobzhansky, pp. 179-86.

Cao, Tian Yu. 2003. "Structural Realism and the Interpretation of Quantum Field Theory." *Synthese* 136: 3-24.

Caplan, Arthur L., ed. 1978. *The Sociobiology Debate: Readings on the Ethical and Scientific Issues Concerning Sociobiology*. New York: Harper & Row.

___. 1988. "Rehabilitating Reductionism." *American Zoologist* 28: 193-203.

Carnap, Rudolf. 1949. "Logical Foundations of the Unity of Science." In Herbert Feigl and Wilfrid Sellars, eds., *Readings in Philosophical Analysis*, pp. 408-422. New York: Appleton, Century, and Crofts.

Cartwright, Nancy. 1979. "Causal Laws and Effective Strategies." *Noûs* 13 (no. 4): 419-38.

___. 1997. "Why Physics?" In Roger Penrose, Abner Shimony, Nancy Cartwright, and Stephen Hawking, *The Large, the Small and the Human Mind*, pp. 161-68. New York: Cambridge Univ. Press.

___. 1999. *A Dappled World: A Study of the Boundaries of Science*. Cambridge: Cambridge Univ. Press.

Castellani, Elena. 2002. "Reductionism, Emergence, and Effective Field Theories." *Studies in the History and Philosophy of Modern Physics* 33 (no. 2): 251-67.

Causey, Robert L. 1977. *The Unity of Science*. Boston: D. Reidel Publishing.

Chakravartty, Anjan. 2003. "The Structuralist Conception of Objects." *Philosophy of Science* 70 (no. 5): 867-78.

Chalmers, David J. 1996. *The Conscious Mind: In Search of a Fundamental Theory*. New York: Oxford Univ. Press.

___. 2010. *The Character of Consciousness*. New York: Oxford Univ. Press.

Churchland, Patricia S. 1986. *Neurophilosophy: Toward a Unified Science of the Mind-Brain*. Cambridge: MIT Press.

___. 1992. *The Computational Brain*. Cambridge: MIT Press.

Churchland, Paul M. and Patricia S. Churchland. 1990. "Could a Machine Think?" *Scientific American* 262 (January): 32-37.

___. 1995. "Intertheoretic Reduction: A Neuroscientist's Field Guide." In Cornwell, pp. 64-77.

Clayton, Philip. 2004. *Mind and Emergence*. New York: Oxford Univ. Press.
___ and Paul Davies. 2006. *The Re-emergence of Emergence: The Emergentist Hypothesis from Science to Religion*. New York: Oxford Univ. Press.
Cole, Stephen. 1996. "Voodoo Sociology: Recent Developments in the Sociology of Science." In Paul R. Gross, Norman Levitt, and Martin W. Lewis, eds., *The Flight From Science and Reason*, pp. 274-86. New York: New York Academic of Sciences.
Collingwood, R. G. 1946. *The Idea of History*. Ed. by T. M. Knox. Oxford: Oxford Univ. Press.
Comte, Auguste. 1975. *Auguste Comte and Positivism: The Essential Writings*. Ed. by Gertrud Lenzer. New York: Harper & Row.
Cornwell, John, ed. 1995. *Nature's Imagination: The Frontiers of Scientific Vision*. New York: Oxford Univ. Press.
Corradani, Antonella and Timothy O'Connor, eds. 2010. *Emergence in Science and Philosophy*. New York: Routledge.
Coveney, Peter and Roger Highfield. 1995. *Frontiers of Complexity: The Search for Order in a Chaotic World*. New York: Fawcett Columbine.
Crane, Timothy. 2001. "The Significance of Emergence." In Gillett & Loewer, pp. 207-224.
___ and D. H. Mellor. 1995. "There is no Question of Physicalism." In Paul K. Moser and J. D. Trout, eds., *Contemporary Materialism: A Reader*, pp. 65-89. New York: Routledge.
Craver, Carl F. 2005. "Beyond Reduction: Mechanisms, Multifield Integration, and the Unity of Neuroscience." *Studies in the History of the Philosophy of Biology and Biomedical Sciences* 36: 375-95.
___ and William Bechtel. 2007. "Top-down Causation Without Top-down Causes." *Biology and Philosophy* 22: 547-63.
Creath, Richard. 1996. "The Unity of Science: Carnap, Neurath, and Beyond." In Galison & Stump, pp. 158-69.
Crick, Francis. 1966. *Of Molecules and Men*. Seattle: Univ. of Washington Press.
___. 1994. *The Astonishing Hypothesis: The Scientific Search for the Soul*. New York: Charles Scribner's Sons.
Crook, Seth and Carl Gillett. 2001. "Why Physics Alone Cannot Define the 'Physical': Materialism, Metaphysics, and the Formulation of Physicalism." *Canadian. Journal of Philosophy*. 31 (September): 333–59.
Darden, Lindley. 2006. *Reasoning in Biological Discoveries: Essays on Mechanisms, Interfield Relations, and Anomaly Resolution*. Cambridge: Cambridge Univ. Press.
___ and Nancy Maull. 1977. "Interfield Theories." *Philosophy of Science* 44 (March): 43-64.
Davidson, Donald. 1970. "Mental Events." Reprinted in his *Essays on Actions and Events*, pp. 207-227. Oxford: Claredon Press, 1980.
Davies, Paul. 1987. *The Cosmic Blueprint*. New York: Simon & Schuster.
___. 1999. *The Fifth Miracle: The Search for the Origin and Meaning of Life*. New York: Simon & Schuster.
___. 2003. "Toward an Emergentist Worldview." In Gregersen, pp. 3-16.
___ and Neil Henrik Gregersen, eds. 2010. *Information and the Nature of Reality: From Physics to Metaphysics*. New York: Cambridge Univ. Press.
Dawkins, Richard. 1976. *The Selfish Gene*. New York: Oxford Univ. Press.
Deacon, Terrence W. 1997. *The Symbolic Species: The Co-Evolution of Language and the Brain*. New York: W. W. Norton.
___. 2012. *Incomplete Nature: How Mind Emerges from Matter*. New York: Norton.

Dennett, Daniel C. 1991. *Consciousness Explained*. Boston: Little Brown.

___. 1995. *Darwin's Dangerous Idea: Evolution and the Meanings of Life*. New York: Simon & Schuster.

Dewey, John. 1934. *A Common Faith*. New Haven: Yale Univ. Press.

Dilthey, Wilhelm. 1976. *Wilhelm Dilthey: Selected Writings*. Ed. and trans. by H. P. Rickman. Cambridge: Cambridge Univ. Press.

Dray, William. 1957. *Laws and Explanations in History*. Oxford: Oxford Univ. Press.

Dreyfus, Hubert L. 1992. *What Computers Still Can't Do: A Critique of Artificial Reason*. Cambridge: MIT Press.

Drozdek, Adam. 1990. "Programabilism: A New Reductionism." *Epistemologia* 13 (July-December): 235-48.

Duerlinger, James. 1993. "Reductionist and Nonreductionist Theories of Persons in Indian Buddhist Philosophy." *Journal of Indian Philosophy* 21 (March): 79-101.

Dupré, John. 1993. *The Disorder of Things: Metaphysical Foundations of the Disunity of Science*. Cambridge: Harvard Univ. Press.

___. 1994. "Methodological Individualism and Reductionism in Biology." In Mohan Matthew and R. X. Ware, eds., *Biology & Society: Reflections on Methodology*, pp. 165-84. Calgary: Univ. of Calgary Press.

___. 1995. "Against Scientific Imperialism." *PSA 1994*, Vol. 2, pp. 374-81. East Lansing: Philosophy of Science Association.

___. 1996. "Metaphysical Disorder and Scientific Disunity." In Galison & Stump, pp. 101-17.

Durkheim, Émile. 1915. *The Elementary Forms of the Religious Life*. Trans. by Joseph Ward Swain. New York: Free Press.

___. 1951. *Suicide: A Study in Sociology*. Trans. by John A. Spaulding and George Simpson. New York: Free Press.

___. 1982. *The Rules of Sociological Method and Selected Texts on Sociology and its Method*. Trans. by W. D. Halls. New York: Free Press.

Eccles, John C. 1989. *Evolution of the Brain: Creation of the Self*. New York: Routledge.

___. 1994. *How the Self Controls its Brain*. New York: Springer-Verlag.

Eddington, Arthur. 1958. *The Nature of the Physical World*. Ann Arbor: Univ. of Michigan Press.

Editorial. 1981. "A Book for Burning?" *Nature* 293 (September 24): 246.

Eliade, Mircea. 1958. *Patterns in Comparative Religion*. Trans. by Rosemary Sheed. New World: Meridian Books.

___. 1959. *The Sacred and the Profane: The Nature of Religion*. New York: Harcourt, Brace & World.

___. 1969a. *Images & Symbols: Studies in Religious Symbolism*. Trans. by Philip Mairet. New York: Sheed and Ward.

___. 1969b. *The Quest: History and Meaning in Religion*. Chicago: Univ. of Chicago Press.

___. 1978. *A History of Religious Ideas*, Vol. 1. Trans. by Willard R. Trask. Chicago: Univ. of Chicago Press.

Emmeche, Claus, Simo Køppe, and Frederik Stjernfelt. 1997. "Explaining Emergence: Towards an Ontology of Levels." *Journal for General Philosophy of Science* 28 (No. 1): 83-119.

___. 2000. "Levels, Emergence, and Three Versions of Downward Causation." In Andersen, pp. 13-24.

Endicott, Ronald P. 1998. "Collapse of the New Wave." *Journal of Philosophy* 95 (February): 53-72.

Eronen, Markus I. 2010-11. "Replacing Functional Reduction with Mechanistic Explanation." *Philosophia Naturalis* 47-48 (nos. 1-2): 125-53.

Esfeld, Michael. 2001. *Holism in Philosophy of Mind and Philosophy of Physics*. Boston:
Kluwer Academic Publishers.

___. 2010-11. "Causal Properties and Conservative Reduction." *Philosophia Naturalis* 47-
48 (nos. 1-2): 9-31.

___ and Christian Sachse. 2007. "Theory Reduction by Means of Functional Sub-types."
International Studies in the Philosophy of Science 21: 1-17.

___. 2011. *Conservative Reductionism*. New York: Routledge.

Evans-Pritchard, Edward E. 1956. *Nuer Religion*. Oxford: Clarendon Press.

___. 1965. *Theories of Primitive Religion*. Oxford: Clarendon Press.

Feigl, Herbert. 1953. "Unity of Science and Unitary Science." In Herbert Feigl and May
Brodbeck, eds., *Readings in the Philosophy of Science*, pp. 382-84. New York:
Appleton-Century-Crofts.

___. 1958. "The 'Mental' and the 'Physical.'" In Herbert Feigl, Michael Scriven, and
Maxwell Grover, eds., *Minnesota Studies in the Philosophy of Science*, Vol. 2, pp. 370-
497. Minneapolis: Univ. of Minnesota Press.

Feuerbach, Ludwig. 1957. *The Essence of Christianity*. Trans. by George Eliot. New York:
Harper & Row.

Feyerabend, Paul. 1999. *Conquest of Abundance: A Tale of Abstraction Versus the Richness
of Being*. Ed. by Bert Terpstra. Chicago: Univ. of Chicago Press.

Field, Hartry. 2003. "Causation in a Physical World." In Michael J. Loux and Dean W.
Zimmerman, eds., *The Oxford Handbook of Metaphysics*, pp. 435-60. New York:
Oxford Univ. Press.

Flanagan, Owen. 1992. *Consciousness Reconsidered*. Cambridge: MIT Press.

Flew, Anthony. 1995. *Thinking About Social Thinking*. 2nd ed. Amherst, NY: Prometheus.

Fodor, Jerry A. 1974. "Special Sciences (Or: The Disunity of Science as a Working
Hypothesis)." *Synthese* 28: 97-115. Reprinted in Fodor 1981b, pp. 127-45.

___. 1997. "Special Sciences: Still Autonomous After All These Years." *Philosophical
Perspectives* 11: 149-63.

Foster, John. 1982. *The Case for Idealism*. Boston: Routledge & Kegan Paul.

___. 1991. *The Immaterial Self: A Defense of the Cartesian Dualist Conception of the Mind*.
New York: Routledge.

Frankl, Viktor E. 1969. "Reductionism and Nihilism." In Koestler & Smythies, pp. 396-408.

French, Steven and James Ladyman. 2003. "Remodelling Structural Realism: Quantum
Physics and the Metaphysics of Structure." *Synthese* 136: 31-56.

Freud, Sigmund. 1950. *Totem and Taboo*. Trans. by James Strachey. New York: W. W.
Norton.

___. 1955. *Moses and Monotheism*. Trans. by Katherine Jones. New York: Vintage.

___. 1964. *The Future of an Illusion*. Trans. by W. D. Robson-Scott; revised by James
Strachey. Garden City: Doubleday/Anchor.

Galison, Peter and David J. Stump, eds. 1996. *The Disunity of Science: Boundaries,
Contexts, and Power*. Stanford: Stanford Univ. Press.

Geertz, Clifford. 1966. "Religion as a Cultural System." Reprinted in Geertz 1973, chap. 4,
pp. 87-125.

___. 1973. *The Interpretation of Cultures*. New York: Basic Books.

Geis, Robert J. 1995. *Personal Existence After Death: Reductionist Circularities and the
Evidence*. Peru, Illinois: Sherwood Sugden.

Gell-Mann, Murray. 1994. *The Quark and the Jaguar: Adventures in the Simple and the

Complex. New York: W. H. Freeman.

Gellner, Ernest. 1973. "Explanations in History." In O'Neill, pp. 248-63.

Gillett, Carl. 2003. "The Metaphysics of Realization, Multiple Realizability, and the Special Sciences." *Journal of Philosophy* (November): 591-603.

___.2006. "The Hidden Battles Over Emergence." In Philip Clayton & Zachary Simpson, eds., *The Oxford Handbook of Religion and Science*, pp. 801-18. New York: Oxford Univ. Press.

___. 2007. "Understanding the New Reductionism: The Metaphysics of Science and Compositional Reduction." *Journal of Philosophy* 104 (April): 193-216.

___ and Barry Loewer, eds. 2001. *Physicalism and its Discontents.* Cambridge: Cambridge Univ. Press.

Gimello, Robert M. 1983. "Mysticism in its Contexts." In Katz, pp. 61-88.

Glock, Charles Y. and Phillip E. Hammond, eds. 1973. *Beyond the Classics? Essays in the Scientific Study of Religion.* New York: Harper & Row.

Grantham, Todd A. 2004. "Conceptualizing the (Dis)unity of Science." *Philosophy of Science* 71 (April): 133-55.

Gregersen, Niels Henrik, ed. 2003. *From Complexity to Life: On Emergence of Life and Meaning.* New York: Oxford Univ. Press.

Grene, Majorie. 1987. "Hierarchies in Biology." *American Scientist* 75: 504-10.

Guthrie, Stewart. 1993. *Faces in the Cloud: A New Theory of Religion.* New York: Oxford Univ. Press.

Gutting, Gary. 2009. *What Philosophers Know: Case Studies in Recent Analytic Philosophy.* New York: Cambridge Univ. Press.

Hacking, Ian. 1996. "The Disunities of the Sciences." In Galison & Stump, pp. 37-74.

Hamnett, Ian. 1973. "Sociology of Religion and Sociology of Error." *Religion* 3 (Spring): 1-12.

Hardcastle, Valarie Gray. 1996a. *How to Build a Theory in Cognitive Science.* Albany: State Univ. of New York Press.

___. 1996b. "The Why of Consciousness: A Non-Issue for Materialists." *Journal of Consciousness* 3 (No. 1): 7-13.

___. 1999. *The Myth of Pain.* Cambridge: MIT Press.

Hardy, Alister. 1983. *The Spiritual Nature of Man.* Oxford: Clarendon Press.

Harris, Marvin. 1979. *Cultural Materialism: The Struggle for a Science of Culture.* New York: Random House.

Hasker, William. 1999. *The Emergent Self.* Ithaca: Cornell Univ. Press.

Haught, John F. 2010. "Information, Theology, and the Universe." In Davies & Gregersen, pp. 300-318.

Hawking, Stephen W. 1980. "Is the End in Sight for Theoretical Physics?" In John Boslough, *Stephen Hawking's Universe*, pp. 131-50. New York: Quill / William Morrow.

___. 1988. *A Brief History of Time: From the Big Bang to Black Holes.* New York: Bantam.

___. 1997. "The Objections of an Unashamed Reductionist." In Roger Penrose, Abner Shimony, Nancy Cartwright, and Stephen Hawking, *The Large, the Small and the Human Mind*, pp. 169-72. New York: Cambridge Univ. Press.

___ and Leonard Mlodinow. 2010. *The Grand Design.* New York: Bantam Books.

Hemelrijk, Charlotte K., ed. 2005. *Self-Organisation and Evolution of Social Systems.* Cambridge: Cambridge Univ. Press.

Hempel, Carl G. 1965. *Aspects of Scientific Explanations and Other Essays in the Philosophy of Science.* New York: Free Press.

___. 1969. "Reduction: Ontological and Linguistic Facets." In Sidney Morgenbesser, Patrick Suppes, and Morton White, eds., *Philosophy, Science, and Method: Essays in Honor of Ernest Nagel*, pp. 179-99. New York: St. Martin's Press.

Hendry, Robin Findlay. 2010. "Emergence vs. Reduction in Chemistry." In Macdonald & Macdonald, pp. 205-31.

___. Forthcoming. *The Metaphysics of Chemistry*. New York: Oxford Univ. Press.

___ and Paul Needham. 2007. "Le Poidevin on the Reduction of Chemistry." *British Journal for the Philosophy of Science* 58 (June): 339-53.

Henle, Paul. 1942. "The Status of Emergence." *Journal of Philosophy* 39 (August 27): 486-93.

Hertzke, Allen D. 1988. "American Religion and Politics: A Review Essay." *Western Political Quarterly* 41 (September): 825-38.

Hesse, Mary. 1988. "Socializing Epistemology." In Ernan McMullin, ed., *Construction and Constraint: The Shaping of Scientific Rationality*, pp. 97-122. Notre Dame, Indiana: Univ. of Notre Dame Press.

Hick, John. 1989. *An Interpretation of Religion: Human Responses to the Transcendent.* New Haven: Yale Univ. Press.

Hodgson, Peter. 1985. "Layers of Matter." In Peacocke, pp. 17-23.

Hoeffer, Carl. 2003. "For Fundamentalism." *Philosophy of Science* 70 (December): 1401-12.

Hohwy, Jakob and Jesper Kallestrup, eds. 2008. *Being Reduced: New Essays on Reduction, Explanation, and Causation.* New York: Oxford Univ. Press.

Holland, John H. 1998. *Emergence: From Chaos to Order.* Reading, Ma.: Helix Books.

Hollis, Martin. 1982. "The Social Destruction of Reality." In Martin Hollis and Steven Lukes, eds., *Rationality and Relativism,* pp. 67-86. Cambridge: MIT Press.

Hood, Ralph W., Jr. 1997. "The Empirical Study of Mysticism." In Bernard Spilka and Daniel N. McIntosh, eds., *The Psychology of Religion: Theoretical Approaches,* pp. 222-32. Boulder: Westview Press.

Hooker, Clifford A. 1981. "Towards a General Theory of Reduction." *Dialogue* 20 (March): 38-59, 20 (June): 201-36, and 20 (September): 496-529.

___. 2004. "Asymptotics, Reduction and Emergence." *British Journal for the Philosophy of Science* 55 (September): 435-79.

Horst, Steven. 2007. *Beyond Reduction: Philosophy of Mind and Post-Reductionist Philosophy of Science.* New York: Oxford Univ. Press.

Hoyingen-Huene, Paul and Franz M. Wuketits, eds. 1989. *Reductionism and Systems Theory in the Life Sciences: Some Problems and Perspectives.* Boston: Kluwer Academic Publishers.

Howard, Don. 2007. "Reduction and Emergence in the Physical Sciences: Some Lessons from the Particle Physics and Condensed Matter Debate." In Murphy & Stoeger, pp. 141-57.

Hull, David L. 1972. "Reduction in Genetics—Biology or Philosophy?" *Philosophy of Science* 39 (December): 491-99.

___. 1974. *Philosophy of Biological Science.* Englewood Cliffs: Prentice-Hall.

___. 2002. "Varieties of Reductionism: Derivation and Gene Selection." In Van Regenmortel, & Hull, pp. 161-72.

Humphreys, Paul. 1996. "Aspects of Emergence." *Philosophical Topics* 24 (Spring): 53-70.

___. 1997a. "Emergence, Not Supervenience." In Lindley Darden, ed., *PSA 1996,* Part 2, pp. 337-45. East Lansing: Philosophy of Science Association.

___. 1997b. "How Properties Emerge." *Philosophy of Science* 64 (March): 1-17.

Hüttemann, Andreas. 2004. *What is Wrong with Microphysicalism?* New York: Routledge.
___. 2005. "Explanation, Emergence, and Quantum Entanglement." *Philosophy of Science* (January): 114-27.
___ and Alan C. Love. 2011. "Comparing Part-Whole Reductive Explanations in Biology and Physics." In Dennis Dieks, et al., eds., *Explanation, Prediction, and Confirmation*, 183-202. New York: Springer-Verlag.
Hüttemann, Andreas and David Papineau. 2005. "Physicalism Decomposed." *Analysis* 65 (January): 33-39.
Idinopulos, Thomas A. and Edward A. Yonan, eds. 1994. *Religion and Reductionism: Essays on Eliade, Segal, and the Challenge of the Social Sciences for the Study of Religion.* New York: E. J. Brill.
James, Susan. 1984. *The Content of Social Explanation.* New York: Cambridge Univ. Press.
James, William. 1958. *The Varieties of Religious Experience: A Study in Human Nature.* New York: Modern Library.
___. 1977. *A Pluralistic Universe.* Cambridge: Harvard Univ. Press.
Johnson, Steven. 2001. *Emergence: The Connected Lives of Ants, Brains, Cities, and Software.* New York: Scribner.
Jong, Huib L. de. 2006. "Explicating Pluralism: Where the Mind to Molecule Pathway Gets Off Track—Reply to Bickle." *Synthese* 151: 435-43.
Jones, Richard H. 1986. *Science and Mysticism.* Lewisburg: Bucknell Univ. Press.
___. 1993. *Mysticism Examined: Philosophical Inquiries Into Mysticism.* Albany: State Univ. of New York Press.
___. 2000. *Reductionism: Analysis and the Fullness of Reality.* Lewisburg: Bucknell Univ. Press.
___. 2009a. *Curing the Philosopher's Disease: Reinstating Mystery in the Heart of Philosophy.* Lanham, Md.: University Press of America.
___. 2009b. *Piercing the Veil: Comparing Science and Mysticism as Ways of Knowing Reality.* New York: Jackson Square Books.
Jung, Carl G. 1938. *Psychology and Religion.* New Haven: Yale Univ. Press.
___. 1964. *Man and His Symbols.* New York: Dell.
___. 1973. *Answer to Job.* Trans. by R. F. C. Hull. Princeton: Princeton Univ. Press.
Katz, Steven T., ed. 1978. *Mysticism and Philosophical Analysis.* New York: Oxford Univ. Press.
___, ed. 1983. *Mysticism and Religious Traditions.* New York: Oxford Univ. Press.
Kauffman, Stuart. 1995. *At Home in the Universe: The Search for Laws of Self-Organization and Complexity.* New York: Oxford Univ. Press.
___. 2008. *Reinventing the Sacred: A New View of Science, Reason and Religion.* New York: Basic Books.
Kemeny, John G. and Paul Oppenheim. 1956. "On Reduction." *Philosophical Studies* 7 (January): 6-19.
Kim, Jaegwon. 1993. *Supervenience and Mind: Selected Philosophical Essays.* New York: Cambridge Univ. Press.
___. 1998. *Mind in a Physical World. An Essay on the Mind-Body Problem and Mental Causation.* Cambridge: MIT Press.
___. 1999. "Making Sense of Emergence." *Philosophical Studies* 95 (nos. 1-2): 3-36.
___. 2000. "Making Sense of Downward Causation." In Andersen, pp. 305-21.
___. 2005. *Physicalism, or Something Near Enough.* Princeton: Princeton Univ. Press.
___. 2006a. "Emergence: Core Ideas." *Synthese* 151: 547-59.
___. 2006b. "Being Realistic About Emergence." In Clayton & Davies, pp. 189-202.

___. 2010. *Essays in the Metaphysics of Mind*. New York: Oxford Univ. Press.

___. 2011. *Philosophy of Mind*. 3rd ed. Boulder: Westview Press.

Kincaid, Harold. 1987. "Supervenience Doesn't Entail Reducibility." *Southern Journal of Philosophy* 25 (No. 3): 343-56.

___. 1997. *Individualism and the Unity of Science: Essays on Reduction, Explanation, and the Special Sciences*. Lanham, Md.: Rowman & Littlefield.

Kitcher, Philip. 1981. "Explanatory Unification." *Philosophy of Science* 48 (December): 507-31.

___. 1984. "1953 and All That: A Tale of Two Sciences." *Philosophical Review* 93 (July): 335-73.

___. 1993. *The Advancement of Science: Science Without Legend, Objectivity Without Illusions*. New York: Oxford Univ. Press.

Klee, Robert L. 1984. "Micro-Determinism and the Concepts of Emergence." *Philosophy of Science* 51 (March): 44-63.

Koestler, Arthur. 1969. "Some General Properties of Self-Regulating Open Hierarchic Order (SOHO)." In Koestler & Smythies, pp. 210-16.

___ and J. R. Smythies, eds. 1969. *Beyond Reductionism: New Perspectives in the Life Sciences*. London: Hutchinson.

Koons, Robert C. And George Bealer, eds. 2010. *The Waning of Materialism*. New York: Oxford Univ. Press.

Krohn, Wolfgang, Günter Küppers, and Helga Nowotny. 1990. *Selforganization: Portrait of a Scientific Revolution*. Boston: Kluwer Academic Publishers.

Kutach, David. 2010-11. "Reductive Identities: An Empirical Fundamentalist Approach." *Philosophia Naturalis* 47-48 (nos. 1-2): 67-101.

Ladyman, James and Don Ross, with David Spurrett and John Collier. 2007. *Every Thing Must Go: Metaphysics Naturalized*. New York: Oxford Univ. Press.

Laszlo, Ervin. 1972. *The Systems View of the World*. New York: George Braziller.

Laughlin, Robert B. 2005. *A Different Universe: Reinventing Physics from the Bottom Down*. New York: Basic Books.

___ and David Pines. 2000. "The Theory of Everything." *Proceedings of the National Academy of Sciences* 97 (January 4): 28-31.

___ et al. 2000. "The Middle Way." *Proceedings of the National Academy of Sciences* 97 (January 4): 32-37.

Lawson, E. Thomas and Robert N. McCauley. 1990. *Rethinking Religion: Connecting Cognition and Culture*. New York: Cambridge Univ. Press.

Le Poidevin, Robin. 2005. "Missing Elements and Missing Premises: A Combinatorial Argument for the Ontological Reduction of Chemistry." *British Journal for the Philosophy of Science* 56 (March): 139-88.

Leach, Edmund. 1954. *Political Systems of Highland Burma*. London: Bell.

Lehn, Jean-Marie. 2002. "Toward Self-organization and Complex Matter." *Science* 295 (March 29): 2400–2403.

Levine, Andrew, Elliot Sober, and Erik Olin Wright. 1987. "Marxism and Methodological Individualism." *New Left Review* 162 (March/April): 67-84.

Lewes, George Henry. 1875. *Problems of Life and Mind*, Vol. 2. London: Kegan Paul, Trench, Turbner.

Lewis, David. 1970. "How to Define Theoretical Terms." Reprinted in his *Philosophical Papers*, Vol. 1, pp. 78-95. Oxford: Oxford Univ. Press, 1983.

___. 1994. "Reduction of Mind." In Samuel D. Guttenplan, ed., *A Companion to Philosophy of Mind*, pp. 412-30. Oxford: Basil Blackwell.

Lewis, I. M. 1989. *Ecstatic Religion: An Anthropological Study of Spirit Possession and Shamanism*. 2nd ed. London: Routledge.

Lewontin, R. C., Steven Rose, and Leon J. Kamin. 1984. *Not in Our Genes: Biology, Ideology, and Human Nature*. New York: Pantheon Books.

Libet, Benjamin. 1996. "Solutions to the Hard Problem of Consciousness." *Journal of Consciousness* 3 (No. 1): 33-35.

___. 2004. *Mind Time: The Temporal Factor in Consciousness*. Cambridge: Harvard Univ. Press.

Loewer, Barry. 2009. "Why is There Anything Except Physics?" *Synthese* 170: 217-33.

Lovejoy, Arthur O. 1936. *The Great Chain of Being: A Study of the History of an Idea*. Cambridge: Harvard Univ. Press.

Lumsden, Charles J. and Edward O. Wilson. 1983. *Promethean Fire: Reflections on the Origin of Mind*. Cambridge: Harvard Univ. Press.

Macdonald, Graham and Cynthia. 2006. "The Metaphysics of Mental Causation." *Journal of Philosophy* 103 (November): 539-76.

___, eds. 2010. *Emergence in Mind*. New York: Oxford Univ. Press.

Machamer, Peter, Lindley Darden, and Carl F. Craver. 2000. "Thinking About Mechanisms." *Philosophy of Science* 67 (March): 1-25.

MacKay, Donald M. 1978. "Selves and Brains." *Neuroscience* 3 (No. 7): 599-606.

___. 1980. *Brains, Machines and Persons*. Grand Rapids: William B. Eerdmans.

___. 1982. *Science and the Quest for Meaning*. Grand Rapids: William B. Eerdmans.

___. 1987. "Brain Science and the Soul." In Richard L. Gregory, ed., *The Oxford Companion to the Mind*, pp. 723-25. Oxford: Oxford Univ. Press.

Mackinnon, Edward. 2008. "The New Reductionism." *Philosophical Forum* 39 (Winter): 439-61.

Macklem, Peter L. 2008. "Emergent Properties and the Secrets of Life." *Journal of Applied Physiology* 104 (June): 1844-46.

Maddox, John. 1983. "Is Biology Now Part of Physics?" *Nature* 306 (24 Nov.): 311.

Maduro, Otto. 1977. "New Marxist Approaches to the Relative Autonomy of Religion." *Sociological Analysis* 38 (Winter): 359-67.

Mandelbaum, Maurice. 1973a. "Societal Facts." In O'Neill, pp. 221-34.

___. 1973b. "Societal Laws." In O'Neill, pp. 235-47.

Maull, Nancy L. 1977. "Unifying Science Without Reduction." *Studies in the History and Philosophy of Science* 8 (No. 2): 143-62. Reprinted in Sober, ed., 1984, pp. 509-27.

Mayr, Ernst. 1988a. *Toward a New Philosophy of Biology: Observations of an Evolutionist*. Cambridge: Harvard Univ. Press.

___. 1988b. "The Limits of Reductionism." *Nature* 331 (February 11): 475.

McCutcheon, Russell. 2006. "It's a Lie. There's No Truth to it! It's a Sin!: On the Limits of the Humanistic Study of Religion and the Costs of Saving Others from Themselves." *Journal of the American Academy of Religion* 74 (December): 720-50.

McGinn, Colin. 1991. *The Problem of Consciousness: Essays Toward a Resolution*. Oxford: Basil Blackwell.

McKown, Delos B. 1975. *The Classical Marxist Critiques of Religion: Marx, Engels, Lenin, Kautsky*. The Hague: Martinus Nijhoff.

McLaughlin, Brian P. 1992. "The Rise and Fall of British Emergentism." In Beckermann, Flohr, & Kim, pp. 49-93.

McMullin, Ernan. 1972. "The Dialectics of Reduction." *Idealistic Studies* 2 (May): 95-115.

___. 2010. "From Matter to Materialism . . . and (Almost) Back." In Davies & Gregersen, pp. 13-37.

Meehl, P. E. and Wilfrid Sellars. 1956. "The Concept of Emergence." In Herbert Feigl and Michael Scriven, eds., *Minnesota Studies in the Philosophy of Science*, Vol. 1, pp. 239-52. Minneapolis: Univ. of Minnesota Press.

Melnyk, Andrew. 1995. "Two Cheers for Reductionism: Or, The Dim Prospects for Non-Reductive Materialism." *Philosophy of Science* 62 (September): 370-88.

___. 2003. *A Physicalist Manifesto: Thoroughly Modern Materialism*. Cambridge: Cambridge Univ. Press.

Midgley, Mary. 1995. "Reductive Megalomania." In Cornwell, pp. 133-47.

___. 2003. "The Aims of Reduction." In her *The Myths We Live By*, pp. 29-35. New York: Routledge.

Mill, John Stuart. 1872. *A System of Logic*. 2 vols. London: Parker & Son.

Monod, Jacques. 1971. *Chance and Necessity: An Essay on the Natural Philosophy of Modern Biology*. Trans. by Austryn Wainhouse. New York: Alfred A. Knopf.

Montalenti, G. 1974. "From Aristotle to Democritus via Darwin: A Short Survey of a Long Historical and Logical Journey." In Ayala & Dobzhansky, pp. 3-19.

Morgan, C. Lloyd. 1927. *Emergent Evolution*. 2nd ed. London: Norgate and Williams.

Morowitz, Harold J. 2002. *The Emergence of Everything: How the World Became Complex*. New York: Oxford Univ. Press.

Morris, Simon Conway. 2003. *Life's Solution: Inevitable Humans in a Lonely Universe*. New York: Cambridge University Press.

Müller, Fredrich Max. 1882. *Introduction to the Science of Religion: Four Lectures*. New ed. London: Longmans, Green.

Murphy, Nancey. 2007. "Introduction." In Murphy & Stoeger, pp. 1-15.

___ and Michael Stoeger, eds. 2007. *Evolution and Emergence: Systems, Organisms, Persons*. New York: Oxford Univ. Press.

Nagel, Ernest. 1961. "The Reduction of Theories." In his *The Structure of Science: Problems in the Logic of Scientific Explanation*, pp. 336-97. New York: Harcourt Brace.

___. 1979. "Issues in the Logic of Reductive Explanations." In his *Teleology Revisited and Other Essays in the Philosophy and History of Science*, pp. 95-117. New York: Columbia Univ. Press.

Nagel, Thomas. 1979. *Mortal Questions*. Cambridge: Cambridge Univ. Press.

___. 1997. *The Last Word*. New York: Oxford Univ. Press.

___. 1998. "Reductionism and Antireductionism." In G. R. Bock & J. A. Goode, eds., *The Limits of Reductionism in Biology*, pp. 3-14. New York: John Wiley & Sons.

Needham, Paul. "What is Water?" *Analysis* 60 (Januray): 13-21.

___. 2009. "Reduction and Emergence: A Critique of Kim." *Philosophical Studies* 146 (no. 1): 93-116.

___. 2010. "Substance and Time." *British Journal for the Philosophy of Science* 61 (December): 485-512.

Nelkin, Dorothy. 2002. "Reductionism and Social Policy." In Van Regenmortel & Hull, pp. 305-17.

Newberg, Andrew, Eugene d'Aquili, and Vince Rause. 2002. *Why God Won't Go Away: Brain Science & the Biology of Belief*. New York: Ballatine Books.

Nickles, Thomas. 1973. "Two Concepts of Intertheoretic Reduction." *Journal of Philosophy* 70 (April 12): 181-201.

___. 1976. "Theory Generalization, Problem Reduction and the Unity of Science." In Robert S. Cohen, Clifford A. Hooker, A. C. Michalos, and J. W. Van Evra, eds., *PSA 1974*, pp. 33-75. Boston: D. Reidel.

Nozick, Robert. 1974. *Anarchy, State and Utopia*. New York: Basic Books.

___. 1981. "Reductionism" and "Nonreductive Understanding." In his *Philosophical Explanations*, pp. 627-45. Cambridge: Harvard Univ. Press.

O'Connor, Timothy. 1994. "Emergent Properties." *American Philosophical Quarterly* 31 (April): 91-104.

___ and Hong Yu Wong. 2005. "The Metaphysics of Emergence." *Noûs* 39 (no. 4): 658-78.

O'Neill, John, ed. 1973. *Modes of Individualism and Collectivism*. London: Heineman.

Oppenheim, Paul and Hilary Putnam. 1958. "Unity of Science as a Working Hypothesis." In Herbert Feigl, Michael Scriven, and Grover Maxwell, eds., *Minnesota Studies in the Philosophy of Science*, Vol. 2, pp. 3-36. Minneapolis: Univ. of Minnesota Press.

Otto, Rudolf. 1958. *The Idea of the Holy*. Trans. by John W. Harvey. Oxford: Oxford Univ. Press.

Pals, Daniel L. 1994. "Explaining, Endorsing, and Reducing Religion: Some Clarifications." In Idinopulos & Yonan, pp. 183-97.

___. 2006. *Eight Theories of Religion*. 2d ed. New York: Oxford Univ. Press.

Parfit, Derek. 1984. *Reasons and Persons*. New York: Oxford Univ. Press.

Pargament, Kenneth I. 2002. "Is Religion Nothing But . . .? Explaining Religion Versus Explaining Religion Away." *Psychological Inquiry* 13 (no. 3): 239-44.

Parsons, Talcott. 1937. *The Structure of Social Action*. New York: Free Press.

Peacocke, Arthur. 1976. "Reductionism: A Review of the Epistemological Issues and Their Relevance to Biology and the Problem of Consciousness." *Zygon: Journal of Religion and Science* 11 (December): 307-36.

___, ed. 1985. *Reductionism in Academic Disciplines*. Guilford, Surrey: The Society for Research into Higher Education.

___. 1986. *God and the New Biology*. New York: Harper & Row.

___. 1993. *Theology for a Scientific Age: Being and Becoming—Natural, Divine, and Human*. Minneapolis: Fortress Press.

___. 2007. *All That Is: A Naturalistic Faith for the Twenty-First Century*. Ed. by Philip Clayton. Minneapolis: Fortress Press.

Penfield, Wilder G. 1975. *The Mystery of the Mind: A Critical Study of Consciousness and the Human Brain*. Princeton: Princeton Univ. Press.

Penner, Hans H. 1989. *Impasse and Resolution: A Critique of the Study of Religion*. New York: Peter Lang.

Penrose, Roger. 1989. *The Emperor's New Mind: Concerning Computers, Minds, and the Laws of Physics*. New York: Oxford Univ. Press.

___. 1994. *Shadows of the Mind: A Search for the Missing Science of Consciousness*. New York: Oxford Univ. Press.

Pepper, Stephen C. 1926. "Emergence." *Journal of Philosophy* 23 (April 29): 241-45.

Pereboom, Derek and Hilary Kornblith. 1991. "The Metaphysics of Irreducibility." *Philosophical Studies* 63 (August): 125-45.

Pettit, Philip. 1993. *The Common Mind: An Essay on Psychology, Society, and Politics*. New York: Oxford Univ. Press.

Pippard, A. Brian. 1988. "The Invincible Ignorance of Science." *Contemporary Physics* 29 (July/August): 393-405.

Place, U. T. 1956. "Is Consciousness a Brain Process?" *British Journal of Psychology* 47 (March): 44-50.

Polanyi, Michael. 1968. "Life's Irreducible Structure." *Science* 160 (June 21): 1308-12.

Polger, Thomas W. 2004. *Natural Minds*. Cambridge: MIT Press.

Popper, Karl R. 1974. "Scientific Reduction and the Essential Incompleteness of All Science." In Ayala & Dobzhansky, pp. 259-84.

___. 1978. "Natural Selection and the Emergence of Mind." *Dialectia* 32 (No. 3-4): 339-55.

___. 1979. *Objective Knowledge: An Evolutionary Approach.* Rev. ed. Oxford: Clarendon Press.

___. 1982. *The Open Universe: An Argument for Indeterminism.* Totowa, N.J.: Rowman and Littlefield.

___. 1994. *Knowledge and the Body-Mind Problem: In Defence of Interaction.* Ed. by M. A. Notturno. New York: Routledge.

___ and John C. Eccles. 1965. *The Self and its Brain: An Argument for Interaction.* New York: Routledge & Kegan Paul.

Prigogine, Ilya and Isabelle Stengers. 1984. *Order Out of Chaos.* New York: Bantam.

Primas, Hans. 1983. *Chemistry, Quantum Mechanics and Reductionism: Perspectives in Theoretical Chemistry.* 2nd ed. New York: Springer-Verlag.

___. 1991. "Reductionism: Palaver Without Precedent." In Agazzi, pp. 161-72.

___. 1998. "Emergence in the Exact Sciences." *Acta Polytechnica Scandinavica* (Electrical Engineering Series) 91: 83-98.

___. 2004. "Can We Reduce Chemistry to Physics?" *World & I* 19 (December).

Proudfoot, Wayne. 1985. *Religious Experience.* Berkeley: Univ. of California Press.

Puligandla, Ramakrishna. 1991. "Is the Central Upanishadic Teaching a Reductionist Thesis?" *Asian Philosophy* 1 (No. 1): 15-20.

Putnam, Hilary. 1994. "Reductionism and the Nature of Psychology." Reprinted in his *Words and Life,* pp. 428-40. Cambridge: Harvard Univ. Press.

___. 1999. *The Threefold Cord: Mind, Body, and World.* New York: Columbia Univ. Press.

Quine, Willard van Orman. 1953. *From a Logical Point of View.* New York: Harper & Row.

___. 1981. *Theories and Things.* Cambridge: Harvard Univ. Press.

Rose, Steven. 1985. "The Roots and Social Functions of Biological Reductionism." In Peacocke, pp. 24-42.

___. 1987. *Molecules and Mind: Essays on Biology and the Social Order.* Philadelphia: Open Univ. Press.

Rosenberg, Alexander. 1992. *Economics: Mathematical Politics or Science of Diminishing Returns?* Chicago: Univ. of Chicago Press.

___. 1994. *Instrumental Biology or the Disunity of Science.* Chicago: Univ. of Chicago Press.

___. 1995. *Philosophy of Social Science.* 2nd ed. Boulder: Westview Press.

___. 2006. *Darwinian Reductionism, or, How to Stop Worrying and Love Molecular Biology.* Chicago: Univ. of Chicago Press.

___. 2011. *The Atheist's Guide to Reality: Enjoying Life Without Illusions.* New York: Norton.

___ and D. M. Kaplan. 2005. "How to Reconcile Physicalism and Antireductionism about Biology." *Philosophy of Science* 72 (January): 43-68.

Ross, Don. 1995. "Real Patterns and the Ontological Foundations of Microeconomics." *Economics and Philosophy* (April): 113-36.

Rue, Loyal. 2005. *Religion is Not About God: How Spiritual Traditions Nurture Our Biological Nature and What to Expect When They Fail.* New Brunswick: Rutgers Univ. Press.

Rueger, Alexander and Patrick McGivern. 2010. "Hierarchies and Levels of Reality." *Synthese* 176: 379-97.

Ruse, Michael. 1971. "Reduction, Replacement, and Molecular Biology." *Dialectica* 25 (No. 1): 38-72.

___. 1988. *Philosophy of Biology Today.* Albany: State Univ. of New York Press.

Ryba, Thomas. 1994. "Are Religious Theories Susceptible to Reduction?" In Idinopulos &Yonan, pp. 15-42.

Ryder, John, ed. 1994. *American Philosophic Naturalism in the Twentieth Century*. Amherst, N.Y.: Prometheus Books.

Ryle, Gilbert. 1949. *The Concept of Mind*. New York: Barnes & Noble.

___. 1954. "The World of Science and the Everyday World." In his *Dilemmas*, pp. 68-81. Cambridge: Cambridge Univ. Press.

Sarkar, Sahotra. 1998. *Genetics and Reductionism*. New York: Cambridge Univ. Press.

Saunders, Simon. 2006. "Are Quantum Particles Objects?" *Analysis* 66 (January): 52-63.

Scerri, Eric. 1994. "Has Chemistry at Least Approximately Been Reduced to Quantum Mechanics?" In David Hull, M. Forbes and R. Burian, eds., *PSA 1994*, Vol. 1, pp. 160-70. East Lansing: Philosophy of Science Association.

Schaffer, Jonathan. 2003. "Is There a Fundamental Level?" *Noûs* (no. 3) 37: 498-517.

___. 2010. "Monism: The Priority of the Whole." *Philosophical Review* 119 (January): 31-76.

Schaffner, Kenneth F. 1984. "Reduction in Biology: Prospects and Problems." In Sober, pp. 428-45.

___. 1993. *Discovery and Explanation in Biology and Medicine*. Chicago: Univ. of Chicago Press.

___. 2006. "Reduction: The Cheshire Cat Problem and a Return to Roots." *Synthese* 151: 377-402.

Schouten, Maurice and Huibert Looren de Jong, eds. 2007. *The Matter of Mind: Philosophical Essays on Psychology, Nueroscience, and Reduction*. Oxford: Basil Blackwell.

Schrödinger, Erwin. 1944. *What is Life? The Physical Aspect of the Living Cell*. New York: Cambridge Univ. Press.

Scott, Alwyn. 1999. *Nonlinear Science: Emergence and Dynamics of Coherent Structures*. New York: Oxford Univ. Press.

___. 2004. "Reductionism Revisited." *Journal of Consciousness Studies* 11 (no. 2): 51-68.

Searle, John. 1984. *Minds, Brains and Science*. Cambridge: Harvard Univ. Press.

___. 1992. *The Rediscovery of Mind*. Cambridge: MIT Press.

___. 1995. "Consciousness, the Brain and the Connection Principle: A Reply." *Philosophy and Phenomenological Research* 55 (March): 217-32.

___. 1997. *The Mystery of Consciousness*. New York: New York Review of Books.

___. 2010. *Making the Social World: The Structure of Human Civilization*. New York: Oxford Univ. Press.

Segal, Robert A. 1989. *Religion and the Social Sciences: Essays on the Confrontation*. Atlanta: Scholars Press.

___. 1992. *Explaining and Interpreting Religion: Essays on the Issue*. New York: Peter Lang.

___. 1994. "Reductionism in the Study of Religion." In Idinopulos & Yonan, pp. 4-14.

Sellars, Roy Wood. 1970. *Principles of Emergent Realism: Philosophical Essays*. Ed. by W. Preston Warren. St. Louis: Warren H. Green.

Sharf, Robert H. 1998. "Experience." In Mark C. Taylor, ed., *Critical Terms in Religious Studies*, pp. 94-116. Chicago: Univ. of Chicago.

Shear, Jonathan, ed. 1997. *Explaining Consciousness—the "Hard Problem."* Cambridge: MIT Press.

Shimony, Abner. 1993a. "The Methodology of Synthesis: Parts and Wholes in Low-Energy

Physics." In his *Search for a Naturalistic World View*, Vol. 2, pp. 191-217. Cambridge: Cambridge Univ. Press.

_____. 1993b. "Some Proposals Concerning Parts and Wholes." In his *Search for a Naturalistic World View*, Vol. 2, pp. 218-227. Cambridge: Cambridge Univ. Press.

Shoemaker, Sydney. 2002. "Kim on Emergence." *Philosophical Studies* 108 (March): 53-63.

Siderits, Mark. 1997. "Buddhist Reductionism." *Philosophy East and West* 47 (October): 455-78.

Silberman, Israela. 2002. "Religion as a Meaning System: Implications for a New Millennium." *Journal of Social Issues* 61 (no. 4): 641-63.

Silberstein, Michael. 2002. "Reduction, Emergence and Explanation." In Michael Silberstein and Peter Machamer, eds., *The Blackwell Guide to Philosophy of Science*, pp. 80-107. Oxford: Basil Blackwell.

_____. 2006. "In Defence of Ontological Emergence and Mental Causation." In Clayton & Davies, pp. 203-26.

_____ and John McGeever. 1999. "The Search for Ontological Emergence." *Philosophical Quarterly* 49 (April): 182-200.

Simon, Herbert A. 1962. "The Architecture of Complexity." Reprinted in his *The Sciences of the Artificial*. 2nd ed., pp. 192-229. Cambridge: MIT Press, 1981.

Sklar, Lawrence. 1993. "The Reduction of Thermodynamics to Statistical Mechanics." In his *Physics and Chance: Philosophical Issues in the Foundations of Statistical Mechanics*, pp. 333-74. New York: Cambridge Univ. Press.

Slingerland, Edward. 2008. "Who's Afraid of Reductionism? The Study of Religion in the Age of Cognitive Science." *Journal of the American Academy of Religion* 76 (June): 375-411.

Smart, J. J. C. 1959. "Sensations and Brain Processes." *Philosophical Review* 68 (April): 141-56.

Smith, Huston. 1965. *The Religions of Man*. New York: Harper & Row.

Sober, Elliot. 1984. "Holism, Individualism, and the Units of Selection." In Sober, ed., 1984, pp. 184-209.

_____. 1993. *Philosophy of Biology*. Boulder/San Francisco: Westview Press.

_____, ed. 1984. *Conceptual Issues in Evolutionary Biology: An Anthology*. Cambridge: MIT Press.

Spencer-Smith, Richard. 1995. "Reductionism and Emergent Properties." *Proceedings of Aristotelian Society* 95 (No. 2): 113-29.

Sperry, Roger W. 1976. "Mental Phenomena as Causal Determinants in Brain Function." In Gordon G. Globus, Grover Maxwell, and Irwin Savodnik, eds., *Consciousness and the Brain: A Scientific and Philosophical Inquiry*, pp. 163-77. New York: Plenum Press.

_____. 1985. *Science and Moral Priority: Merging Mind, Brain, and Human Values*. New York: Praeger.

_____. 1991. "Search for Beliefs to Live by Consistent with Science." *Zygon: Journal of Religion and Science* 26 (June): 237-58.

_____. 1995. "The Riddle of Consciousness and the Changing Scientific Worldview." *Journal of Humanistic Psychology* 35 (Spring): 7-33.

Spiro, Melford E. 1966. "Religion: Problems of Definition and Explanation." In Michael Banton, ed., *Anthropological Approaches to the Study of Religion*, pp. 85-126. London: Tavistock.

Stapp, Henry P. 2007. "Quantum Mechanical Theories of Consciousness." In Max Velmens, et al., eds., *The Blackwell Companion to Consciousness*, pp. 300-12. Oxford: Basil Blackwell.

Sterelny, Kim and Philip Kitcher. 1988. "The Return of the Gene." *Journal of Philosophy* 85 (July): 339-61.

Stich, Stephen P. 1983. *From Folk Psychology to Cognitive Science: The Case Against Belief.* Cambridge: MIT Press.

___. 1996. *Deconstructing the Mind.* New York: Oxford Univ. Press.

Stöckler, Manfred. 1991. "A Short History of Emergence and Reductionism." In Agazzi, pp. 71-90.

Suppes, Patrick. 1981. "The Plurality of Science." In Peter D. Asquith and Ian Hacking, eds., *PSA 1978*, Vol. 2, pp. 3-16. East Lansing: Philosophy of Science Association.

Tännsjö, Torbjörn. 1990. "Methodological Individualism." *Inquiry* 33 (March): 69-80.

Tauber, Alfred I. 1992. "The Human Genome Project: Has Blind Reductionism Gone Too Far?" *Perspectives in Biology & Medicine* 35 (Winter): 220-35.

Taves, Ann. 2009. *Religious Experience Reconsidered: A Building-Block Approach to the Study of Religion and Other Special Things.* Princeton: Princeton Univ. Press.

Teller, Paul. 1992. "A Contemporary Look at Emergence." In Beckermann, Flohr, & Kim, pp. 139-53.

Tloczynski, Joseph. 1993. "Is the Self Essential? Handling Reductionism." *Perceptual and Motor Skills* 76 (June): 723-32.

Tylor, Edward B. 1871. *Primitive Cultures.* 2 Vols. London: Murray.

Van Brakel, Jaap . 2010. "Chemistry and Physics: No Need for Metaphysical Glue." *Foundations of Chemistry* 12 (no. 2): 123-36.

Van Gulick, Robert. 2001. "Reduction, Emergence and Other Recent Options on the Mind/Body Problem: A Philosophic Overview." *Journal of Consciousness Studies* 8 (nos. 9-10): 1-34.

___. 2010-11. "Non-Reductive Physicalism and the Teleo-Pragmatic Theory of the Mind." *Philosophia Naturalis* 47-48 (nos. 1-2): 103-24.

Van Regenmortel, Marc H. V. and David L. Hull, eds. 2002. *Promises and Limits of Reductionism in the Biomedical Sciences.* New York: John Wiley & Sons.

Van Riel, Raphael. 2010-11. "Identity-based Reduction and Reductive Explanation." *Philosophia Naturalis* 47-48 (nos. 1-2): 185-221.

___. 2011. "Nagelian Reduction Beyond the Nagel Model." *Philosophy of Science* 78 (no. 3): 353-75.

Vedral, Vlatko. 2010. *Decoding Reality: The Universe as Quantum Information.* New York: Oxford Univ. Press.

Vision, Gerald. 2010. *Re-emergence: Locating Consciousness in a Material World.* Cambridge: MIT Press.

Vitzthum, Richard C. 1995. *Materialism: An Affirmative History and Definition.* Amherst, NY: Prometheus Books.

Wade, Nicholas. 1976. "Sociobiology: Troubled Birth for New Discipline." *Science* 191 (19 March): 1151-55.

Ward, Keith. 2010. "God as the Ultimate Informational Principle." In Davies & Gregersen, pp. 282-300.

Weber, Max. 1963. *The Sociology of Religion.* Trans. by E. Fischoff. Boston: Beacon Press.

___. 1968. *Economy and Society: An Outline of Interpretive Sociology.* Ed. by Guenther Roth and Claus Wittich. New York: Bedminster Press.

___. 1984. *The Protestant Ethic and the Spirit of Capitalism.* Trans. by Talcott Parsons. London: Unwin.

Wegner, Daniel M. 2002. *The Illusion of Conscious Will*. Cambridge: MIT Press.

Weinberg, Steven. 1977. *The First Three Minutes of the Universe*. New York: Basic Books.

___. 1992. *Dreams of a Final Theory*. New York: Pantheon Books.

___. 1995. "Reductionism Redux." *New York Review of Books* (October 5): 39-42.

Weiss, Paul A. 1969. "The Living System: Determinism Sratified." In Koestler & Smythies, pp. 3-42.

Weissman, David. 2000. *A Social Ontology*. New Haven: Yale Univ. Press.

Whitehead, Alfred North. 1967. *Science and the Modern World*. New York: Free Press.

Whitesides, George M. and Bartosz Grzybowski. 2002. "Self-Assembly At All Scales." *Science* 295 (March 29): 2418–2421.

Wiebe, Donald. 1998. *The Politics of Religious Studies: The Continuing Conflict with Theology in the Academy*. New York: St. Martin's.

Williams, Nigel. 1997. "Biologists Cut Reductionist Approach Down to Size." *Science* 277 (July 25): 476-77.

Wilson, David Sloan. 2002. *Darwin's Cathedral: Evolution, Religion, and the Nature of Society*. Chicago: Univ. of Chicago Press..

Wilson, Edward O. 1975. *Sociobiology: The Modern Synthesis*. Cambridge: Harvard Univ. Press.

___. 1978. *On Human Nature*. Cambridge: Harvard Univ. Press.

___. 1996. "Culture as a Biological Product." In his *In Search of Nature*, pp. 107-26. Washington, D.C.: Island Press.

___. 1998. *Consilience: The Unity of Knowledge*. New York: Alfred A. Knopf.

Wimsatt, William C. 1976. "Reductionism, Levels of Organization, and the Mind-Body Problem." In Gordon G. Globus, Grover Maxwell, and Irwin Savodnik, eds., *Consciousness and the Brain: A Scientific and Philosophical Inquiry*, pp. 205-67. New York: Plenum Press.

___. 1984. "Reductive Explanation: A Functional Account." In Sober, ed., pp. 477-508.

___.1994. "The Ontology of Complex Systems: Levels of Organization, Perspectives, and Causal Thickets." In Mohan Matthew and R. X. Ware, eds., *Biology & Society: Reflections on Methodology*, pp. 207-74. Calgary: Univ. of Calgary Press.

___. 1997. "Aggregativity: Reductive Heuristics for Finding Emergence." In Lindley Darden, ed., *PSA 1996*, Part 2, pp. 372-84. East Lansing: Philosophy of Science Association.

___. 2006. "Reductionism and its Heuristics: Making Methodological Reductionism Honest." *Synthese* 151: 445-75.

___. 2007. *Re-Engineering Philosophy for Limited Beings: Piecewise Approximations to Reality*. Cambridge: Harvard Univ. Press.

Winch, Peter. 1958. *The Idea of a Social Science and its Relation to Philosophy*. London: Routledge & Kegan Paul.

Wolfram, Stephen. 2002. *A New Kind of Science*. Champaign, Ill.: Wolfram Media.

Wright, Cory D. 2000. "Eliminativist Undercurrents in the New Wave Model of Psychoneural Reduction." *Journal of Mind and Behavior* 21 (no. 4): 413-36.

Yates, F. Eugene, ed. 1987. *Self-Organizing Systems: The Emergence of Order*. New York: Plenum Press.

Zeleny, Milan, ed. 1981. *Autopoiesis: A Theory of Living Organization*. New York: North Holland.

Index

Printed in Poland
by Amazon Fulfillment
Poland Sp. z o.o., Wrocław

35327136R00139